CLIMATE AND THE MAKING OF WORLDS

CLIMATE AND THE MAKING OF WORLDS

Toward a Geohistorical Poetics

TOBIAS MENELY

THE UNIVERSITY OF CHICAGO PRESS

CHICAGO AND LONDON

The University of Chicago Press, Chicago 60637
The University of Chicago Press, Ltd., London
© 2021 by The University of Chicago
Published 2021
Printed in the United States of America

30 29 28 27 26 25 24 23 22 21   1 2 3 4 5

ISBN-13: 978-0-226-77614-9 (cloth)
ISBN-13: 978-0-226-77628-6 (paper)
ISBN-13: 978-0-226-77631-6 (e-book)
DOI: https://doi.org/10.7208/chicago/9780226776316.001.0001

The University of Chicago Press gratefully acknowledges the generous support of
the Office of Research and the College of Letters and Science at the University of
California, Davis, toward the publication of this book.

Library of Congress Cataloging-in-Publication Data

Names: Menely, Tobias, author.
Title: Climate and the making of worlds : toward a geohistorical poetics /
    Tobias Menely.
Other titles: Toward a geohistorical poetics
Description: Chicago ; London : The University of Chicago Press, 2021. |
    Includes bibliographical references and index.
Identifiers: LCCN 2021004016 | ISBN 9780226776149 (cloth) |
    ISBN 9780226776286 (paperback) | ISBN 9780226776316 (ebook)
Subjects: LCSH: English poetry—18th century—History and criticism. |
    English poetry—17th century—History and criticism. | Ecology in literature. |
    Seasons in literature. | Climatic changes in literature. | Human ecology in
    literature. | Climate and civilization—Great Britain.
Classification: LCC PR551 .M46 2021 | DDC 821/.50936—dc23
LC record available at https://lccn.loc.gov/2021004016

Thus altering Age leads on the World to Fate,
The Earth is different from her former state.
   —Lucretius, *De rerum natura* (Thomas Creech translation, 1682)

CONTENTS

Stratigraphic Criticism

It is now a commonplace that the speed and scale of planetary change in the present can be understood only in the context of the Earth's long history, unimaginable durations of slow sedimentation and erosion punctuated by sudden cataclysmic phase shifts.[1] In the critical humanities, however, there is a pervasive sense that the cultural past has been rendered antique, the ruins and remainders of Holocene civilization superseded by the urgent exigencies of a "no-analogue" present.[2] Inherited cultural forms—not unlike our institutions of knowledge, modes of governance, and economic systems—appear unable to adequately represent and respond to this state of emergency, the intensifying crisis in the Earth system. We seek new genres, new disciplines, and a new politics suitable to this catastrophic conjuncture of human and planetary history. That such an account of our Anthropocene predicament—as a total rupture with existing vocabularies and institutions—simply reiterates the trope of modernity, even as it widens its frame, further evinces the limited range of our historical categories, as does persistent recourse to a rhetoric of apocalyptic finality that has its roots in ancient religious traditions.

The work of reading and teaching centuries- or millennia-old poems— and, not only that, but reading as well what so many others have written about those poems—can, in this time, feel like further evidence of the inadequacy of received forms of inquiry. The patience required for archival research and the dispassionate poise that is the norm of scholarly writing are punctured by a sense of urgency and dread. To read at all, these days, is to read "under duress," as Jennifer Wenzel writes, to read pressed up against the "hardness" of planetary history and the pressure of imminent calamity.[3] Yet in this others have gone before us. In 1939, Walter Benjamin—stateless and writing with what he called "the courage of desperation"—asked: "How, in this day and age, can one read lyric poetry at all?" How can one read with "the knowledge that tomorrow could bring destruction on such a scale that yesterday's texts and creations might seem as distant from us as centuries-old artifacts."[4] His response to the approach of a catastrophe that would divide the present from itself, leaving a rift in history, was to treat Brecht's lyric poetry as if it were already a "classical text," to consider what is contemporary as if it were an ancient relic reclaimed from the Earth.

Benjamin has been taken up by so many as a theorist of planetary crisis *avant le lettre* because of the insistence with which he sought alternatives to a positivist historiography that characterizes time as a unilinear sequence of events.[5] We are coming to recognize the abstract—"homogeneous, empty"—temporality of historical progress, the passing away of the past, to be itself an expression of fossil-powered modernity and our (supposed) escape from planetary exigencies.[6] The past remains, not least as carbon dioxide accumulated in the atmosphere. In his 1940 essay on Baudelaire's "lyrics of modern life," Benjamin asserts that the "structure of . . . experience"—including memory, the faculty with which we perceive what endures and what gives way—is subject to alteration.[7] With its jostling novelty and information overload, modern urban life estranges temporal perception, producing a state of hyperalertness to a present decoupled from past and future. For Benjamin, Baudelaire's lyrics enfold—and so mutually illuminate—different structures of historical experience. The "isolated experience" (*Erlebnis*) of modern life comes to be recognizable from within the archaic forms of experience—ritualistic, elemental, allegorical—invoked by the lyric poem, "long experience" (*Erfahrung*) of the sort "that accompanies one to the far reaches of time, that fills and articulates time" ("Motifs in Baudelaire," 331). In his treatment of lyric poetry as noncontemporaneous with itself, at once modern and antiquated, Benjamin establishes a model for the antipositivist philosophy of history he explores in his late work, including his identification of the sudden "constellation saturated with tension" that enables a recognition of "a present [that] is not a transition," a form of memory, or retrieval, that would make an obscured present newly recognizable ("On the Concept," 396).

Unacknowledged by scholars looking to Benjamin for insight relevant to our disastrous present is his tendency of referring to climate as that which sustains, with the palpability of long experience, a continuous baseline against which historical change might be measured. In "The Storyteller," for example, he writes of the First World War: "A generation that had gone to school on horse-drawn streetcars now stood under the open sky in a landscape where nothing remained unchanged but the clouds and, beneath those clouds, in a force field of destructive torrents and explosions, the tiny,

fragile human body."[8] Atmospheric tropes stand for the cumulative and cy-
clic experience against which the immediacy of the passing instant can be
known. The clouds, the air, and the sun are witnesses to history's tumult,
palpable figures for the "splinters of messianic time" that sustain the possi-
bility of revelatory interruption. Benjamin writes of how that which has ap-
parently passed can be reintroduced as that which illuminates and so alters
the present: "The past carries with it a secret index by which it is referred
to redemption. Doesn't a breath of the air that pervaded earlier days caress
us as well?" ("On the Concept," 397, 390). The unchanging air sustains
a continuity of human experience, an elemental consistency immune to
those conditions that lead to the radical reorganization of perception and
memory in capitalist modernity. A "breath of lost time" enables us to break
the illusion of progress, of time's inexorable passing within "the sequence of
days," and so to realize the solidarity among generations and commence the
work of reparative remembrance ("Motifs in Baudelaire," 354). This atmo-
spheric index—a countervailing temporal order, archive of the other times
that remain—reappears as the "open air of history" and the "sun which is
rising in the sky of history." It is a blast of wind that bears "the fullness of
[the] past" ("On the Concept," 395, 390), driving the clouds before it: "In
every true work of art there is a place where, for one who removes there,
it blows cool like the wind of a coming dawn. . . . Progress has its seat not
in the continuity of elapsing time but in its interferences—where the truly
new makes itself felt for the first time, with the sobriety of dawn."[9] Benja-
min's redemptive "now-time" (Jetztzeit), in other words, assumes the con-
tinuity and legibility of climate, a planetary temporality that endures and so
measures historical alteration ("On the Concept," 395). Benjamin diagnoses
the temporal disorders that make the modern present unavailable yet holds
out hope, expressed in metaphors of climatic constancy, that, buffeted by
arctic winds, the clouds will still part, unveiling other destinies.

Benjamin's investigations of allegory in his early work on the Trauerspiel
and of lyric in his late studies of Baudelaire are major touchstones for this
book. Yet, in the passages examined above, Benjamin figures the climate as
an unchanging and so salvific counterpoint to history. This oversight in his
bold materialist exploration of alternatives to positive facticity and progressive
temporality is the first instance, in this study, of what I call the climatological
unconscious. The climate, for Benjamin, stands for that which is untouched
by history and so for the dream of an emancipation from historical necessity.

The idealization of an untouched atmosphere and a revitalizing wind is
a romantic inheritance. Consider the culminating stanza of Wordsworth's
"Lines, Written a Few Miles above Tintern Abbey" (1798), in which the

poet directs his lyric address so that it includes not only his sister, Doro-
thy, but the mountain wind as well: "And let the misty mountain winds
be free / To blow against thee" (137–38). A poet calling on the wind to do
what it does naturally is a familiar, if still enigmatic, lyric conceit. "If ask-
ing winds to blow," as Jonathan Culler observes of such apostrophes, is the
poet's way of dramatizing his own vocation, it seems no less to stage the
nonefficacy, "the gratuitous action," of poetic labor.[10] The concluding turn
to Dorothy is often read as an effort to reintegrate the world of human oth-
ers, to compensate for the "suppression of the social"—the "social, histori-
cal, ideological"—that Marjorie Levinson famously identified as the poem's
governing ideological presentation of "culture as Nature."[11] What enables a
new "secular" sociality, in the final lines of the poem, is the nondetermina-
tion embodied by the windswept mountains, an alternative to powerful so-
cial institutions, a wilderness in which any individual can discover himself
or herself.[12] "There is no cycle of air," claims Northrop Frye, endorsing such
romantic atmospherics. "The wind bloweth where it listeth."[13]

Apostrophe is an insistently literary convention, as much an invoca-
tion of the poetic past as an addressed other. If we look to the poets whose
words so often echo in Wordsworth's verse, however, we discover a different
treatment of the wind. Rather than standing for a freedom beyond historical
determination, the wind presses in on and disastrously unsettles human
projects. In *The Seasons* (1726–46), James Thomson directs his address to
the winds, not to command them to do what they would do regardless, but
to pose the question of their origin, of the hidden forces they manifest: "Ye
too, ye winds! that now begin to blow / With boisterous sweep, I raise my
voice to you. / Where are your stores, ye powerful beings! say, / Where your
aerial magazines reserved / To swell the brooding terrors of the storm?" (*Wi*,
111–15). Thomson regards the wind as part of a natural cycle and a global
system. Trade winds support international commerce, but the circulation of
air becomes dangerous when it intensifies in "hurricanes" and the "circling
typhon" (*Sp*, 326; *Su*, 984). In *Paradise Lost* (1667), Adam and Eve call on
"ye winds that from four quarters blow" (5.192) to join them in devotional
praise. For Milton, however, the "winds / Blown vagabond" (11.15–16) rep-
resent not freedom but constraint. After the Fall, Adam and Eve, soon to
be expelled from Paradise, come to recognize their new exposure to "the
inclement seasons," which, Adam observes, "the sky with various face be-
gins / To show us in this mountain while the winds / Blow moist and keen,
shattering the graceful locks / Of these fair spreading trees" (10.1063–67).

Before Milton and Thomson, there was Lucretius, who for British poets
from the seventeenth century on modeled the possibility that verse was

the most felicitous medium for the most daring philosophical inquiry, a "knowledgeable practice," in the words of Amanda Jo Goldstein, "whose figurative work brought it closer to, not farther from, the physical nature of things." Lucretius stood, in particular, for an understanding of multicausal determination, what Goldstein terms "associative emergence,"[14] a principle of creative disorder, contrasted with providential design and teleology, which Lucretius often figured meteorologically, as in the "strange storm" that precipitates the formation of the Earth (5.436).[15] For Lucretius, verse discloses the workings of hidden forces, processes of change, and principles of causation only partially perceivable, evident in phenomena such as evaporation and erosion, the growth of organisms, and the spread of disease. He offers the wind of an example of an enigmatic planetary flux perceivable in its destructive implications for human world making:

> The wind, its might aroused, lashes the sea
> And sinks great ships and tears the clouds apart.
> With whirling tempests sweeping across the plains
> It strews them with great trees, the mountain tops
> It rocks amain with forest-felling blasts,
> So fierce the howling fury of the gale,
> So wild and menacing the wind's deep roar.
> Therefore for sure there are unseen bodies of wind
> Which sweep the seas, the lands, the clouds of heaven,
> With sudden whirlwinds tossing, ravaging. (1.271–79)

The contrast between such devastating blasts and the redemptive breeze in Wordsworth's lyric corresponds with a changing conception of the aesthetic, from a philosophical didacticism to Wordsworth's prototypically romantic enacting of an address that seems to stage only the noninstrumentality of the poet's voice. This contrast also reveals a different understanding of climate. What is, for the earlier poets, a shaping condition of human activity, a hazard of planetary existence, is, for Wordsworth and Benjamin, a symbol of undetermination.

THE END OF THE LITTLE ICE AGE

In recent years, under the looming pressure of the climate crisis, historians have begun to ask "how," in the words of John Brooke, "the history of the earth system" has "shaped the history of the human condition?"[16] In 1982, Hubert Lamb linked his search for "evidence of climatic impact in the course of history" with a renewed awareness of human precarity: "We live in a world that is increasingly vulnerable to climatic shocks. After some decades in which it seemed that technological advance had conferred on mankind a considerable degree of immunity to the harvest failures and famines that afflicted our forefathers, population pressure and some other features of the modern world have changed the situation."[17] Following Lamb and other pioneers such as Emmanuel Le Roy Ladurie and Gustav Utterström, historians are exploring the complex interplay between the Earth's fluctuating climate and social world making, tracking the vectors linking climate with famines and epidemics, demographic trends and patterns of migration, economic development and geopolitical conflict.[18] Such research challenges the dominant historiographic paradigm in which social change is explained by social factors. Climate, in these studies, is recognized as a catalyst of social change, an intensifier of conflict, a variable force of production. Historians have identified climate shifts as triggers for a multitude of historical events from prehistory to the present, from the fall of the Akkadian and Roman Empires to the French Revolution and the recent civil war in Syria. As Lamb notes, even a relatively stable climate can shape human activity, particularly in marginal areas such as uplands, deserts, and polar regions (*Climate, History and the Modern World*, 3).

This book focuses on a particular phase of planetary history, the latter half of the Little Ice Age. There is much debate about the chronological and geographic scope of this period of modest cooling, about its social consequences, and even about its geophysical causes. Shifts in solar activity and ocean circulation as well as increased volcanic activity have been proposed as natural sources of climate forcing, but researchers have also identified two potential anthropogenic triggers for reduced atmospheric carbon dioxide and so lower temperatures: diminished agriculture, and the resultant reforestation, following the Black Death and forest regrowth after the genocide of native peoples in the Americas.[19] What is clear is that the seventeenth and eighteenth centuries, especially in the temperate zones of the Northern Hemisphere, saw lower average temperatures, heightened temperature variability, and increased extreme weather, adding up to the "most pronounced climate anomaly of the past 8,000 years (until contemporary global warming)."[20] Historians have, in recent years, drawn connections between the adverse climate in this period and conflict in the Ottoman Empire, the Dutch Golden Age, European settlement in North America, the African slave trade, Hindu liturgical practice, and the development of capitalism.[21] The most ambitious argument for a global Little Ice Age is that advanced by Geoffrey Parker, who contends that climatic deterioration contributed to the General Crisis of the seventeenth century, a period of worldwide geopolitical upheaval.[22]

My study begins during the coldest phase of the Little Ice Age, the Maunder Minimum, roughly 1645–1715. Milton wrote *Paradise Lost* in the aftermath of a civil conflict that was, as Parker shows, thoroughly shaped by climatic conditions, from early skirmishes over control of the Newcastle coal trade to the failure of Cromwell's Western Design. Thomson, the subject of chapter 2, was born in Scotland shortly after the seven ill years, the period of extreme weather and harvest failures in the 1690s often identified as the climax of the Little Ice Age. The first half of the eighteenth century saw ongoing climatic disruption, including the Great Storm of 1703, the Great Winter of 1709, and the coldest year overall (1740) in British history, a record unlikely to be broken. Near the end of my period, the eruption of the Laki Craters in 1783 shifted global weather patterns for a half decade and caused substantial localized devastation, as would the Tambora eruption in 1815.

What marks the transition out of the Little Ice Age and into the Anthropocene was not the return of stable climatic conditions but rather the development of infrastructures of production and transportation that insulated society from climate shocks. In Parker's account, the "fatal synergy" between climate and society was "broken" at the end of the seventeenth century with the emergence of a strong fiscal-military state, international trade networks, and increased agricultural productivity through enclosure, crop rotation, and selective breeding (*Global Crisis*, xxviii).[23] In somewhat different terms, Kenneth Pomeranz's "colonies and coal"—outward and downward expansion—allowed Britain and then Europe to transcend environmental constraints, reducing exposure to dearth and disaster while enabling an economic system based on accelerating growth.[24] Extending David Harvey's principle of the "spatial fix," Jason Moore calls these infrastructures of production and exchange "climate fixes," solutions to climatic crises of social reproduction that facilitated (temporary) escape from environmental vicissitude.[25] Like capitalist agriculture and colonial expansion, the epochal transition to a coal-based energy economy can be understood as a climate fix. Ji-Hyung Cho is, as far as I know, the one historian to identify the connection between the Little Ice Age and the coal takeoff directly. "The irreversible transition from renewable organic energy to nonrenewable inorganic energy," he asserts, "was experienced by Britain as an *active response* to the coldest weather in the last ten thousand years."[26] By the end of the seventeenth century, London had grown into the largest city in Europe because of its access to coal shipped from the northeast of

England. The seventeenth and eighteenth centuries saw the development of new coal-powered manufacturing industries and a shift from charcoal to coal in metal smelting, innovations that culminated in the fossil-powered factories and transportation networks of the Industrial Revolution. By the middle of the nineteenth century, if not earlier, the uptick in atmospheric carbon from coal combustion brought to an end the conditions of the Little Ice Age. Global warming replaced global cooling.

Climate and the Making of Worlds takes up the problem of narrating this story: of the end of the Little Ice Age, which is also the birth of the Anthropocene; of climate as a shaping force in human world making; but also of the development of productive forces that served as insulation from climatic exposure. It is a study of "geohistory," the complex interplay between a dynamic Earth system and dynamic social formations. Elaborating on what Moore defines as "the journey from geology to geohistory," it pursues a "historical method that grasps the material-symbolic formation of power in human organization" as "itself already constituted relationally in the web of life."[27] At the same time, this book explores the reasons why it is difficult to narrate a "geostory" in which the Earth and social institutions are coequal actors.[28] Again and again in the course of writing, I found myself emphasizing, even at the level of syntax, one agent or another: planetary or social causality, climate shocks or human adaptations, precarity or resilience, necessity or freedom, "the forces of nature" or "the forces of man," the naturally given or the human-made, *physis* or *poiesis*.

GEOHISTORICAL POETICS

Poetry, this book argues, offers a uniquely sensitive register of geohistorical conjuncture. My archive is a lineage of British blank-verse poetry, beginning with *Paradise Lost* (1667) and concluding with Charlotte Smith's "Beachy Head" (1807). Integrating new forms of knowledge into ancient literary genres, these ambitious poems aspired to encompass the whole of space and time, to describe what in *The Seasons* Thomson refers to as the "system . . . entire" (*Su*, 99). They were written over the course of a momentous century and a half during which Britain, emerging from decades of national conflict intensified by the Little Ice Age, as part of a dual process established the largest empire in world history and instigated the Industrial Revolution. I propose a geohistorical interpretation of the shifts that have long been associated with three phases in the history of English poetry: baroque allegory, Augustan description, and romantic lyric. A mode is a method, a way of accomplishing something, and I argue that shifts in the ways these poems solve the modal problem of defining their work and their mimetic relation to the world give expression to geohistorical transition. Critics have long recognized that poetry undergoes a series of seismic changes across this historical period, a story variously told as the decline of allegory, analogy, or personification; as a georgic renaissance and a georgic crisis; as the classic and the romantic, or the mirror and the lamp, or imitation giving way to expression; as lyricization. It is the project of this book to show how such modal change indexes several key stages in an epochal transition as Britain developed from an agrarian society, embedded in the climate system and subject to its shocks, to an industrial-imperial state that had begun to decouple from the concrete spatiotemporality of the planetary climate system.

So why should a poem, of all things, turn out to be a sundial telling the time of geohistory, providing an archive distinct from that offered by other artifacts, symbolic (paintings, weather diaries, sermons, travelogues) or material (landscapes, buildings, tools)? My answer begins with an observation about what poems share with these other made things. A poem, like any object of labor, evinces, in some partial way, the conditions of its creation. From its early emergence in Greek antiquity, poetics has been concerned with making: *poiesis* as work, energetic expenditure, a changing of form. Andrew Ford shows that the simultaneous "invention of poetry" and of poetics as a mode of criticism in the fifth and fourth centuries BCE involved the application of a "craftsmanly conception of making" to the labor of composing songs, newly distinguished from the activity of performing them. Such a conception highlights the technical skill involved in producing the *poiēma* as a tangible, if verbal, object. Ford relates the emergence of this critical language of poetic making to Herodotus's historical investigations of "past and present cultural forms." The poem, as a "made thing," is defined by its provenance at a specific point in secular linear time, as opposed to ever-renewed sacred time. In turn, having developed a materialist account of language and human perception, the atomist Democritus characterized poetry as a "human contrivance." Homer "constructed," as would a builder, "a universe [*kosmos*] of all sorts of words." *Kosmos* refers not only to an "ordered structure" or "ensemble" but also to a coherent whole, an enclosed worldlike object. The implied analogy between poem and house, both built objects, is unsettled by Democritus's materialist revision of an older account of creative "inspiration," of the *pneuma* as, if not divine breath, then the "moving stream of atoms in the air," the "influx of something airlike and volatile" that enables imaginative creation.[29] This understanding of air as the medium of an energy transition and so the

engine of creative activity will recur frequently in accounts of *poiesis*.
Poems, like plants, are objects made in the capture and channeling of
atmospheric energy, which is one reason why poems may be, not unlike
tree rings and ice-core samples, particularly sensitive records for tracking
the history of climate, at least as it intersects with the history of human
making.[30]

Across its long history, poetics takes up the familiar problem not only of
the mimetic relation of the poem (as imitation, representation, figuration,
fiction, fable) to the world but also of the poet's world making to other
practices of human labor and other instances of planetary energy flux. In his
Defense of Poesy (1595), Sir Philip Sidney draws attention to the suggestive
etymology of *poet*, "wherein," he writes, "I know not whether by luck or
wisdom we Englishmen have met with the Greeks in calling him a maker."
Sidney, however, inverts the materialist conception of poetry as artisanal
making developed by the early Greek critics, comparing the poet's trans-
formative activity to divine creation ex nihilo (the poet, "with the force of
divine breath . . . bringeth things forth"), an act independent of any preex-
isting materials and conditions other than the animating air. He compares
the poet's making with the arts of the astronomer or the physician wherein
"the works of nature . . . without which they could not consist, and on
which they so depend," establish the conditions and constraints of activity.
By contrast:

> Only the poet, disdaining to be tied to any such subjection [to the "depth
> of nature"], lifted up with the vigor of his own invention, doth grow, in
> effect, into another nature, in making things either better than nature
> bringeth forth, or quite anew, forms such as never were in nature . . . so
> as he goeth hand in hand with nature, not enclosed within the narrow
> warrant of her gifts, but freely ranging within the zodiac of his own wit.
> Nature never set forth the earth in so rich tapestry as divers poets have
> done; neither with pleasant rivers, fruitful trees, sweet-smelling flowers,
> nor whatsoever else may make the too-much-loved earth more lovely;
> her world is brazen, the poets only deliver a golden.

The poet, as maker, is unlike the farmer, who arduously cultivates the
Earth, but like the plant that raises itself from the soil into the air. Yet, for
Sidney, the difference between the poet's golden world and brazen reality
turns out to be a matter of idealization, "making things . . . better," rather
than sheer invention, bringing "forth" new "forms." After all, the golden
world that germinates in the poet's imagination shares with the world of

brass a hydrologic cycle (pleasant rivers), a biosphere (trees and flowers), and an atmosphere. It is no wonder, then, that, in the culminating passage of the *Defense*, Sidney refers to "the planet-like music of poetry."[31] Poetic making is, for Sidney, a kind of labor that disavows, even if it cannot fully escape, the instrumental logic of economic exchange, just as it imaginatively overcomes natural hardship, transforming floods into pleasant rivers, dearth into fecundity. This idealization of the Earth is oriented not toward a future, of projects and progress, but toward a past known retrospectively, a lost golden age.[32]

In his "Defense" (1821), Shelley unites the materialist historicism of the early Greek critics with Sidney's idealizing conception of *poiesis* as noninstrumental labor. Shelley's favored metaphor for the real—the shaping externality and the material of making—is the wind. "Poetry," he asserts, "is connate with the origin of man. Man is an instrument over which a series of external and internal impressions are driven like the alternations of an ever-changing wind over an Aeolian lyre." Later, the lyre, as a metaphor for the mind, is replaced with an image of combustion: "The mind in creation is as a fading coal, which some invisible influence, like an inconstant wind, awakens to transitory brightness." Figures of poetic making as planetary energy flux proliferate: "a spark, a burning atom"; "the first acorn, which contained all oaks potentially"; "a fountain forever overflowing"; "the root and blossom"; "a wind over the sea."[33] Heidegger, in turn, revisits the Greek artisanal language of *poiesis*. He compares the work of the poet not to the cultivator but the builder, "erecting things that cannot come into being and subsist by growing." Heidegger rejects the atmospheric figure of poetic making, linking *poiesis* not with inspired breath or flight but with inhabitation: "Poetry does not fly above and surmount the earth in order to escape it and hover over it. Poetry is what first brings man onto the earth, making him belong to it, and thus brings him into dwelling."[34]

In all these accounts, *poiesis* is defined by analogy with other examples of energy transition—work as the changing of form, as incipience and accomplishment, as capture and release, as flow and flame—that occur in the Earth's interlocking spheres of activity. The poet makes on a planet that is itself dynamic and eventful, the *oikos* in which he or she labors to create. Endeavoring to develop a "genuine poetics," Frye generalizes this condition as an axiom of criticism:

> The archetypal critic studies the poem as part of poetry, and poetry as part of the total human imitation of nature that we call civilization. Civilization is not merely an imitation of nature, but the process of

making a total human form out of nature, and it is impelled by the force
that we have . . . called desire. The desire for food and shelter is not con-
tent with roots and caves: it produces the human forms of nature that
we call farming and architecture. Desire is thus not a simple response to
need, for an animal may need food without planting a garden to get it,
nor is it a simple response to want, or desire *for* something in particular.
It is neither limited to nor satisfied by objects, but is the energy that
leads human society to develop its own form. . . . The form of desire,
similarly, is liberated and made apparent by civilization. The efficient
cause of civilization is work, and poetry in its social aspect has the func-
tion of expressing, as a verbal hypothesis, a vision of the goal of work and
the forms of desire.

Nature, for Frye, embodies not determination or formlessness but scarcity,
the inadequacy of the given—roots to eat, caves for shelter—that must be
transformed to fulfill human desire. Poetry then gives expression to a uto-
pian project, "the process of making a human form out of nature" (*Anatomy
of Criticism*, 105–6, 112). The mimetic problem—of *poiesis* as imitation or
idealization—is redirected through the governing metaphor of poetic mak-
ing as an act of labor comparable to cultivation and construction; *poiesis*
is not about the world as it is but about the world as it might be. But, in a
key sense, this possible world, the outcome of labor, is still very much the
world. Frye conflates the two forms of teleological activity that Heidegger
distinguishes, cultivation and construction, both of which are negotiations
with the climatic energy flowing through the Earth. Cultivation captures
the solar energy photosynthesized by plants. Construction is the making of
shelter that protects us from elemental forces.

Fredric Jameson, across a fifty-year career dedicated to the development
of a "poetics of social forms," returns often to Frye's claim that poetry inter-
nalizes a "vision of the goal of work." We can see this as early as the 1971
PMLA article "Metacommentary," in which he claims that "experience has
as its most fundamental structure *work* itself, as the production of value
and the transformation of the world."[35] The insurmountable necessity of la-
bor, the imperative to participate in an ecology or an economy, to appropri-
ate and expend energy as a condition of survival, is the existential condition
that any work of art will, as itself an outcome of labor, both acknowledge
and repress. We can see a version of this axiom in Jameson's recent *Alle-
gory and Ideology* (2019), in which he commends the return, in speculative
thought, to the "the aesthetic, in the sense of poesis or making, of creation
rather than of being or knowing." "Aesthetics," he affirms, "is indeed the

very allegory of production! It is constructivism which is at stake here in poesis and not consumption."[36] In *The Political Unconscious* (1981)—"a dialectical critique" but also a "fulfillment" of Frye's "methods" in *Anatomy of Criticism*—Jameson cites the long passage on poetry as civilizational activity.[37] He rejects Frye's ahistorical assertion of an "unbroken continuity between the social relations and narrative forms of primitive society" and those that prevail under capitalism as well as Frye's identification of private desire rather than the "destiny of community" as the utopian horizon of art. His materialist poetics shares with Frye's archetypal criticism an understanding of imaginative activity as expressing a "vision of the goal of work," but the final referent of this vision is the totality of social labor. The "work" of the symbolic object—what it represents, assembles, and resolves—is to be understood less in terms of the dialectic of alienation and utopia in any act of human making than in its relation to the particular historical forms taken by the world-creating labor of society, the "ultimate determination by the mode of production" (68–70, 45).

That the materialist critic limits totality to the form given to it by capitalism (or communism)—social labor—rather than the energetic transitions occurring in the biosphere or atmosphere is itself a symptom of the climatological unconscious, the positing of a social internality that can be conceptualized as independent of the Earth system. It is no wonder that, in *Allegory and Ideology*, Jameson turns so quickly from aesthetics as an allegory of production to a fantastic vision of the good Anthropocene: "the transmutation of ecological disaster into the terra-forming of earth, and of the population explosion into a genuine human age, an Anthropocene to be celebrated rather than caricatured in second-rate dystopias" (37). This failure to recognize planetary necessity—"nature" or, more precisely, the Earth system—as impinging on human making is pervasive across Jameson's oeuvre. "The external world is," as he writes in *Marxism and Form*, "the product of human labor and human history."[38] This assertion underwrites a method of reading literary history—the "decipherment of the Utopian impulses" within "ideological cultural texts" (*The Political Unconscious*, 296), with "utopia" standing for the transcendence of planetary necessity—that, as a work of Jameson-inspired metacommentary, this book historicizes as a symptom of carbon modernity.

The method I develop, geohistorical poetics, begins with the supposition that a poem will reflexively condense a broader set of mediations that, exceeding human identities and relations, give expression to the individual poet's and his or her society's inescapable imbrication in the Earth system, the condition of all productive activity. My contention, in essence, is that, as a symbolic mediation of the work that made it, any poem can be understood, in its world making and time shaping, to offer a meditation on the enigmatic yet omnipresent nature of energy, in its planetary and social manifestations. Even if we take alienated social labor as the "scandal . . . everywhere known, everywhere repressed," in acknowledging that such labor takes different forms under different modes of production we must also acknowledge that the moment labor is recognized as something more than sheer physiological exertion—the moment it is processed symbolically (conceptualized, figured, narrated in relation to an end)—it is known by comparison with other instances of work and change that are not necessarily human or social or even directed toward human goals.[39]

As a precedent for this work, then, I offer a final example from the history of poetics, one in which climate appears not as a displaced figure for human activity but as the shaping context of poetic world making. In his "An Essay on the Georgics," prefixed to Dryden's 1697 translation, Joseph Addison keys in on the famous passage in book 2 where Virgil compares his vocation to that of the farmer. The poet reflects on his own work, including the demanding Lucretian mandate to study nature's underlying forces ("rerum cognoscere causas"), such as "the moon's many labors," the "tremblings of the earth," and the "force to make deep seas swell and burst their barriers" (Georgics, 171). But he pulls back from such ambition, longing only to enjoy the shady woods and cool flowing waters of Haemus, a mountainous region in northern Greece associated with Orpheus. Addison, writing at the climax of the Little Ice Age, reflects on the exotic situation of a poet fantasizing about not warmth but coolness: "We may, I think, read the Poet's Clime in his Description, for he seems to have been in a sweat at the Writing of it. . . . And is everywhere mentioning among his chief pleasures the coolness of his shades and rivers, vales and grottos, which a more northern poet would have omitted for the description of a sunny hill and fire-side."[40] The poet's mimesis and the poet's desire, Addison suggests, reflects his climatic situation.

In the course of the Georgics, Virgil articulates a number of roles for poetry: as idealizing panegyric, in the celebration of glorious Italy (147), its happy farmers (169), and powerful sovereign (135); as consolation, as it is for Orpheus (251), or in the "song" with which the farmer's wife "solaces . . . her long toil" (119), or in the dream image of the "cool glens of Haemus" (171); and as a didactic investigation of the conditions of "unrelenting Toil, and Want that pinches when life is hard" ("labor . . . improbus, et duris urgens in rebus egestas") (109). Poetic labor is, in this last sense, associated not with the civilizational transcendence of natural conditions, or with the wishing away of difficult realities, but with the Lucretian imperative to acknowledge planetary necessity, what Virgil refers to as nature's "laws and eternal covenants" (103), what Lucretius calls the "manner" in which "each thing has a power / That's limited, and deep-set boundary stone" (*On the Nature*, 1.77–78).[41] In the passage analyzed by Addison, which provides a leitmotif for this study and a touchstone for the British poets I discuss, these competing ideas of poetry's task are placed in explicit and heightened tension, vividly staging what Frye calls the "conflict of desire and reality" (*Anatomy of Criticism*, 105).

Poetry offers an archive of geohistory because poems formalize the activity of making as a transformative redirection of planetary energy. I have foregrounded this metacritical proposition and shown that the long history of poetics as a significant tributary of criticism returns to this problem, if not conceptually, then at least in its figures of creation. I recognize, however, that the poetic tradition I examine in this book may be particularly amenable to supporting such a metacritical claim. If there is something distinct about the period I discuss, it has to do with the initial concurrence of two profoundly divergent energy regimes, the way a poetic apprehension of energy, as that which binds human societies to the Earth, appears, before the hegemony of fossil fuels and the thermodynamic physics that is its theoretical expression, in the comparison between free-flowing solar radiance and combustible minerals channeled through a furnace or engine. Yet what is distinct about the imaginative world making at the end of the Little Ice Age—as recording a stratigraphic break, boundary, unconformity—comes into focus only insofar as we define it in relation to a much longer genealogy, one extending back at least to early agriculture and the formation of monotheism and forward to a present in which we look toward the future with grave trepidation.[42] With this claim in mind, I turn to a second metacritical proposition about why poems might constitute a distinct register of geohistorical transition. In their allusive density, they are, like the Earth's strata, diachronic objects that record change and continuity across relatively long (in human time scales) durations of geohistory.

STRATIGRAPHIC CRITICISM

A periodizing argument such as the one developed in this book is possible only because poetry is a cumulative tradition. As Frye puts it: "Poetry can only be made out of other poems" (*Anatomy of Criticism*, 97). The symbolic material from which the poet forms a world is inherited from the literary past, which is why, as we have seen in Benjamin's approach to lyric poetry, poems can be understood to be layered with nonsynchronous time, what Reinhard Koselleck calls "time strata" (*Zeitschichen*).[43] What makes a literary work—and perhaps a poem most distinctly—compelling as a historical artifact is its capacity to give expression to historical diachronicity, the intersecting forces of change and continuity within the present that can be defined only with respect to the past and future. We continue to study literary history because—far from being simply "embedded in specific historical occasions," understood through ever-more finely grained historical contextualization[44]—any given work bears multiple strata, a layering of time, an archive of endurance and incipience. Any text preserves, revitalizes, and refigures symbolic material inherited from earlier phases of history in its weave of allusions and generic affiliations, patterns, as Wai Chee Dimock writes, of "cumulative reuse, an alluvial process, sedimentary as well as migratory." "In its suppleness of receiving," she adds, "poetry is probably a special case."[45] Drawing on a similarly geologic idiom, Kevis Goodman observes of Virgil's *Georgics* that "every line teems with the buried and multiple voices of other poets." This textual condition is figured in one of Virgil's most memorable images, that of the farmer's plow uncovering artifacts buried by time, an exemplary figure not only of human labor mixing with an Earth that is itself incessantly active but also of reading as an act of sifting through layers of allusion.[46]

In turn, the history of a poem's reception—the rewriting it inspires (or fails to inspire), the readers it finds (or fails to find), the manner in which it is taught or critically interpreted—provides further strata of meaning, up to and including the choice of a given scholar to teach it or write about it. When we interpret a literary work, Jameson writes, we are reading through the "sedimented layers of previous interpretations" as well as "sedimented reading habits and categories developed by those inherited interpretive traditions" (*The Political Unconscious*, 9). Critical reading requires us to consider earlier readings, a situation literary studies shares with constitutional law and talmudic hermeneutics. The poems discussed in my first two chapters, *Paradise Lost* and *The Seasons*, are the subject of reception histories of immense—perhaps unequaled—ambition, John Leonard's *Faithful Labourers* (2013) and Ralph Cohen's *The Art of Discrimination* (1964). Leonard introduces his two-volume study with a series of geologic metaphors, many of which derive from Milton. Critics are laborers who work the "pregnant soile" of *Paradise Lost*, their collective accomplishment producing a "mountain" of sediment that threatens to "bury" the poem.[47] No less than the allusions "buried" within a poem, its reception, popular as well as critical, contributes to its stratigraphic density, not an occluding top layer to be bulldozed away in search of an original text or in support of an original interpretation, but rather a more compendious archive of cultural continuity and change.

In this study, I return often to the stratigraphic tropology within the language of criticism, the figuration of texts as sedimented and fissured, crisscrossed by fault lines and strata, subject to processes of accretion and erosion, volatility and hardening. Such earthly figures of textuality have come under scrutiny in recent decades, often among scholars who cite the climate crisis as justification for a more positivist—"descriptive," "surface"—approach to the literary text, one that would bring criticism into epistemological alignment with the Earth sciences. As Wenzel notes, there is an irony, itself symptomatic of the predicaments we face, in the fact that critics concerned with climate change have rejected the figurative idiom literary studies borrows from geology.

The "postcritical" turn—the metacritical rejection of the hermeneutical methods closely associated with Jameson and historical materialist criticism—has been coincident with the mainstreaming of ecocriticism. In *Romantic Ecology* (1991), Jonathan Bate identified two events as context for the emergence of a "literary ecocriticism": the fall of Eastern Bloc communism and the publication of research linking extreme weather with global warming.[48] If, as the actual existing possibility of an alternative to liberal capitalism, history had come to an end, geohistory had reemerged as the inescapable condition of human world making. Bate polemically defines ecocriticism by contrasting its mode of textual interpretation with that of an earlier generation of "Althusserian" critics who read the romantic idealization of nature as an ideological suppression of sociopolitical conflict. Though he draws attention to the need to connect economic modes of production with the "economy of nature," the emphasis in his readings of Wordsworth's poetry and prose is the staging of individual experience, particularly the existential solace that can be discovered in wild nature. Romantic aesthetics provides an "education into ecological consciousness," an affirmative corrective to industrial modernity's reified and delocalized patterns of thought (84). Three years after Bate, Karl Kroeber published *Ecological Literary Criticism*, which similarly repudiates the "Cold War psychology" of earlier scholarship. Where Jerome McGann and Marjorie Levinson had seen a romanticism burdened by the experience of social contradiction and revolutionary failure, Kroeber, like Bate, characterizes the romantic poets as anticipating modern ecological science and developing a corollary aesthetic of "freedom and personal fulfillment" sustained "through conscious engagement with a dynamic cosmos."[49]

In this new millennium, the most tendentiously audible voices in criticism have carried on this first-wave ecocritical project, seeking to move beyond the "symptomatic" mode of interpretation exemplified by Althusser and Jameson, deemed by its detractors as "suspicious" or "paranoid," and to develop "postcritical" reading practices more in line with scientific modes of inquiry, such as paraphrase, description, and quantification.[50] It was Bruno Latour who in a 2004 *Critical Inquiry* article argued that in the age of climate crisis the "danger" comes not from those ideological surfaces that repress the real work beneath but from "an excessive distrust of good matters of fact," above all the "fact" of "global warming."[51] Sharon Marcus and Stephen Best draw on Latour's method of tracking the "assemblages" in which facts are produced, a project, they note, given urgency by the climate crisis. They call for an interpretive practice concerned with textual surfaces, asking readers to "stay close to our objects of study." For them, this means that the critic must "let go of the belief that texts and their readers have an unconscious," the latent and unspoken forms of meaning so central to Jameson's hermeneutic.[52] Rita Felski rejects critical modes that "interrogate, unmask, expose, subvert, unravel, demystify, destabilize" reading for "what lies concealed in . . . recesses and margins."[53] She singles out the stratigraphic figuration of reading as an act of "digging" and of texts as "composed of strata" where the "faults, cracks, rifts, fissures, and fractures" evince "subterranean forces" (the very metaphors of temporal disjuncture that criticism shares with archaeology and geology) (62). Channeling Latour, she contends that critical suspicion of positive knowledge and literal meaning is not viable in an age when "arguments about the social construction of truth are used to dismiss evidence of global warming" (45).

Postcritical readers such as Felski have, I believe, misrepresented the concept of the unconscious and the implications of stratigraphic metaphors in criticism. Far from claiming mastery, dialectical reading assumes a position of historical reflexivity vis-à-vis a text, what in a recent survey of three decades of romanticist criticism ("a geological core sample of that field—a deep-drilled cylindrical section of a historically layered domain"), Levinson calls a recognition of "the interdependent blindness and insight peculiar to one's moment of writing."[54] The principle that there is something that the text does not know about itself, evident in its gaps and incompletion, is inseparable from the principle that the text knows something about us, its readers, that we do not know about ourselves. Though Levinson defines her intellectual trajectory in terms of a "shift from a historical to an ontological materialism" (1), a shift she claims is exemplary of literary studies more generally, she defends the concept of the unconscious. The unconscious is not a "deep truth," hidden below the surface, but "one element in a dynamic process through which different kinds and degrees of knowledge . . . are related to each other" (9).[55]

Five years after Latour issued his call in *Critical Inquiry* for a renewal of critical realism in light of the climate crisis, Dipesh Chakrabarty published a groundbreaking article in the same journal in which he reached a very different conclusion. Individuals and nations, classes and races, are the protagonists in our genealogies of modernity, yet, Chakrabarty argues, our newfound status as "geologic agent[s]" on a global scale—a "shared catastrophe"—requires us to regard humankind as a single "species," a "natural condition." Such conceptualization, however, eludes both our inherited ways of "connecting pasts with futures" and the "phenomenology" of experience itself, throwing our inherited modes of historical understanding "into a deep contradiction and confusion."[56] Rather than affirming managerial and scientific reason, Chakrabarty calls for an renewed critical mode, oriented toward a "figure of the universal"—associated now with planetary catastrophe rather than classless society—"that escapes our capacity to experience the world" (222). In literary studies, even as some critics have used the climate crisis to justify more modest or positivist reading practices, others have expanded on Chakrabarty's work in claiming that the now indispensable dialogue with the Earth sciences does not require the critical humanities to relinquish its concern with speculative and negative knowledge, with figurative and nonreferential modes of representation, with absent causality, and with a stratigraphic understanding of texts as layered and fractured, symbolic objects not only formed but deformed in their composition and passage through time.[57]

In this book, I argue that—as a problem of historical understanding, of knowing (and not knowing) our place in geohistory—climate change requires a deepening, rather than a slackening, of symptomatic reading practices. I make a case for the ongoing relevance of the method of reading exemplified in Jameson's *Political Unconscious*, yet I identify planetary determinations, including the climate, as lacunae in materialist approaches to literary history. *Climate and the Making of Worlds* advances a mode of reading and an interpretation of the history of English poetry concerned with the relation between the positivity of representation and the unconscious as an absence, break, or negation. Literary studies, it argues, is best able to contribute to the cross-disciplinary conversation organized around the climate crisis in its sensitivity to the limits of knowledge, the way

silence and omission shadow saying, the exclusions that enable a represen-
tation of the world to be assembled, the conditions of synthesis but also
nonresolution. To read critically, in light of the Anthropocene proposal, is
to identify textual symptoms that express not historical but socioecological
or even geohistorical contradiction, to recognize not only energy systems
but also the Earth system as internal to the structural whole ("totality") and
so as providing a horizon of interpretation by which the historicity of the
symbolic object—in its dialectic of disclosure and nondisclosure, knowing
and not knowing—might come to be intelligible.

Not unlike the lithostratigraphic "signatures" that divide epochs in the
Geologic Time Scale, a poem achieves meaning in its mediation of disjunc-
tive temporal orders. It is this sense of a layering of nonsynchronous time,
of accretion and erosion as conditions of meaning making, that justifies the
long-standing analogy between literary texts and geologic strata as objects
of study, literary history and geology as modes of inquiry.[58] Geology draws
on the vast scales and improbable events of epic and romance.[59] Historicist
criticism, in turn, borrows from geology a stratigraphic language of spatial-
ized time, in Nigel Clark's words "a lexicon of seismic shifts, fault lines,
eruptions, upheavals, fractures, fissures, abysses, chasms and rifts."[60] As in
a cross section of the Earth, in a text multiple periods and forms of time
can be present. In a uniquely reflexive treatment of such geologic tropes,
Eric Gidal models his study of the "poetic unconformity"—the unrecon-
ciled languages of progress and loss in Macpherson's Ossian poems—on
James Hutton's concept of the geologic unconformity. Unconformities are,
in Gidal's words, "angular disjunctions in the stratigraphic record that dem-
onstrate breaks in the geological history of a region . . . physical manifesta-
tions of heterogeneous time, compressions of distinct eras of sedimentation
caused by orogenic shifts and subsequent erosions that have produced radi-
cally discordant appearances in the layering, or 'superposition,' of strata."[61]
The unconformity embodies the shifting forces at work in the Earth's his-
tory, periods of deformation, erosion, or sea-level change that produce varia-
tions and gaps in the geologic record. An unconformity is a mark of what is
absent, a discordance that registers different episodes in the Earth's history.
Offering a "bibliostratigraphic" reading, Gidal, in turn, applies the con-
cept to Macpherson's poetry and its reception among those eighteenth- and
nineteenth-century critics who read Ossian's mythic landscapes in order to
make sense of their experience of living across "two distinct epochs" (7).

   Notwithstanding Foucault's influential claim about the static structures
of *historia naturalis* in the "classical" episteme, geohistoricism, and the

analogical thinking it licenses, has a long history.[62] One of the arguments of this book, in fact, is that, prior to the development of nineteenth-century "comparative historicism," analogy was already being used, in the words of Devin Griffiths, as a "tool that brings the relation between previous ages and the present into focus, seeking the origins of contemporary social and natural order within the patterns of past events."[63] As Martin Rudwick observes in his study of the disciplinary history of geology, the discovery of the Earth's dynamic prehuman past actually required a historiographic sensibility derived from the study of human history, what he calls the "transposition from culture to nature": "Ideas, concepts, and methods for analyzing evidence and for reconstructing the past were deliberately and explicitly *transposed* from the human world into the world of nature, often with telling use of the metaphors of *nature*'s documents and archives, coins and monuments, annals and chronologies."[64] As we will see, this metaphoric traffic goes both ways.

What Thomas Ford calls a "new conception of time" that emerges at the end of the eighteenth century—the "radical temporalisation of nature" as defined by "a dynamical causal process of changes and disruptions"—has, in fact, a long prehistory.[65] An approach to reading the Earth's superimposed layers and discordant forms as an archive of planetary change can be said to extend at least a century before Hutton, to Thomas Burnet's four-book *Sacred Theory of the Earth* (1681–90). Burnet was a "world maker" in the sense given by John Keill, in his critical review of *Sacred Theory*, to refer to those who dared to speculate about the physics of biblical cosmogony, inspired by Descartes's hypotheses about Earth's formation by mechanical processes in *Principia philosophiae* (1644).[66] In fact, the first world makers were, as Burnet acknowledges, the Epicurean atomists. Lucretius describes a process of planetary genesis without supernatural steering in the fifth book of *De rerum natura*.[67] Following Lucretius, Burnet and other savants recognized planetary geomorphology as the outcome of processes of change.[68] For Burnet, the Earth's "broken form" (*Sacred Theory*, 99) invites the speculative reconstruction of a cataclysmic history, "the Rise and Fall, and all the Revolutions, not of a Monarchy or an Empire . . . but"—scaling up— "of an entire World" (25). Burnet starts with a problem of deformation or displacement: how did planetary matter come to be arranged as it is, asymmetrically? He considers three "irregularities" in the Earth's "present form and composition": subterranean chasms, mountains, and the oceanic abyss. Of the latter, he writes: "So deep and hollow, and vast; so broken and confus'd. . . . This would effectually waken our Imagination, and make us inquire . . . how such a thing came in Nature; from what causes, by what force or engines could the Earth be torn in this prodigious manner? did they dig the Sea with Spades, and carry out the molds in hand-baskets?" (104). To reconcile biblical chronology with a geohistorical narrative based on physical causality, to see the Noahic Deluge as the scripturally given "Force" that rearranged the Earth's face, is only to confront what Burnet calls a "great difficulty": accounting, naturalistically, for the sudden appearance of sufficient water to envelope the planet and alter its shape (39). His solution is to hypothesize that the surface of the antediluvian Earth was uniform and that a subterranean vault of water was released when, dried by the "heat of the sun," the Earth's crust ruptured, leaving behind the Earth's variegated mountains and oceans, this "Heap of Ruines" (67, 231).

Examining the Earth's broken forms, Burnet developed an account of the historicity of the Earth, and he speculated about the relation between the Earth's epochs and the ages of man.[69] A planet, he asserts, does "differ . . . from itself, in different periods of its duration," and "every new state of Nature doth introduce a new Civil Order, and a new face and Oeconomy of Humane affairs" (Sacred Theory, 140). Two centuries later, geology and political economy had both matured into recognizable disciplines, yet each continued to compare stages in the Earth's history and stages in human history, the forces of planetary change and the forces of production. Geologists modeled the study of the Earth's history on archaeology, the revolutions of time recorded in the ruin of human-made artifacts compared with the stochastic forces at work in deep time. Karl Marx, in turn, drew on geology to develop a new way of thinking about epochs of human history, as defined by the technologies and relations organizing production. In chapter 15 of Capital, "Machinery and Large-Scale Industry," the longest chapter in the first volume, he draws an analogy very much at odds with the current stratigraphic imperative to identify the Anthropocene epoch in terms of what Simon Lewis and Mark Maslin call a "clear, datable marker."[70] "Epochs in the history of society," Marx observes, "are no more separated from each other by strict and abstract lines of demarcation than are geological epochs."[71] It is in this chapter, concerned with the role of machinery in mediating the relation of natural forces to labor productivity, that Marx establishes a parallel between historical and geologic periodization. The specific implication is of a Lyellian uniformitarianism, no single transformative event but a cumulative process of change.[72] Like Lyell, however, Marx cannot not periodize, even as he recognizes that periodization imposes strict boundaries in place of complex dynamics of change.

The question of labor's relation to natural forces is persistent through Capital. In the opening chapter on the commodity, Marx observes: "When man engages in production, he can only proceed as nature does herself, i.e., he can only change the form of the materials. Furthermore, even in this work of modification he is constantly helped by natural forces [*Naturkräften*]" (133–34). In chapter 7, labor is defined as the process wherein man "confronts the materials of nature as a force of nature": "He sets in motion the natural forces which belong to his own body" (283). This setting in motion requires the intermediary agency of the "instrument," which converts planetary and bodily energy into directed "work." "The earth itself," Marx writes, "is an instrument of labor," but to be employed as such, whether in agriculture or other modes of production, "presupposes a whole series of other instruments" (285). The instrument also "serves as a conductor" between the worker and the "object of labor," leading to its transformation (287). In relating these "instruments of labor" to the succession of socioeconomic formations (*Gesellschaftsformationen*), Marx was again drawing on Lyell. In a note, he observes that historians have paid little attention to "the development of material production, which is the basis of all life," whereas the "investigations of natural science" have delineated "prehistoric times" "according to the material used to make tools and weapons, into the Stone Age, the Bronze Age, and the Iron Age" (286). Such investigations were the subject of Lyell's *Geological Evidences of the Antiquity of Man* (1863), which Marx read during the months in 1863 when he was actively grappling with the role of technology in organizing economic periods. The analogy between historical and geologic periodization is even more explicit when he asserts: "Relics of bygone instruments of labour possess the same importance for the investigation of extinct economic formations of society as do fossil bones for the determination of extinct species of animals. It is not what is made but how, and by what instruments of labour, that distinguishes different economic epochs" (286). Fossilized bones are to extinct organisms as superseded tools are to their socioeconomic epoch. Bones are instruments, forms that organize the channeling of force by a given species, just as a human being conducts "natural forces" via his "own body, his arms, legs, head, and hands" (283).

I have detailed this unlikely genealogy of geohistorical analogy across disciplines and in crucial moments of discipline formation first as a reminder that the problem of strata as materializations of time, what Gidal calls the "spatial exposure of temporal dislocations" (*Ossianic Unconformities*, 139), has long informed historical and scientific inquiry alike. When literary critics reject figures of spatialized time in order to align criticism more closely with science, they overlook the fact that such metaphors play a crucial role in the development of both geologic and materialist historicism. What a symbolic object such as a poem shares with the "broken form" of the Earth, a fossil embedded in sediment, or an outmoded tool is diachronicity, an existence that endures even as it is changed—broken up, made residual, buried—through history.

Second, for Marx and Lyell at least, periodization, the identification of "epochs in the history of society," no less than geologic epochs, confronts an irreducible contradiction within what Jameson calls "the narrative structure of historicity." Any account of diachronic change entails both continuity and rupture, a duration that is also a break.[73] This same narrative predicament—the imperative and impossibility of periodization—is evident in the deliberations of the Anthropocene Working Group, which is tasked with the particular challenge of reuniting the disciplines the formation of which I have been discussing. In a recent publication on the relation of Earth-system science to stratigraphy, several members of the group make it clear that the case for the new epoch is based not on nuclear weapons or industrial agriculture or the expansion of human infrastructure but on anthropogenic climate change. The Earth system involves numerous interlocking spheres of activity, but its key principle of homeostasis is, they write, the "highly systemic nature" of the climate, the interconnections between the atmosphere, the hydrosphere, and the biosphere that maintain a consistent planetary energy balance.[74] The Earth's history, then, is understood in terms of long phases of relative systemic stability, "a distinct mode of operation persisting for tens of thousands to millions of years within some envelope of intrinsic variability," punctuated by transformative events, "a transition from one fundamental state of the Earth System to another, . . . a regime shift" (325–26). In this account, we are in such a period of transition "outside the Holocene norm," the prevailing climatic conditions over the past twelve thousand years (335). The current "rates of change of the climate system," driven by human activity, far exceed the natural variability of the Holocene. Owing to carbon dioxide and methane emissions, the Earth system has entered "a *trajectory* away from the Holocene," "crossing . . . a threshold into the trajectory of the Anthropocene" (337). For the Anthropocene Working Group, *trajectory* implies a condition of indeterminacy—in the sense of both contingency and unknowability—within a transitional present. Its members assume that the Earth system will, at some undetermined point in the future, enter a new "state" of relative climatic stability. "The ultimate nature of the Anthropocene," they write, "cannot yet be determined." In other words, the current geologic epoch is neither the Holocene nor the Anthropocene. We are, as Davies writes, "living in the fissures between one epoch and another" (*Birth of the Anthropocene*, 2).

ENERGY CRITICISM AND THE STRATIGRAPHIC TEXT

With this brief history of the circulation of figures of stratigraphic periodiza-
tion between planetary and social registers in mind, I return to the implica-
tions of such figures for literary criticism. Attention to the multiple strata
registered in the text's fractured form—its failure to cohere as a fully self-
present object, its contradictions or "fault lines"—turns out to be the prin-
ciple that motivates Jameson's famous, if often misunderstood, injunction,
"Always historicize!"[75] As early as "Metacommentary," Jameson identifies
the nonunity of the text with the diachronic situation of reading. Any at-
tempt to understand interpretation, he argues, must begin by acknowledging
what he calls the "strangeness . . . of the hermeneutic situation," the very
"need" to interpret (10). Interpretation must interpret itself, the difficulty it
faces in defining its struggle for meaning, the sheer labor of reading as well
as its incompletion, its incertitude, and its inability, finally, to distinguish
itself from its object of study, as a proper analytic method should, since a text
requires a reader before it can begin to mean anything at all. To confront
this puzzling situation, to ask *why* we read critically before we ask *how*,
requires us, Jameson suggests, to consider the temporal lapse that separates
the production and the reception of any text. Hermeneutics, he argues, be-
gins in the imperative to account for historical (and cultural) difference, to
"assimilate monuments of other times and places" (10) in cases where the
text's world (period, context) is not that of the reader. The example he often
cites as the model of his own interpretive method is patristic and medieval
exegesis, where the story of the nation of Israel recounted in Jewish scrip-
ture is interpreted allegorically to prefigure Christ's redemptive sacrifice.
The manifest content of the Old Testament is retrospectively granted a la-
tent anticipatory significance. Jameson compares such exegesis, in which
meaning is discovered as much in what is not said as in what is said, to the
"Freudian hermeneutic," but, whereas for psychoanalysis the distinction
between surface and depth symptomatizes psychosocial repression, for the
"traditional hermeneutic" the principle of partial meaning that requires in-
terpretive reconstruction "was ultimately History itself" (15).

In *The Political Unconscious*, Jameson identifies three horizons of in-
terpretation, each of which corresponds with a given context of textual pro-
duction: the individual "political" speech act, the collective discourses of
class antagonism, and history itself, the "mode of production," the relations
and forces by which humans organize the work of reproducing social life.
Drawing connections between the "time scheme" that defines a given text
(97) and the mode of production as a "total system," however, does not

allow the reader to stabilize meaning but instead offers an explanation for
the multiple and irresolvable strata of mimetic activity within a text. Be-
cause any social formation contains "several modes of production," some
vestigial and some emergent, literary texts are "crisscrossed and intersected
by a variety of impulses from contradictory modes of cultural production"
(95). As an example, we might think about how late capitalism, structured
in relation to immaterial flows and algorithmic logics, still depends on not
only concrete and steel but also that ancient mode of production: agricul-
ture. Social reproduction in the twenty-first century is still built on a pri-
mary biospheric energy chain: autotrophs capturing sunlight and hetero-
trophs, including humans, metabolizing that energy. For Jameson, it is the
concurrence of modes of production, the noncontinuity between coexistent
modes of production with "relative autonomy," that explains why literary
texts are layered with surfaces and depths, are—far from being cohesive
formal objects—characterized by "rifts and discontinuities" (56), their at-
tempts at resolution always (interestingly, symptomatically) impossible.
The reader must tease apart "a host of distinct generic messages—some of
them objectified survivals of older modes of cultural production, some an-
ticipatory." Certainly, it can be said of many cultural objects that they give
expression to "*a field of force* in which the dynamics of sign systems of sev-
eral distinct modes of production can be registered" (99), but literary texts,
and poems in particular, are distinctly amenable to this internalization of
diachronicity because of their semantic density and layers of allusion.

Introducing a groundbreaking cluster of articles in *PMLA*, Patricia Yae-
ger returns to this account of textual "rifts and discontinuities" as she
proposes that the "uneven" history of "energy sources" might provide the
basis for a reperiodization of the cultural past. "Perhaps energy sources,"
she writes, "enter texts as fields of force that have causalities outside (or in
addition to) class conflicts and commodity wars."[76] Human labor, whether
as existential condition or social relation, is itself meaningful only as it is
imbricated in the broader history of energy sources, energy "converters,"
and the infrastructures and social relations that connect them.[77] Yaeger and
other scholars working in the emerging field of the energy humanities ask
us to link textual layers and lacunae with the energy regimes that organize
society, giving a more literal significance to the question Marcus and Best
associate with suspicious reading: "What those absences mean, *what forces
create them*" ("Surface Reading," 175; my emphasis). Recent scholarship
has investigated not only the ways texts explicitly represent fuel and in-
frastructure but also, more ambitiously, the manner in which what Heidi

Scott calls a society's "energy imaginary"—its manner of valuing labor, of delineating boundaries, its principles of causality and change, its economies of surplus and scarcity, its figures of the manifest and the hidden, of concentration and dispersal—reflects an "energy ontology," "the nature of surviving, working, and consuming" within "specific fuel regimes."[78] Since it is, in fact, the source of all activity and change, any society will develop ways of naming and narrating energy. Such energy imaginaries, we can speculate, contain intuitions both about the commensurability of energy forms and about the entropic reduction of usable energy in closed systems since these are the underlying conditions of all production, all making, and all change.

Much of the research on the social and literary implications of energy regimes has focused on fossil fuels, particularly petroleum.[79] Owing to their energy density and transportability, oil and other fossil fuels enable an abstraction of space and time, a disaggregation of extraction, consumption, and disposal, a decoupling of cause and effect that makes it impossible to connect the phenomenology of modern life with the geologic consequences of mass fossil-fuel consumption. The Anthropocene concept updates (and complicates) a long-standing story that identifies the rise of fossil fuels as the definitive feature of modernity, with Watt's double-acting steam engine serving as the iconic turning point. In the short article initially proposing the recognition of the Anthropocene as an epoch in the Geologic Time Scale, Paul Crutzen and Eugene Stoermer traced it to atmospheric changes caused by rising coal combustion in the "latter part of the eighteenth century" that can be tracked through the isotopic analysis of ice cores. They correlate this stratigraphic signal with a historical event, "James Watt's invention of the steam engine in 1784."[80] The science of thermodynamics, the "self-sustaining economic growth" of "fossil capitalism," Marx's materialist historicism, and anthropogenic global warming all developed, in tandem, in the century after that invention.[81] The steam engine served as the exemplary technology for nineteenth-century energy physics because it both manifestly organizes energy conversion—heat transformed into pressure, pressure transformed into kinesis—and offers a closed system in which the input (coal) and the output (work) can be precisely quantified. As Cara New Daggett, Allen MacDuffie, Nigel Clark, Kathryn Yusoff, and others have observed, one of the inheritances of the Industrial Revolution is a conception of energy as fuel, converted and channeled toward mechanical "work," the transformation of matter toward human ends.[82] Modern social theory, including Marxism, gives theoretical expression to a concept of energy—as capturable, quantifiable, and commodifiable—materially instantiated in the coal-powered steam engine and the factory system. This concept is a key building block for the notion of society as a closed system, fully independent of the Earth system.

So what might it mean to conceptualize energy and the relation of energy to society prior to the hegemony of mineral power and prior to Thomas Young's use of *energy* in 1807 to refer to a quantifiable unit of work? E. A. Wrigley asserts that the "equivalence" between mechanical and thermal energy "was not suspected by people in the eighteenth century; the notion that a horse pulling a treadmill and a coal fire heating a lime kiln were in some sense doing the same thing would have appeared absurd to them."[83] As we have seen with Burnet, however, prior to thermodynamic physics it was entirely possible to recognize an equivalence between heat, kinesis, and work. In the course of this book, I consider a number of other examples of prethermodynamic intuitions of energy commensurability, above all in a poetic language in which solar radiance is said to gleam, stream, glow, pour, brighten, illumine, melt, shake, strike, swell, awaken, ferment, and concoct. This book tracks what Daggett calls the "expansive, multidimensional figuration of preindustrial, poetic energy" (*Birth of Energy*, 4), a vernacular understanding of energy that takes as its source of input not the finite stock of subterranean coal but the flow of solar radiation and takes as its exemplary converter not the steam engine but the planetary climate system. This climatic energy imaginary reflects a social world still largely embedded in diurnal and seasonal rhythms, an economic world defined more by agricultural production and the global circulation of commodities than labor markets or machines.

Climate, in this sense, is a primary source of energy input: solar radiation as flows through the atmosphere (as wind and heat), the hydrosphere (as ocean currents and the hydrologic cycle), and the biosphere (in the growth of plants and so animals). Such a conception of climate corresponds with a point made by Emmanuel Le Roy Ladurie. "La nature et le climat avec ses fluctuations," he maintains, are among "les forces de production."[84] Dagomar Degroot develops a similar claim in his study of the Netherlands during the Little Ice Age. "Climate change," he observes, "influenced pre-industrial societies by affecting how much energy people could extract from local environments, and how they could use it. Energy that bore the imprint of weather, and over the course of decades climate change, sustained human lives and enabled complex civilizations. . . . By altering the material world—including human bodies—it influenced how people thought and created culture" (*The Frigid Golden Age*, 302). In preindustrial societies, patterns of light and darkness, heat and cold, moisture and aridity, the everyday weather and the occasional storm, the circulation of air and water, the growth and change of living things, are not only the immediately perceivable elements of everyday experience but also the direct context of human productive activity.

Recognizing the Earth's climate as the total context of human world making, however, requires us to push further still, identifying climate as a primary manifestation of energy scarcity and energy surplus, determining human projects and so leaving a mark in the symbolic domain even when it is not directed toward social reproduction, captured or put to work within a given mode of production. Here, it is useful to turn to Bataille's distinction between a "restricted economy," in which energy can be captured, calculated, and made available for exchange, and the "general economy," the basis of which is the abundant and unceasing flow of solar energy that powers nearly all activity on Earth.[85] Social relations, for Bataille, begin in neither scarcity nor exchange but rather in an originary surplus. Any ecosystem or economy is, like the planet itself, an open system, constantly renewed and agitated by the solar radiance that enters from without. Thus "human community," as Nigel Clark observes, must be understood "as an extension of the tumultuous and excessive energy of the sun" (Inhuman Nature, 110). The argument of this book—one developed through a sustained reading of poetry written during a period of momentous energy transition—is that the general economy and the restricted economy, the climate system and the infrastructures of energy production, must be conceptualized in their interconnection. The ineluctable difficulty of such conceptualization—of narrating history as the interrelation of energy forms that are planetary givens and social artifacts—is a further symptom of the climatological unconscious.

MODAL HISTORY: POETRY AND PRODUCTION

Christophe Bonneuil and Jean-Baptiste Fressoz remind us that "the history of energy is not one of transitions, but rather of successive additions of new sources of primary energy."[86] The thesis that underlies my reading of British poetry written between the Restoration and the romantic period extends this insight to the diachronicity sedimented in changing poetic modes. It is the superimposition of flow-based "solar" and stock-based "mineral" energy economies that produces, in the poems I treat, the antinomies, rifts, and displacements that enable the poem to constitute its symbolic world.[87] To literalize the topographical figure of reading, it is, at least in part, the concurrence of energy systems in this period—of the sunlit atmosphere and ripening fields; of trade winds, flowing rivers, and distant plantations;

of subterranean mines and the hidden interiors of the furnace, factory, or engine—that creates the dynamics of *surface* and *depth* in the poems I discuss. Disjunctures between seasonal or diurnal forms of time consciousness and the accelerative abstract temporality of industrialization produce apprehensions of geohistorical change, of living through an epochal transition. This is not formalized or disciplinary knowledge. It is, rather, the more capacious and sensitive type of understanding that manifests in figure and form and even (or especially) in negation, in the manner in which what is not or cannot be represented leaves a textual trace.

The poems I discuss in this book describe the heat of summer and the cold of winter, the cycles of wind and water, the labor of fields, factories, mines, and plantations. However, geohistorical transition is expressed not only in what poets write about, what they are able to describe, but also in changing modes of poetic representation, the manner in which a poem establishes a mimetic relation to the world in its principles of figuration and referentiality, expansion and contraction. *Mode* is a broader category of critical distinction than *genre*, though less abstract than *form*, and all three concepts are notoriously slippery. From the Latin *modus*, mode refers to a measure or method, a way of accomplishing something, a manner of producing an effect, of directing material toward an end. Frye, the critic most closely associated with a "theory of modes," differentiates modes according to the degree of agency shown by the protagonist, the relation of the hero to "other men and to the environment" (*Anatomy of Criticism*, 33). Although my account of modal change—allegory, description, lyric—does not correspond, exactly, to Frye's declensionist "five epochs of Western literature" (35), beginning with ancient myth and concluding with modern irony, it draws on his sense that modes best express the relation between human production and natural givens.[88]

In chapter 1, I read *Paradise Lost* as a baroque allegory collapsing under the weight of a history that turns out to be geohistorical, not least in the "cold / Climate" that, in his final address to the muse, the poet worries will "damp" his "intended wing" before he can finish his Protestant epic (9.44–45). Milton appropriates this pagan genre in order to narrate the creation story of Hebrew scripture, which itself encodes a mythopoetic inheritance of the long Holocene, featuring the veneration of a solar deity, an origin myth (the Fall) in which the sudden deterioration of the climate necessitates a new regime of hard agricultural labor, and (perhaps the oldest story) the narrative of the Deluge.[89] I follow Benjamin in emphasizing the discordant naturalism of baroque allegory, its internalization of a natural-historical sense of time as entropic flux and unidirectional emergence, a heightened awareness of diachronic change contrasted with the "mystical instant" of symbolic revelation.[90] In Milton's naturalistic retelling of sacred history, the allegorical signifier, the poem's manifest content, comes to mean in excess of any allegorical signified. The moral architecture of the allegory is, in fact, sustained through the persistent contrast between two regimes of energy, the "pure ethereal stream" of heavenly light and the "materials dark and crude, / Of spiritous and fiery spume" found "deep underground" (3.7, 6.478–79). The action of *Paradise Lost* begins with Satan recognizing a change of one clime (Heaven) for another (Hell) and then convincing his comrades to continue their revolt against God by invading the "happy isle" Earth, either to "possess" it or "with hell fire / To waste" (2.410, 364–65). This initial instance of climate "change" anticipates the diachronic catastrophe that is, with the Fall, the beginning of Earth's disequilibrium. The postlapsarian "air that now / Must suffer change," bringing "change / Of seasons to each clime," is a definitive symptom of the uncertain planetary order that spells the end of analogical knowledge and the beginning of a form of descriptive knowledge rooted in the hard georgic labor of cultivating a recalcitrant Earth (10.212–13, 677–78).

Descriptive poems, such as Thomson's *The Seasons*, proceed by parataxis, the multiplication of concrete particulars, ranging across diverse scales and orders. This mimetic imperative is rooted in the principle that any comprehensive view of the world's interlinked economies and climates requires attention to the distinguishing detail, the specificity of the region or climate, the season or time of day. Description is, I argue, the mode of an energy economy organized around the geographic and annual variance in the availability of sunlight. Descriptive realism is most closely associated with the rise of the novel, culminating in the novel's totalizing ambitions as the modern epic. By telling the story of Augustan descriptive poetics, I establish a less familiar genealogy of realism, offering a perspective on the current debate about the novel's resources for representing the climate crisis by returning to poetry's history as a medium of knowledge transmission.

The focus of chapter 2 is Thomson's *The Seasons*, the preeminent long poem of eighteenth-century Britain, a work translated and emulated across Europe. As its title suggests, Thomson's mixed-genre descriptive poem gives form to the idea of a consistent climate, the texture of the circling year, annual oscillations in access to solar efflux. The formal expansiveness of descriptive verse represents a period of mercantilist expansion in which the British economy grew by gaining access to foreign climes. Yet, like Milton, Thomson also emphasizes the "severer sway" of the seasons and the "flux" of planetary history that undermine human projects (*Sp*, 317;

Su, 35). In chapter 3, I discuss three long blank-verse poems that test the limits of description in their attempts to represent emerging sites of industrial production: *The Fleece* (1757), John Dyer's georgic of wool manufacturing and trade; *The Sugar-Cane* (1764), James Grainger's georgic of the Caribbean sugar plantation; and *Edge Hill* (1767), Richard Jago's locodescriptive account of Black Country coal mining and Birmingham metal manufacturing. I identify the representational pressures and infelicities that emerge when poets try to extend ancient genres, concerned with nature's variability and limits, to modes of production that render nature abstract and delocalized, when they attempt to reconcile fantasies of accumulation decoupled from environmental constraint with literary conventions oriented around virtuous labor and seasonal recurrence. These industrial georgics fail—to find an audience, to count as good poetry—precisely insofar as they succeed in intimating the hazards of industrial-scale production.

In the first chapter, description manifests as an imperative within baroque allegory, an expression of the insistence of geohistory, Earth's spatiotemporal variability, in the story of human world making. In the concluding chapter, I show how lyricization—as a modal principle of poetic expansion, association, and resolution—emerges within descriptive poetics, offering a solution to the inadequacy of inherited conventions in an industrial age. Since Hegel, it has been recognized that—like the novel and unlike other verse modes—lyric invites a theory because its development, or at least its claim to literary preeminence, occurs under the pressure of modernization. To read lyric as the definitive genre of the early Anthropocene is to restate, in geohistorical terms, a long-standing account of the lyric as an expression, in Benjamin's words, of the "alienating, blinding experience of the age of large-scale industrialism" ("Motifs in Baudelaire," 314). In lyric, the narrator's individual consciousness, buffeted by the shock and obscurity of modern life, provides the scale and focal point of the poem. The poet—often seeking refuge, in untouched nature, from an increasingly reified world—replaces the economy of nature and nation as the focalizing scale of poetic world making. I begin with Cowper's lyricized georgic *The Task* (1785), written over two years in which the catastrophic effects of the Laki eruption made many observers wonder whether Judgment Day had arrived. As a volcanogenic haze migrates from Cowper's descriptions of the countryside to the greenhouse and the city, he finds himself unable to distinguish nature's seasonal "revolvency" from eschatological presages or the modernization process itself, the historical "revolution" embodied by worsening urban pollution (*The Task*, 1.372, 462).[91] Because *The Task* is unable to sustain its symbolic moral topography—"God made the country, and man made the town" (749)—the narrator's own search for a calling, a redemptive vision of what it means to know or create a world, offers the only viable principle of formal closure. I turn next to Wordsworth's "Tintern Abbey," the locodescriptive poem that closes the first edition of *Lyrical Ballads* (1798) and stands so often as the paradigmatic example of the romantic lyric. The condition of possibility for Wordsworth's lyric, wherein the individual finds relief from the psychic damage of modern life in an imagined reciprocity with nature, is, I argue, an etherealization of the atmosphere and a mystification of the planetary energy flows that support production. This study concludes with a reading of Charlotte Smith's "Beachy Head" (1807), a sweeping topographical poem that in its attention to the Earth's dynamic history brings together, stratigraphically, the poetic modes I discuss. Smith fluently links theories of the Earth with the climatic exigencies of conquest and commerce, rural labor with precise descriptions of the time sequences of flora, even as she also explores the lyric impulse to escape from an oppressive climate—and "human crimes" as well.[92]

From a certain perspective, the three poetic modes (allegory, description, lyric) could not be more distinct, which is why in so many accounts of literary history they are seen to correspond with well-delineated literary periods, sequestered as autonomous kingdoms of professional literary studies. Such genealogies support certain judgments about what literature ought to accomplish, about who we are now as readers and how we should read old poems.[93] Yet the poets I treat in this study, writing across three literary "epochs," were part of a continuous tradition.[94] All of them returned to and revised topoi received from the Latin poets, especially Lucretius, Ovid, and Virgil. All of them adopted Milton's blank verse. And all of them read one another. Indeed, it is likely that every poem I discuss in detail was composed with knowledge of every earlier poem. For the purposes of my stratigraphic argument, then, the most important figure of speech is among the least flamboyant: allusion. I track a number of motifs that reappear in these poems, most of which have classical precedents: the poet overcome by heat, the revitalizing effects of a shady bower or an inspiring breath of fresh air, the sun passing through an opaque and disturbed atmosphere, the agriculturalist watching his fields destroyed in a flood, the sailor on a storm-tossed sea. It is because verse is so intertextual that we can locate stratigraphic density within it.

Moreover, elements of allegory, of description, and of lyric coexist in all these poems. "Once we have learned to distinguish the modes," Frye observes, "we must learn to recombine them" (*Anatomy of Criticism*, 50).

Epochs in literary history, to put this another way, "are no more separated from each other by strict and abstract lines of demarcation" than are epochs in the history of the Earth or of societies. This is an argument about uneven transitions in modes of production and in poetic modes rather than clean breaks. All the poems I treat are descriptive. Description is based on the principle that minute variations in concrete time and space have causal significance. The roots of description can be found in the classical epic; in Lucretius's insistence that the smallest deviation in the trajectory of an atom is the source, at once, of emergent causality and historical contingency; and in Virgil's argument, in the *Georgics*, that successful husbandry requires attention to seasonal and regional variations, "what each clime yields and what each disowns" (*Georgics*, 103). If description gives expression to historical succession and geographic variation, allegory seeks to assemble the particulars of manifest reality in an all-encompassing story: providence, or progress, or the anagogic expectation of a salvific end of time. For eighteenth-century critics, personification—and above all the poetic "address to inanimate objects personified," which Hugh Blair called "the boldest of all rhetorical Figures"—was an inheritance from an allegorical past that persisted, somewhat unaccountably, in descriptive poetry.[95] Such personification appears in all the poems I discuss, from Milton's deifying address to light to Wordsworth's apostrophe to the River Wye. "As soon as descriptive impulses strive for accuracy," Angus Fletcher writes, "personifications arise, like will-o'-the-wisps rising from the ground, to invest the material descriptions with spiritual meanings."[96] (And, as I argue in the first chapter, *spiritual meaning* is best understood as the absent presence of energy itself, as that which endows matter with motion and animacy.) Finally, all the poems examined in this study feature lyric moments in which the poet's embodied consciousness, mental labor, and shaping environment are foregrounded as conditions of poetic composition and historical knowing.

This book, as I have noted, not only develops geohistorical readings of these poems, as individual works and exemplars of modal shifts, but also offers a history of critical reception, as another layer within which to register geohistorical diachronicity. I identify certain patterns of interpretation—changing ways of reading these old poems—as expressions of the disavowal of planetary determination that I see as the defining ideological reflex of industrial modernity. Though the materialist heterodoxies of *Paradise Lost* were widely recognized in the century after its publication, as John Leonard has shown, critics came increasingly to insist on the epic's coherence as a statement of Protestant orthodoxy, dismissing or ignoring Milton's strange personifications and flirtation with Lucretian materialism. If the critical tendency in reading *Paradise Lost* has been an ascription of theological unity that displaces its layer of descriptive naturalism, its abiding concern with the Earth, readers of *The Seasons* have taken the opposite tack, questioning the unity of a poem that describes the "circling year" (*Su*, 14). What is at stake, I suggest, in interpretations such as Samuel Johnson's that complain of the poem's "want of method" is the question of whether seasonal recurrence and so climate can lend formal unity to Thomson's diverse topoi. In other words, assigning formal coherence to *Paradise Lost* and denying it to *The Seasons* accomplish similar ends: negating the planetary as the ultimate referent. The largely forgotten but fascinating industrial georgics discussed in the third chapter have suffered a different fate. From their very first publication, critics asserted that the new modes of production—mining, manufacturing, and the plantation system—were infelicitous subjects for verse. While these ambitious poems were quickly relegated to the poetic past, romantic-era lyric poems, such as Wordsworth's "Tintern Abbey," that find personal solace in unproductive nature and an anodyne climate have come to be read as exemplifying an ecological aesthetics that continues to have relevance for us today.

This reception history, in turn, returns us to the question of poetics as a critical enterprise and so one of method, how we ought to read literary history in this time of climatic upheaval. Dialectical criticism, Jameson writes, includes an "essentially critical, negative, rectifying moment, one which forces upon us an abrupt self-consciousness with respect to our own critical instruments and literary categories" (*Marxism and Form*, 375). It combines the familiar gesture of retrospectively identifying textual symptoms—fissures, evasions, or contradictions that express an element of history unfixed or incipient, incompletely experienced or symbolized—with an appreciation for what the fullness of the past might disclose about the conditions of our own nonknowledge, the conditions that determine what we notice and fail to notice when we read. After Jameson, and as a corrective to Jameson's project, in this book I define this negative moment in terms of modern criticism's climatological unconscious, suppositions about literary mediation and historical context premised on the analytic separation of society from the Earth. The climatological unconscious is, as I show, a symptom of the fossil-fuel-enabled fantasy of an escape from planetary vicissitude. It also reflects the more fundamental challenge of thinking multicausality, or overdetermination, across scales, in the conjuncture of the planetary and the social. The "structural causality" that is nowhere present but everywhere constitutive, existing not as an underlying foundation or totalizing enclosure but in "the entire system of *relationships* among . . . levels" (Jameson, *The Political Unconscious*, 35–36), is best understood as the metabolic relation between the institutions organizing social reproduction and the biogeophysical systems channeling energy flux through the Earth.

"Earth Trembled": *Paradise Lost*, the Little Ice Age, and the Climate of Allegory

CLIMATIC INFLUENCE

The action in *Paradise Lost* begins with a fiery journey from one world to another and so with a question about why worlds matter. The apostate angels plunge to Hell, "hurled headlong flaming from the ethereal sky / With hideous ruin and combustion" (1.45–46). Satan and his "horrid crew" lay "in the fiery gulf," reckoning with the consequences of their rebellion (51–54). We see their new world through the "eyes" of Satan as "he views / The dismal situation waste and wild, / A dungeon horrible, on all sides round / As one great furnace flamed" (55–62). The first action undertaken by Satan and Beelzebub, in book 1, is to seek relief in this infernal environment. They alight from the "fiery waves," finding refuge on a "dreary plain, forlorn and wild," "glorying to have scaped the Stygian flood / . . . by their own recovered strength" (180–84, 239–40). Satan studies his surroundings like a settler surveying an unknown land. Turning to Beelzebub, he asks: "'Is this the region, this the soil, the clime / . . . / That we must change for Heaven, this mournful gloom / For that celestial light?'" (242–45).

Clime, in this instance, implies atmospheric conditions: the "dusky air" (1.226), "rolling smoke" (671), "floods and whirlwinds of tempestuous fire" (77). Hell's climate is thick, smoky, and hot, like the interior of a furnace. As Ken Hiltner notes, Milton's depiction of its noxious air, produced by "ever-burning sulfur" (69), echoes contemporary complaints about London's atmosphere, polluted by highly sulfuric sea coal.[1] England was, by the Restoration, burning five times as much coal as the rest of the world combined. During the seventeenth century, the average rate of increase in London's use of coal was comparable to that of industrial Britain in the nineteenth century. Mineral coal, imported from Newcastle, was burned for domestic heating and cooking, "the staple fuel of the capital," a replacement for increasingly rare and expensive charcoal and firewood.[2] Coal was also finding new uses in manufacturing industries, leading to an "early Industrial Revolution" and the beginnings of an economy organized around mineral energy.[3] In 1661, as Milton was composing *Paradise Lost*, John Evelyn published his jeremiad on coal pollution, *Fumifugium*, addressed to the recently restored Charles II. He compares London—with "its Hellish and dismall Cloud of SEA-COAL"—to "the Suburbs of *Hell*." "For when in all other places the *Aer* is most Serene and Pure," he writes, "it is here Ecclipsed with such a Cloud of Sulphure, as the Sun it self . . . is hardly able to penetrate and impart it here."[4]

The association of climate with atmosphere was fairly novel in the seventeenth century. We can detect in Satan's use of *clime* an older meaning as well. *Klima*, for the Greeks, referred to a latitudinal band, an inclination of the Earth with respect to the sun. Climate was, in this earliest sense, a differential concept, a geometric principle of planetary variation. "A Clime is properly a space of the Earth comprehended between two Parallels," as Patrick Hume glosses Satan's line in the 1695 annotated edition of *Paradise Lost*.[5] By the seventeenth century, if not earlier, this cosmographic idea of climate had begun to coalesce with a Hippocratic understanding of the relation of bodily health to regional environments, including seasonal patterns, temperature, and winds as well as the distinct properties of the water, air, and soil.[6] A clime is a place more or less wholesome, more or less fertile, more or less conducive to human flourishing. *Climate* is thus a comparative term contrasting fixed places with respect to physical features but also salubriousness, fitness for inhabitation, cultivation, and prosperity. "Satan's is a Fiery Climate, a Torrid Zone," Hume observes. Examining his surroundings, Satan acknowledges the consequences of his actions, a "dire" outcome to the rebellion, "as this place testifies" (1.625). Losing Heaven, he gains perspective, realizing that there exists an alternative to the now lost "happy realms of light" (85). As the narrator affirms: "O how unlike the place from whence they fell!" (75). Heaven, as the reader will discover, also has a climate— "climes of bliss" (11.708)—with "ambrosial" air and "cool winds" blowing at night (5.642, 655).

The pride that fuels Satan's rebellion, explored retrospectively in the middle of the epic, is based on an ontopolitical conception of identity: Satan "affecting all equality with God" (5.763). The narrative action begins, however, only when the conflict with Heaven becomes territorial. The refusal to recognize divine sovereignty is transposed, in the epic's opening scene, into a refusal to be influenced by the torrid clime. Having studied the "infernal world," Satan professes to be one who "brings / A mind not to be changed by place or time" (1.251–53). "What matter where," he asks, "if I be still the same . . . ?" (256–58). This is a characteristic statement, one that echoes Satan's claim during the War in Heaven to be, with the other rebels, "self-begot, self-raised / By our own quickening power" (5.860–61). The poet, however, undercuts this assertion of autonomy. Using his spear for support, Satan walks unsteadily over the burning soil, "and the torrid clime / Smote on him sore besides" (1.297–98). As William Cowper notes in glossing these lines, Milton had a habit of conveying "the effect of violent heat by the verb *smite*" (a word that is striking and requires a gloss because it expresses a thermodynamic intuition of the equivalence of heat and force).[7] Angelic bodies turn out to be vulnerable to extreme temperatures, immortal but still ruled by the climate. The dramatic irony—the gap between Satan's stoic avowal and the reality of his situation—evinces a form of unacknowledged determination, not ontological or political but climatic.[8] An inventor and explorer, associated with concentrated energy and transoceanic empire, Satan imagines himself acting independently of spatiotemporal exigency. In undercutting his hubristic claim to exist separately from his "dismal world" (2.572), Milton stages a version of what I call the *climatological unconscious*.

Throughout his life, Milton grappled with theories of climatic influence, from the sway of the seasons on poetic inspiration to the role of climate in shaping the character and destiny of nations.[9] Milton's nephew Edward Philips famously reported that the poet's inspiration was curtailed during the warmer months: "His Vein never happily flow'd, but from the *Autumnal Equinoctial* to the *Vernal*, and that whatever he attempted was never to his satisfaction, though he courted his fancy never so much."[10] Another early biographer, John Toland, asserted, to the contrary, that Milton's creativity was awakened in the springtime, citing his early Latin poem "In adventum veris," in which the young poet writes: "Earth, with her strength renewed, is donning her brief youth and the frost-free soil is putting forth its green sweetness. Am I deluded? Or are my powers of song returning? . . . My breast is aflame with the excitement of its mysterious impulse and I am driven on by the madness and the divine sounds within me."[11]

Milton was particularly concerned with the notion that the cool, wet climate of England induced mental sluggishness and a conflictual national character, a theory influentially promoted in Jean Bodin's *République* (1576) and Giovanni Botero's *Relationi universali* (1591–96). Fink identifies eight references, across Milton's oeuvre, to the "adverse effect of cold climates" ("Milton and the Theory of Climatic Influence," 71). In the "Digression" of the *History of Britain* (written around 1648, published in 1681),

Milton looked to the harsh northern climate to explain the failure of his countrymen—ancient Britons as well as his contemporaries—to preserve the political liberty for which they so valiantly fought. Britons never lack the courage or ferocity to claim their freedom; rather, he suggests, they lack the civic virtue and intelligence to retain it: "For the Sun, which we want, ripens Wits as well as Fruits."[12] Milton's journey to Italy in 1638 had sharpened his sense of this climatic difference, the contrast between "fruitful Italy," as he wrote in a poem addressed to Giovanni Salzilli, and his home country, "where the worse of the winds, powerless to control its crazy breath, pants in cold blasts."[13] In the *Reason of Church-Government*, published in 1642, Milton named his own resolution to adopt the "Epick form" to English if, he says, there be nothing "advers in our climat" that would check this ambition.[14] Then, of course, the narrator of *Paradise Lost* worries, in the final address to the muse, that the "cold / Climate" will "damp" his "intended wing," keeping him from completing the epic (9.44–45). The poem culminates with a significant climate shift, one implication of which, as Michael tells Adam, is humoral: "in thy blood will reign / A melancholy damp of cold and dry / To weigh thy spirits down" (11.543–45).

In his "Life of Milton," Samuel Johnson rejected such accounts of climatic influence, Milton's "fancy" that "the *climate* of his country might be *too cold* for flights of imagination" (*Lives*, 1:99). As we will see, Johnson often takes this skeptical position, ridiculing the notion that authors or nations are susceptible to the weather, the seasons, or the climate. "This dependence of the soul upon the seasons," he writes, "those temporary and periodical ebbs and flows of intellect, may, I suppose, justly be derided as the fumes of vain imagination. *Sapiens dominabitur astris*. The author that thinks himself weather-bound will find, with a little help from hellebore, that he is only idle or exhausted." It is the theory of climatic determinism, not climate itself, that impinges on human agency: "But while this notion has possession of the head, it produces the inability which it supposes. Our powers owe much of their energy to our hopes . . . when it is admitted that the faculties are suppressed by a cross wind, or a cloudy sky, the day is given up without resistance; for who can contend with the course of Nature?" (98).

Johnson's dismissal of climatic causality seems to have shaped subsequent generations of Milton critics, few of whom have seriously considered the persistent problem of climate and so of the relation of "Nature" to "our powers" in Milton's verse. This chapter examines the broad range of pagan myth, sacred history, and early modern natural philosophy on which Milton draws as he represents the climate and the Earth in his great epic. My aim, however, is to develop a geohistorical reading of *Paradise Lost*, to ask whether the poem itself, as allegory, has been marked by its geohistorical context in ways that exceed the poet's capacity for intentional, explicit, or cohesive representation within inherited frameworks of knowledge. Milton's "cold / Climate" is, rightly, glossed as a geographic reference, alluding to England's location at the far reaches of the temperate zone. *Climate* is, in its early modern sense, a term of synchronic, spatial comparison. In this chapter, however, I propose that we register a diachronic meaning in the phrase; that, in *Paradise Lost*, *climate* implies geographic but also geohistorical variance; that, like Lucretius and other world makers, Milton recognized that the Earth is a planet with a history; and that such historicity could be seen as a cause and a consequence of human action. The diachronic understanding of climate finds support in ancient texts, including *De rerum natura*, Ovid's *Metamorphoses*, and the Deluge narrative in Genesis. It also, I believe, reflects the fact that climatic variability during Milton's lifetime was unusually intense.

Milton began composing *Paradise Lost* during the winter of 1657–58, which John Evelyn called the "severest winter that any man alive had known in England."[15] The frigid winter was followed by an atypically hot and dry summer, caused by the same blocking ridge. In the years during which he wrote *Paradise Lost*, Milton not only lived through the disintegration of the Protestant Commonwealth, the restoration of the monarchy, the Great Plague, and the Great Fire of London; he also experienced one of the most acute phases of the Little Ice Age. Between 1646 and 1661, England suffered ten failed harvests, fatally undermining the Commonwealth.

If Milton expresses uncertainty about the influence of climate on his creative output and on the aptitude of his countrymen for self-governance and projects this uncertainty into the narrative structure of *Paradise Lost*, historical retrospection has done little to clarify the vectors of climatic causality in the seventeenth century. While there is near consensus that the period between 1400 and 1850 saw a statistically significant decrease in planetary mean temperatures, reaching a low point between the 1570s and the 1690s, there remains significant disagreement about the scope and causes of the Little Ice Age.[16] Even more controversial are attempts to discern connections between climatic variability and historical eventfulness: famines and food riots, patterns of settlement and migration, pandemics and wars. The Swedish historian Gustav Utterström is often credited with establishing modern climate history in several articles published in the mid-1950s in which he identified connections between climate, agricultural productivity, and demographic change in early modern Europe. He argues that Fernand Braudel failed to recognize the decisive role of climate in late seventeenth-century famines in southern Europe, an oversight that reflects not only the inherent difficulty of reconstructing past climates but also "the common tendency among historians to try to explain social phenomena exclusively in terms of political and economic causes."[17] This is the "Durkheimian principle," as Wolfgang Behringer puts it, "whereby the social is explained by the social."[18]

In turn, one of Braudel's students, Emmanuel Le Roy Ladurie, took up the project of advancing the climate history of early modern Europe, but he did so, in his early work, by downplaying what he called "the climatic interpretation of human history" as proposed by "climatic romancers" such as Utterström (a claim that echoes Johnson on Milton's climate "fancy," suggesting an essentially literary and imaginative quality of climatic explanations).[19] In limiting himself to "facts which are strictly climatic," in avoiding positing direct linkages between climate and famine or migration, Ladurie aimed to make the case for the historiographic reconstruction of climatic variation itself (17). Recently, however, Ladurie published the extensive *Histoire humaine et comparée du climat*,[20] making explicit the connections that were left obscure in *Times of Feast, Times of Famine*. He even acknowledged elsewhere that Braudel had warned him not to put forward a thesis that "claimed that climate affected the course of history, but he thought I could get away with a book in which all the data pointed that way, provided my conclusions minimized the link."[21]

Geoffrey Parker's *Global Crisis* represents the most ambitious attempt to identify the "fatal synergy" between the climatic perturbations of the Little Ice Age and systemic sociopolitical unrest on a global scale, "the general crisis" of the seventeenth century (xxv). Parker adopts the language of Earth-system scientists in describing how climatic pressures on social reproduction led to unpredictable "tipping points that end the existing social, economic, and political equilibrium"; a period of crisis ensues, followed by the eventual "emergence of a new equilibrium" (xxx). Extreme weather serves as an "intensifier," putting pressure on vulnerable sites such as marginal agricultural lands and cities and so increasing the likelihood of famine, pandemic, and political conflict. The cumulative effect was a one-third reduction of the population in Europe and Asia during the seventeenth century. Of particular relevance to the reconstruction of Milton's experience, Parker shows that bad weather and drought contributed to Charles's failed campaign against Scotland in 1639, leading to the armistice that gave Scotland control of Newcastle coal, a major source of leverage as Londoners struggled through the cold winters of the 1640s. During the Republic, climatic exigencies, Parker argues, played a significant role in the failure of Cromwell's effort to seize control of the Caribbean. This failure, along with a series of hard winters, harvest failures, and disease outbreaks in the 1650s, paved the way for the Restoration. While Parker's account has been highly influential, it has also been controversial. Paul Warde, for example, argues that Parker relies on "the accumulation of examples" rather than "repeated clear-cut demonstrations of cause and effect," a "synergistic *alchemy*" magically linking climate change with sociopolitical crisis at scales ranging from the local to the global.[22]

ALLEGORICAL STRATA

This chapter proposes that the historiographic problem of tracking causality in the synergistic alchemy linking climate and society can be productively compared to the critical problem of reading allegory. "It is by virtue of a strange combination of nature and history that the allegorical mode of expression is born," writes Benjamin (*The Origin of German Tragic Drama*, 167). Allegory, for Benjamin, registers an apprehension of natural-historical "transience" that can be captured only in a literary mode that stages its own insufficiency such that "the false appearance of totality is extinguished" (176–77). Allegory stages a displacement or deferral of a principle of mediation that would synthesize fact and meaning, the perceived world and its underlying forces, a principle that can exist only—if at all—in the interpretive code brought by the reader.

Critical accounts of *Paradise Lost* as allegory confront the poem's proliferating levels or strata of meaning, the challenge, in reading a purportedly orthodox Protestant poem, of reconciling its cacophony of voices and diverse modes of figuration, generic commitments, and forms of reference. In his discussion of *Paradise Lost*, Johnson extends René Le Bossu's influential account of allegory, arguing that Milton began with a "moral," the vindication of providence, which the story, "a narration artfully constructed," serves to illustrate (*Lives*, 1:122). The moral is "essential and intrinsick"; the epic action is secondary, a blend of biblical fact and imaginative fiction that points toward a truth ("providence") irreducible to its particular instances ("history"). Johnson identifies the issue that Milton's readers inevitably confront. In choosing to narrate revealed history, to tell of "the fate of worlds, the revolutions of heavens and of earth," Milton introduces numerous elements of his own imagining. By sending his "faculties out upon discovery, into worlds where only imagination can travel," he risks the

confusion of the literally true with the "licentiousness of fiction" (127, 131).
Johnson's solution to this problem is a common one. The poem achieves
its theological aims only by implication, in the manner in which charac-
ters and events exemplify the moral: divine grace actualized in our human
freedom to choose. For Johnson, however, the relation between manifest
narrative and latent moral is destabilized by various other figurative op-
erations, including the "mythological allusions," the similes that expand
"beyond the dimensions which the occasion required," and the Spenserian
personifications, abstract figures such as Death and Sin granted "material
agency" (128, 133). Such extraneous figuration intensifies the ambiguity
produced by the rift between matter and spirit, description and doctrine. If
not in the very attempt to renarrate sacred history then in this unsettling
proliferation of figurative layers, Johnson maintains, "Milton's allegory . . .
is undoubtedly faulty" (133). And, when personifications become agential,
"allegory is broken."

The status of *Paradise Lost* as an allegorical poem remains a major
source of critical debate, as does the conceptualization of allegory itself, as
a distinct mode or a more fundamental hermeneutical imperative insepara-
ble from *poiesis* or even representation as such. It was neoclassical critics
such as Johnson who established the correlation between allegory and person-
ified abstractions like those that populate Spenser's *Faerie Queene*.[23] After
his return from Italy, Milton began to plan a series of ambitious literary
projects, including a dramatic retelling of the Fall. In the first outline for
a work to be titled "Paradise Lost," he foresaw a fifth act in which, in his
words, Adam and Eve are shown "personifications of the consequences of the
Fall, but also Faith, Hope, and Charity."[24] It is sometimes suggested—inaccu-
rately, as my discussion of the personified Earth will show—that only two
such personified abstractions remain in *Paradise Lost*: Satan's offspring, Sin
and Death. The rejection of a wider cast of personified figures is taken as
evidence of the "antiallegorical nature" of the poem.[25] Indeed, Johnson ob-
serves that Milton's original design would have "produced *only* an allegory"
(*Lives*, 1:89).

Other readers continue to grapple with the interpretive burden imposed
by the poem's proliferating modes and levels of figuration, its insistence on
indirect or nonmimetic forms of meaning. Since allegory is often assumed
to require meta-allegorical cues—if not "instructions for its own interpre-
tation" (Teskey, *Allegory and Violence*, 3), then at least acknowledgment
of the representational dilemma that necessitates indirection—accounts of
Paradise Lost as allegory often turn to Raphael's response to Adam's request

for a "full relation" of what "hath passed in Heaven" (5.554, 556). "Sad task and hard," Raphael responds, "for how shall I relate / To human sense the invisible exploits / Of warring spirits" (564–66). Coming not long after his monist avowal of "one first matter all" (472), here Raphael promotes a more heterogeneous ontology: forms more or less corporeal, more or less visible, more or less accessible to human comprehension.[26] The assertion of a discontinuous reality that exceeds description and so requires figuration, with its unique resources for representing difference as well as similitude, is, of course, an inevitable implication of any belief in a supernatural deity. Thus, Raphael's "difficult" task, within the poem, becomes a way of meta-allegorically representing Milton's own task, to "see and tell / Of things invisible to mortal sight" (3.54–55), to justify the ways of an "invisible king" (7.122). Despite his monism, Milton rejects empiricism, a knowledge grounded in direct perception. Just because we perceive the Sun to revolve around the Earth, Raphael reminds Adam, does not mean that it does so.

As Mindele Anne Treip observes, Raphael's pledge to accommodate his representation of Heaven (5.570–76) to the needs of Adam's sensible perception and "process of speech" (7.178)—in short, to say one thing as a means of suggesting something else—is the promise of allegory itself. For Treip, the "diverse *strata* of 'truth' and fiction in the poem, diverse *levels* of language and figuration," including its "anthropomorphic" depictions of God, are themselves the essential condition of its allegorical procedure.[27] Much as Milton came to emphasize the role of "inner conscience" in guiding the interpretation of scripture (Poole, *Milton and the Making of "Paradise Lost"* 102), so, according to Treip, does any reconciliation of these multiple strata, any stabilization of literal and figural reference, occur only in the "fit" audience's capacity for introspective reading. Allegorical resolution occurs in the Protestant reader's difficult but generative experience of negotiating "many kinds and levels of realism and non-realism" (*Allegorical Poetics*, 242). Treip recognizes that allegory is best understood as a crisis of meaning expressed in the proliferation of mimetic strata. What requires more careful (geo)historicization is this "authentic Protestant aesthetic" itself (229), which would see in introspection and individual choice the solution to the problem of theodicy—an explanation for cosmic disorder and planetary transience—as well as to the hermeneutical predicament posed by allegory itself. As Christopher Kendrick persuasively argues, Milton, writing in a period of "emergent capitalism," gives expression to an ideology organized around individual self-determination in his opposition to feudal and absolutist forms of political sovereignty no less than in a theodicy according to which God made man "Sufficient to have stood, though free to fall" (3.99). Arminian theology corresponds to an ideology of possessive individualism.[28]

In her revisionist approach to Miltonic allegory, Catherine Gimelli Martin places *Paradise Lost* in "the transitional cosmos of baroque poetics," where rapid historical change and the emergence of new sciences attentive to incomplete knowledge ruptured the allegorical translation of nature into spirit.[29] Allegory is, thus, a decidedly postlapsarian genre, the story of history as "an emergent pattern of meaningfulness," its "uncertain symbolic register embracing at once the Fall's effect on the poet in his poem, and on the unpredictabilities of our responses" (21–22). Far from representing a stable and coherent "cosmic hierarchy" (Fletcher, *Allegory*, 139), baroque allegory expresses, according to Martin, historical discontinuity, "the transition from one great epoch to another," a "phase shift" (*The Ruins of Allegory*, 24). In particular, it seeks to reconcile the new incertitude—grounded in attention to a desacralized, chaotic, and stochastic nature that no longer signifies providence, if it ever did—with the older eschatological promise of a complete history, given spatial form in the medieval system of correspondence between superlunary and sublunary spheres. Divine presence can, according to Martin, be discovered only in its fragmented residue in the vitalistic and atomic activity of Milton's "expanded naturalism" (28). Since my ultimate emphasis here is metacritical, it is worth quoting at length the crucial statement of method that distinguishes Martin's study from the mainline of Milton criticism, which attributes to his texts an "ontological consistency" (Fallon, *Milton among the Philosophers*, 169), a "religious coherence" (Poole, *Milton and the Making of "Paradise Lost"* 161), or a "coherent aesthetic scheme" (Treip, *Allegorical Poetics*, 249). Martin writes: "In the very act of encoding the abstract ideals of a culture, the aims of allegory necessarily exceed the mimetic range of the probable. In the process, its analogies, like its referents, become entangled, not only with the systematization of cultural values, but also with their contradictions. For this reason alone, any insistence that Milton's epic-allegory should have a consistent, that is, a determinate or certain as against an indeterminate or uncertain, sense would seem to misunderstand its construction, which by definition cannot be univocal" (*The Ruins of Allegory*, 29). Only by accepting the polyvocality of *Paradise Lost*, she argues, is it possible to read the poem—as the poet insists we must—as a reparative work composed amid "the ruines" left by "our first parents."[30]

Martin's approach to allegory—as a mode that in its formalization of generic incertitude gives expression to an experience of historical rupture—

draws on what is now rightly acknowledged to be the twentieth-century critical text responsible for revitalizing our understanding of allegory after the mystifications and denigration of neoclassical and romantic critics: Benjamin's famously unsuccessful habilitation dissertation on the German *Trauerspiel*.[31] What distinguishes baroque allegory is, according to Benjamin, its insistent internalization of a natural-historical temporality. While the symbolic logic of sacrament unites substance and spirit according to the world-annihilating, world-renovating "*light* of redemption" (*The Origin of German Tragic Drama*, 173; my emphasis), baroque allegory confronts a landscape that in its disorder fails to signify a divinely given origin or end.[32] With confidence in neither transcendental empowerment nor Baconian projects of human world making, baroque allegory is, Benjamin asserts, "the form in which man's subjection to nature is most obvious" (166). He links baroque allegory's antitranscendental stance with the naturalistic justification of sovereign absolutism. A geohistorical perspective might, however, relate the images of a mortal and ruined world in baroque allegory to the catastrophic weather events, famines, epidemics, wars, and political insecurity that predominated during the depths of the Little Ice Age.

Fredric Jameson articulates in precise terms the hermeneutical dilemma in allegorical interpretation and opens it up to the widest possible significance. As Johnson noticed, the challenge of reading *Paradise Lost* is to reconcile its multiple layers of reference and figuration, truth and fiction, concrete description and abstract implication. With its "structure of multiple meanings," Jameson claims, allegory gives expression to antinomies— for example, in theology between narrative and doctrine or individual and collective salvation—intensified by the differentiation of classes and modes of production and the emergence of a world system that exceeds not only direct perception but ideation itself. In its suspension of the drive toward synthesis, it emerges as a "solution" when "beneath this or that seemingly stable or unified reality *the tectonic plates of deeper contradictory levels* of the Real shift and grate ominously against each other and demand a representation, or at least an acknowledgment, they are unable to find in the *Schein* or illusory surfaces of existential or social life": "Allegory does not reunify those *incommensurable forces*, but it sets them in relationship with one other in a way which, as with all art, all aesthetic experience, can lead either to ideological comfort or the restless anxieties of a more expansive knowledge" (*Allegory and Ideology*, 34; my emphasis).

Allegory, then, is the name for the text's refusal to offer the reader an interpretive code—a principle of reconciliation, of mediation—that would satisfactorily stabilize levels of meaning at the same time that the text continues to assert some possibility of truth that exists in the relation among the levels. The reference to "incommensurable forces" recalls Jameson's definition in *The Political Unconscious* of *allegory* in terms of Althusserian "expressive causality," "the opening up of the text to multiple meanings" (28–29), "a host of distinct generic messages—some of them objectified survivals from older modes of cultural production, some anticipatory, but all together projecting a formal conjuncture through which the 'conjuncture' of coexisting modes of production at a given historical moment can be detected and allegorically articulated" (99). Though his touchstone is the development of thermodynamic physics rather than changing modes of production, Bruce Clarke suggests something similar in describing energy as a "powerful allegorical operator," concerned with a latent similitude that underlies manifest difference, mediation between levels or systems, and the entropic dispersal of meaning or potential (as does Martin in an allegorical reading of *Paradise Lost* concerned with its incipient recognition of the first and second laws of thermodynamics).[33]

In this book, I am proposing a reading practice in which the ultimate horizon of intelligibility is provided not by the emergence of the capitalist mode of production but by the broader interchange between social forms, including capitalism as a world ecology, and planetary energy flux. From the standpoint of a geohistorical materialism, the "incommensurable forces" at work in history are (1) the energy flows in the Earth system that are a condition of possibility for social reproduction yet always exceed and potentially destabilize such reproduction and (2) the infrastructures and institutions by which societies organize their relations and modes of production in connection with those planetary forces. In Milton's England, the harsh climate of the Little Ice Age—"cold and heat / Scarce tolerable" (10.653–54)—put pressure on social reproduction, limiting the productivity of marginal land, and increasing costs for food and fuel as well as the likelihood of harvest failures, disease outbreaks, and civil turmoil.

In the rest of this chapter, I show how other mimetic strata within *Paradise Lost*—the epic plot, the naturalistic similes, the personification of the Earth, the theological antinomy between free-flowing light and combustible minerals, and the representation of the Fall as a climate shift—give expression to these "incommensurable forces": planetary vicissitude and human world making. I have already hinted at one such climate fix: downward expansion, the exploitation of mineral coal, the atmospheric trace of which we encountered in the depiction of Hell as a furnace and will consider again when we examine Satan as a personification of concentrated energy. A second climate fix, to which I now turn, is the traditional theme of epic, outward expansion: the colonization of a "new world" (2.403) and the exploitation of new resource frontiers. Jameson makes the Earth's lithosphere the concrete vehicle for his abstract theory of allegory. But what if, along with other manifestations of energy flux in the Earth system, those "tectonic plates" are themselves among the "incommensurable forces" that demand "acknowledgment"? What if Jameson's metaphor is read literally, much as I will read Milton's account of the Fall as actually a story of climatic deterioration, such that the theological moral and the eschatological promise are seen to offer imaginary resolution to real geohistorical contradictions? Notably, Simon Lewis and Mark Maslin literalize the figure of tectonic plates that Jameson employs metaphorically. They describe the process that begins with the European colonization of the Americas—the annihilation of between 70 and 90 percent of indigenous people through disease and violent conquest as well as the global homogenization of flora and fauna—as "playing the same role as plate tectonics has in the past . . . knitting the continents and oceans together."[34] They argue, as well, that the biotic regrowth that followed the violent depopulation of the Americas produced a carbon minimum, a potential golden spike for the Anthropocene. Others have suggested that this anthropogenic alteration of the carbon cycle may have, in turn, intensified the second phase of the Little Ice Age, though both these claims are difficult to verify definitively.[35]

CLIMATE AND EPIC

On the level of narrative action, Milton's epic recasts Genesis as a conflict over territory, the grave consequences of which include a catastrophic deterioration of the Earth's climate. That Satan's difficult transit through Chaos will be comparable to the voyages of discovery across the Indian and Atlantic Oceans is anticipated after the infernal debate, when Satan promises to make his way "through all the coasts of dark destruction" (2.464), undertaking a "dreadful voyage" (426). He is, in this sense, associated with two explorers alluded to in the poem, Vasco da Gama and Christopher Columbus, both of whom crossed oceans relatively uncharted by Europeans. Adam and Eve are likened to the "American" natives, "naked . . . and wild / Among the trees on isles and woody shores" (11.1116–18). The conquest of the Earth was complete when Sin and Death "found a path / Over this main from hell to that new world" (256–57).[36]

Milton's life closely paralleled the first wave of English expansion, a process in which Milton was indirectly involved in his service as secretary for foreign tongues to the Commonwealth Council of State. Despite significant setbacks in Cromwell's Western Design, by the Restoration England had become the preeminent European power in North America, the population of its colonies in New England and Virginia having quadrupled during the 1650s.

For J. Martin Evans, the colonial plot imposes an interpretive problem, that of "describing the *relationship* between the colonial and the biblical elements in the poem without resorting to a crudely allegorical reading of a story that Milton certainly believed to be the literal truth."[37] Although he observes that the Old Testament was widely invoked to justify New World settlement, in the association of America with Canaan, Evans deflects the underlying hermeneutical problem, replacing the question of the relationship among levels with the idea of a palimpsestic form, the anxieties and attractions of New World settlement filling "the spaces *between* the biblical worlds." In his conclusion, however, he argues that the imperial themes and metaphors actually contribute to the meaning of the scriptural story: "Europe's colonial adventures offer . . . a continuous simile, a rich cultural stockpile of ideas and images, by means of which the ancient rivalry between good and evil can be related directly to the political experience of the poet's contemporaries" (147). Such an account parallels the reading I am developing in which it is in the most literal and historical level of the allegory—and finally in simile itself—that the geohistorical real is encoded. In this sense, history, or geohistory, is not what is hidden or erased but what appears on the surface of the text, like a purloined letter.

In the first two books of *Paradise Lost*, the Earth is a rumored place, a potential alternative to the infernal world. The consult in Hell is less about the sort of ontopolitical issues favored by Satan—whether God's sovereignty is just, what it means to be "free" (1.259)—than about the habitability of Hell. The first speaker, the warrior Moloch, advocates the continuation of outright war. The rebels are "fugitives" (2.57), their "dwelling place" a "dark opprobrious den" (57–58). "What can be worse," Moloch asks, "Than to dwell here . . . / In this abhorrèd deep" (85–87). In response, the sensualist Belial observes that Hell not only is habitable but also offers a "refuge" from the worst of God's punishment (168). Belial is a climate realist. The rebels must accept both the constraint imposed by their environment and that they remain subject to God's retribution insofar as he controls the temperature of Hell. Belial answers Moloch's question, imagining a worse fate. "What," he asks, "if the breath that kindled those grim fires / Awaked should blow them into sevenfold rage" (170–71). Instead of continuing a war that would exacerbate their environmental precarity—subjecting them to "a fiery tempest," "racking whirlwinds," and the "boiling ocean" (180–83)—he asks his comrades to foresee a future in which God's anger abates and "these raging fires / Will slacken" (213–14). Not only might Hell's extreme climate be tempered, but their own angelic natures may become habituated: "Our purer essence then will overcome / Their noxious vapor; . . . / Or, changed at length, and to the place conformed / In temper and in nature, will receive / Familiar the fierce heat" (215–19). Belial echoes an idea common in the literature of early colonization: seasoning, the adjustment of the body's humors, after a period of illness, to an alien climate.[38]

Mammon's speech builds on Belial's, while also emphasizing the possibility that the rebels might further refashion Hell, as they have by building the great hall Pandaemonium. Mammon calls on them to "seek / Our own good from ourselves, . . . though in this vast recess" (2.252–54). He observes that there are "thick clouds" in Heaven, just as there are in "This deep world / Of darkness" (262–64). The fallen angels can, by their labor and ingenuity, re-create the world they have lost, even that most crucial feature: "cannot we his light / Imitate when we please?" (269–70). Mammon is, throughout the poem, associated with industrial activity, such as mining, metal smelting, and construction. It is he, the narrator reports, who instructed men to ransack "the bowels of their mother earth / For treasures better hid" (1.687–88). Though he echoes Belial in envisaging a future in which their angelic bodies become conditioned to the infernal elements, "our temper changed / Into their temper" (2.276–77), his emphasis is on environmental intervention. Though the critique of mining goes back to Ovid, Milton clearly associates Mammon with the emergent industrial classes—miners and artisans—and with the infrastructure projects and manufacturing industries contributing to the atmospheric pollution Evelyn rallied against.[39] Mammon's rhetoric also invokes the idea that new settlements offer unique opportunities for environmental intervention, including the amelioration of intemperate climates through deforestation. The rebels endorse Mammon's vision, compelled by his plan to "found this nether empire" (296).

In his rejoinder, Beelzebub rejects Belial's plan to "build up here / A growing empire" because, he claims, the "king of Heaven" retains his "high jurisdiction" over Hell (2.314–19). Having shifted the debate from environmental to political terms (captivity, rule, and revolt), he returns to the problem of territory, perhaps recognizing that the worldly conditions of existence matter more to his fellows than "revenge" (337). Echoing Satan in book 1, he observes: "There is a place / . . . another world, the happy seat / Of some new race called man" (345–48). As Satan had in his earlier address, here Beelzebub turns the attention of the rebels to Earth, inviting them to imagine it as a world, to see it from afar. Their design with respect to this place remains ambiguous, whether as a field in their proxy war with God or as a site of potential colonization, an alternative to Hell. "Here perhaps," Beelzebub proposes, "Some advantageous act may be achieved / By sudden onset, either with hell fire / To waste his whole creation or possess / All as our own" (362–66). After the devils assent to his plan, he brings to the fore the environmental factors that might motivate their enterprise: "we may chance . . . in some *mild zone* / Dwell, not unvisited of Heaven's fair light, / Secure, and the brightening orient beam / Purge off this gloom; the soft delicious air, / To heal the scar of these corrosive fires, / Shall breathe her balm" (397–402; my emphasis). The debate and the decision to send Satan on his "adventure" hinges on a sense of the difference between Hell, a dismal world with a poisoned atmosphere, and the new world, with its wholesome air conducive to life.

There are significant echoes between Beelzebub's depiction of the Earth as a "happy isle" (2.410), with a mild and healthful climate, and the early promotion of English settlement in America. The North American colonies did not offer settlers access to the vast mineral wealth the Spanish had appropriated from their gold and silver mines, and there was significant anxiety that northeastern North America was barren and its climate extreme.[40] To counter such concerns, promoters of New World colonization emphasized the salubrious climate and fertile soils to be found in New England and Virginia. In his *Briefe and True Report of the New Found Land of Virginia* (1588), advocating new explorations around Roanoke, Thomas Hariot extolled the "excellent temperature of the ayre there at all seasons, much warmer then [*sic*] in England, and never so violently hot, as sometimes is under & between the Tropikes, or neere them."[41] In his influential *Principal Navigations, Voyages, Traffiques, and Discoveries of the English Nation* (1589–1600), Richard Hakluyt wrote in support of the establishment of a colony in Virginia. He records an early settler's account of the benign "temperature of Climate," "the most sweet and healthfullest climate, and therewithall the most fertile soyle (being manured) in the world."[42] Such promotional rhetoric—the idealization of a more salubrious climate—goes back to the earliest European explorers of the New World.

Before we follow Satan's flight through Chaos toward the Earth and the real action of the epic, there is a curious scene in which, like settlers in a new world, the fallen angels explore the diverse territories and climes of Hell. Ancient climate theory is based on the idea that, as a sphere, the Earth is divided into different climatic zones, some of which are salubrious and some of which are uninhabitable. Several squadrons set out to survey the "dismal world," seeking to determine "if any clime perhaps / Might yield them easier habitation" (2.572–73). They undertake a mission in Hell not unlike that promoted by Beelzebub, and what they discover is a treacherous climate similar to that experienced by the first colonists in New England and Virginia. The rebels discover no promised land, but they do learn that, like a spherical world, Hell features intense temperature variation as well as severe season-like oscillations (594–600).

The guileful Satan, like the propagandists of New World colonization, recognizes the rhetorical currency of environmental justifications, including the promise of a better climate. In his meeting with his horrid offspring, Sin and Death, Satan, needing to convince Sin to unlock Hell's gate, promises "to set free" his children "from out this dark and dismal house of pain" (2.822–23). As Beelzebub had with the rebels, he presents Sin and Death with an idealized image of Earth's climate, a place "created vast and round—a place of bliss" (832), with "buxom air" (842). Sin agrees to open the gates on the basis of the promise of being brought to "that new world of light" (867). Later, Satan tells the guardian angel Gabriel that he came to Eden "in hope to find / Better abode" (4.938–39). There remains a not altogether explicable ambiguity in Satan's self-presentation. Though he clearly uses such rhetoric to manipulate others, once he arrives in Eden he seems to recognize the importance of place in a new way. He is repeatedly struck by the Earth's beauty and fertility. In book 9, he addresses Paradise directly: "With what delight could I have walked thee round, / If I could joy in aught, sweet interchange / Of hill and valley, rivers, woods, and plains, / Now land, now sea, and shores with forest crowned, / Rocks, dens, and caves" (9.114–18). The irony that I identified at the beginning of this chapter—the gap between Satan's self-representation and his actual situation—begins to shape his sense of identity. After his rage-filled address to the Sun in book 4, Satan claims "myself am Hell" (4.75). The orthodox reading supports this idea, an essentially psychological understanding of the torment of sin as alienation from God. "Hell," writes Robert Crosman, "is the creature's voluntary self-exile from his Creator."[43] Some readers go further, arguing that the disordered environment of Hell should be read as standing for Satan's internal disequilibrium. Such conflations derealize the literal, turning environment into a metaphor for psychology, repeating Satan's own error in claiming to be one who "brings / A mind not to be changed by place or time." In his epic, however, Milton continues to insist that motive and action cannot be separated from setting.[44]

EPIC SIMILES

Milton audaciously places the "dismal world" (2.573) of Hell not deep in the Earth's lithosphere but in the "gulf" of Chaos (1027), an infinite realm of primordial matter beyond the "circumference" of the universe (7.231). This cosmic geography widens the scope for the epic action, and it represents Milton's attempt to materialize the entire Christian universe—or "multi-verse," as Dennis Danielson suggests—providing coordinates for places often treated as allegorical.[45] Milton depicts a continuous cosmos where not only celestial bodies (the Earth, the Sun, and the Moon) but also Hell and Heaven and Chaos are subject to the same physical laws. This sense of cosmic conti-nuity is developed on another figurative level within the poem: Milton's epic similes. These naturalistic similes establish a layer of referential meaning, associating "this frail world" (2.1030) with processes of dynamic change and disequilibrium.

Immediately after Satan is "Smote" by Hell's "torrid clime," his vain-glorious self-assertion confounded by the reality of his furnace-like world, he calls out to the other defeated rebels. The brief reference to the throng of angelic bodies, initially motionless and dazed by the seven-day fall through Chaos, is magnified in a compounding series of environmental similes. They are likened, first and famously, to "autumnal leaves" thickly strewn among "the brooks / In Vallombrosa" (1.302–3). The comparison is highly specific, in the reference to the Benedictine monastery Milton may have visited dur-ing his stay in Florence in 1636, and densely layered with allusion.[46] As ex-tended similes often do, the naturalistic description works to familiarize an otherwise fantastic scene, bringing the "infernal world" (251), the Hell that Milton chose to imagine on the basis of the scantiest of scriptural support, nearer to our world. Yet the tangible image of streams thickened with fallen leaves in a valley of shadows also performs allegorical work, referring not only back to the specific tenor, the angels who have themselves just fallen, but also to the poem's broader narrative of the Fall, the human lapse that introduces seasonal extremes and history itself into the planetary order.

It is appropriate, then, that the next simile involves a winter scene. The prostrate rebels on the sea of fire are likened to "scattered sedge / Afloat, when with fierce winds Orion armed / Hath vexed the Red Sea coast" (1.304–6). No less layered with allusion, this simile contains an archaic personification of the constellation Orion, a conspicuously bright star formation often deified in ancient Near Eastern myth and associated with winter storms and floods. The reference recalls the opening book of the *Aeneid*, when Ilioneus tells Dido of the tempest that dispersed the Trojan fleet: "Rising with sudden swell, stormy Orion bore us on hidden shoals and with fierce blasts scat-tered us afar amid pathless rocks and waves of overwhelming surge" (299). Like the *Aeneid*, *Paradise Lost* begins in the aftermath of a storm—"The sulphurous hail, / Shot after us in storm, o'erblown hath laid / The fiery surge" (171–73)—as the survivors regroup and take stock. Orion makes three appearances in the Old Testament, most notably in the book of Amos, where the deified constellation has been subsumed by Yahweh: "He who made the Pleiades and Orion, . . . who summons the waters of the sea and pours them over the earth" (5:8). As the simile expands, the winter floods associated with Orion are conflated with the destruction of Pharaoh's army in Exodus. The fallen angels are linked first with the storm-tossed reeds and then with "Busiris and his Memphian chivalry" who lay "thick bestrewn / Abject" after pursuing the Israelites (1.307–12).[47] Not unlike Virgil's Juno and Aeolus, the Hebrew deity intervenes in human affairs through his control of the skies.[48] Once again, the simile's naturalistic vehicle, reeds tossed about on the winter seas, turns back toward the specific tenor, the fallen angels, but also a broader typological referent, the Flood, when a retributive God will make the rain pour "till inundation rise / Above the highest hills" (11.828–29).

A conventional epic device, Milton's naturalistic similes play a significant role in the poem's complex figurative orchestration.[49] Extended similes bring two relatively concrete phenomena—often, for Milton, scenes of action, of bodies in a landscape, sometimes paused, mostly in motion—into direct comparison. They suspend the unfolding of the plot, introducing a comparison and so drawing attention to the act of narration, the role of the narrator, and even the dilemma of representation itself insofar as mimesis seems to require a figurative supplement, a clarifying comparison. While the implied relation of the first image to the second is never stable—similes may shift perspective, amplify or diminish, anticipate or recall—the most common effect of the extended simile is not to estrange but to familiarize, "to bring the terrible sublime," as Hartman writes of the early similes in *Paradise Lost*, "home to the reader's imagination."[50] This is generally how earlier epic poets use extended similes. In the *Iliad*, for instance, the ever-growing pile of exchanged missiles is likened to the shrouding drifts of a snowstorm.[51] Aeneas compares the experience of watching Troy's conflagration to that of a shepherd who observes a windblown fire destroy a cornfield or a mountain torrent as it "lays low the glad crops and labours of oxen and drags down forests headlong" (*Aeneid*, 337). In these instances, the simile sharpens the reader's apprehension of an extraordinary epic event—annihilative warfare—by comparing it with what would have been more familiar: a winter storm, a destructive wildfire or flood.

Unfurling a cosmic epic canvas and writing about events from the creation to the apocalypse, Milton employs such naturalistic similes—images of an unsettled Earth, a hazardous home planet—far more frequently than Homer or Virgil. In Hell, Satan's gigantic body slams down on the burning marl

> As when the force
> Of subterranean wind transports a hill
> Torn from Pelorus or the shattered side
> Of thundering Etna, whose combustible
> And fueled entrails thence conceiving fire,
> Sublimed with mineral fury, aid the winds
> And leave a singèd bottom all involved
> With stench and smoke. (1.230–37)

Another exhalation, this one atmospheric rather than subterranean, underlies the notorious simile in which Satan appears before his legions

> as when the sun new risen
> Looks through the horizontal misty air
> Shorn of his beams, or from behind the moon
> In dim eclipse disastrous twilight sheds
> On half the nations and, with fear of change,
> Perplexes monarchs. (594–99)

This image—of disorder in the atmosphere signaling disorder in the polity—echoes Evelyn's description of London's smog. It is supposedly the one passage in the epic to invite the scrutiny of the royal censor (and, as we will see, it echoed in the minds of several later observers trying to make sense of disquieting atmospheric phenomena). In other meteoric similes, the rebels arrayed faithfully before their leader are compared with forests singed by lightning strikes but still standing (612–15). Posed for battle, Satan and his offspring Death are like two thunderclouds on the Caspian Sea (2.714–18). Later, Death and Sin push the disordered matter of Chaos into a bridge-like mass, as "when two polar winds blowing" in opposite directions across the Arctic Ocean "together drive / Mountains of Ice" that block any northwest passage (10.289–93). More peculiarly, when Raphael (taking over the role of narrator) recounts the War in Heaven to Adam, he employs such naturalistic similes despite the fact that Adam, his prelapsarian auditor, has not yet experienced such planetary disequilibrium. In Raphael's words, the steadfast and pious Abdiel strikes Satan "as if on earth / Winds under ground or waters forcing way / Sidelong had pushed a mountain from his seat / Half sunk with all his pines" (6.195–98).

In these similes, the dynamic Earth system—its cycles, its unpredictable meteors and exhalations—establishes a layer of referential meaning, a form of planetary mimesis that supports the poem's ambitious cosmologic flights. One might term this layer the referential *bedrock* or *ground*, but, of course, neither figure captures Milton's emphasis on a disordered rather than a stable planet. Many natural phenomena, such as mountains and the starry firmament, embody endurance. Milton's similes, however, depict an Earth riven by constant change. Even the occasional reference to stillness, as when Beelzebub's audience of rebels stands "still as night / Or summer's noontide air" (2.308–9), involves only a brief pause in a transitory world. Indeed, the appearance of stability may itself be a form of demonic deception, as in the poem's first extended simile—of an island anchorage that is actually a sleeping sea monster (1.200–209). The Earth of Milton's epic similes is, as many readers have noted, definitively postlapsarian, subject to the profound changes introduced by the Fall, the intensification not only of the elemental strife but also of the unpredictability that Satan will experience in the realm of Chaos. It is a ruined Earth, subject to the force of fierce winds and pounding waves, a place of earthquakes and volcanoes and landslides, insect swarms and forest fires, blizzards and heat waves.

In a series of essays published in the *Monthly Magazine* between 1796 and 1798, John Aikin (perhaps the first ecocritic) observes of Milton's similes involving wind and storms: "The sensible effects . . . are more striking and terrible, considering their frequency, than those of any other phenomena of nature."[52] Whatever allusive or allegorical resonance may be discovered in epic similes, Aikin suggests that they work because of their familiarity and concrete immediacy. Extended simile redoubles mimesis in order to make the distant familiar. Milton compares the concord achieved by the rebels after their long debate with the "radiant sun" suddenly breaking through a "louring" sky that had threatened "snow or shower," revitalizing the living landscape (2.488–95). While this evocative simile has a precedent in the *Iliad*, the eighteenth-century French critic Jean-Bernard Le Blanc saw Milton's attention to the changeable skies as rooted in firsthand experience: "One can't read his *Paradise Lost*, without perceiving, that he had a hundred times in his life, taken pleasure in seeing the sun, sometimes gild the horison, and reanimate all nature; and at others, withdraw its rays, and leave her buried in the horrors of darkness."[53]

Often implied in Milton's naturalistic similes is the idea that the disordered Earth—with its unpredictable exhalations, its varied climates and geographies—is the shaping condition of human experience and action. Anne Ferry reads the temporal and geographic specificity in the highly allusive similes as expressing a soft environmental determinism, a sense of being irrevocably embedded in the natural world. Such similes, she writes, convey "the quality of experience which the narrator and the reader share": "As human beings we are always *bound by time and space*. . . . We can *never escape* the seasons; our lives are *controlled* by the weather, light and darkness, all the cycles of nature" (*Milton's Epic Voice*, 78; my emphasis). This climatic influence is particularly explicit in another of the early extended similes, the description of the massing rebels. The angels course through the air until, directed by Satan's spear, they touch down on the plain, "A multitude like which the populous north / Poured never from her frozen loins to pass / Rhine or the Danube when her barbarous sons / Came like a deluge on the south" (1.351–54). The notion that the barbarian invasions originated in northern overpopulation is often credited to the eighth-century Benedictine monk Paul the Deacon. He begins his *History of the Langobards* by asserting: "The region of the north, in proportion as it is removed from the heat of the sun and is chilled with snow and frost, is so much the more healthful to the bodies of man and fitted for the propagation of nations, just as, on the other hand, every southern region, the nearer it is to the heat of the sun, the more it abounds in diseases and is less fitted for the bringing up of the human race. From this it happens that such great multitudes of people spring up in the north."[54] Several scholars have suggested that Milton's reference probably came from Paul's account of climate history as it is reworked in the opening pages of Machiavelli's *Istorie fiorentine* (1532). In the simile, however, Milton's language seems closest to that of Giovanni Botero, who observes: "And as the Northerne-man by nature is hot and moyst, (the Elements of faecunditie) so there is no question, but that of al people they are, and have bin, the most populous. For from the *Goths*, the *Scithians*, the *German*, and the *Scandians*, not onely vast deserts and goodly cities have been founded, and inhabited, but from their loynes also, have Colonies beene derived throughout all Europe. . . . the North [is] the Store-house of Mankind."[55] Milton's simile, comparing the rebel angels to the barbarian hordes, inverts the logic of climatic causation at work in Hell, where there are not (yet) population pressures and where it is the inhospitably torrid clime that justifies outward migration.[56] On a more general level, however, it aligns with the epic plot in linking climatic variation with the founding of colonies and the expropriation of territory.

There is a comparable simile in book 3 as Satan, the unrelenting storms of Chaos at his back, gazes in the direction of Earth:

As when a vulture on Imaus bred,
Whose snowy ridge the roving Tartar bounds,
Dislodging from a region scarce of prey
To gorge the flesh of lambs or yeanling kids
On hills where flocks are fed, flies toward the springs
Of Ganges or Hydaspes, Indian streams. (3.431–36)

The association between Satan and the starving bird searching for prey may appear obvious, as in a later simile in which Satan entering Eden is compared to a "prowling wolf / Whom hunger drives to seek new haunt for prey" (4.183–84). Less evident is how seriously we should take the implication that Satan is compelled by an experience of dearth, as in the difference between the barren massif and the bounteous plains. Indeed, the images of the hungry vulture and the Vandal hordes are not dissimilar from those of the Israelites escaping Pharaoh to wander in the desert or the homeless Trojans, refugees on a perilous Mediterranean. Extended simile is a device of epic because the organizing principle of the genre is displacement and expansion, movement outward across the Earth's various territories. This is not a matter of mere ornamentation or exoticism. *Paradise Lost* is a poem in which territorial and climatic differences generate the vectors of movement that spark epic action.

THE FIGURE OF THE EARTH

A similar sense of planetary heterogeneity as a condition shaping human activity can be identified in another mimetic stratum, one that has received far less critical attention than Milton's similes. *Paradise Lost* treats the Earth as a physical body, a material object with a history, one among many worlds in what Milton, it is said, was the first to call interstellar "space" (1.650). The only contemporary personage named in the poem is Galileo, alluded to three times. In each instance, he is said to gaze on other celestial bodies: the Sun with its "spots," the Moon, "whose orb / Through optic glass [he] views / . . . to descry new lands, / Rivers, or mountains in her spotty globe" (287–91). In showing that other worlds are heterogeneous bodies—in seeing rivers and mountains on the moon and spots on the sun—Galileo positions the Earth as one sphere in space, no longer the mutable center (or "sump") of the cosmos, contrasted with an ethereal and perfectly regular celestial domain.[57] As the most infamous of the world builders, Thomas Burnet, would write several decades later, the Earth is "such a body as the Moon appears to us": "Rude and ragged . . . such a thing would the Earth appear if it was seen from the moon" (*Sacred Theory*, 91).

In *Paradise Lost*, Milton draws on the imaginative resources of poetry to intrepidly enlarge the Galilean perspective, "with no middle flight . . . to soar / Above the Aonian mount" (1.14–15). Satan traverses Chaos and outer space, Adam and Eve look to the heavens, and all the characters in the poem survey the Earth from high vantages. In his epic retelling of Genesis, Milton rises to the challenge set in his third prolusion, written as a student at Christ's College (1625–32), in which he contrasts the scholasticism of the Cambridge curriculum with a more worldly pedagogy: "Let your eyes wander . . . over all the lands depicted on the map . . . traverse the stormy Adriatic . . . climb unharmed the slopes of fiery Etna . . . and do not shrink from taking your flight into the skies and gazing upon the manifold shapes of the clouds, the mighty piles of snow, and the source of the dews of the morning . . . yes, even follow close upon the sun . . . and ask account of time itself."[58]

In the exordium to *Paradise Lost*, the poet calls for inspiration from the same muse who "on the secret top / Of Oreb, or of Sinai," revealed to Moses "in the beginning how the heavens and earth / Rose out of chaos" (1.6–10). Milton's syntax just teases at world-making heresy, perhaps a Lucretian cosmogenesis without a deity, the Earth rising out of the fortuitous collision of atoms. God's role in the Earth's formation is made explicit in the cosmogenic accounts given later by the angel Uriel, speaking to the disguised Satan in book 3, and then by Raphael, speaking to Adam in book 7. As Ayesha Ramachandran notes, however, *Paradise Lost* multiplies narratives of creation rather than settling on a single definitive account, drawing attention to cosmogenic narration itself, the diverse perspectives of those who tell and the curiosity of those who seek to hear. This narrative reflexivity contrasts with the unified creation story given in Du Bartas's *Semaines* (1578–84), the key precursor to Milton's attempt to synthesize natural philosophy and the hexameral tradition.[59] Ramachandran traces the uncertainty in Milton's accounts of cosmogenesis to the "fault lines" evident in the opening two chapters of Genesis, the first of which depends on the world-creating power of the divine Word, the second of which describes a "vital impregnation and prolonged gestation that gradually shapes matter" (204–5).[60] This fault line, as Theodore Hiebert explains, itself reflects the composite identity of Genesis, with Genesis 1:1–2:3—the "Priestly" account, likely composed after the return from the Babylonian exile—offering an encompassing cosmology meant to sanctify a stratified state religion, and Genesis 2:4–3:24—the Yahwist account, written as early as the tenth century BCE—expressing an agriculture-based worldview with close affinities to other Near Eastern fertility religions.[61]

In *Paradise Lost*, Milton introduces an initial phase of creation, without scriptural precedent, in which the Father withdraws his being from primordial matter, leaving it "free / To act or not," governed not by divine decree but by "necessity and chance" (7.171–72). This is the realm of Chaos, the disordered potentiality of primal matter, the "fighting elements" (2.1015) that are "this world's material mold" (3.709). The creation of "new worlds" (7.209) and the ordered cosmos is then described, variously, as a giving of form, a demarcation of boundaries, a process of elemental or alchemical separation, a generative infusion, a purging, a founding, a conglobing, a spinning. The theological problem—much discussed but unresolved—is why Milton insists on aligning his multiple angelic accounts of cosmogenesis with those pagan cosmologies that begin with dynamic and disordered elemental matter.[62] Milton's Chaos—"hot, cold, moist, and dry, four champions fierce, / Strive here for mastery, and to battle bring / Their embryon atoms" (2.898–900)—is clearly influenced by Ovid's *Metamorphoses* and Lucretius's *De rerum natura*. The epic identifies in Chaos a creative and destructive potential: "the womb of nature and perhaps her grave, / Of neither sea, nor shore, nor air, nor fire, / But all these in their pregnant causes mixed / Confusedly" (911–14).[63] This dynamism within Chaos does not align with Milton's account of primal matter in *Christian Doctrine*, where the emphasis is on its passive state, awaiting God's "virtue and efficiency": "It was necessary that something should have existed previously, so that it could be *acted upon* by his *supremely powerful active efficacy*" (307; my emphasis). One explanation for Milton's flirtation with atomism is that it offered a way of reconciling mechanical determination with free will, thus supporting the poem's Arminian alignment of divine justice with man's status as one "free" to "swerve" (5.235–38).[64] It is, of course, Lucretius who directly links the "atoms" that "Swerve slightly" with the "free will / Possessed by living creatures" (*On the Nature*, 2.242–43, 256–57). Even before the Fall introduces the "ever-threatening storms" (*Paradise Lost*, 3.425) of Chaos onto the Earth, the cost of human freedom, for Milton, is that we share with our turbulent planetary home a dangerous and unpredictable dynamism, a creativity that emerges from disequilibrium.

When Satan reaches the border of Chaos, he beholds "this pendant world" (2.1052). To compensate for this disconcerting image of Satan viewing our home from afar, in book 3 Milton regroups in Heaven, where the Father "bent down his eye, / His own works . . . to view" (3.58–59). This literal God's-eye view, promising order and justice, is again contrasted with Satan's perspective, when, on the Sun, Uriel directs Satan's attention to Earth: "Look downward on that globe whose hither side / With light from hence, though but reflected, shines; / That place is earth, the seat of man" (722–24). These heavenly vantages on the Earth, offering the reader the exotic opportunity to see it as a world, anticipate Eve's dream vision. In book 5, Eve narrates to Adam her dream of an angel who encourages her to eat from the forbidden tree: "'Taste this and be henceforth among the gods / Thyself a goddess, not to earth confined, / But sometimes in the air as we sometimes / Ascend to Heaven'" (5.77–80). She appears to taste the fruit, and, in her words, "Forthwith up to the clouds / With him I flew and underneath beheld / The earth outstretched immense, a prospect wide / And various" (86–89). Satan identifies the earthbound condition as a privation, but what Eve experiences after she tastes the fruit is not proximity to God but a bird's-eye view of Earth. There are good reasons to interpret such prospects, echoed at a number of points in the poem, in terms of what Milton calls the "lordly eye" (3.578): seeing as possessing.[65] But I am not in agreement with ecocritical readings that regard the desire to see the Earth from a high point as sinful temptation. After all, the effect of such a perspective is never quite one of encompassing totality. As Ramachandran remarks, "Milton inherits the challenge of comprehending the whole," as much a scientific imperative as a theological one, yet he persistently stages the "fundamental impossibility of that task" (*The Worldmakers*, 183). The enlarged perspective, whether demonic or divine, reveals planetary heterogeneity and the incompleteness of any given view. To see the Earth from above is to see not totality but partiality, variety, and complexity.

Even before her dream ascent, Eve had begun speculating about the nature of her world, asking Adam a probing cosmologic question about the "glittering starlight": "wherefore all night long shine these?" (4.656, 657). This question inspires in the stolid Adam a "desire to know" (7.61), which leads him to ask Raphael: "How first began this heaven which we behold / Distant so high with moving fires adorned / Innumerable, and this which yields or fills / All space, the ambient air, wide interfused / Embracing round this florid earth?" (86–90). What follows is Raphael's account of the Earth's formation, the making of a world: a sequence of separations, the emergence of its encompassing layers, the "elemental air," the "circumfluous waters" (265, 270). With the flowing ocean, however, the agency of creation diffuses, as if in the relation of earth and water and heat a new actor emerges, the personified sea: "over all the face of earth / Main ocean flowed, not idle, but with warm / Prolific humor softening all *her* globe, / *Fermented* the *great mother* to conceive, / Satiate with *genial* moisture" (278–82; my emphases).

Expanding on Genesis 1:12, according to which "the earth produced grow-
ing things," Milton next depicts God calling on the Earth to "put forth the
verdant grass, herb yielding seed / And fruit tree yielding fruit" (310–11). In
turn, the "bare earth . . . / Brought forth the tender grass" (313–15). Then,
after the appearance of hydrology and the creation of the Sun, which "all the
horizon round / Invested with bright rays" (371–72), God again speaks, and
a more fully personified "earth *obeyed* and straight, / *Opening her fertile
womb*, teemed at a birth / Innumerous living creatures" (453–55; my em-
phases). After the appearance of the autotrophic plants, which convert solar
radiance into living matter, Raphael introduces this personified Earth, like
the ocean a generative agent. In personifying the Earth, Milton represents
a composite agency that emerges in the entangled loops of solar and atmo-
spheric, hydrologic and biological activity.

Barbara Kiefer Lewalski identifies the close parallels between Rapha-
el's account of the creation and Lucretius's description of the Earth "as a
marvellously fecund and prolific *magna mater*" generating life, although
she downplays the heretical implications of Milton incorporating so many
echoes of an atheistic cosmogenesis.[66] But just as strange as Milton's al-
lusions to *De rerum natura* is Lucretius's own use of the personification,
which he takes the trouble to justify: "the earth does well deserve / The
name of mother which we give to her / Since from the earth all things have
been created" (*On the Nature*, 5.794–96). For Lucretius and Milton alike, it
is not enough to describe the Earth as an object of vision, an amalgamation
of diverse agents, or an encompassing totality. There is, for both poets, an
imperative to personify it, an imperative that fits uneasily with their other
cosmologic commitments. And it is not only Raphael, in his account of cos-
mogenesis, who personifies. In book 9 of *Paradise Lost*, the narrator follows
the angelic narrator in personifying the Earth. In an extraordinary sequence,
in the instant immediately after Eve eats from the Tree of Knowledge, the
narrator reports: "Earth felt the wound, and nature, from her seat / Sighing,
through all her works gave signs of woe" (9.782–83).[67] Of these lines, Hugh
Blair observed: "No Personification, in any author, is more striking, or in-
troduced on a more proper occasion" (*Lectures on Rhetoric*, 176). Milton's
narrator describes the changed state of the Earth before recounting the ac-
tions of the serpent and the enjoyment Eve takes in the fruit's delectable
taste. Then, when Adam eats, "Earth trembled from her entrails as again /
In pangs, and nature gave a second groan; / Sky loured and, muttering thun-
der, some sad drops / Wept" (9.1000–1003). The Fall is a phase shift in the
planetary system, like the initial birth of the living world, first registered in
the personified Earth.

Jameson claims that the rejection of personification, and with it the decline of allegory as an explicit literary mode, is a symptom of modernization: "When allegory as a literary form begins to lose its vocation and retreat into the past, thrust like some incomprehensible structure cast into the deepest shadow by the rising sun of the symbol and of symbolism, what can be most tangibly measured and demonstrated of this world-historical transition is the falling into disrepute of personification as such" (*Allegory and Ideology*, 39). Yet, despite its disrepute, personification persists into modernity, and understanding why may help us understand its appearance in *Paradise Lost*. In his 2013 Gifford Lecture on natural theology, Bruno Latour compares James Lovelock's episteme-shifting contribution (in *Gaia: A New Look at Life on Earth* [1979]) to that of Galileo three centuries earlier. Whereas Galileo recognized that the Earth is a planet similar to other planets, a physical sphere in space, Lovelock recognized that it is "a planet like no other," or, at least, a very unusual one, where the biosphere supports the highly specific conditions for its own continuance through a series of reciprocal connections, loops of molecular and thermodynamic exchange with the lithosphere, the hydrosphere, and the atmosphere.[68] For Latour, the personified figure of Gaia allows Lovelock to negotiate a narrow rhetorical path between vitalist "overanimation" and reductionist "deanimation" (*Facing Gaia*, 85). Lovelock, reflecting on the reception of *Gaia*, identified his rhetorical challenge, that of justifying a new scientific paradigm, which would study the emergent and self-regulating qualities of the Earth, while also offering a sufficiently evocative vision of our planet as an object worthy of "love and respect" (viii). Scientists, he notes, largely dismissed his theory, at least in name, owing to its association with "poetry and myth" (x), even as they came in the 1980s and 1990s to accept the new paradigm concerned with the Earth as a self-organizing system tending toward homeostasis yet capable of sudden phase shifts.

For Milton, personification—the attribution of a composite identity, of connection without organic unity or apprehensible totality, of a capacity to shape and be shaped, of continuity despite change, of an "agency" that is "multiplicative" (Swarbrick, *Queer Milton*, 282)—emerges as a necessary supplement to that which is empirically seen and that which is known by the inner light of faith. Such personifications seem just as out of place—residual and excessive, if also insistent—in Milton's Protestant epic as in Lovelock's paradigm-shifting approach to the Earth system. Milton's readers often ignore or repudiate them, not unlike the Earth scientists influenced by Lovelock. Personification, an exemplary signature of allegory, registers a principle of activity beyond the surface (the persona), the noncoincident relation of appearance and reality. "Allegory is itself allegorical," Jameson observes. "It contaminates its environment with a *disturbing ferment*" (*Allegory and Ideology*, 19; my emphasis). In my reading, I have been returning to the metaphoric vehicle, or to the most historical level within the allegory, and suggesting that the vehicle or the historical level insists in ways that forestall sublimation by the tenor or the more abstract levels of meaning. As an example, let me propose, with respect to Jameson's own figures of allegory, that the energetic "ferment" of interlaced planetary systems—of the living world as it interacts with the lithosphere, the atmosphere, and the hydrosphere—is the condition and referential horizon of all allegory, and that the Sun, the radiance of which drives all planetary activity, is what is at stake in the shift from allegory to symbol as the exemplary mode of figuration, a historical shift that coincides with the epochal transition from a solar to a fossil-fuel energy regime.

ENERGY AND THEOLOGY

At the end of book 2, Satan reaches the border where Chaos meets the outermost extent of the created cosmos, and there "at last the sacred influence / Of light appears . . . / A glimmering dawn; here nature first begins / Her farthest verge" (2.1034–38). Chaos is the lightless domain from which God has withdrawn; nature is the realm of light and life. In the prologue to book 3, the narrator, celebrating a safe return to the realm of celestial light after his "dark descent" (3.20), directs his address not to the heavenly muse of book 1 but to radiance itself:

> Hail holy light, offspring of Heaven firstborn;
> Or of the eternal coeternal beam
> May I express thee unblamed, since God is light,
> And never but in unapproachèd light
> Dwelt from eternity, dwelt then in thee,
> Bright effluence of bright essence increate? (1–6)

Even more than the description of the heavens and the Earth rising from chaos in book 1, these lines are, in their questioning and equivocation, heterodox. In Genesis, after all, light is, definitively, created after Heaven and the Earth (though before the Sun, much as dawn appears before the solar orb is visible), whereas Milton identifies light as either the first creation or "coeternal"—which is to say, "increate" (uncreated)—a suggestion echoed in Raphael's account of cosmogenesis, when, at God's command, "light, /

Ethereal, first of things, quintessence pure, / Sprung from the deep" (7.243–45). There is, unsurprisingly, a great deal of exegetical debate about the nature and theological implications of the light to which Milton's apostrophe is addressed, especially in its association with Milton's Arianism and his representation of the Son as "the radiant image" (3.63). There is no need to parse theology, however, to recognize that sunlight, the "pure ethereal stream" (7), more than any other earthly phenomenon, including the atmospheric *pneuma*, accomplishes the figurative work of connecting physical, perceivable reality with divinity, of supporting the figurative sublimation of the knowable into the ineffable.

The invocation in book 3 effects this transformation of physical into spiritual light in terms that are distinctly personal, reminding us of Le Blanc's observation about Milton's experience of the "horrors of darkness." The poet, blind for a half decade when he began composing *Paradise Lost*, returns to the realm of light and warmth. The apostrophic address here subtly shifts, from light to the Sun. The narrator feels heat, "thy sovereign vital lamp," but his eyes cannot "find thy piercing ray and find no dawn" (3.22, 24). The poet must discover his "powers" (52) in his privation, his loss of a recurrent temporality marked by the oscillating annual and diurnal patterns of light, now available only in memory (40–44). This light—the source of earthly sustenance, the flux of which structures time, the illumination of which makes visible "the book of knowledge fair / . . . / Of nature's works" (47–49)—is transmuted into the celestial light available to the blind but devout poet who will follow his muse into the "pure empyrean" (57) in order to "tell / Of things invisible to mortal sight" (54–55). As David Quint observes, Milton is here revising his fifth Latin elegy, "In adventum veris" (written in 1629), in which he finds creative inspiration in the return of the springtime Sun.[69] In the same year, Milton decisively rejects Apollonian solar worship in "On the Morning of Christ's Nativity." The birth of the Son leads to the abandonment of the pagan gods, and the "Sun himself . . . / . . . hid his head for shame, / As his inferiour flame, / The new-enlighten'd world no more should need; / He saw a greater Sun appear."[70] These lines anticipate John's eschatological vision of the New Jerusalem: "The city did not need the sun or the moon to shine on it, for the glory of God gave it light" (Rev. 21:23).

Milton's attempt to distinguish physical from divine light and to repudiate pagan solar veneration even as he continues to personify the Sun is a reminder of how deeply the symbolic association between the deity and light—and above all sunlight—is woven into Christianity and other monotheisms.[71] This association is a source of symbolic resonance—from the figuration of God as "a sun and shield" (Ps. 84:11) to Christ's claim, "I am the light of the world" (John 8:12)—but also theological anxiety. Danielson notes that in Genesis God may create the "greater" and "lesser lights" rather than the Sun and the Moon because the Hebrew word for *sun, shemesh*, sounds too much like the Mesopotamian sun god, Shamash (*"Paradise Lost" and the Cosmological Revolution*, 133). There remains in the Bible an uncomfortably close association between God and the provision and privation of solar energy. Job, for example, must show regret for his worship of the celestial lights: "If I ever look on the sun in splendor or the moon moving in her glory . . . this would have been an offence before the law, for I should have been unfaithful to God on high" (31:26–28).

Readings of the symbol of light in *Paradise Lost* seek to define the theological terms in which Milton is able to secure the difference between physical and celestial light—*lumen* and *lux*, effluence and essence, "offspring" and "coeternal"—often, unsurprisingly, with the Son, on whom "Impressed the effulgence of his glory abides," as the mediator (3.388).[72] To interpret Miltonic sunlight as referring to the Son is to assume, hermeneutically, that the physical manifestation (solar radiance) is simply an epiphenomenal vehicle that successfully points toward a personal, if also an abstract, tenor, an anthropomorphic God concerned with human affairs. To read *Paradise Lost* from a geohistorical perspective requires us to treat Milton's theology not on its own terms, connecting doctrinal statement with poetic practice, but anthropologically. Milton himself would have recognized such an approach in Lucretius's account of the origin of religion, when the mysterious activity of the heavens—"Moon, day, and night . . . / flying flames, / Clouds, sun, rain, snow, winds, lightnings, hail, / And thunderclaps"—was "to the gods / Ascribe[d]" (*On the Nature*, 5.1190–95). Lucretius's account of supernatural beliefs as a psychological "refuge" (1186) was taken up by Hobbes in chapter 12 of *Leviathan* (1651), where religion is seen to be rooted in the same fear of death that compels subjection to the sovereign. In the seventeenth century, there emerged a Protestant account of idolatry, including John Selden's *De diis Syris syntagmata* (1617) and Gerhard Vossius's influential *De theologia gentili* (1641), both of which link pagan idolatry with animistic sky worship. Samuel Parker's *Tentamina physico-theologica de Deo* (1665) traces solar worship to the Sun's role in biological generation. As Dimitri Levitin writes of Parker's genealogy: "The sun was said first to be omniscient, then omnipotent, and to predetermine everything. From there it was only a short step to asserting the deity's omnipresence and to equating God with nature."[73] This was an animism that, according to Parker, led to the development of Greek physics. Edward Herbert's work of radical deism, *De religione gentilium* (1663), offers an extensive investigation of the origins of divinization in solar veneration. "The adoration of the Sun," he writes, "was both ancient and universal."[74]

Such approaches to religion—however one defines *idolatry*[75]—as originating in the divinization of natural forces have been largely discredited under the Durkheimian paradigm, which regards religion as a sociological phenomenon: society knowing and organizing itself. Since my aim is not to reconstruct the terms in which Milton would have distinguished idolatrous solar veneration from the celestial light of true religion but rather to offer a geohistorical interpretation of Milton's representation of God, I turn to the German-born Oxford philologist Max Müller, a scholar of comparative religion whose work represents the fullest expression of the pre-Durkheimian paradigm. Between 1888 and 1892, Müller gave the first Gifford Lectures, part of the same series in which Latour recently called for a revitalized theory of religion able to account for its extrasocial dimension, a comparative "cosmology" that defines all knowledge, scientific and religious, in terms of a "principle of organization" that "distributes agency" among human and nonhuman actors (Latour, *Facing Gaia*, 150–52). The value of Müller's approach to religious symbolism is his insistence that, before the worship of deified figures takes on its "psychological" (subjective) and "anthropological" (social) dimensions, it is rooted in a relation to the physical world that is the source of human sustenance and the shaping context of all social reproduction. This "physical" component of religious worship can be identified in "scattered fragments" of theological symbolism across global cultures.[76]

According to Müller, however, it is only in the study of the Sanskrit Vedas that we gain full access to the "geological stratum"—a "stratum of thought and language"—in which we can discern directly "the process of deification" in its formation (*Physical Religion*, 11, 118). On the basis of his study of the Vedas, he asserts that the root of religion is solar veneration, the acknowledgment of an extraperceptual "infinitude" in the life-sustaining flows of sunlight:

> *Deus* in Latin means god and nothing but god. But *deva* in Sanskrit means first bright and brilliant. The sun, the dawn, the sky, the day, all are *deva* in the sense of bright, from the same root which yielded in Sanskrit *Dyaus*, sky, and Zeus in Greek. Here then we catch a glimpse of the origin of the concept of god. It was because all these beneficent and joyful phenomena had been called *deva*, bright, that, after dropping the phenomena of which it could be predicated, *deva* itself remained with

the meaning of brightness, raised to the more general and higher concept which now belongs to it, namely deity.[77]

Müller sees the formation of the idea of God as a process of abstraction in which the dawn light, the direct light of the Sun, the reflected light of the Moon, the stars in the heavens, and, finally, fire all came to be associated with a shared quality: "brightness," "an awakening, shining, illuminating, and warming light" (*Physical Religion*, 140). In its variable (diurnal, annual) flux, light is worshiped because it is the condition for the reproduction of life, the source of all sustenance. "What better subjects could there have been in an early state of society," Müller writes, "than . . . the daily return of the sun, which means the return of light and warmth, that is the possibility of life and the joy of life,—or the yearly return of the sun, which meant again the return of spring and summer after the horrors of winter, that is, the possibility of life and the joy of life" (12).[78] For Müller, deification begins in our sensory perception of the "great phenomena of nature"—light, the Sun, the Moon, storms, and fire, then the wind and rivers—in their activeness, their life-giving energy (8). Within this perception, there is an apprehension of a horizon, something "indefinite" that exceeds apprehension. What Müller calls "myth" or the "poetical imagination" or "personification" is the attribution of identity—modeled on our sense of our human capacity for meaningful action, which he takes to be the first subject of language—to these "undefined, infinite agents or agencies" (*Natural Religion*, 195).

As I have discussed, Milton justifies his anthropomorphic representation of God—as embodied, with eyes and ears, as one who speaks, sees, creates—by referring to God's choice to "represent" himself in this way in scripture and so to accommodate his human creatures. Light is then the medium of divine ineffability, this hiddenness in presence. In book 3, the angels sing a hymn of worship in which they address the Father, a deity invisible even to the angels, perceivable only in the light that emanates from him:

> Fountain of light, thyself invisible
> Amidst the glorious brightness where thou sit'st
> Throned inaccessible, but when thou shad'st
> The full blaze of thy beams and through a cloud
> Drawn round about thee like a radiant shrine,
> Dark with excessive bright thy skirts appear
> Yet dazzle Heaven that brightest seraphim
> Approach not but with both wings veil their eyes. (3.375–82)

This is the hidden God who speaks to Moses from behind a cloud, who "dwelling in unapproachable light . . . no one has ever or can ever see" (1 Tim. 6:16), who is "enfolded in a robe of light" (Ps. 104:2). This is the Christian God knowable, in his unknowability, by the very flows of energy divinized in pagan solar veneration. We return to the problem that my reading hinges on: celestial light depends on physical light.

Milton often characterizes the Sun as the embodiment of providence, that which provides. In *Christian Doctrine*, he cites James 1:17 on providence: "every good gift and every perfect gift is from above, descending from the Father of lights" (327). In book 3, Satan flies through space toward the "golden sun," the "great luminary," the "all-cheering lamp" that "gently warms / The universe, and to each inward part / With gentle penetration, though unseen, / Shoots invisible virtue" (3.572, 576, 581, 583–86). In Eden, "the sun / . . . spreads / His orient beams on herb, tree, fruit, and flower" (4.642–44), but its influence extends even underground, where it "produces with terrestrial humor mixed, / Here in the dark so many precious things" (3.610–11). Laying out the doctrine of monism, according to which angels themselves consume and digest food, Raphael describes at length a circulatory solar energy economy, by which matter "corporeal to incorporeal turn" (5.413), that begins and ends with the Sun: "that light imparts to all, receives / From all his alimental recompense / In humid exhalations" (423–25). When Michael comes to expel Adam and Eve from Paradise, he reassures them that divine "omnipresence fills / Land, sea, and air, and every kind that lives, / Fomented by his virtual power and warmed" (11.336–38).

So how can a reader distinguish the physical embodiment of life-giving virtue, of nurturance and influence, from God in his "glorious brightness" (3.376), especially since even seventeenth-century savants such as Parker and Herbert had linked pagan solar deities with the life-giving powers of the Sun? In several scenes, Milton depicts the natural history of religious devotion, an original propensity toward solar worship that must be redirected toward the transcendent Father. Adam and Eve's daily "orisons" follow the coming of dawn, the diurnal reappearance of "sacred light" (11.137, 134). The first parents address their apostrophic address to the personified Sun before redirecting it to God. Light, the dawn (134–35), the morn (174–75), and the Sun are personified, given a face and even a capacity for response, not unlike the apostrophized deity posited as the subject of address in prayer, worship, and entreaty. In encouraging Raphael to narrate the creation, Adam observes that there remains plenty of daylight, here speaking of the Sun: "thy potent voice he hears / And longer will delay to hear thee tell / His generation and the rising birth / Of nature from the unapparent deep" (7.100–103). Even the narrator enlists the Sun, as the subject of his address, to join him in his worship, substantiating my point that, in this divine metaphor, the tenor cannot exist without the vehicle: "Thou Sun, of this great world both eye and soul, / Acknowledge him thy greater, sound his praise / In thy eternal course" (5.171–73).

Milton stages the development of natural theology in Eden when Adam recounts to Raphael his earliest awareness as a newly created being: "Soft on the flowery herb I found me laid / In balmy sweat, which with his beams the sun / Soon dried and on the reeking moisture fed" (8.254–56). Even as he identifies it as a typological anticipation of the Fall, after which Adam will sweat as he labors in the fields, Geoffrey Hartman points to an "excess" in this exorbitant image of sweat and reeking moisture, an excess that reflects the curious fact that the prefallen climate of Eden is itself subject to oppressive extremes, supplying "more warmth than Adam needs" (5.302).[79] Newly created under the midday Sun, Adam sweats, and, like the blind poet, he feels the Sun's heat on his skin, instinctively turning his gaze toward Heaven. He observes the role of light in the living world, the "shady woods and sunny plains" (8.262) (figure 1). The flow of radiance through the biosphere and the "liquid lapse of murmuring stream" correspond with the "vigor" he discovers in his own capacity for motion (263, 269). That such flowing presence should suggest absence and so ontological uncertainty ("who I was . . . from what cause" [270]) is surely related to his discovery of his capacity to name: "My tongue obeyed and readily could name / Whate'er I saw. 'Thou sun,' said I, 'fair light, / And thou enlightened earth so fresh and gay / . . . Tell if ye saw, how came I thus, how here?'" (272–77).

Speech is vocative before it is descriptive. In naming the Sun and the Earth first, Adam identifies them not as objects of perception but as subjects of address, like him insofar as they appear to "live and move" (8.276), and so, perhaps, like him insofar as they might see and know and speak. Readers often identify his naming of the animals as the first act of speech.[80] But his first speech is not a naming that instantiates his dominion but a clearly misdirected address to the Sun and the Earth, a primal act of apostrophic personification. His demand for a human companion with whom he can engage in "social communication" (429) is an attempt to redirect speech, yet the persistence of personification suggests that such a channeling of meaning making into the closed circuit of human community never fully succeeds. If there is a hint of idolatry in his address to the Sun and the Earth, there is also, in the newly awakened Adam, a compensatory intuition of something beyond what is immediately manifest. Unlike Satan, Adam does not claim to be self-begot. He recognizes that his life, his vigor, depends

Fig. 1. Sir John Baptist Medina, "Book 8," in John Milton, *Paradise Lost* (1688).
Photograph: The British Library.

on the world around him, "where I first *drew air* and first beheld / This
happy light" (284–85; my emphasis), and he intuits a principle of creation
that precedes the life-giving air and light, an intuition confirmed when his
author does reveal himself, leading him to a high prospect and granting him
dominion over the Earth.

I am not suggesting, exactly, that Milton's Protestantism is simply a
rarefied form of solar worship. I am claiming, however, that, like other dei-

ties, Milton's God is knowable and representable through association with planetary processes, atmospheric activity, and, above all, sunlight. Moreover, ancient solar deification, refracted through Christian monotheism, received new support from Copernican heliocentrism. As Harinder Marjara writes: "Milton resisted the temptation of adopting the heliocentric hypothesis, but he found it hard to withstand the surging tide of sun-worship that resulted from this hypothesis" (*Contemplation of Created Things*, 46). While the poem refuses to decide between the heliocentric and the geocentric hypotheses, the angelic visitor Raphael, reminding Adam that the Sun and the heavens only "seem" to move "to thee who hast thy dwelling here on earth," asks: "What if the sun / Be the center to the world"? (8.117, 118, 122–23).

So if Milton's God is a personification made, at once, more concrete and more abstract in his association with solar radiance, what does that make Satan? In a striking parallel with the narrator's address to light in book 3 and Adam and Eve's address to the Sun in book 5, in book 4, Satan, on Earth, looks heavenward and addresses the "full-blazing sun" (4.29):[81]

> "O thou that, with surpassing glory crowned,
> Look'st from thy sole dominion like the god
> Of this new world, at whose sight all the stars
> Hide their diminished heads, to thee I call,
> But with no friendly voice, and add thy name,
> O sun, to tell thee how I hate thy beams
> That bring to my remembrance from what state
> I fell." (32–39)

The sunlight reminds Satan of the "bright eminence" he has lost (44). In his soliloquy, we can detect the same ambiguity that defines his initial experience of Hell and his motives in traveling to Earth, as to whether "state" and "place" refer simply to ontopolitical relations—of "subjection," "submission," "debt"—or whether such relations are meaningful only insofar as they are defined by an environment. Later, in his temptation of Eve, Satan observes: "The gods are first and that advantage use / On our belief that all from them proceeds; / I question it, for this fair earth I see, / Warmed by the sun, producing every kind; / Them, nothing" (9.718–22). This is his countertheology, his rejection of Adam's spontaneous recognition of a creator. Adam intuits that his own "vigor" is continuous with the flow of energy he sees in planetary activity. Satan, by contrast, begins his rebellion against God by asserting that he and the other angels are "self-begot, self-raised / By our own quickening power": "Our puissance is our own" (5.860–64). He imagines himself to exist independently of the solar energy economy that Raphael outlines for Adam (404–30). He claims to contain his own energy, which is why he is undetermined by spatiotemporal exigency, much as societies built on fossil fuels understand themselves to be undetermined by climate.

If God is associated with the flow of sunlight, Satan is defined, on the level of both figure and plot, in his relation to concentrated energy, combustible subterranean fuel. In Hell, Satan "Springs upward like a pyramid of fire" (2.1013). When he is discovered in Eden, he startles as "a spark / Lights on a heap of nitrous powder laid / Fit for the tun some magazine to store / Against a rumored war, the smutty grain / With sudden blaze diffused inflames the air" (4.814–18). In the form of the serpent, he leads Eve to the Tree of Knowledge "as when a wandering fire / Compact of unctuous vapor which the night / Condenses and the cold environs round, / Kindled through agitation to a flame" (9.634–37). Surely it is with such similes in mind that Shelley asserted: "Nothing can exceed the energy and magnificence of Satan as expressed in *Paradise Lost*" ("A Defense of Poetry," 290).

Satan is the principle of change, introducing disequilibrium into what are otherwise stable and closed systems. Such generative disequilibria already exist in Chaos, and they play a crucial role in facilitating Satan's "voyage" to Earth in what may be the most disconcerting event in all of *Paradise Lost*. Having escaped through Hell's gate, Satan leaps into Chaos and is uplifted by "surging smoke." He "meets / A vast vacuity," dropping down "and to this hour / Down had been falling had not by ill chance / The strong rebuff of some tumultuous cloud / Instinct with fire and niter hurried him / As many miles aloft" (2:928, 931–32, 934–38). This passage closely echoes Lucretius's famous depiction of the atomic swerve, given here in Lucy Hutchinson's translation, produced and circulated in the 1650s and 1660s:

> Tis further to be known
> Bodies in a streight line, with their own weight
> Borne down, in the vast space alter their state,
> When both in an uncerteine time, and place,
> Suddaine concussions force them to give space;
> For if they were not thus us'd to decline,
> Like drops of raine, they all in a streight line
> Would fall into the vast profoundie.[82]

Satan's journey toward Earth is a chance Lucretian swerve produced not by a concussive collision of two material bodies but by a fiery explosion of combustible matter. The entire theological allegory hangs on a random blast of niter and the updraft it generates, a protothermodynamic physics that aligns with the depiction of meteors and exhalations in the similes.[83] In his energy physics, Milton is drawing on alchemical theories that characterized niter (saltpeter) and sulfur, especially in their explosive combination, as the source of all combustion and fermentation.[84] These same reactive, spiritous particles cause lightning in the atmosphere, subterranean earthquakes, volcanic eruptions, the explosive power of gunpowder, the combustibility of sea coal, and the infernal "circling fire / Yet unconsumed" (2.647–48).

The blast of niter in Chaos is a fluke, but, even before his daring escape from Hell, Satan is defined by his technological mastery of these sources of concentrated energy. During the War in Heaven, he proposes that the rebels invent "Weapons more violent" (6.439). Beneath "the bright surface" of Heaven's soil, he observes, there are, "Deep underground, materials dark and crude, / Of spirituous and fiery spume": "These in their dark nativity the deep / Shall yield us pregnant with infernal flame" (472, 478–79, 482–83). That such dangerous compounds grow in Heaven's soil is evidence of Milton's commitment to a monist ontology; Heaven, like Hell, is a world. Having "turned / Wide the celestial soil," the rebels discover the same explosive matter that later pushes Satan toward Earth: "The originals of nature in their crude / Conception: sulphurous and nitrous foam / They found" (509–10, 511–13). With "subtle art" (513), they transform the subterranean compounds into gunpowder and then refine metal to shape into cannons. Milton modernizes the epic, as Neil Forsyth observes, associating material prowess not with heroism but with the development of advanced weaponry.[85] Satan's mastery of gunpowder and artillery, "devilish enginery" (6.553), is prelude to a whole series of further technological developments, advancements in energy conversion overseen by the rebel angels Mulciber and Mammon with the building of Pandemonium and then taken up in human history by the forge master Tubal-Cain (11.564–73). The mining and smelting of metal and the construction of Pandemonium put into practice Mammon's promise that, with technology, the rebels can replace the divine light that has been lost: "As he our darkness, cannot we his light / Imitate when we please" (2.269–70). As Hiltner notes, the fallen angels approach Hell as abstracted and "featureless space" awaiting transformation (*Milton and Ecology*, 24).

The moral architecture of *Paradise Lost*—the antinomy between providential benevolence and satanic temptation, good and evil, grace and sin—is pervasively figured in terms of the difference between free-flowing solar energy ("realms of light") and concentrated mineral energy ("materials dark and crude"). On the figurative level that sustains the theology, the poem encodes an allegory of the epochal transition from a solar to a mineral energy economy. I am not suggesting that Milton is inventing a new energy imaginary wholesale. Rather, *Paradise Lost* draws on and reworks long-existing figurative associations, including the association of God with sunlight, in ways that symptomatize the energy transition in progress, not least the development of London, in the mid-seventeenth century, into "a hive of mechanized industrial activity," producing armaments, munitions, and a multitude of manufactured goods.[86] We can speculate that an apprehension of comparative solar- and mineral-based energy regimes—on one level emergent, on another level symbolically organizing the poem's theology—is the condition of possibility for the development of the concept of energy as such, a concept that is already implicit in the most elemental religious abstraction, the deification of light.[87]

THE CLIMATIC FALL

In this chapter, I have been analyzing a narrative in which climate is a synchronic category, one manifestation of the geographic variety that serves as an impetus to action and conflict. In his representation of the Fall, Milton introduces a diachronic conception of climate change, one without precedent in the opening books of Genesis. The geophysical description of the Fall is recounted by the narrator directly, not by the angelic intermediaries who tell of the creation and postlapsarian history. The same radiant Sun that is the medium of providence is also the agent whereby the punishing Father transforms life on the planet:

> The sun
> Had first his precept so to move, so shine,
> As might affect the earth with cold and heat
> Scarce tolerable, and from the north to call
> Decrepit winter, from the south to bring
> Solstitial summer's heat. (10.651–56)

Planetary disorder and temperature extremes, the physical correlates of sin, begin in the variance of solar efflux. Milton expresses ambivalence in accounting for the postlapsarian introduction "of seasons to each clime" (678), whether produced (as "some say" [671]) by the Earth's axial tilt or by a Ptolemaic shift in the Sun's orbital plane. In either case, the diurnal phases of the edenic climate, the hot days and cool nights, are now matched by annual "inclement seasons" (1063): "pinching cold and scorching heat" (691). The amplification of temperature extremes introduces a cascade of further shifts in the atmosphere and the hydrosphere, with dire effects on the living world: "These changes in the heavens, though slow, produced / Like change on sea and land, . . . / Vapor and mist and exhalation hot, / Corrupt and pestilent" (692–95). The air, once "Wholesome and cool and mild," now harbors "damps and dreadful gloom" (847, 848). With the Fall, the conditions of elemental conflict that Satan discovers in the domain of Chaos—"hot, cold, moist, and dry, four champions fierce, / Strive here for mastery" (2.898–99)—have been transposed to the Earth. Henceforth, the winds "with bluster . . . confound / Sea, air, and shore," blowing from the north "armed with ice, / And snow and hail" (10.665–66, 697–98).

The idea that Adam and Eve's disobedience made nature less fertile and more recalcitrant to human need was widely held in the seventeenth century. Such an understanding derives from Genesis 3:17–19, where, having cursed Eve with the labor of reproduction, God tells Adam: "On your account the earth will be cursed . . . it will yield thorns and thistles for you. You will eat of the produce of the field, and only by the sweat of your brow will you win your bread." In *Christian Doctrine*, Milton cites these lines in defining the planetary consequences of the Fall—"the curse of death extends to the whole of nature, because of man"—yet he adds no further detail (399). One widely recognized influence on Milton's representation of the creation and the Fall is Du Bartas's *Semaines*, yet, while the description there of a "woeful alteration" extending through the cosmos is echoed in Milton's gloss of book 10, when God "commands his Angels to make several alterations in the Heavens and the Elements," in describing the geophysical and climatic consequences of the Fall, as one scholar notes, "as is very rarely the case, Milton goes more into detail than Du Bartas."[88] Another source is Robert Burton's *Anatomy of Melancholy* (1638), which directly links "the fall of our first parent Adam" with "the earth accursed." Citing Ecclesiasticus 39:29—"Fire, and hail, and famine, and dearth, all these are created for vengeance"—Burton characterizes the postlapsarian Earth in terms of its hazardous atmosphere: "the air with his meteors, thunder and lightning, intemperate heat and cold, mighty winds, tempests, unseasonable weather; from which proceed dearth, famine, plague, and all sorts of epidemical diseases."[89]

While there is little scriptural precedent for Milton's detailed depiction of the Fall as a cascade of geophysical events that transform the planetary climate, there are important precursors in pagan myth, stories of epochal shifts in the climate that, like pervasive flood stories, suggest a basic connection between climatic instability and the human narrative impulse.[90] It is often asserted that the Holocene was a stable epoch after the wild oscillations of the Pleistocene, a "long summer" in which agriculture and civilization could flourish. Yet the twelve thousand years since the last glacial age are best characterized in terms of punctuated equilibria: periods of relative homeostasis interrupted by sudden catastrophic events and phase shifts. The warming of the early Holocene supported the establishment of permanent settlements among the Natufian people in Anatolia, settlements that became untenable during the return of near glacial conditions during the Younger Dryas. A great aridification event around 2200 BC brought down the Old Kingdom in Egypt, the Akkadian Empire, and possibly the Indus Valley Civilization. A thousand years later, another extended drought contributed to the Late Bronze Age collapse. Climate change was a persistent feature of the Holocene, leaving its mark not only in widespread flood stories but also in mythic accounts of epochal change. The Aztecs described themselves as living under the Fifth Sun, the earlier epochs having ended in a period of darkness, a hurricane, a drought, and a flood. Hinduism divides planetary time into stages, from the gentle weather of the Satya Yuga to the drought and scarcity of the present Kali Yuga. In *Works and Days*, Hesiod describes humanity's tenure across a series of successive ages. Ovid expands on Hesiod, emphasizing the geophysical alterations that characterize these epochs. Ovid's Golden Age features an Earth of such fertility that labor is unnecessary and, as in Milton's Eden, "springtime lasted all the yeare."[91] The defining change of the Silver Age is the introduction of the seasons, extremes of hot and cold:

> the olde
> And auncient spring did Jove abridge, and made therof anon
> Foure seasons: winter, sommer, spring, and autumne off and on.
> Then first of all began the ayre with fervent heate to swelt,
> Then isycles hung roping downe; then, for the colde was felt
> Men gan to shroud themselves in house. (1.132–37)

The Bronze Age, in turn, intensifies conditions of scarcity, competition, enclosure ("Which was as common as the ayre and light of sunne before" [153]), and extraction ("Not onely corne and other fruites, for sustance and for store / Were now exacted of the Earth" [154–55]), much as, in *Paradise*

Lost, the Fall leads not only to agricultural toil but also to mining and metal-working (11.565–74).

So, beyond Christian scripture, Milton was able to draw on Greek and Roman myths that depict climatic phase shifts in the Earth's history. But why introduce such disreputable pagan stories into Christian sacred history? Why narrate the Fall as a climate event, an epochal shift in planetary history? One possibility is that Milton was drawing on knowledge of the environmental and climatic transformations brought about by European colonization. During the consult in Hell, Beelzebub had proposed that the rebels might colonize the Earth or "with hell fire / . . . waste [God's] whole creation" (2.364–65). Satan later reiterates that his plan is "to have marred" the Earth as much as it is to tempt Adam and Eve to sin (9.136). Considering this colonial subtext, one potential basis for Milton's depiction of climatic deterioration is the European experience of colonizing Atlantic islands. These tropical "Edens" were quickly transformed by deforestation and desiccation, offering, as Richard Grove has shown, early laboratories for theories of anthropogenic climate change.[92]

Another possible explanation for Milton's choice to depict the Fall in such detailed climatic terms is his experience of living in a period of unprecedented climatic perturbation. It is especially notable that Milton links the Fall with a flux in solar radiation. In Geoffrey Parker's analysis, the clearest example of a direct awareness among seventeenth-century observers that "they lived in the middle of a major climate change" is in the conjectures of astronomers that the period's "extreme weather" might be related to "fluctuations in the number of sunspots" (*Global Crisis*, 8, 12).[93] Galileo's report of spots on the Sun and thus of the variability of solar activity had undermined Aristotle's account of superlunary phenomena as incorruptible and unchanging.[94] Milton acknowledges this revolutionary new understanding of the heterogeneous solar body when Satan descends to "the archchemic sun": "Not all parts like, but all alike informed / With radiant light" (3.609, 592–93). So Milton's explanation for a climatic Fall—"the sun / Had first his precept so to move, *so shine*"—offered a not inaccurate interpretation of the "cold / Climate" that coincided with his lifetime. Recognizing this emphasis on climate in Milton's audacious retelling of sacred history requires us to think differently about the (geo)historical context of poetic composition and the symbolic work of Protestant epic.

In a revisionist ecological reading of the Hebrew Bible, Theodore Hiebert describes the nearly hegemonic interpretation of the singularity of Jewish monotheism, which goes back to Hegel's theory of the evolution "from religions of nature to religions of history" (*The Yahwist's Landscape*, 15). This transition involves the subordination of cyclic nature, the desacralization of which paves the way for the development of a properly historical consciousness, one embodied in the story of the election and redemption of the Jewish people by a transcendentalized deity. In his study, Hiebert recovers the socioecological context of the Yahwist narrative, grounded in the rain-based dryland agriculture of the Mediterranean highlands. He claims that the "curse on arable soil" is the organizing climax of the stories of the Fall and of Cain and Abel: "The soil's curse is an element around which narrative tension is built, and it is the only issue ultimately resolved by the flood. The Yahwist's primeval narrative might be described, without exaggeration, as a drama of the soil, a narrative *designed to explain and define* the relation between arable land and its farmers" (68; my emphasis). "The agricultural setting of this drama," he insists, "is not a mere stage upon which the events of the divine-human relationship unfold. It is rather the theme of the drama itself, providing the terms by which culture is defined and the relationship between humanity and God is played out for the world" (72). Hiebert's project offers a precedent for my reading of *Paradise Lost* as a poem in which the Earth is not simply the setting for a historical epic or a theological allegory but the source of the actual contradictions that the sacralization of history seeks to resolve. His study also offers a useful comparison because it shows the extent to which, in retelling Genesis, Milton emphasizes climate rather than soil as the thematic crux.

Much as *Paradise Lost* begins with Satan reflecting on his changed "clime," so does it close by considering how our first parents will compose themselves in a world that everywhere speaks of the ruin they have wrought. Eve, sublimely, proposes to Adam that they forebear reproduction and so break the curse of death that will otherwise be passed on to future generations. Adam attempts to reconcile Eve to a human future in the now intemperate world, reminding her that when God had confronted them in the garden, "Pitying how they stood / Before him naked to the air that now / Must suffer change" (10.211–13), he had provided them with clothing, "lest cold / Or heat should injure us" (1056–57). The God who punishes also preserves. With further entreating prayer, Adam claims, the Father will "teach us further by what means to shun / The inclement seasons, rain, ice, hail, and snow," a new climatic order Adam senses already in the "winds" that "Blow moist and keen" (1062–66). Against the frigid nights to come, they will learn to "with matter sere foment, / Or by collision of two bodies grind / The air attrite to fire," mastering the same elemental powers that "tine the slant lightning," allowing them to "supply"—temporarily replace—"the sun" (1071–73, 1075, 1078). Having intensified the planet's climatic disorder, God's pity for his vulnerable creatures leads him to grant them the resources they need to protect themselves, not least "such fire to use" (1078). Knowledge ("by what means") is now defined in terms that are worldly and instrumental, as a matter of survival in a distempered world.

In book 11, the angel Michael is sent by God to "without remorse drive out" the humans from Paradise (11.105). In justifying this expulsion, the Father refers not only to the authority of his judgment but also to natural law, which dictates that the "tainted" (52) humans can no longer abide in the pure air of Eden.[95] Again, the question of place, of climate and why it matters for human world making, is brought to the fore. While Adam responds to the sentence of an unforeseen exile with frozen "sorrow," Eve turns to Eden itself and its floral inhabitants, in another act of personifying address: "Must I thus leave thee, Paradise?" (269); "O flowers, / That never will in other climate grow, / . . . which I bred up with tender hand / From the first opening bud and gave ye names, / Who now shall rear ye to the sun"? (273–78). The detail about Eve's naming of the flowers is an astonishing act of feminist revision on Milton's part, but it is also a reminder of how much naming in this poem is connected not only with possessing but also with the labor of cultivation.[96] Eve asks, finally: "How shall we breathe in other air, / Less pure, accustomed to immortal fruits?" (284–85). Michael interrupts her interrogative apostrophes to the world around her, directing her to find recompense for her loss in her human bond with Adam: "Where he abides think there thy native soil" (292). Ecological relations are, once again, redirected into human social bonds.

Michael leads Adam to the highest hill in Eden, "from whose top / The hemisphere of earth in clearest ken / Stretched out to amplest reach of prospect lay" (11.378–80). The expanded vision afforded by the mountain overlook facilitates, in this case, not cosmogenic speculations or claims of possession but a prophecy of planetary catastrophe, "what shall come in future days" (357). It is a chastening vision of ongoing socioecological calamity, the "many shapes / Of death," including "fire, flood, famine" (467–72), biting scarcity and "luxurious wealth" (788), and the Deluge: "Down rushed the rain / Impetuous and continued till the earth / No more was seen" (743–45), a cataclysm of such magnitude that the very mountain where they stand shall "by might of waves be moved" (830). To read Milton's account of Adam's vision today is to be reminded of Srinivas Aravamudan's definition of *catachronism*: our experience in an age of accelerating climate change of learning to regard "the past and the present in terms of a future proclaimed as determinate," "a known and inevitable outcome" rather than a result of open-ended agency.[97] Michael's prophetic vision serves to stabilize the allegory, above all by teaching Adam to interpret the role of providence properly, in the redemptive appearance of Christ and the eschatological promise of a final judgment but also in God's covenant to limit his vengeance and maintain the regularity of nature. After the Flood, God promises "never to destroy / The earth again by flood" (892–93): "day and night, / Seed time and harvest, heat and hoary frost / Shall hold their course, till fire purge all things new, / Both heaven and earth, wherein the just shall dwell" (898–901). The covenant and the eschatology are two sides of the same solution to the problem to which the Fall and Adam's vision of postlapsarian history so acutely testify: the dangerous volatility of "this transient world" (12.554).

The poem's final scene—Adam and Eve's removal from Eden—returns to the problem of climatic influence. In his parting advice, Michael echoes Satan's assertion in the opening scene when he faced an inhospitable world. Michael promises Adam and Eve that, in the divinity of their human selves and in their relation to one another and the generations they will bear, they will find recompense for the world they ruined: "then wilt though not be loath / To leave this Paradise but shalt possess / A paradise within thee" (12.585–87), a statement echoed by Eve when she assures Adam: "Thou to me / . . . all places thou" (617–18). As he does in showing Satan's feet singed by Hell's burning soil, or his wistful apostrophe to Eden, or Adam and Eve grappling with the unbearable loss they face, Milton unsettles this vision of a social relation independent of place and clime. He describes forebodingly, in the poem's final image, the changed world Adam and Eve will enter: the "brandished sword of God before them blazed / Fierce as a comet, which with torrid heat / And vapor, as the Libyan air adust, / Began to parch that temperate clime" (633–36).

On a formal level, the two instances of climate change that open and resolve the epic appear to foreground climate's consequentiality. In *Paradise Lost*, this chapter has argued, climate—the variance between climes, some more habitable than others, as well as the difference between one climate epoch and another—impels narrative action and contributes to narrative resolution. Most readers have, however, been comfortable with the implication of Michael's advice, that an "inner" paradise can compensate for the loss of "the happy garden" (3.66), that spiritual succor matters more than any "mere place," as one influential editor puts it.[98] Yet, if, as readers traveling through the cosmic territories of Milton's epic, we are, in the words

of Joanna Picciotto, "never allowed to forget that we are traversing inte-
rior spaces, spiritual conditions," we might say, with no less confidence,
that the poem never allows us to forget the significance of exterior places:
worlds, regions, and climes.[99] That the poem stages this consequentiality as
uncertain offers, in my view, a meta-allegorical wink no less important than
Raphael's promise to accommodate his narrative to his human auditors,
highlighting the way in which the most literal level within the allegori-
cal schema insists on a natural-historical significance that cannot be fully
sublimated into more abstract (moral, anagogic) levels of meaning. Indeed,
there is nothing keeping the reader from inverting the significance Johnson
attributed to the allegorical tenor and vehicle, the moral and the history:
seeing the anagogic as an expression of a "desire" that serves to negate an
apprehension of "the real." Considering that the Father has instructed Mi-
chael to "dismiss them not disconsolate" (11.113), one wonders whether
the angel's mollifying words—like "the light of salvation" itself, the escha-
tological promise of a redemptive end to history—should be understood as
evidence of the enormity of the loss and the psychological impossibility of
Adam and Eve, the first climate refugees, facing it squarely.

"The Works of Nature": Descriptive Poetry and the History of the Earth in Thomson's *The Seasons*

"UNREMITTING ENERGY"

"The subject of the work," Wordsworth observed nearly a century after the first publication of *The Seasons*, "is the changes produced in the appearances of nature by the revolution of the year." "Thomson," he added, "was fortunate in the very title of his poem, which seemed to bring it home to the prepared sympathies of every one."[1] It did indeed. Into the nineteenth century, Thomson remained, in Hazlitt's words, "perhaps the most popular" English poet, *The Seasons* having been reprinted, anthologized, and translated on an unprecedented scale.[2] Writing in 1779, John Aikin claimed that *The Seasons* had established a new "aera" in the history of British poetry as an "original" work responsible for the conventions according to which "modern descriptive poets" represented "natural objects."[3] Any reader of *The Seasons* recognizes the dynamism of Thomson's song of the "varied year" (*Wi*, 1), the distinct lexical and figural innovations he employed to describe "sun, and water, earth, and air, / In ever-changing composition mixed" (*Au*, 635–36).[4] In 1774, a critic prophesized that Thomson's "matchless song" would find an audience as long as "the circling seasons still appear."[5]

The Seasons, however, is not a poem simply about the reassuring pattern of annual recurrence, "the glories of the circling year" (*Su*, 14), what Sarah Dimick calls "seasonal form," "rhythmic configurations, phenological beats and accents that cohere into recognizable temporal patterns."[6] *The Seasons* is no less about atmospheric disorder and climatic extremes, the planetary flux that necessitates and thwarts human projects. Born in 1700, Thomson grew up in the border county of Roxburghshire as Scotland sought to recover from the disaster of its seven ill years. The 1690s are considered the climax of the Little Ice Age, with extreme winters and widespread famines in northern Europe. Scotland was hit hard. Cold, wet, and irregular weather caused harvest failures on a regional level every year between 1688 and 1698, leading to famine and outward migration.[7] The desolate landscape of the Cheviots, where the poet in the "morn of life" enjoyed a "careless solitude" (Wi, 7, 8), was the result of depopulation caused by the famines of the 1690s. It also reflected a longer phase of farm abandonment in the uplands of southeastern Scotland as the viable altitude of oat cultivation dropped by 150 meters during the seventeenth century, which surely served for those affected as an acute example of perceivable climate change.[8] In Scotland, the decade of frigid temperatures and dearth, along with the financial devastation brought about by the failure of the Darien Scheme in 1700, paved the way for the 1707 Act of Union. Scotland's union with its prosperous neighbor to the south was itself a way of adapting to the rigors of the Little Ice Age. Like a number of Scots of his generation seeking opportunity, Thomson moved south to London, in February 1725, leading to his achievement as the first great poet of Great Britain. In this chapter, I identify climatic upheaval and Britain's innovative ways of responding to it as the shaping context in which Thomson, refiguring a classical inheritance, forged a new mode of poetic description.

In a September 1725 letter to his lifelong friend William Cranstoun, Thomson, writing from East Barnet, a suburb north of London where he had taken a position as a tutor, included lines of verse that would appear in the first edition of *Winter*, an address to the personified season: "Welcom! kindred Glooms! / Drear awfull wintry horrors, welcome all!"[9] The lines echo Satan's assertive address to Hell: "Hail horrors, hail / Infernal world, and thou profoundest Hell / Receive thy new possessor." Yet Thomson does not lay claim to "a mind not to be changed by place or time" (*Paradise Lost*, 1.250–52, 253). He welcomes winter as "kindred" because it reminds him of the harsh seasons of his Scottish childhood. Indeed, it was the appearance of extreme weather, he tells Cranstoun, that inspired his versifying. It was the "terrible floods, and high winds, that usually happen about this time of year, and have already happen'd here . . . that first produced the enclosed lines." Several weeks later, the cold had become intolerable. He wrote to David Mallet, explaining that he had resigned his tutoring position and would return to the city: "Flesh and blood cannot endure, to be expos'd here, as in the Bell-house of a steeple, to the raging elements. . . .'Tis so cold that the pen is like to drop out of my hand" (*Letters and Documents*, 20–21).

In *Winter*, first published in a 405-line edition in March 1726, Thomson identifies an earlier biographical source for his verse, his youthful saunters through the season's "rough Domains," when he listened to "the Winds roar, and the big Torrent burst," and beheld "the deep, fermenting, Tempest brew'd / In the red, evening, Sky" (*Wi*, 10–14 [1726 ed.]). As the wintery weather threatens, the poet is drawn by "forming *Fancy*" to visionary "Worlds remote," abstracted from "outward Sense" (*Wi*, 68–79). He refuses such idealizing flight, returning instead to the phenomenal world of rolling fogs and stagnant marshes. This sort of reflexive staging of the problem of the muse's attention is a hallmark of Thomson's verse, as is the insistence on attending, against the lure of fancy, to a harsh and hazardous world. Winter announces itself with a rainstorm, which floods the fields and swells the river. Creatures of the air and land seek shelter. The narrator addresses "NATURE! Great Parent" (143), associating the poet's apostrophizing "Voice" (149) with the experience of sublimity and the enigmatic status of natural forces. At sea, pounding wind and billowing waves engulf the sailor, an embodiment of "feeble Man" (169) (figure 2). A more orthodox prayer to the "FATHER of Light, and Life" follows (210), a plea for "never-fading Bliss" (215). The deistic apostrophe to nature has been recognized as insufficient in the face of wintry annihilation. A blizzard arrives, rendering the earth "one, dazzling, Waste" (228). The address shifts again, as the poet calls on "*Shepherds*" to shelter and feed their "helpless Charge" (242), the "Rigours of the Year" demanding that religious solace be supplemented with a more practical ethics (253). The poet retreats to shelter, where, warmed by the "ruddy Fire" (257), he holds "Converse with the mighty Dead / *Sages* of ancient Time" (258–60). Though *Winter* has many devotional elements, here pagan writing—the worthies, "as Gods rever'd," who "humaniz'd a World" (260–62)—offers another source of meditation and solace during the inhospitable season. Yet, for those exposed to the hardships of the year, such consolatory retreat is unavailable. "Can human Hearts endure / Th' assembled *Mischiefs*, that besiege them round: / Unlist'ning *Hunger*, fainting *Weariness*, / The *Roar* of Winds, and Waves[?]" the poet asks (341–44). The final solution to this vulnerability to nature's forces is eschatological, the solace of a faith that promises the conversion of cyclic time into a linear time that achieves completion, the "Glorious *Morn*! the second Birth / Of Heaven, and Earth" (378–79). Like *Paradise Lost*, *Winter* claims its poetic mandate as theodicy, recognizing providence in the Earth's disorder and anticipating a restoration to come, "Life undecaying" (405).

In *Winter*, climatic extremes are the explicit context for the poet's search for a literary vocation. The poem finds resolution to its Joban theodicy in millennialist expectation, in line with a genre of "eschatological odes" popular in the 1720s.[10] In *Winter*, however, we see already the countervailing ten-

Fig. 2. William Kent, "Winter," in James Thomson, *The Seasons* (1730). Photograph:
Special Collections, University of California, Davis, Library.

dencies that would characterize *The Seasons*: engagement with a classical
inheritance and an insistently materialist attention to natural phenomena.
Indeed, Thomson came to see natural philosophy, rather than scripture, as the
foundation of his poetic authority.[11] The muse, as he later writes in *Liberty*
(1735–36), is guided by "her tutor Science."[12] Even in revised and expanded
versions, *Winter* retains hints of a "punitive theology," as Blanford Parker
notes, "an elegy for the possibility of a fully moralized landscape," while the
rest of *The Seasons* eschews "teleological morality" for empirical expansive-
ness.[13] Though Newtonian physicotheology came to offer Thomson a way of
reconciling religious devotion with science, I argue in this chapter that the
poet continued to insist on the stochastic volatility in nature's "great eternal
scheme," in terms that owe as much to Lucretius as to Job and as much to
his own experiences of an unsettled climate as to any literary forbearers.

When Thomson includes Milton in his list of British worthies in *The Seasons*, he points not only to his predecessor's accomplishment in equaling the epic bards of antiquity but also to the naturalism with which Milton daringly materializes the Christian cosmos: "Is not each great, each amiable muse / Of classic ages in thy Milton met? / A genius universal as his theme, / Astonishing as chaos, as the bloom / Of blowing Eden fair, as heaven sublime" (*Su*, 1567–71). He follows Milton in this ambition to bring all time and space within the ambit of his poem. Our experience as ephemeral earthbound creatures is contrasted with the vast temporal and spatial scale of the solar system, as is suggested in the account of cosmogenesis early in *Summer*:

> With what an awful world-revolving power
> Were first the unwieldy planets launched along
> The illimitable void!—thus to remain,
> Amid the flux of many thousand years
> That oft has swept the toiling race of men,
> And all their laboured monuments away,
> Firm, unremitting, matchless in their course;
> To the kind-tempered change of night and day,
> And of the seasons ever stealing round,
> Minutely faithful. (32–42)

The heliocentrism that remains ambiguous in *Paradise Lost* is explicit in *The Seasons*. Temporal recurrence, which provides the poem with its structuring form, derives from the steady rotation of the Earth on its internal axis and in its solar orbit. The Sun is recognized as the source of life-giving radiance, and the Earth is a living planet: "Informer of the planetary train! / Without whose quickening glance their cumbrous orbs / Were brute unlovely mass, inert and dead, / And not, as now, the green abodes of life!" (104–7). Like Milton's characters and narrator, Thomson is prone to directing his devotional address not to a deified (and anthropomorphic) Father but to the light by which he is known and the beneficent orb that is his intermediary: "O Sun!" "Prime cheerer, Light! / Of all material beings first and best! / Efflux divine!" (94, 90–92).[14]

What Thomson adds to Milton's cosmology in addition to this unequivocal heliocentrism is the force of gravity. Again, he addresses the Sun: "'Tis by thy secret, strong, attractive force / As with a chain indissoluble bound / Thy system rolls entire" (*Su*, 97–99). The emanation of heat, "the effulgence of thy blaze" (103), and light, along with the "attractive force" of gravitation, constitute a total system. Drawing on Newton's monumental account of celestial mechanics, Thomson claims a unified vision of nature's "works," its "motions, periods, and . . . laws" (*Au*, 1357). In May 1727, he paused work on *Summer* to compose the commemorative poem *To the Memory of Sir Isaac Newton*. The scientist had died in March. The first edition includes an epigraph from *De rerum natura*, lines praising Epicurus: "Nature thus by your power has been so manifestly laid open and uncovered in every part" (*On the Nature*, 3.28–30).[15] Like Epicurus, Newton proposed a physics in which simple underlying principles of causality could explain a vast multitude of effects. In Thomson's words: "to call / From a few causes such a scheme of things, / Effects so various, beautiful, and great, / An universe complete!"[16] Gravity played a role similar to that of atomic particles, as a cause perceivable only in its effects, an unchanging foundation that both produces and limits flux. Indeed, Newton worried that the very regularity of a clockwork cosmos would displace providence, which is why, at least publicly, he avoided speculating about the exact nature of gravity, allowing it to be defined, in Richard Bentley's words, as "Divine energy and impression."[17] Unlike the occult agencies at work in alchemical metamorphoses or a contingent history of atomic collision and assemblage, gravitation, a force empirically and mathematically verifiable yet perceivable only through its effects, could be easily aligned with Christian orthodoxy as the basis for a new physicotheological consensus. After a century of dangerous speculation, "knowledge" of cosmic harmony was found, in Thomson's words, to be compatible with "devotion" (*Newton*, 137–38).

The tension in *Summer* between entropic flux as the condition of human labor and the steady recurrence of planetary motion is anticipated in *Newton*. "While on this dim spot where mortals toil / Clouded in dust," the natural philosopher "from motion's simple laws / Could trace the secret hand of Providence" (*Newton*, 13–15). The initial image recalls Lucretius's well-known analogy between colliding atoms and the particles of dust "mingling in a multitude of ways" that are visible in a beam of sunlight (*On the Nature*, 2.117). For Thomson, the dusty air is not, as Lucretius put it, a "small thing" that by analogy illuminates "great things" (124–25). It is, rather, evidence of the earthbound atmospheric obscurity that Newton's philosophic gaze had pierced. The naturalist explained the role played by the moon's gravitational pull in controlling the tides, the pulse of the ocean "heaving on the broken rocks" (*Newton*, 53). The wearing away of earthly matter is at once caused by and contrasted with the regular motion of the "harmonious system." A "single power" is at work in the multitude of solar systems and "the stone projected to the ground" (65–67). This same distinction provides the governing metaphor in the poem's concluding lines. The poet addresses the "mouldering stones" out of which the pyramids and arches of ancient civilizations were constructed, each "monument effaced / By ruthless ruin," ground "to the dust" (174–79). By contrast, Newton, who had discovered the "unremitting" principle of planetary motion, "lifts his column to the skies, / Beyond the waste of time" (180–81). Newtonian time, which reconciles cyclic recurrence and millennial completion "when time shall be no more" (208), is contrasted with the entropic arrow of planetary change described in the fifth book of *De rerum natura*, in which Lucretius observes that "the monuments of men collapsed" because of "the strong force of time" (*On the Nature*, 5.311–14). In the passage in *Summer*, Thomson returned to this distinction between the planetary cycles that steadfastly "remain" and "the flux of many thousand years / That oft has swept the toiling race of men, / And all their labored monuments away" (*Su*, 34, 35–37).

After publishing *Winter* and *Newton*, Thomson returned to his grand project, finishing *Spring* (1727) and *Summer* (1728) and then in 1730 the first complete edition of *The Seasons* (along with a separate quarto edition of *Autumn*), which was followed by revised editions in 1744 and 1746. In *Spring*, Thomson revisits the language of divine power in *Newton*. What, he asks, is the nature of the instinct that inspires animals to reproduce in springtime? "What, but God? / Inspiring God! who, boundless spirit all / And unremitting energy, pervades, / Adjusts, sustains, and agitates the whole" (*Sp*, 852–55). These lines closely echo a passage in *Newton* linking the scientist's discoveries with his devotion: "For could he / whose piercing mental eye diffusive saw / The finished university of things, / In all its order, magnitude, and parts / Forbear to adore that Power / Who fills, sustains, and actuates the whole?" (*Newton*, 138–43). Yet, in *Spring*, Thomson introduces the word *energy* (which appears nowhere in *Paradise Lost*) as a synonym for divine power.

In adopting this neologism, Thomson is riffing on the concluding paragraph of Joseph Addison's essay in *Spectator* no. 120, one of a series, each prefaced with an epigraph from Virgil's *Georgics*, in which the author makes observations on rural life. Addison considers the "instinct in animals," which, like human reason, seems to exceed "any properties in matter." He compares instinct with "the principle of gravitation in bodies, which is not to be explained by any known qualities inherent in the bodies themselves, nor from any laws of mechanism, but, according to the best notions of the greatest philosophers, is an immediate impression from the first mover, and the divine energy acting in the creatures."[18] Previously a term of rhetoric, *energy* had in the seventeenth century begun to stand as a mediating

principle, neither spirit nor matter but the activity by which the one re-
veals itself in the other. Energy takes the place of other phenomena such
as air (*spiritus, pneuma*) and light that had traditionally figured spirit but
had been increasingly materialized. As Anne Janowitz observes, however,
in such formulations the very imperative to preserve a role for divinity may
have the countervailing effect of making God indistinguishable from the
energy of gravitation, producing an anxiety similar to that explored in the
previous chapter: a God knowable as light can be reduced to light.[19]

In revising the passage from *Newton*, Thomson replaces *fills* with *per-
vades*. The latter was another neologism, one that, as Gerard Passannante
explains, derives from Henry More, who uses it to describe an omnipresent
spiritual substance that, in More's words, awakens "that immense mist of
Atoms into several energies."[20] Thomson's addition of *adjust* to the list of
verbs reflects a question among Newton's contemporaries as to whether the
deity must intervene in the cosmos to compensate for matter's tendency to
decay. Accepting an entropic principle despite its association with atomism
could justify a countervailing principle of divine renewal and adjustment.
A more surprising addition, *agitate*—to disturb, put into violent motion—
appears nowhere else in *The Seasons*.[21] A variant occurs once in *Paradise
Lost*, in the description of Satan's temptation of Eve, when he is compared
to the *ignis fatuus*, "kindled through agitation to a flame" (9.637). In this
passage in *Spring*, Thomson insists on the (almost demonic) disorder in
the Newtonian cosmos. In the 1744 edition of *The Seasons*, he removed
twelve lines following the reference to "unremitting energy" that charac-
terized God as the punishing storm deity of Job (e.g., "The Tempest blows
his Wrath"). While, in the revision, Thomson diminishes the role of special
providence and the Joban theodicy of *Winter*, it is evident that he was not
comfortable with what he took to be the implication of perfect order in a
clockwork cosmos. "The Seasons thus," he insists, ". . . ceaseless round a
jarring world they roll" (*Sp*, 1166–67).

Like *Winter*, *Spring*, the opening book of the complete *Seasons*, begins by
acknowledging the capriciousness of the weather. The transition from "surly
Winter" (*Sp*, 11) to "gentle Spring" (1) is uncertain: "As yet the trembling
year is unconfirmed, / And Winter oft at eve resumes the breeze, / Chills
the pale morn, and bids his driving sleets / Deform the day delightless" (18–
21). Having plowed and planted his fields, the farmer must contend with a
multitude of dangers: an "Untimely frost" (117); or, "brushed from Russian
wilds, a cutting gale" (114); or "insect armies" (121), the arrival of which
will lead to "Corrosive famine" (126); or the "deepening clouds on clouds,
surcharged with rain, / That o'er the vast Atlantic hither borne / In endless

train would quench the Summer blaze, / And cheerless drown the crude un-
ripened year" (139–42). While *Spring* explores the same sort of atmospheric
unpredictability and potential hardship that infuses *Winter*, we also see
Thomson working to integrate a scientific understanding of weather as a
global system of circulation, with cold fronts pushing in from the Eurasian
interior and moisture carried from the Atlantic.

For Thomson, meteoric disorder, along with the extremes of planetary
geography and season, are characteristics of the current phase of the Earth's
history. *The Seasons* veers, as many readers have observed, between a Whig-
gish belief in historical progress and an idealization of the primitive Earth,
when the vegetarian virtue of early man was made possible by a salubrious
climate. In the Ovidian "golden age" (*Sp*, 273), the "youthful Sun / Shot his
best rays" (260–61), and men "rose as vigorous as the sun" (246). Nota-
bly, Thomson characterizes this idealization as a retrospective projection
of "fabling poets" living "amid these iron times" (273–74). He recognizes,
in other words, that the fable of an earlier benign climate constitutes what
Robert Markley calls a "back formation," a fiction built to reverse "the
negative consequences of a climatologically unstable and often hostile
world."[22] Though such visions of an ideal climate may be "sung in Alle-
goric Phraze" (297 [1728 ed.]), Thomson weaves myth together with natural
philosophy to identify a turning point in planetary history, drawing on the
most influential work of the speculative world builders, Burnet's *Sacred
Theory of the Earth*.[23]

As I noted in the introduction, Burnet characterized the asymmetries of
the Earth as a consequence of the Flood. The surface of the primeval Earth
was uniform, "not a wrinkle, scar or fracture in all its body" (*Sacred Theory*,
64), its smooth crust overlaying a vault of water. The agent of change is "the
Sun, that great workman of Nature" (44), activating subterranean moisture
and weakening the mantle: "as the heat of the Sun gave force to these Va-
pours more and more, and made them more strong and violent, so . . . it also
weaken'd more and more the Arch of the Earth . . . drying it immoderately,"
until it finally ruptures at the time of the Deluge (68). Here is how Thomson
describes the effects of the Flood:

> Hence, in old dusky times, a deluge came:
> When the deep-cleft disparting orb, that arched
> The central waters round, impetuous rushed
> With universal burst into the gulf,
> And o'er the high-piled hills of fractured earth
> Wide-dashed the waves in undulation vast,

Till, from the centre to the streaming clouds,
A shoreless ocean tumbled round the globe. (*Sp*, 309–16)

According to Burnet, there were no violent exhalations in the antediluvian world: "The smoothness of the Earth made the face of the Heavens so too; the Air was calm and serene; none of those tumultuary motions and conflicts of vapours, which the Mountains and the Winds cause in ours: 'Twas suited to a golden Age" (*Sacred Theory*, 64). In Thomson's rendition, the "winds and waters flowed / In consonance" (*Sp*, 270–71). The air was calm and pure, and "Great Spring . . . / Greened all the year" (320–21). Burnet had argued that the Flood caused the Earth to tilt on its axis with respect to its ecliptic plane—"it lost its equal poise" (*Sacred Theory*, 147)—introducing seasonal "alternation" and a more dynamic equilibrium, "the contrary seasons balancing one another" (67). In Thomson's version, we hear echoes of Burnet as well as Milton's depiction of intensified seasonal extremes after the Fall: "The Seasons since have, with severer sway, / Oppressed a broken world: the Winter keen / Shook forth his waste of snows; and Summer shot / His pestilential heats" (317–20).

Paolo Rossi distinguishes two approaches to natural philosophy that emerge at the end of the seventeenth century. One approach, exemplified by Burnet, took up the Epicurean speculations about the mechanical processes that would account for the formation and evolution of the Earth. Abandoning any Aristotelian idea of "eternal structures," Burnet began to ask, as Rossi writes, "How has nature produced a particular object during the course of time?" (*The Dark Abyss of Time*, 17). The second approach is exemplified by Newton, who, according to Rossi, describes a "stable and harmonious" cosmos (43). Like Boyle before him, Rossi notes, Newton draws, at least in his published writings, a sharp division between the investigation of nature's laws and any "scientific reconstruction of the formation of the world" (43). While Rossi may overstate Newton's commitment to nature's fixity, his distinction captures a tension in Thomson's poetic treatment of natural philosophy between a Newtonian energy that accounts for the unremitting constancy of diurnal and seasonal recurrence and an awareness of a stochastic agitation embodied not only in meteorologic extremes and unpredictability but also in the changing epochs of the Earth.[24]

GEORGIC DESCRIPTION AND PLANETARY CIRCULATION

Thomson's early readers certainly would have understood his insistence on the "severer sway" of the seasons. The first half of the eighteenth century saw ongoing climatic volatility. The Great Storm of 1703 caused widespread devastation as well as an early meteorologic media sensation.[25] The winter of 1708–9 is widely regarded as the coldest in the Northern Hemisphere during the past half millennium; temperatures in London reached –12° C during the Great Frost. The Thames froze over again in 1716. The summer of 1725, the very year Thomson began composing *The Seasons*, has the record for the lowest June-to-August period in the Central England Temperature Index (which begins in 1659), while 1740 stands as the coldest year overall recorded in the index. As Hubert Lamb notes, the challenging climate included not only unusually low temperatures and increased storminess but also the "enhanced variability of temperature level"—intense heat as well as cold along with general unpredictability—"which must have badly upset harvest expectations" (*Climate, History and the Modern World*, 220).

Yet the historian Geoffrey Parker describes this period as one in which, in Britain at least, the "fatal synergy" between climate and crisis was "broken." For Parker, the 1688 Revolution in England stands as the decisive turning point, leading to a "permanent escape from both the General Crisis and the Little Ice Age" (*Global Crisis*, 395). The crucial factor, according to Parker, is the emergence of centralized state institutions, which support the expansion of transportation infrastructure and so regional and global trade networks. Historians have also identified the Agricultural Revolution as a response to the rigors of the Little Ice Age, which, in Brian Fagan's words, "insulated the English from the worst effects of sudden climatic change."[26] Higher agricultural yields (the result of better tools and techniques), crop diversification, the enclosure of common land, and a growing understanding of nutrient cycling created resilience in the face of climate shocks.[27]

That the imperative to improve agricultural practices and raise productivity constitutes a response to climatic adversity, a "climate fix," helps explain the immense resonance during the eighteenth century of Virgil's *Georgics*, which treats the "Science of Husbandry," as Joseph Addison observes in his preface to Dryden's 1697 translation of the poem, "set off with all the Beauties and Embellishments of poetry" ("An Essay on the Georgics," 146).[28] In an Iron Age subject to "the blazing sun's fierce tyranny" and "the North Wind's piercing cold," Virgil writes, Jove has determined "that the path of husbandry should not run smooth, . . . sharpening men's wits by care" (*Georgics*, 105–7). According to Virgil's theodicy, the harsh climate and recalcitrant soil are not a punishment but an incitement to human self-development.[29] Seasonal extremes and meteorologic capriciousness necessitate *labor improbus*, "unrelenting Toil," but also lead to experience and "thought," which together "might little by little forge all manner of skills" and technologies (109), allowing the farmer to turn stubborn natural forces toward human ends.

The guiding principle of the *Georgics* is that successful cultivation requires attention to the distinct economy of atmosphere and weather, soil and water. Knowledge of specific regional conditions directs action: "And ere our iron cleaves an unknown plain, be it first our care to learn the winds and the wavering moods of the sky, the wonted tillage and nature of the ground, what each clime yields and what each disowns" (103). Satan echoes these lines when he first studies Hell: "is this the region, this the soil, the clime / . . . that we must change for Heaven?" The georgic insists on what remains unresolved in *Paradise Lost*, the consequentiality of the Earth's variation, what Kurt Heinzelman calls "the complexity of the local: how, out of the particulars of place, the need arises to work, to persevere—or to be conquered."[30] Just as every day and every season varies, so all regions vary, and these concrete variations of time and space are the condition of husbandry. Invoking Lucretius, Virgil writes: "Nature laid these laws and eternal covenants on certain lands" (103). Understanding a place—its soil and climate, its laws and limits—is what allows the farmer to direct the forces of nature toward human goals. Indeed, *georgic* and *energy* share an etymological root. *Georgic* derives from the Greek *ge* (meaning Earth) plus *ergon* (work): cultivation as a directing of energy that reworks the Earth, but also the energy that the Earth—nature's work—contributes to production.

Thomson identifies the "Mantuan swain" (*Sp*, 456) and his middle poem as the inspiration for *The Seasons*, which John Chalker calls "the most thorough-going, the most complex, and the most sensitively serious eighteenth-century imitation of the *Georgics*."[31] In July 1726, Thomson published an expanded edition of *Winter* along with a new preface, audaciously placing his ambition in a line that runs "from Moses down to Milton." He addresses the "enemies of poetry" as "weak-sighted gentleman" who "cannot bear" its "strong light."[32] If Pope had asserted that "the proper study of mankind is man," Thomson returns to an earlier theme: "It was this devotion to the works of Nature that, in his Georgics, inspired the rural Virgil to write so inimitably" (241). Here, Thomson translates the passage from the second book of the *Georgics* in which Virgil positions his project in relation to the ambitious Lucretian mandate for poetry:

Me may the Muses, my supreme delight!
Whose priest I am, smit with immense desire,
Snatch to their care; the starry tracts disclose,

The sun's distress, the labours of the moon:
Whence the earth quakes: and by what force the deeps
Heave at the rocks, then on themselves reflow:
Why winter-suns to plunge in ocean speed:
And what retards the lazy summer-night.[33]

More than a medium for recounting the pains and pleasures of rural life, po-
etry seeks to discern the forces that underlie manifest reality, nature's hidden
machinery, its "works." Of course, the didactic aim of the *Georgics* is more
practical than the invocation of the Lucretian muse would suggest. Where
Lucretius explores underlying causality—"The order of the heavens / And
visage of the sky must be my theme / And storm and lightning flash must be
my song, / Both what they do and from what cause they spring" (*On the Na-
ture*, 6.83–85)—Virgil is concerned with the signs that predict meteorologic
change and allow the cultivator to coordinate his labor with a changeable
climate: "that through unfailing signs we might learn these dangers—the
heat, and the rain, and the cold-bringing winds" (*Georgics*, 123).

In his poem of the "changeful year" (*Wi*, 107), Thomson explores this
georgic process whereby human labor, the growth of plants, and the activi-
ties of animals are coordinated in diurnal and seasonal time. Husbandry
oversees the process whereby solar radiance, "fluid gold" (*Su*, 84), is, in its
annual flux, captured for "Britannia's weal" (*Sp*, 930). The georgic formal-
izes the physiocratic principle that agricultural production yields social
surplus as a result of the "uncompensated work of nature."[34] The opening
of *The Seasons* depicts just such a process of transmutation. The ravag-
ing "blasts" of winter give way, intermittently, to a nature "blooming and
benevolent" (*Sp*, 10). The "bounteous sun" (26) warms the "atmosphere,"
"unbinding" the "earth," "vivifying" the living world. This is the first of
numerous accounts of the role of sunlight—in concert with soil, air, and
moisture—in the growth of plants. Later in *Spring*, "the various vegetative
tribes / . . . / Draw the live ether and imbibe the dew" (561–63), and "the
vernal sun awakes / The torpid sap" (567–68). In *Autumn*, the muse travels
to France and views the "vigorous soils and climes . . . / Where, by the po-
tent sun elated high, / The vineyard swells refulgent on the day, / . . . and
drinks . . . the heightened blaze" (*Au*, 684–89).

Thomson wrote a half century before the discovery of photosynthe-
sis, yet any agriculturalist knows that it is, in Thomson's words, the Sun's
"quickening glance" that generates "the green abodes of life" (*Su*, 105, 107).
Thomson drew extensively on the research of Stephen Hales, famous for his
account of the circulation of sap and moisture in plants, facilitated by pres-

sure and attraction, but fueled by the light and warmth absorbed by leaves and roots. Hales proved experimentally that air and light, as much as soil, contribute to vegetable growth. "These new combinations of air, sulphur and acid spirit, which are constantly forming in the air, are doubtless very serviceable, in promoting *the work of vegetation*," he wrote in *Vegetable Staticks* (1727).[35] According to Hales, a plant is a kind of "machinery" (361), a tree a "complicated engine" (353), and he speculated that sunlight energizes this living machinery. Picking up on hints in Lucretius and Newton, Hales wondered whether "light also, by freely entering the expanded surfaces of leaves and flowers," might contribute to the "ennobling principles of vegetation" (327).[36] As Paul Warde observes, Hales proved that the "living world" was "part of a greater set of flows" that included the hydrologic cycle, the atmosphere, and sunlight itself.[37] Hales even adopted the term *energy* to describe the force of circulation: "We find a considerable energy in the root to push up sap in the bleeding season" (*Vegetable Staticks*, 103). And, lacking access to enlivening "particles of light" (356), plants fail to flourish. Hales noted that "in the year 1726 when by reason of the extreme wetness and coldness of the preceding summer"—the intemperate summer in the aftermath of which Thomson began a poem about seasonal order and disorder—"the unripe shoots produced generally very little fruit" (373).

In the opening sequence of *Spring*, Thomson describes how the energy supplied by the light and warmth of the sun and by the igneous particles absorbed from the air and soil are coordinated with the labor of humans and animals. Such coordination is the basis of culture. The husbandman drives his steers as they pull the plow, their shared "toil" preparing the field for the sower (*Sp*, 39). The work of humans and animals is understood as a continuation of solar activity, and after "laborious man / Has done his part" it is the role of the "world-reviving sun" to "temper all" (48–49, 51). Calling on "Britons" to "venerate the plough" (67), Thomson foresees the culmination of this tempering:

> Let Autumn spread his treasures to the sun,
> Luxuriant and unbounded. As the sea
> Far through his azure turbulent domain
> Your empire owns, and from a thousand shores
> Wafts all the pomp of life into your ports;
> So with superior boon may your rich soil,
> Exuberant, Nature's better blessings pour
> O'er every land, the naked nations clothe,
> And be the exhaustless granary of a world! (69–77)

Both production and exchange—the growth of plants and animals, the transoceanic trade in commodities—are traced back to the passage of the sun's energy through the Earth system. The completion of one process, the transformation of "seed" into "treasure," initiates another, global commerce, itself energized by the currents and trade winds that "waft" ships of commerce from distant lands to British ports. While wool still constituted more than two-thirds of Britain's total exports, the first decades of the eighteenth century saw the rapid growth of grain exports from southern England, making Britain the major source of food surplus in northwestern Europe. Along with falling food prices, these exports facilitated the development of Britain's consumer economy, including the importation of "the pomp of life": spices and silk, coffee and tea, sugar and tobacco.[38]

In *The Seasons*, Thomson describes a national economy in which production depends on the "ability to capture some part of the flow of energy reaching the earth," as E.A. Wrigley characterizes Britain's eighteenth-century "advanced organic" energy regime (*Continuity, Chance and Change*, 51). Wrigley's emphasis on the circulation of solar energy, as a force of production, helps us think about the status of *The Seasons* as the paradigmatic poem of description, "the classic of descriptive poetry," as Edmund Gosse writes, "the specimen which the literature of the world presents which must be considered as the most important and the most successful." "A great part of Thomson's poem," Gosse added, "is nothing more nor less than a skilfully varied catalogue of natural phenomena."[39] In 1756, Joseph Warton named Thomson as the poet who first superseded the hackneyed conventions of natural description, "a set of hereditary objects" that have been passed "from one poet to another, . . . without any propriety as to age or climate."[40] Thomson, by contrast, offered "a variety of new and original images, which he painted from nature itself, and from his own actual observations."[41] Hugh Blair refers to descriptive poetry as "the great test of a Poet's imagination," in which "the highest exertions of genius may be displayed." "Of all professed Descriptive Compositions," he adds, "the largest and fullest that I am acquainted with, in any language, is Mr. Thomson's *Seasons*" (*Lectures on Rhetoric*, 457–58). In 1779, John Aikin called *The Seasons* the "first capital work in which natural description was professedly the principle object." "Every grand and beautiful appearance in nature, that distinguishes one portion of the annual circuit from another," he continued, "is the proper source of materials" ("Essay on the Plan and Character," viii, xiv).

My contention is that the imperative to describe the works of nature, to detail the Earth's shaping forces, reflects an energy economy organized around concrete temporal and geographic variations in access to solar radiation. This interpretation elaborates on a point made by Angus Fletcher in what is surely the most substantive critical study of poetic description. Fletcher identifies Thomson as an originator of descriptive poetics, the foundation for the "environment poem." Description, he writes, is rooted in diurnal experience, "knowledge of the sun's presence and absence, creating a daily round, giving earth its vital energy" (A New Theory for American Poetry, 77). The work of description in The Seasons is to delineate the phases of the seasons and the climates of the Earth, the fluctuations and variations that are the condition of economic production. The all-embracing expansiveness of Thomson's description—"My muse is not selective but greedy," he wrote to Mallet (quoted in Parker, The Triumph of Augustan Poetics, 150)—reflects the "advanced" phase of the organic energy economy, in which production is supplemented by new industrial technology and growing mercantile empire.

The (never complete) modal transition from allegory to description is evident in the way Thomson, notwithstanding Warton's claim that the poet's images of nature are rooted in direct observation, insistently reworks Milton's epic similes. "Objects which are the vehicles of heroic metaphor in Paradise Lost," James Sambrook notes, "have a way of reappearing in the Seasons simply as themselves; scraps of Milton's epic are naturalized into the georgic mode."[42] Consider the famous comparison in which Satan appears before the rebels "as when the sun new risen / Looks through the horizontal misty air / Shorn of his beams." As with any extended simile, the reader is invited to pause, draw up in the mind's eye an image of the rays of the morning sun passing through the thickened atmosphere, and reflect on the tenor, the fallen angel, still charismatic yet now diminished. In Milton's similes, I argued, the naturalistic vehicle insists, in its particularity and exorbitant materiality, in a manner that forestalls its reabsorption in the tenor. Thomson exploits this possibility, literalizing and deallegorizing Milton's similes, appropriating Milton's language so that the allusion is inescapable, but using it as the basis of empirical description: the winter "sun / Scarce spreads o'er ether the dejected day. / Faint are his gleams, and ineffectual shoot / His struggling rays in horizontal lines / Through the thick air" (Wi, 44–48). While the two images of a thickened atmosphere evince a modal contrast, Thomson's language is not straightforwardly mimetic. The Sun is personified. Like the Protestant epic Paradise Lost, The Seasons is, despite its empiricism, brimming with out-of-place "persons," including the various seasons, day and night, inspiration, heat, a maternal nature, and a patriarchal sun. Personification endures in Augustan poetry, Heather

Keenleyside explains, because the modern distinction between agential persons and passive things remained insecure in the eighteenth century.[43] Personification is continuous with description insofar as description represents an animacy in the world, not discrete objects but forces and processes. In his 1777 study of the poem, John More argued that personification was a natural feature of speech intensified by "poetical imaginations," which, "like the sun, diffuse peculiar energy and animation wherever they move."[44]

When we think about poetic description, it is not personification but the field of vision that comes to mind, what Parker in his account of "descriptive poetry" calls "the world of incidental appearances" (*Triumph of Augustan Poetics*, 18). Thomson internalized the empiricist epistemology of the new sciences, above all the equation of seeing with knowing. The first stanza of the 1726 edition of *Winter* begins with an injunction: "SEE!" The third stanza echoes this: "Behold." Or as Thomson writes in the first complete edition of *The Seasons*: "Scrutinous Philosophy looks deep / With piercing eye, into the latent cause; / Nor can she swallow what she does not see" (*Su*, 1131–33 [1730 ed.]). The poet observes and describes, but—aided by the Lucretian "philosophic eye" (*Su*, 102–3 [1746 ed.])—he "looks deep," seeking causes that underlie manifest and multitudinous reality. This is what the laboring-class poet Robert Story meant when he wrote in 1842: "The philosophic Muse of the 'Seasons' taught me to look not only on the surface of things, but beneath it."[45]

John Barrell's influential reading of *The Seasons* compares Thomson's descriptions with landscape paintings. The distance between the observer, stationed on a high prospect, and the landscape, "detached from him, *over there*," substantiates the poet's authority. "Thomson," Barrell asserts, "feels he must control nature in order not to be controlled by it."[46] Such prospect views embody, according to Barrell, the ostensibly disinterested perspective of the gentleman landowners whose patronage is celebrated throughout the poem and who provide "an equal, wide survey" of an increasingly economically differentiated society (*Su*, 1617), transforming ideological conflict into picturesque synthesis.[47] His account, however, misses the dynamism of Thomson's descriptions, the emphasis on shifting conditions and uncertain boundaries, what W. B. Hutchings calls "nature in process."[48] Better than any later critic, John More pinpoints the dynamic transformation and interanimation in Thomson's verse: "The Seasons abounds in descriptions, where the objects which occupy several scenes, are specifically enumerated; not separately, as in a state of disjunction, but as possessing certain relative connections, as partly dependant on each other, as constituent particulars of one whole; as contributing their respective shares, in producing the general effect" (*Strictures*, 54). To characterize this mode of processual description, Hutchings refers to Lessing's account of Homer's famous description of the forging of the shield of Achilles, where language depicts not static objects but Vulcan's laborious refashioning of matter.

For Thomson it is not the forge master but the Earth, and the radiance that flows through it, that organizes the unceasing metamorphosis of form. Verbs rather than nouns—or nouns turned into verbs—are the grammatical engines of description. A river "boils, and wheels, and foams, and thunders" (*Wi*, 105). Rarely does Thomson depict a discrete object or enclosed scene.[49] He describes processes of transformation that are alchemical (congealing, fermenting, putrefying, melting, freezing, rarefying, dissolving) and mechanical (diffusing, rolling, gathering, pouring, bending). The effect is a sense of successive time as it manifests in the shifting states of matter, flowing, percolating, eddying, slowing, accelerating. We detect the planetary forces that animate Thomson's landscapes in frequent images of overabundance, proliferation, matter spreading out and spilling over. In *Autumn*, the sky spreads, sheaves "swell" (*Au*, 137). A "view" is "diffusive" (657), a "prospect" "boundless" (658). In *Winter*, "the low-bent clouds / Pour flood on flood, yet unexhausted" (*Wi*, 77–78), and, in turn, the river "Wide o'er the brim, with many a torrent swelled, / . . . its banks o'erspread" (94–95). Despite Barrell's claim about visual command, often what Thomson describes are scenes of visual confusion, as in *Autumn* when the "general fog" in a "formless grey confusions covers all" (*Au*, 729–31), a condition he compares to the first "Chaos" (733). Landscapes are indistinct; changing weather and atmospheric conditions estrange familiar scenes. Night falls, and "Order confounded lies" (1141).

It is in the depiction of air—of the atmosphere as itself a medium and a system of circulation, of that *anima* that animates the living world—that we best understand Thomson's descriptive technique. A poetry of visual description confronts a unique challenge when it attempts to depict such barely tangible matter.[50] Thomson recognizes air's representational recalcitrance: "expression cannot paint, / The breath of Nature" (*Sp*, 554–55). "Though one transparent vacancy it seem," however, the "lucid air" is not "Void," Thomson writes in the famous "microscopic eye" passage (*Su*, 309–11, 288). It was the vacuum pump, not the microscope, that had inaugurated the Restoration-era science of air in the hands of Robert Boyle, the chemist whom Thomson lists among the British worthies (1556). It was Boyle who, as Keats complained, first "emptied the haunted air" by experimentally confirming the corporeality of a substance so readily available to occult imaginings. Air, for Boyle, was neither intelligent nor inert. It was an elastic, corpuscular fluid, with temperature and humidity, mass and spring, and a role in combustion, respiration, and the conveyance of sound. A century before the identification of its component gases, Boyle even speculated, in his wonderfully titled *Suspicions about Some Hidden Realities of the Air*, about air's "Ingredients," its "aggregate of effluviams." "Perhaps there is scarce a more heterogeneous body in the world," he wrote.[51]

What Thomson inherits from Boyle is a sense of the metamorphic variability of air as a subtle substance knowable by its sensible qualities and its transmission of force. Thomson, however, was interested in air's behavior not in the vacuum pump but in the atmosphere. Here, he takes a cue from Burnet, who linked the postdiluvian seasonal vicissitudes with what he called the "inconstancy of the Air" (*Sacred Theory*, 153): "The different pressure of the Atmosphere, sometimes heavier, sometimes lighter, more rare or more dense, moist or dry, and *agitated* with different degrees of motions, and in different manners" (157; my emphasis). It is this agitated air—itself the medium of light, moisture, and sound—that most vividly announces time's passage in the "circling year" (*Su*, 14). In *Spring*, the air swells and expands: "Forth fly the tepid airs" (*Sp*, 32). This "liberal" (98), "lenient" (78), "light" (752), "soft" (510), and "vital air" (583) engenders movement and growth. The glittering "coloured" air (86) of the dawn in *Summer* gives way as the "the potent sun / Melts into limpid air the high-raised clouds / And morning fogs" (*Su*, 199–201). The air of *Autumn* is "ruffled" by wind (*Au*, 34) and leaf littered (992). This is the season of "roving mists" (734) and "doubling fogs," when the "vapour-burdened" and "plume-dark air" (869) confuses vision. The frigid winds in *Winter* bear "thick air" (*Wi*, 47). The moon is seen through "turbid, fluctuating air" (126). The air is "troubled" (82), "precipitated" (153), "burdened" with "groans . . . shrill sounds, and distant sighs" (191–92). Only with the falling snow is the air "hushed" (229) and "darkened" (277).

Thomson describes the Earth as a circulatory system operating by means of the diffusion and metamorphosis of solar radiance passing through a variable "atmosphere" (*Sp*, 28; *Su*, 318; *Wi*, 697), driving the hydrologic cycle, and supporting the living world and so human projects. The most significant addition to *Autumn* in the 1744 edition concerns the atmospheric circulation of moisture, offering an eighty-line correction to the earlier account of the hydrologic cycle and the origin of springs and rivers. The entire section follows the description of autumnal fog, "copious exhalations" "condensed" (*Au*, 707–8). In earlier editions, Thomson endorsed the percolation theory, according to which ocean water seeps into "the sandy stratum," and, cleansed of salt, "mounting still," it rises to "spouting rills"

(745–56). Lucretius had granted evaporation a role in the hydrologic cycle (*On the Nature*, 6.616–23) but follows Plato in his account of seawater filtered through underground caverns and raised to mountain springs by subterranean pressure (6.631–39), a theory endorsed by Ovid and Seneca. The percolation hypothesis remained dominant through the seventeenth century, supported by Robert Plot in *De origine fontium* (1684). In revising *The Seasons*, Thomson realized that this theory was an "Amusive dream" (*Au*, 757). The new model of the hydrologic cycle recognizes the role solar radiance plays in powering planetary circulation. In a 1686 *Philosophical Transactions* paper, "An Account of the Circulation of the Watry Vapours," Edmund Halley argued that evaporation, "the rising of Vapour by warmth," could account for all springs and rivers. "The Sun warming the air and rais-ing a more plentiful Vapour" from the ocean, the vapors are pushed by wind toward mountains, where they condense into clouds and precipitate, accu-mulating in the soil, and forming springs. Solar "heat" is a pump that drives "the Circulation" of water through the Earth.[52] This is the system of ener-getic circulation Thomson describes in his revised account: "United thus, / The exhaling sun, the vapour-burdened air, / The gelid mountains, that to rain condensed, / These vapours in continual current draw, / And send them o'er the fair-divided earth / In bounteous rivers to the deep again" (*Au*, 828–33). While Thomson refutes the percolation hypothesis associated with Lu-cretius, Gertrude Greene Cronk argues that the Lucretian search for hidden causes as well as the epicurean poet's specific diction describing vapors rising and condensing infuses the entire section, a Lucretian influence that "per-meates" Thomson's thought.[53] Certainly this influence can be detected in the apostrophe to natural knowledge that introduces the corrected hypoth-esis: "O thou pervading genius, given to man, / To trace the secrets of the dark abyss! / Oh! lay the mountains bare, and wide display / Their hidden structure to the astonished view" (*Au*, 777–80). Thomas Reisner, who asserts that Thomson's rejection of the percolation hypothesis reflected his growing understanding of "the forces of capillary attraction," notes that his reference, a few lines later, to "the leaning strata, artful ranged" (810), in the same pas-sage reflects John Strachey's identification in 1719 of the superpositioning of mineral strata and the distinction between vertical and horizontal strata.[54] *The Seasons*, then, includes not only an updated account of the hydrologic cycle, the first of the Earth systems to be fully understood, but also what may be the first poetic incorporation of this essential principle of geology.

Autumn concludes with a deistic apostrophe that reiterates the Virgilian invocation of Lucretian knowledge Thomson had cited in the preface to

Winter: "O Nature! . . . / Enrich me with the knowledge of thy works"
(*Au*, 1352–53). Such knowledge begins with the Newtonian "World beyond
world" of the "rolling" heavens, before descending to the "deep," "the min-
eral strata" (1354, 1359). It then ascends, like moisture raised by heat into
the atmosphere, through the "rising system" to "the vegetable world" and
beyond to human mind and passions (1352–73). Here, however, Thomson,
following Virgil, acknowledges a limit to his own philosophical vision. This
impediment is geohumoral, the tradition according to which human bod-
ies and minds, no less than plants and animals, are shaped by temperature
and atmospheric conditions: "if to that unequal—if the blood / In sluggish
streams about my heart forbid / That best ambition—under closing shades /
Inglorious lay me by the lowly brook, / And whisper to my dreams" (1367–
71). The lines in *Autumn* recall a passage in *Spring* in which the poet rec-
ommends that those subject to "listless languor" caused by the noontime
heat retreat to the shaded bank of a creek and "There let the classic page thy
fancy lead / Through rural scenes, such as the Mantuan swain / Paints in
the matchless harmony of song" (*Sp*, 455–57). The climatic implications of
the passage in *Autumn* in which Thomson most explicitly recalls "the clas-
sic page" are murky, though worth unpacking. In the *Georgics*, the climatic
context for the poet's "chill blood" ("*frigidus . . . sanguis*") and the resulting
mental sluggishness that justifies his turn from philosophical speculation
to pastoral pleasures seems to be extreme heat, which leads the poet to
dream of visiting "the cool glens of Haemus," where he might take refuge
in the forest shade (*Georgics*, 171).[55] It is not entirely clear whether Thom-
son's reference to his "sluggish" blood is meant to foreground seasonality
or climate, the theory that northerners had thick blood and so lethargic
minds, which Milton had invoked in worrying about the "cold / Climate."
What is clear is that, here, Thomson calls attention to his own embod-
ied susceptibility and the relation of climate to mental labor. A narratorial
persona that usually remains in the background appears only in order to
retreat into the solitary forest and from the Lucretian call to learn "the
laws of nature's working" (*Georgics*, 171). In a study of the lyricism of *The
Seasons*, Christopher Miller claims that Thomson "creates an independent-
minded poetic self who abides through all seasons and weathers," showcas-
ing "mental adaptation to seasonal change."[56] In this instance, however, the
poet shows himself in order to show his vulnerability, an environmental
susceptibility that checks his attempt to understand the forces of planetary
flux. Yet the reader can also see that there is no retreat, no place outside the
global system of circulation: the smallest brook is part of the just-theorized
hydrologic cycle.[57]

INDUSTRY AND EMPIRE AS CLIMATE FIXES

Thomson considers the relation of climate to human world making early in *Autumn*, in a sequence that begins with an apostrophe to "Industry, rough power," which raises "human kind" by teaching men to utilize the "Materials infinite" given by nature (*Au*, 43–52). Before industry, the "shivering wretch" was exposed to "Hail, rain, and snow" (59–62). The days "rolled . . . along"

> A waste of time! till Industry approached,
> And roused him from his miserable sloth;
> His faculties unfolded; pointed out,
> Where lavish Nature the directing hand
> Of Art demanded; showed him how to raise
> His feeble force by the mechanic powers,
> To dig the mineral from the vaulted earth,
> On what to turn the piercing rage of fire,
> On what the torrent, and the gathered blast;
> Gave the tall ancient forests to his ax. (72–81)

This passage revisits Lucretius's account of the historical evolution of toolmaking and the early development of metallurgy (*On the Nature*, 5.1241–97). In Thomson's version, "Industry" enables humans to overcome climatic exigency, the "rude inclement elements." "Industry" means industriousness, the postlapsarian "sweat, and pain" (*Au*, 44) required to tame recalcitrant nature. But the personified Industry also holds some of its modern connotations: human labor augmented by technological contrivances, "mechanic powers" that capture and direct natural forces.

Coal was in this period playing an increasingly important role in Britain's energy economy. Wrigley estimates that, in 1700, Britain was generating 50 percent of its total consumed energy from coal, a percentage that rises to 60 percent by the middle of the century (Wrigley, *Energy and the English Industrial Revolution*, 36–38). The traces of this new energy economy in *The Seasons* are subtle. Thomson is vague about the "mineral" extracted from the Earth, although the capacity "to raise / His feeble force by the mechanic powers" (*Au*, 76–77) suggests the coal-powered Newcomen engines, used beginning in 1712 to pump water from coal mines. The most overt reference to coal comes shortly after the address to Industry, in a reference to a Newcastle collier sailing up the Thames—the "sooty hulk / Steered sluggish on" (126–27)—an image that foregrounds the power of wind rather than mineral combustion. Owing to the "gifts" of Industry, Thomson writes, "Pensive Winter, cheered by him, / Sits at the social fire"—almost certainly coal fueled—"and happy hears / The excluded tempest idly rave along" (143–45). Here, it is worth recalling Ji-Hyung Cho's argument that Britain's growing use of coal—first and foremost for domestic heating—should be understood as a response to the cold of the Little Ice Age.

When Thomson moved to London in 1725, it was the largest metropolis in Europe, its growth enabled by coal shipped from Newcastle. Despite living in and near the capital for the majority of his adult life, Thomson wrote a poem that strives to encompass "the system . . . entire" yet largely ignores the crowded and polluted city. Early in *Spring*, he narrates his departure from the capital as a change of atmosphere: "Now from the town, / Buried in smoke and sleep and noisome damps / Oft let me wander o'er the dewy fields / Where freshness breathes" (*Sp*, 101–4). Every day he observed the activity of grimy and busy London, but almost none of that provided material for his greatest poem, which he continued to revise until the end of his life. For Thomson's contemporaries, London's self-evidently anthropogenic, coal-thickened air stood as an acute embodiment of what William Cavert calls a "new kind of economy, one in which abundant energy made possible new kinds of work, life, and urban space."[58] In his *Tour through the Whole Island of Great Britain* (1724–27), Defoe describes London as a city of "smoke and dirt, sin and seacoal." He climbs to a high point near Clapham and takes in the view of the capital, focusing on the grand houses on the city's outskirts, places of "retreat" where the elite can "draw their breath in a clean air."[59] Thomson echoes this passage in *Summer* when he climbs Richmond Hill and looks toward the city: "what a goodly prospect spreads around, / Of hills, and dales, and woods, and lawns, and spires, / And glittering towns, and gilded streams, till all / The stretching landskip into smoke decays!" (*Su*, 1438–41). The view foreshortened by smoke does not unsettle the poet's sense of a harmonious landscape, emphasized with an atypical alliteration. The city's murky atmosphere is safely circumscribed, and what follows is an apostrophe to a providentially favored "Happy Brittannia" (1442): "Thy country teems with wealth" (1454). I am not suggesting that Thomson willfully obscures the mineral energy regime in *The Seasons*. Rather, the condition of possibility for his "rural song" (*Su*, 29)—and for the poem's ideological promise that historical progress can be reconciled with seasonal recurrence—is a turn away from the forces of change embodied in London. In the eighteenth century, the poetic treatment of the city required a satiric eye, as in Swift's "A Description of a City Shower" (1710), Gay's *Trivia* (1716), and Johnson's *London* (1738). For a poet with philosophical and patriotic ambitions, a more felicitous subject was the advanced organic energy regime embodied in "the power of cultivation" (*Su*, 1436) and Britain's global commerce: "Thy crowded ports, / where rising masts an endless prospect yield" and the "hurried sailor . . . loosening every sheet, / Resigns the spreading vessel to the wind" (1461–66).

While Thomson has little to say about what is closest to home—the smoky metropole—he has much to say about distant lands and climes. A descriptive mode that fails when confronted with furnaces and factories flourishes in representing mercantile empire. The Sun's "effulgence" (*Su*, 103) is distributed unevenly across the spherical Earth, and seasonal extremes have their geographic parallel in the range of climatic zones. As Virgil had written (in Dryden's translation), "Earth in several climes divides," and between the equator and the poles "the gods assigned / Two habitable seats for human kind."[60] Virgil's own brief excursions to the planet's extreme climes were widely renowned. As Warton observes: "The contrast is very strong between the scenes of Africa and Scythia, and has a fine effect. This variety, this magic art of conveying the reader from one climate to another, constitutes one of the great beauties of poetry."[61] Thomson's explorations of the "frigid zone" (*Wi*, 796) and the "torrid zone" (*Su*, 632) and the societies they support were widely regarded as among the most sublime passages in *The Seasons*. The connection, for Thomson, between extreme climates and national development, however, is not straightforward, as is evident in his treatment of the northern climes. Northern Europe—Milton's "populous North"—is home to the Scythians, a "boisterous race" hardened by the frigid northwest wind, whose invasion of "enfeebled" Rome "gave the vanquished world another form" (*Wi*, 835–42). Here, Thomson invokes the idea, explored in the previous chapter, that the barbarian invasions were precipitated by resource scarcity and overpopulation in the cold north. The north is also home to the Laplanders, who eschew war and "ask no more than simple Nature gives" (845). Violent expansion and frugal self-sufficiency are two responses to the rigorous northern clime. A third is offered by Russia. Despite "the distant sun, / That rears and ripens man as well as plants" (938–39), Peter the Great, the Russian tsar, has "his stubborn country tamed" (956). Not unlike the narrator, Peter journeyed through "every land." He learned to utilize the "mechanic tool" and "Gathered the seeds of trade, of useful arts" (967–70). Compensating for the frigid climate, his improving ethos can be seen as a model for another northern nation in need of development. In *Autumn*, the poet describes the natural abundance of his native "Caledonia" (*Au*, 880)—"forests huge," "watery wealth" (883, 886)—and calls for a patriot to "cheer dejected Industry, to give / A double harvest to the pining swain" (914–15), to protect the native fisheries and develop wool and linen manufacturing. Thomson anticipates the rhetoric of "civil cameralism" that Fredrik Albritton Jonsson has identified in later eighteenth-century natural-historical and agricultural writing, where visions of Scotland's fertility, diverse resources, and "unexploited potential"—not least its herring fisheries—were linked with "projects of improvement."[62]

In *Winter*, the poet, sheltered and warmed by a "ruddy fire," considers the role climate plays in the fate of nations:

> The sage historic Muse
> Should next conduct us through the deeps of time,
> Show us how empire grew, declined, and fell
> In scattered states; what makes the nations smile,
> Improves their soil, and gives them double suns;
> And why they pine beneath the brightest skies
> In nature's richest lap. (*Wi*, 587–93)

Thomson's conception of "active government" (*Wi*, 949), of which Peter serves as an exemplar, reiterates the Virgilian theodicy that interprets climatic hardship as a goad to ingenuity and activity. By contrast, the tropics, with their salubrious climate and ready bounty, induce passivity in their inhabitants. Thomson navigates divided imperatives in depicting Britain's climate. In some instances, it is favorable and even providentially favored. He echoes the *laudes Italiae* passage in the *Georgics* ("here spring is perpetual" [147]) when he asserts of Britain: "Rich is thy soil, and merciful thy clime; / Thy streams unfailing in the Summer's drought" (*Su*, 1446–47). Yet he also must emphasize the deficiencies that necessitate labor, ingenuity, and active government. The surest way to generate "double suns"—increasing production within the fixed limits of the organic energy economy—is by gaining access to foreign resource frontiers. Thomson contrasts Britain's cool climate with that of the tropics, where abundant sunlight produces immense fertility not only on "the surface of the enlivened earth" but also underground in the metals and minerals Thomson believed were generated by the sun's "mighty power" (130–34).[63] As we saw in the previous chapter, proponents of British expansion had since the seventeenth century justified commerce and colonization in climatic terms, as means of acquiring commodities unavailable in Britain's northern climate. Thomson's progress poem *Liberty* includes a vision of a mercantile empire prophesized by the "Genius of the Deep," in which, by commanding the seas, Britain would

have access to every climate, from "those that, profuse / Drunk by equa-
tor suns, severely shine" to "those . . . to the poles approaching" (4.412–
14). Britain transcends the limits of its climate and the finite extent of its
bounds by controlling trade with foreign nations.

Even with the increasing grain and manufacturing trade, England's
export economy was still largely dependent on wool. In *Summer*, having
tracked the sun's "effulgence" as it vivifies "the vegetable world" (*Su*, 112)
and, in turn, supports animal life—"of mellow fruit the nameless nations
feed" (302)—Thomson turns to sheep husbandry. Washed in a creek, the
sheep "spread / Their swelling treasures to the sunny ray" (388–89) before
being shorn. Thus, through its wool production, he observes, Britain "com-
mands / The exalted stores of every brighter clime, / The treasures of the
sun without his rage" (424–26). This passage was added in 1744, as were the
martial lines that follow: "Hence fervent all with culture, toil, and arts, /
Wide glows her land: her dreadful thunder hence / Rides o'er the waves sub-
lime, and now, even now, / Impending hangs o'er Gallia's humbled coast; /
Hence rules the circling deep, and awes the world" (427–31). Affiliated
with the Whig opposition, Thomson had associated Walpole's regime,
which fell in 1742, with corruption and the decline of British naval power,
and his poetry—most notoriously *Britannia* and the famous ode "Rule
Britannia!"—often celebrates naval aggression against Spain and France in
support of Britain's mercantile interests.

The paean to Britain's naval supremacy is followed by an acknowl-
edgment of its subjection to climatic extremes. This lyric passage closely
echoes the culminating sequence of *Autumn*. The season's "all-conquering
heat" (*Su*, 451) impairs the poet's perception: "In vain I sigh, / And restless
turn" (455–56). Like Virgil dreaming of Haemus, Thomson nostalgically
recalls the mountains of the north with their ever-flowing streams. Like
Adam in Eden, he seeks shelter in a shaded bower. A creature of climate
no less than the animals who find relief in cool water, the narrator finds
that his senses are renewed: "the fresh-expanded eye / And ear resume their
watch" (477–78). The poet continues his saunter, ascending "the mount"
where he breathes "the freshness of the humid air" (623): "Now, while I
taste the sweetness of the shade, / . . . / Now come, bold fancy, spread a dar-
ing flight / And view the wonders of the torrid zone: / Climes unrelenting!
with whose rage compared, / Yon blaze is feeble and yon skies are cool"
(629–34). He ascends into the atmosphere, like Eve in her dream, and begins
his survey of the tropics, over eight hundred lines of detailed description.

I have accounted for Thomson's specifying tendency with respect to the
atmosphere as an example of a descriptive poetics that gives expression to

an energy economy in which the variability of concrete time and space is the context of production. The atmospheric flight in *Summer* shows how such specifying description is transformed into a generalizing and idealizing movement. As Leo Spitzer observes, concepts like atmosphere, air, and climate all serve to localize, to identify the particular "characteristic which distinguishes one place"—or age—"from another."[64] Yet, as Spitzer notes, the sense in which one is "embraced" by a given atmosphere is elusive, unavailable to empirical perception. The atmosphere that is a source of spatiotemporal distinction also encircles and circulates, a principle of totalizing generalization. This duality is related to the auratic quality of air, a substance pervasive but perceptually elusive, life-giving but ghostly. It is this tangible intangibility that is implied when we speak of air or atmosphere as a distinctive ambience, a mood or tone that exceeds empirical sense perception and is available only to imaginative or esoteric ways of knowing. The blowing wind and the inspiring breath both exemplify the auratic quality of air; indeed, in Latin *aura* refers to a gentle breeze or a breath of air.[65]

In the auratic atmosphere, Thomson navigates what Kevis Goodman calls the poem's "dialectic[s] of distance and proximity" (*Georgic Modernity*, 40). Consider the effect of the autumnal air on the narrator: "in every breeze the Power / Of Philosophic Melancholy comes! / . . . / O'er all the soul his sacred influence breathes; / Inflames imagination . . . and far / Beyond the dim earth exalts the swelling thought" (*Au*, 1004–13). In this invigorating air, the poet secures a historical gaze, referring, in short order, to the "remotest time" past and "future times" to come. At the end of *Summer*, it is "Philosophy" itself—which encompasses the arts of human knowing and not least the skill of "Navigation" that "fearless braves / The burning line or dares the wintry pole" (1768–69)—that is associated with "the liberal breath / Of potent heaven, invisible, the sail" that "swells out, and bears the inferior world along" (1778–79, 1781). The wind is metaphorically associated with the uniquely human forms of ratiocination—what Thomson calls "the rising mind" (1805)—that lift us from the state of nature into history and enable us to know more than the particular: "Nor to this evanescent speck of earth / Poorly confined" (1782–83).

Thomson defines wind as a source of energy in much more literal terms as well. At the beginning of his global flight in *Summer*, he observes that the sun "sends / . . . the general breeze to mitigate his fire / And breathe refreshment on a fainting world" (*Su*, 639–42). By *mitigate*, Thomson means not a cool breeze on a hot day but, as his own note explains, the way in which the atmospheric mantle of winds enables the global circulation of goods, the mixing of distinct climes. "The general breeze," he explains, refers to the trade wind, "which blows constantly . . . from the east."[66] Wrigley's model of the organic energy economy emphasizes the conversion of solar radiance into biomass, but for Thomson the hydrologic cycle and the trade winds represent other manifestations of solar energy, converted into planetary flow, that can be directed toward human need.

In *Summer*, the narrator takes "flight / And view[s] the wonders of the torrid zone: / Climes unrelenting!" (*Su*, 631–33). In the phantasmagoric global reverie that follows, what he imagines under the "bright effulgent sun" and "dazzling air" (635, 638) of the tropics is a "wondrous waste of wealth" (860): "mountains big with mines" (646), profuse timber and exotic fruit, silk and gold. This imaginative geography of imperial ambition and desire is definitively climatic, for it is climatic variation—the temperate conditions of English wool production, the "spicy Gales" of the Orient, the heat-ripened minerals of Africa and South America—that makes the globe conceivable as a rich tapestry of commodities and markets. Wealth is generated not only in the uncompensated work of nature in agricultural production, as in physiocratic political economy, but also, as in a mercantilist account of value, in the global movement of commodities. Because transport involved intense energy expenditure, and because different commodities were associated with different climates, value was understood to be generated, as Wolfram Schmidgen explains, less in the "exploitation of human labor" than in the "circulation of goods."[67] What energizes such circulation are the flows—trade winds, ocean currents, and the hydrologic cycle—that link British locales with distant lands. The pervasive "images of rivers, torrents, floods, oceans, and seas" in descriptive verse express, Laura Brown observes, the "fluidity and energy" that enabled "mercantile capitalist expansion."[68]

There is in Thomson's long description of tropical nature a key moment of historical differentiation: the rich flora and fauna of Africa and the Americas were "to ancient song unknown" (*Su*, 653). In a poem in which not only natural history but also human history are often conceived to be cyclic, global exploration and trade give progressive directionality to historic time, a rise without a fall: "From ancient gloom emerged / the rising world of trade" (1006–7) and "in unbounded commerce mixed the world" (1012). Thomson rewrites Milton, whose Satan had apostrophized the Sun, recalling his prelapsarian state: "I had stood / Then happy; no unbounded hope had raised / Ambition" (*Paradise Lost*, 4.59–61). In the "boundless" air of Thomson's global flight, "unbounded" commerce is seen to rise. Through such lexical repetitions, Thomson links the cyclic time of seasonal recurrence and global circulation with the progressive time of history, the development of capitalism as a world ecology. The atmosphere particularizes, generating climatic distinction, and universalizes, which is why the air through which the narrator soars has the quality of a general equivalent, a domain of abstraction that renders the produce of different climates exchangeable. Air is the pervasive matter that enables Thomson to conceive of planetary totality and so to foretell the emergence of a globalized world system. The atmosphere is the medium in which he scales up his image of the human, envisioning a world market, "the round of nations" (Su, 139), inconceivable to the ancients.

In The Seasons, the annual oscillation in access to solar "efflux" (Su, 92) provides the poem's organizational principle. In this extraordinary sequence in Summer interweaving the local and the global, as in the opening lines of Spring, Thomson sutures this seasonal energy differentiality to its geographic equivalent: variation among the planet's climes along with the flows of air and water that link them. The result is a striking depiction of cornucopian abundance.[69] Robert Markley points to John Locke's formative role in depicting nature as a source of "limitless resources," an "abstract, econometric space." Such ideas, he argues, resonated widely between the late 1660s and 1691, a "comparatively benign" period climatically that allowed the natural world to be seen "as a storehouse of potential wealth that can be exploited indefinitely."[70] The Seasons, I have been arguing, is marked by an acute awareness of seasonal uncertainty and climatic extremity. Yet, in this prophetic vision of global trade, Thomson depicts a future of unchecked accumulation, an economy decoupled from fixed environmental limits. He foresees a form of cornucopianism in which surplus derived from the "boundless furnace of the sky" (Su, 962), as it manifests the "gay profusion" of the tropics (861), can be accumulated in "unbounded commerce." The essential ideological claim The Seasons instantiates on the level of form is that the historical time of rising commerce and the coming of a global world system is knowable, progressive, and even providentially sanctioned insofar as it expresses an imperative in nature itself, in the climatic distribution of commodities and the trade winds that enable their circulation. The poem's cornucopian optimism is rooted in its account of the role that a strong state, a powerful navy, and global commerce can play in overcoming natural constraint.

LUXURY AND WASTE

Thomson was, at least in private, not so sanguine about the effects of boundless commerce. In a 1736 letter to Aaron Hill, he writes that Britons find themselves living in "Times of Putrefaction" brought on not only by the corruption of the Walpole regime but also by "the Super-abundance" of successful commerce. As had happened in Rome, the very wealth brought by industry and trade, "the continual Tide of Riches, pour'd in upon this Nation by Commerce," produced luxury and an insatiable desire for further gain (*Letters and Documents*, 104–7). Under capitalism, surplus simply begets the drive for greater accumulation. The abundance that in a cool climate such as Britain's can be acquired only with labor and commerce brings about a condition, not unlike that innate to the tropics, of luxurious profusion and decadence that undermines liberty and industry. Human projects are reabsorbed into the cycles of nature. In the letter to Hill, Thomson is unable to foresee any condition of permanent growth. Such ideas—of a planetary flux that cannot be overcome by active government—are only hinted at in *The Seasons*, as in the claim in *Summer* that "Revolving ages sweep the changeful earth, / And empires rise and fall" (*Su*, 724–25).

In *Liberty*—which Thomson considered his greatest poem, an opinion universally contradicted by critics and readers—the poet offered a more vexed representation of the historical implications of cornucopian abundance and the relation between climate and nation.[71] The poem had its roots in Thomson's journey through France and Italy in 1730–32, when he served as traveling companion for Charles Richard Talbot on his Grand Tour. "I long to see the fields whence Virgil gathered his immortal honey," he wrote to George Dodington (*Letters and Documents*, 73–74). In contrast with Milton, he was disappointed with the Continent. He contrasted the poverty of France with the state of England, where "industry and liberty mutually support and inspirit each other" (77–78). He was especially shocked by Italy and particularly Rome, the immediate environs of which had been depopulated by an outbreak of malaria. Writing to Lady Hertford, he asserted: "The bad Government in Italy . . . has not only extirpated almost [all] human Arts and Industry, but even disfigured Nature herself" (*Letters and Documents*, 81–84).[72] In the land of perpetual spring, the natural abundance of which Virgil had so famously sung—"filled with teeming crops . . . the home of the olive, the home of fattened flocks" (*Georgics*, 147)—Thomson found destitution and ruin, evidence, for him, of the importance of government in securing nature's gifts. "The gracious sun indeed still dispenses to them his powerful smiles," he writes to Lady Hertford, "but him they are afraid of" (*Letters and Documents*, 81–82). In *Liberty*, Thomson instructs Britons to learn from the example of Rome, which fell—"In spite of climes / Whose sun-enlivened ether wakes the soul," where "treasures teem, to thy cold clime unknown" (1.325–29)—because of its corrupt and oppressive government. He even addresses Virgil, holding him responsible for his idealizing praise of Augustus—"First from your flattered Caesars this began" (286)—a rich complaint from a poet whose encomiums on favored patrons stain the pages of *The Seasons*. The poem follows a personified Liberty as she appears and disappears through history, culminating in her presence in Britain. The lesson is that liberal governance—divided power, republican virtue, and public works—matters more than any climatic inheritance. Liberty is a "better sun" (5.553). But, as Thomson's letter to Hill suggests, the vision of Britain's progress is haunted by an anxiety, supported by the evidence of past empires, that accumulation creates the conditions of its undoing, that a nation "puffed with power and gorged with wealth" (381) tends toward the same lassitude and corruption that impedes tropical nations.

In 1744, George Lyttelton, one of the patrons praised in *The Seasons*, secured Thomson an appointment as surveyor general of the Leeward Islands, the center of British trade and sugar production in the eastern Caribbean. This was the very sort of sinecure that had, in the previous decade, exemplified the corruption of the Walpole regime. Thomson's lifelong friend William Patterson was granted the position of Thomson's deputy, taking up residence in Bridgetown, Barbados. In a long letter to Patterson, Thomson imagined his friend's life of tropical ease, "reclining under Cedars, and Palmettoes; and there enjoying more magnificent Slumbers than are known to the pale Climates of the North" (*Letters and Documents*, 194–98). It is not hard to detect here an echo of *Liberty*, where Thomson envisions a Britain fattened with spoils, its citizenry "immersed in sloth" (5.310). Thomson proposed to Patterson a plan for bringing some of the floral luxuriance of the tropics to the northern climate. He requests:

> Send me some Seeds of Things that might succeed here during the Summer, tho they cannot perfect their Seeds sufficiently, in this to them ungenial Climate to propagate. In the which case is the calliloo, which, from the seed it bore here, came up puny, rickety, and good [for] Nothing. There are other Things certainly with you, not yet brought over hither, that might flourish here in the Summer Time, and live tolerably well, provided they be sheltered in an hospitable Stove or Green-House during the Winter. You will give me no small Pleasure by sending me, from Time to Time, some of these Seeds, if it were not more to amuse me in making the Tryal . . . [of] the Transplanting of the Vegetable into distant dangerous Climates.

Thomson seeks to participate in the project of seed collecting and transplantation taken up by Linnaeus and others in the second half of the eigh-

teenth century, testing the limits of acclimatization, and working to pro-
duce what Alan Bewell calls a "global nature."[73] Yet he is motivated by
pleasure and curiosity rather than plans of national improvement. Notably,
in *Liberty*, he had used similar botanical language to envisage a nation in
which private interests had supplanted "passion for the commonweal." The
"portion" of social surplus that might be dedicated to "the smiling public"
instead "serves but to nurse / A locust band within, and in the bud / Leaves
starved each work of dignity and use" (5.346–51).

A comparison of Thomson's images of "puny, rickety, and good [for] noth-
ing" exotics growing in the urban greenhouse, of the "rank uncultivated
growth" of contemporary Italy (*Liberty*, 1.137), of Africa's "blooming wilds, /
And fruitful deserts" (*Su*, 860), and of Britain's "Nature wide and wild"
(*Sp*, 505) does suggest an unreconciled tension in his solar cornucopianism.
Raymond Williams notices an "ambiguity, growing toward actual contra-
diction, in Thomson's simultaneous celebration of improvement and of ro-
mantic wastes."[74] For Williams, this contradiction evinces Thomson's am-
bivalence about "the actual social relationships" developing under agrarian
capitalism (*The Country and the City*, 70). Yet, I would suggest, the poet's
"melancholy and thoughtful withdrawal" (71) can also be characterized as a
positive relation to "nature's works" not subject to the improving or enclos-
ing hand, not abstracted as a potential resource, not capturable as wealth.

The Seasons is replete with images of a self-sufficiency and self-
organization in the living world's sovereign "kingdoms" and "nations," as
Thomson periphrastically refers to species of birds and insects and fish. The
ideology of improvement characterizes unenclosed land as underutilized, even
wasted. Sustained labor and ownership are required to bring it to a flourishing
state.[75] Thomson expresses real ambivalence about this ideology, an ambiva-
lence that has its biographical origins in his childhood experience of the de-
populated Scottish uplands and its philosophical roots in Theocles's rapturous
survey of the Earth in Shaftesbury's *The Moralists*, which provides much of
the material for Thomson's global excursion in *Summer*. In a striking state-
ment of nonanthropocentrism, Theocles rhapsodizes: "The wildness pleases.
We seem to live alone with nature. We view her in her inmost recesses, and
contemplate her with more delight in these original wilds than in the artificial
labyrinths and feigned wildernesses of the palace. The objects of this place, the
scaly serpents, the savage beasts, and poisonous insects, how terrible soever or
how contrary to human nature, are beauteous in themselves."[76]

In attending to "Nature's common bounty" (*Au*, 189)—its "gay profu-
sion" (*Su*, 860), its "blooming wilds" (847), its "boundless deep immensity

of shade" (652)—Thomson depicts what, in a reflection on vegetable cornu-copianism, Michael Marder calls a "bounty . . . beyond our receptive capac-ity."[77] In contrast to a mineral energy economy dependent on a finite reserve of subterranean fuel, a solar energy economy is sustained by the "unremit-ting" (if fluctuating) constancy of solar radiance. Rather than finding actual-ization only in the discrete instance of combustion in a furnace or a firebox, energy is everywhere active: in a breeze and the flow of a river, in "the living herbs, profusely wild" that grow "O'er all the deep-green earth" (*Sp*, 222, 223), in the murmuring insects and the plovers who "sing their wild notes to the listening waste" (25). I certainly do not want to elide the extent to which Thomson imagines those untapped African commodities—a "won-drous waste of wealth" (*Su*, 860)—as something like a standing reserve, a stock awaiting realization in trade and human use. I am suggesting only that there is an active tension, crucial for understanding the reception of a poem about the works of nature that came to be read as a poem about the love of nature, between this sense of waste (nature's productivity not yet channeled toward human ends) and an appreciation for what Thomson calls "the beauty of the waste" (919), life's lavish exuberance as an expen-diture without retention or capture. As John Veitch observed of *The Sea-sons* in 1887: "No man can be drawn to the varied aspects of the outward world without rising to a sympathy and tender love for the creatures of the wilds—of . . . all the gentle living beings which rejoice in nature's care, and are sustained by her free bounteousness."[78]

"DISASTERED"

In a solar energy economy, the very flows that manifest in natural bounty, captured in the form of national wealth, also produce a destructive excess that exceeds and destabilizes human projects. In the course of *The Seasons*, Thomson depicts a Saharan sandstorm, an Atlantic typhoon, an avalanche destroying a Swiss village, an earthquake razing Palermo, a forest fire, sev-eral rainstorms, thunderstorms, and snowstorms, and a number of plagues and shipwrecks. The image of optimistic expectation that opens the poem, the bounteous fields of grain foreseen in *Spring*, is transformed in *Autumn* into disaster: "Defeating oft the labours of the year, / The sultry south col-lects a potent blast" (*Au*, 311–12). In an example of what Ralph Cohen calls the "Augustan double view," Thomson employs the same words to describe the growth of crops and the storm that sweeps them away.[79] Fields, forests, flocks, and vines swell until, in *Autumn*, "the aerial tempest fuller swells" (316). The fields are a "sea" (326), a "flood of corn" (42), until the "ditches swell" (336) with runoff and the harvest is ruined in the "rushing tide" of an autumn flood (339). Whereas, in southern Europe, drought was the primary cause of crop failure, in Britain overprecipitation was the main cause of diminished and lost harvests.[80] As Thomson writes, with the flooding "all that the winds had spared / In one wild moment [is] ruined" (341–42). From a hill, the farmer watches his fields turned into a "miserable wreck" (345), and his thoughts turn to "winter unprovided, and a train / Of claimant children dear" (349–50). Thomson, in turn, directs a moralistic address to "Ye masters" (350), calling on landowners to recognize their dependence on the rural laborer and not "cruelly demand what the deep rains / And all involving winds have swept away" (358–59).

There are in *De rerum natura* and the *Georgics* antecedents for Thomson's destructive autumn flood. Lucretius treats the disasters faced by the agriculturalist in a passage here given in the Creech translation:

> Nay often too, when Man with pains and toil
> Hath plough'd and conquer'd the unwilling Soil;
> When flowers put forth, and budding branches shoot,
> Look gay and promise the desired Fruit;
> The scorching Sun, with his too busie beams,
> Burns up the fruits, or clouds do drown with streams;
> Or chill'd by too much Snow they soon decay,
> Or Storms blow them, and all our hopes away.[81]

Unsurprisingly, Creech downplays the epicurean lesson here, that destructive storms and other catastrophes reveal "That in no way for us the power of gods / Fashioned the world and brought it into being" (*On the Nature*, 5.197–98). Virgil's concern is less with the physical cause of the storms than with the presages that announce them. Virgil asks: "Why need I tell of autumn's changes and stars, and for what our workers must watch[?]" (*Georgics*, 121). Nature is unpredictable, he answers, and it is only by studying its "unfailing signs" that the cultivator can hope for success, hope not always realized: "Often, too, there appears in the sky a mighty column of waters, and clouds mustered from on high roll up a murky tempest of black showers: down falls the lofty heaven, and with its deluge of rain washes away the gladsome crops and the labours of oxen." Virgil concludes with a lesson opposite to Lucretius's. The life of the farmer is one of constant fear; to alleviate this fear, the agriculturalist must "worship the gods, and pay great Ceres her yearly rites" (123).

Thomson generally rejects a moralized understanding of disasters as allegories of divine providence or punishment and seeks instead physical

explanations for their causes. He shows an epicurean interest in the psycho-
logical response of individuals suffering calamity, such as the mind's refusal
to accept sudden disastrous change or the driving imperative to discover
design in accident. Conditions are often deceiving. A calm precedes the sud-
den storm "of roaring winds and flame and rushing floods" (*Su*, 996), and
the sailor is too slow to recognize the threat. Unlike Virgil, who describes
the signs that make the atmosphere predictable, Thomson draws attention
to the confusion brought about by disaster, the way a familiar landscape can
be so altered as to become unintelligible. Panic and uncertainty attenuate
the human capacity for sympathy, a theme he found in two of the source
texts for his graphic descriptions of pandemics, the account of the Athenian
plague that concludes *De rerum natura* and Defoe's *Journal of the Plague
Year*. The problem of interpreting disaster is staged in the description of
summer thunderstorms. Thomson first explores physical causes, echoing
Milton in ascribing electrical storms to the influence of "nitre, sulphur
and the fiery spume / Of fat bitumen" (*Su*, 1108–9) rising into the atmo-
sphere, where they, "a magazine of fate, / Ferment; till, by the touch ethe-
real roused, / . . . / They furious spring" (1112–16). Here, he introduces the
tale of Celadon and Amelia, two lovers of "equal virtue formed" (1173).
Caught in a thunderstorm, Amelia is overcome with fear. Celadon reas-
sures her because "he, who yon skies involves / In frowns of darkness, ever
smiles on thee / With kind regard" (1206–8). Yet—"Mysterious Heaven!"
(1215)—at that very instant "A blackened corse, was struck the beauteous
maid" (1216). What is most interpretively vexing about the episode is that
Celadon's very act of seeing divine justice in the storm seems itself to call
forth the strike, as if he is being punished (by proxy) for his claim to know
divine will. What Thomson does insist on is that we look for physical ex-
planations for atmospheric events, much as Lucretius asserts that, to un-
derstand the "true nature of the thunderbolt" (*On the Nature*, 6.379), we
must not "search in vain the hidden minds of gods" (382) but rather seek
a simple geophysical explanation: thunderstorms are produced when "the
years rough straits mix cold and hot" (364).

The thunderstorm caps an extensive catalog of "horrors" in *Summer*.
It begins with a sandstorm burying a desert caravan (*Su*, 961–79), which
is followed by the "circling typhon" and "dire ecnephia" (984). (Thomson
included a note clarifying that these are "terms for particular storms or
hurricanes known only between the tropics" [986].) The "terrors of these
storms" (1013) are increased by the presence of sharks, which follow slave
ships, "that cruel trade" (1019), awaiting the tempest that will subject
"Tyrants and slaves" (1022) to "one death" (1023). Here, as in the autumn

storm, disaster is indiscriminate. Thomson next turns to the "pestilent dis-
ease" (1035) that appears when the summer sun "draws the copious stream
from swampy fens / Where putrefaction into life ferments" (1028–29). Ac-
counting for contagions, he follows Lucretius in assuming that infection
comes either "down from above, / Like clouds and mists, or often forms
and springs / From the earth itself, when damp has made it rot, / Struck
by unseasonable rains and sun" (On the Nature, 6.1099–1103). In the final
edition, Thomson supplied a note, referring the reader to Richard Mead's A
Short Discourse Concerning Pestilential Contagion (1722 [8th ed.]), which
links the transmission of the plague in North Africa to the unsanitary con-
ditions of Cairo, its "filth, and fetid Fields" (Su, 1056), and to what Mead
called the "Intemperance of the Climate," particularly the "violent Rains"
and "sultry Heats" of summer.[82] Lucretius asserts that those who travel to
"climates" to which they are "unaccustomed" are particularly susceptible
to the "power of pestilence and plague" (On the Nature, 1098, 1103–4). In the
final edition of The Seasons, Thomson includes a reference to a recent event
that reveals the dangers of foreign adventures, the plague that afflicted Lord
Vernon's fleet at Cartagena in 1741, halting Britain's campaign against the
Spanish. In depicting the African plague, Thomson had echoed Mead in con-
demning the "dreadful policy . . . / Inhuman and unwise" (Su, 1076–77) of
confining the families of those infected with the plague and limiting travel.
In a time of disaster, good governance—"Princely wisdom" (1065)—fails.
Lord Vernon is an admirable exception, one who "pitying" (1042) observed
the progress of the plague. Glynnis Ridley argues that Thomson implies
that the cause of the failed campaign was corruption and a lack of govern-
ment support, rejecting a "natural explanation of events in favour of a po-
litical one."[83] Yet here, as in other representations of disaster, Thomson is
wrestling with the imbrication of natural and social forces, a point made by
Denys Van Renen, who argues that the Cartagena plague reveals that, when
"colonials penetrate alien environments and spread these effluvia, they dis-
rupt fragile ecosystems and spread infectious disease."[84]

Similar interpretive issues confront the reader of the famous account
in Winter of the "swain / Disastered" (Wi, 278–79), lost in his "own loose-
revolving fields" (278) when a snowstorm transforms a familiar environ-
ment into a "land unknown" (301). The shepherd pushes through the grow-
ing drifts, driven by "thoughts of home" (286), but as his terror grows, as
"fancy feigned" (290) visions of his cottage confront the actuality of the
"middle waste" (292), "busy shapes" (297)—of unseen cliffs and chasms and
bogs—"check his fearful steps; and down he sinks" (305). In Tim Fulford's
interpretation, Thomson positions the reader at a distance from the swain,

close enough for a momentary identification, but sufficiently removed by the mediation of the poem to feel not only secure but powerful in his alignment "with the narratorial energy with which nature's crushing force is represented" (*Landscape, Liberty and Authority*, 18). The fact that Thomson shifts perspective from the freezing field worker to the family awaiting his return—"In vain for him the officious wife prepares / The fire fair-blazing and the vestment warm; / In vain his little children, peeping out / Into the mingling storm, demand their sire, / With tears of artless innocence" (311–15)—complicates Fulford's argument that the distance between reader and sufferer is reassuringly stable. The shift in perspective, from the dying man to his apprehensive family, derives directly from Lucretius, who considers, in book 3, the way we are taught to imagine what we lose when we die: "No longer now a happy home will greet you / Nor loving wife, nor your sweet children run / To snatch your kisses and to touch your heart / With silent sweet content" (*On the Nature*, 3.894–97). Yet, Lucretius adds, when you die, "the desire / Of things like these hangs over you no more" (900–901). In *The Seasons*, the integration of the family's perspective suggests that Thomson's interest is less in the fate of the swain than in the loss experienced by his family. But the Lucretian influence can be detected in the lack of any reference, in this instance, to the consolation of an afterlife, as the narrator returns to the swain buried in snow, "o'er his inmost vitals creeping cold . . . a stiffened corse, / Stretched out, and bleaching in the northern blast" (*Wi*, 318–21).[85]

Fulford's critique is premised on the claim that Thomson misconstrues as natural a condition of vulnerability—rural poverty—that is properly understood as social.[86] The implication is that the domain of social responsibility is potentially infinite, that, with equitable institutions, natural disaster can be avoided. The ideological work of Thomson's poem manifests in an overemphasis on natural causality. The poet's "social imagination is," in Fulford's words, "limited, however, by his assumption that the shepherd died from unavoidable natural causes" (*Landscape, Liberty and Authority*, 26). Yet, as Fulford acknowledges, Thomson goes on to foreground "man-made oppression" and the possibilities of amelioration, echoing the emphasis on government in *Liberty*. The "swain / Disastered" scene is followed by the poet's most explicit statement of reformist politics. He condemns the "gay licentious proud" (322) who dance in ignorance while others "sink in the devouring flood, / Or more devouring flame" (329–30). He then commends the work of the Jail Committee, appointed in 1729 to improve the condition of prisons. Inmates had been "Shut from the common air" (333). The tyrannical jailors tear "from cold wintry limbs the tattered weed" (369), and their rapacity is compared with a "raging" wolf pack descending on an alpine village in winter. The "redressive" (360) work of the committee is then figured as an extension of georgic cultivation: "in this rank age, / Much is the patriot's weeding hand required" (382–83).

In his representation of disaster, Thomson emphasizes the role of natural forces—rainstorms and snowstorms, lightning, sharks, plague—which can, to some extent, be understood but never fully predicted or controlled. He also identifies the role played by social institutions—such as the slave trade, the prison system, and policies governing quarantine—in intensifying or diminishing human vulnerability to disaster. With respect to disaster, he navigates a tension similar to the one I have been identifying in his conception of climate, in which both planetary forces and "active government" play determining roles. Fulford sees Thomson's depictions of natural chaos as subsumed within a "structure of order" (22), the authoritative prospect view described by Barrell, which is itself an extension of the order of divine providence. The argument developed in this chapter is, however, that Thomson recognized conditions of disequilibrium in nature that could not be fully incorporated within the harmonious universe of Newtonian physicotheology or confident proclamations of national progress. Human communities are formed in a "broken world" (*Sp*, 318), littered with the ruins of previous civilizations. All achievements are temporary.

Thomson was himself vulnerable to hidden atmospheric influence, the "sickly damps and cold autumnal fogs" (*Sp*, 329) that, in this tumultuous epoch, hang "on the springs of life" (330). In the mid-1730s, he moved to the suburb of Richmond, close to Pope's villa in Twickenham, to escape "the smoke and noise of the metropolis" (Sambrook, *James Thomson*, 137). He often walked into the city. As his first biographer, Patrick Murdoch, reports, "one summer evening," in August 1748, "he had overheated himself" returning to Richmond "and in that condition, imprudently took a boat to carry him to Kew; apprehending no bad consequences from the chill air on the river": "Now, the cold had so seized him, the next day he found himself in a high fever." After a brief recovery and further exposure to "evening dews," he relapsed and died.[87] John Armstrong, a physician and close friend of Thomson's and the author of the medical georgic *The Art of Preserving Health* (1744), reported that Thomson died of "a malignant nervous fever, that came upon the back of a tertian" (quoted in Sambrook, *James Thomson*, 277). Such symptoms—a chill followed by a fever, a brief recovery, and a relapse (the "tertian")—suggest malaria, a disease common in England in late summer and early autumn, even during the cold centuries of the Little

Ice Age.[88] The "noisome damps" (*Sp*, 100) of the city, which were widely associated with the ague—"The hoary fen / [which] in putrid streams emits the living cloud / Of pestilence" (*Su*, 292–94)—were, in fact, the habitat for malaria-transmitting mosquitoes. Thomson shared this fate with Virgil, who, striving to complete the *Aeneid*, journeyed to Greece, hoping that a change of scenery would restore his vitality and inspire his verse. He contracted a malarial fever in Megara and died at Brindisi at the age of fifty-one.

"LAST-CENTURYNESS": THE RECEPTION OF *THE SEASONS*

To read *The Seasons* as a poem of planetary circulation is to emphasize a characteristic of the text on which Thomson insists yet that many subsequent readers have seen as absent: the integration of its varied parts, its ambition to describe the "system . . . entire." The work of following the flow of "unremitting energy"—as it takes planetary form in the movement of wind and vapors, the climatic distribution of heat and cold, the growth of plants and animals, the labor of men, the dearth and wealth of nations—requires a belief in the systemic consistency of different elements. Interlinked spheres—the Earth, its varied climes bound together by the flow of water and air, its rotations around the Sun giving seasonal variation to the year, its internal rotation structuring day and night—are the weave that underlies the poem's associative drift. Recognizing the principle of planetary form that underlies the poem's historical vision offers a way of contextualizing critical debates on the poem as well as the trajectory of its popular reception, how a poem reprinted more than a hundred times in the century after its publication could be out of print and largely forgotten today. What is at stake in the reception of *The Seasons* is the adequacy of seasonal order and disorder as an organizing structure and thus climate and its consequences for human world making as an organizing theme, a formal and thematic alignment that would enable the synthesis of the divergent temporalities—stochastic, recurrent, progressive—explored in this chapter.

Of *The Seasons*, Jonathan Swift wrote: "I am not over fond of them, because they are all description, and nothing is doing; whereas Milton engages me in actions of the highest importance."[89] Swift distinguishes an epic centered on human choice and the consequences of human action from a poem dedicated to the description of nature's works, and he finds the latter lacking. In 1753, Thomson's biographer Robert Shiels gave voice to what has become the paradigmatic critical complaint: "There appears no particular design . . . nor is there any connection or dependence throughout. . . . [E]ach season may rather be called an assemblage of poetical ideas."[90] In his biography of Thomson, Samuel Johnson famously reiterated this criticism of the poem's lack of associative unity: "The great defect of the *Seasons* is want of method. . . . Of many appearances subsisting all at once, no rule can be given why one should be mentioned before another" (*Lives*, 2.376-77).[91] Its capaciousness adds up to an "enumeration of circumstantial varieties." Johnson is reputed to have read several passages from *The Seasons* aloud to Shiels, noting after both had praised the verse: "Well, sir, I have omitted every other line."[92]

It is unsurprising that it should be Johnson who most forcefully articulated what has become the definitive criticism *The Seasons*, for it was he who in the *Idler* no. 11 rebuked his Georgian contemporaries for their preoccupation with atmospheric effects: "Surely nothing is more reproachful to a being endowed with reason, than to resign its powers to the influence of the air."[93] To inhabit an "age of inquiry and knowledge," according to Johnson, requires one to distinguish "custom" from "climate" categorically. He mocks those who "derive the civil institutions of every country from its climate, who impute freedom and slavery to the temperature of the air," just as sternly as he does those poets who "will imagine the fancy exalted by vernal breezes" (59, 63). To imagine that the climate shapes the course of nations or that the weather inspires creativity is to fall prey to the delusion experienced by the mad astronomer in *The History of Rasselas*, who is convinced that his thoughts control the weather. It is to confuse the domain of natural causality with that of human control, as Johnson asserts: "He that shall resolutely excite his faculties, or exert his virtues, will soon make himself superior to the seasons, and may set at defiance the morning mist, and the evening damp, the blasts of the east, and the clouds of the south" (63-64). The *Idler* essay helps us see that it is not that *The Seasons* lacks a method. It is that, from Johnson's perspective, the poem's self-evident narrative principle—it "leads us through the appearances of things as they are successively varied by the vicissitudes of the year" (*Lives*, 2:376)—appeared inadequate because it prioritizes natural causality and so diminishes human agency.

Johnson did endorse one interpretive approach emphasizing environmental influence that retains currency in readings of *The Seasons*. He identified the imprint of the landscape around Jedburgh on *Autumn*, asserting that, as Thomson, settled in London, continued to revise the poem, it lost some of its original "*race*; a word which, applied to wines, in its primitive sense, means the flavor of the soil" (*Lives*, 2:377). Future readers would develop this idea that Thomson's boyhood in the Scottish border country shaped *The Seasons*, not only in the depiction of specific upland landscapes, but also in Thomson's manner of seeing and describing the dynamism of nature. In 1777,

John More connected Thomson's innovative close attention to the passage of seasonal time with his Scottish roots: "It was reserved for him, who had his birth and education among the bleak and desert wilds and hills of North Britain, to present the world with a graphical map of the year" (*Strictures*, 17–18). He defended Thomson's depiction of the peasant lost in the snow, pointing out that such accidents were frequent in southern Scotland, where there were few roads and houses were often connected by faint footpaths (48). A century later, Veitch argued that Thomson's poetic originality derived from "the strong impressions made on him in youth, and carried to a southern clime from his native streams and hills" (*The Feeling for Nature*, 39). Had Thomson grown up beside the Thames in Richmond, Veitch speculates, he never would have learned to appreciate the variety of landscapes or to notice the atmospheric activity for which his verse is known. Writing in 1868, John Wilson argued that the "one Great Poem" written in English was written by a Scot, about seasons that—"without insult, injury, or injustice [meant] to the rest of the globe"—had themselves been rendered Scottish. Of Thomson's singular poetic genius, he adds: "He effulged all at once sunlike—like Scotland's storm-loving, mist-enamoured sun, which till you have seen on a day of thunder, you cannot be said ever to have seen the sun."[94] A number of critics and biographers in the twentieth century have reiterated this form of environmental interpretation, one that, we can surmise, would have been amenable to a poet who himself emphasizes the shaping role of climate. As Harko Gerrit de Maar writes of Roxburghshire: "It was in this rugged and lonely district that Thomson gained his experience of natural scenery and it was from this region that he derived his conception of landscape."[95]

In the 1770s, two critics, John More and John Aikin, dedicated significant critical attention to the task of rebutting Johnson's claim about the "want of method" in *The Seasons*.[96] More insisted on the coherence of the poem and the propriety of the transitions, although he did note that with respect to "unity of subject" the notoriously changeable climate of Britain presented difficulties:

> Distinct as the seasons of the year may seem to a superficial observer, the weather, the objects, and the sentiments which distinguish them most, yet run into one another, especially in our variable climate. . . . How often are we not almost as cold and uncomfortable in some days of Summer, as in many of Winter; little less languid in Spring, than in Summer; and hardly more spiritless and exhausted in Autumn, perhaps, on many occasions, than in any other month of the year. No wonder our Poet is sometimes betrayed into slips of this kind. Hence he stumbles on the

very threshold, and speaks in the first period of his *Spring*, of *Music veil'd in a shower of shadowing roses*. These delicate and tender flowers are not certainly quite so early in our island. Had he wrote in a warmer climate, where vegetation is much more forward than here, fact, perhaps, might have countenanced this beautiful exordium. (*Strictures*, 33–34)

More, however, defends the unity of the poem precisely in terms of its commitment to the sort of regionalist knowledge so central to the *Georgics*: "Wherever he carries you, it is nature all, genuine and uncorrupted throughout. No exotics are forced on your view. Every spot under the genial and propitious influence of his descriptive talents, abounds with its own productions" (41).

In the *Essay on the Application of Natural History to Poetry* (1777), Aikin identified Thomson, along with Milton and Virgil, as one of the rare poets to offer truly original observations of natural history. He then composed the "Essay on the Plan and Character of the Poem" for a 1779 edition of *The Seasons*, in which he argues, contra Johnson, that the seasons provide a perfectly capacious organizing principle for the poem when it is considered that "all mankind" establish their "computations of time" on the solar year and, in "temperate climates," on "the four seasons" ("Essay on the Plan and Character," x). He emphasizes the poem's temporal form. The natural logic of seasonal succession, "incipient, confirmed, and receding," organizes the "progressive series of descriptions, . . . all parts of a general plan" (xi). For Aikin, the study of natural history involves attending to "the distinctions, resemblances, and changes of all the bodies, both animate and inanimate, which nature offers to us" (xvii). It is precisely in this enumeration of small variations that the poet is able to account for a complete system. Thomson, Aikin argues, had some "idea of the *oeconomy of nature*, as enabled him to preserve regularity of method and uniformity of design through all the variety of his descriptions" (xxi).

Aikin's reading of the poem's unity in terms of an "*oeconomy of nature*" led him to deemphasize those elements pertaining to the economy of the nation and the empire. More similarly defines "descriptive poetry" as that which refers to "external nature" and "has no direct or immediate connection either with the human character, or any department of social life" (*Strictures*, 33).[97] As this chapter has argued, for Thomson these economies are inseparably intertwined. Yet, by the end of the eighteenth century, readers appear less able to recognize the flows of sunlight, wind, and water as meaningful features of economic production. *The Seasons* came to be read as a poem about an autonomous and unproductive nature contrasted with the human-made world and productive activity, an interpretation that selectively emphasizes Thomson's turn away from the city and his appreciation of "Nature wide and wild." In 1798, Anna Seward wrote a series of letters to Thomas Park examining Thomson's revisions of the poem. She echoes More in complaining of the "striking inaccuracy" in the inclusion of blooming roses in *Spring*, but her sharpest criticism was aimed at the address to Argyle in *Autumn*, where Thomson calls for the development of manufacturing in his native country. After such fine depictions of the wild Scottish landscape, "how vexed we feel," she writes, "to see a curtain suddenly dropt on the scenery of the waning year, that we may attend to the patriotism of introducing the muslin manufacture into Scotland, and of looking better after the herrings." Of the return to Thomson's proper subject, "the fading many-coloured woods" (*Au*, 950), she adds: "Ah! How glad we are to escape from the muslin-looms, the herrings, and the duke, into the woods and wilds."[98] Thomson's natural descriptions are seen as discontinuous with human labor, promising a salutary escape from urban life and economic activity. By the late nineteenth century, James Russell Lowell observes of Thomson: "He was the inventor of cheap amusement for the million, to be had of All-out-doors for the asking." The "love of Nature . . . is a modern thing," Lowell argues, because "so long as men had slender means, whether of keeping out cold or checkmating it with artificial heat," they were unable to appreciate winter for its scenic beauty.[99] The geologist Hugh Miller makes a similar point, though with a greater appreciation for Thomson's verse. He attributes the "strong appetite for the rural intensified into poetry" to the "influence of great cities." "Nowhere have Thomson, Cowper, and Crabbe," he writes, "given a larger amount of pleasure, than in London."[100]

If critics and readers have, since the mid-nineteenth century, lost the capacity to appreciate Thomson's "wandering song" (*Au*, 150), it may be because the experience of planetary order and disorder that shaped the poem's composition and underlies its formal structure has been attenuated in fossil-powered modernity.[101] In a review of a new edition of *The Seasons* in 1897, a critic in *The Academy* relegated Thomson to "last-centuryness." Thomson's vaunted observations of seasonal time, he claimed, amounted to little more than knowledge of "the time-sequence of snowdrop, crocus, primrose, and 'violet darkly blue.'" In the accelerated urban imaginary of this late Victorian, a knowable climatic order as the basis for social and economic life is only an anachronism, beyond even nostalgia, anticipating our own age, in which the annual "time-sequence" is itself altering owing to global warming. Thomson, the reviewer added, speaks "to us from another world than ours."[102]

Mine, Factory, and Plantation: The Industrial Georgic and the Crisis of Description

DESCRIPTION AND ABSTRACT SOCIAL NATURE

In the previous chapter, I argued that, while agrarian labor and global commerce could be accommodated within descriptive convention, Thomson recognized that London—its population density, economic activity, commodity culture, and air pollution all manifestations of an emergent energy regime—offered an infelicitous topos for a poet inspired by the "classic page" (*Sp*, 452). The middle decades of the eighteenth century saw the publication of a series of ambitious blank-verse descriptive poems that attempted to represent new sites of industrial-scale production, including Robert Dodsley's *Agriculture* (1753), John Dyer's *The Fleece* (1757), James Grainger's *The Sugar-Cane* (1764), and Richard Jago's *Edge Hill* (1767). These patriotic and formally expansive poems sought, not always with felicity, to reconcile the Virgilian virtues of rural life and labor with the sort of complex industrial processes that Milton had represented as definitively postlapsarian, if not positively demonic.

The second half of the eighteenth century was a period of rapid expansion, with more than two-thirds of the total economic growth in Europe occurring in Britain (Wrigley, *Continuity, Chance and Change*, 13). This period remains difficult to characterize, however, because it lacks an emblematic site such as the steam-powered cotton factories that so powerfully evoke the Industrial Revolution. The decades before Watt's invention of the double-acting steam engine saw not only rising agricultural yields and growing global commerce but also the development of two properly industrial modes of production, in the coal-fueled metal manufacturing towns of the west Midlands and the Caribbean sugar plantations. By midcentury, parliamentary enclosure had accelerated the rate of land privatization, which, along with scientific management practices and the conversion of wastes to arable land, significantly raised productivity. By the end of the century, only two in five male workers were directly involved in the agricultural sector, the lowest rate in Europe. Many of these laborers found employment in the growing cities of the Midlands, where proximity to rich seams of coal and metal ore enabled the growth of mechanized industries, in what Paul Hohenberg and Lynn Hollen Lees call the "explosive concentrated effects of the first, or paleotechnic phase, of modern economic change."[1] In the second half of the century, much of Britain's growth was occurring in manufacturing cities, such as Birmingham and Leeds, and in port cities reaping the benefits of the triangular trade, such as Bristol and Liverpool. Britain's sugar plantations in the Caribbean, with their unique "synthesis of field and factory" and violent labor discipline, were generating significantly more profit than were the North American colonies, as well as a source of dense calories to feed the urban labor force.[2] These emergent industrial sectors of the economy worked in tandem, a global infrastructure of positive feedback based on energy surpluses and capital surpluses feeding further investment.

Unlike the rest of this book, this chapter examines three poems that were never especially popular and have been largely forgotten. I begin with Dyer's *The Fleece*, which treats sheep husbandry, wool manufacturing, and global wool markets. I next turn to Grainger's georgic of the Caribbean sugar plantations, *The Sugar-Cane*, like the *Fleece* a single-commodity georgic modeled on John Philips's *Cyder* (1708). I conclude with Jago's *Edge Hill*, a locodescriptive poem that includes a georgic account, replete with direct allusions to Virgil, of coal mining, iron smelting, and metal manufacturing in the Black Country and Birmingham. In the first two poems, intensified regimes of biological production are linked with intensified systems of labor discipline, including child labor and chattel slavery, and expanding networks of global trade. In *Edge Hill*, it is the dense energy of coal, conjoined with the malleability of iron, that generates new relations of labor, principles of value, and configurations of geopolitical power. All three poems culminate with optimistic visions of sustained future growth partially decoupled from environmental constraints. All three also hint at the socioecological crises introduced by industrial production and the speculative investment that supports it.

The defining representational challenge for a poet—or political economist or statesman—in the eighteenth century was growing social and economic differentiation. As "society becomes more various," John Barrell observes, it becomes less possible for anyone to claim to "comprehend the range and organization of activities necessary for its survival and progress." The rhetorical problem, for the descriptive poet, was to show how an "increasingly differentiated society" could still be seen as "unified."[3] *The Seasons* sought to describe the "whole," with a unifying vision enabled not by a prospect view but by attention to the planetary variation and circulation that facilitate production in an advanced organic energy regime. In this chapter, I read these industrial georgics for evidence of modal strain, often acknowledged by the poets themselves, that attests to the inadequacy of descriptive verse for representing socioecological differentiation related to the development of modes of production partially decoupled from the concrete temporalities and geographies of a solar energy economy.

This is also an argument about reception, about changes during this period in what readers expected from poetry. Dyer, Grainger, and Jago saw their ambitious projects as continuous with a tradition of patriotic descriptive verse that ran from Virgil to Thomson. Yet critics—Samuel Johnson famously among them—saw descriptive verse, with its high diction and classical allusions, as an entirely infelicitous medium for representing industrial production and a developing world market. Of Dyer's georgic treatment of the wool industry, Johnson observed, "the subject . . . cannot be made poetical." The ridicule he directed at *The Sugar-Cane* was, as Boswell recounted, even more pointed: "What could he make of a sugar-cane? One might as well write the 'Parsley-bed, a Poem,' or 'The Cabbage-garden, a Poem.'"[4] One of the defining features of romanticism is, as I argue in the next chapter, a redefinition of poetic vocation as defined by its opposition to industrial modes of production (with certain notable exceptions, such as Erasmus Darwin's georgic celebrations of modern science and industry). Readers and critics were coming to expect poems that stood at a remove from modern life.

Scholars have long recognized that, having achieved unique prominence in the Augustan age, georgic and locodescription fall into disrepair and disrepute by the end of the eighteenth century, remaining, as Kevis Goodman writes of the georgic, only as a "rhizomatic underpresence" (*Georgic Modernity*, 1). Kurt Heinzelman describes "the disappearance [after 1770] of the georgic as an acknowledged literary form" as constituting an epistemic "fissure or disjunction" ("Roman Georgic in the Georgian Age," 199). Markman Ellis claims that Grainger's attempt to represent a slave-based production rendered the georgic a "ruined poetic form."[5] A stratigraphic break in poetic form and vocation appears as the descriptive genres are pushed underground or abandoned as relics of an earlier age in the very decades in which Crutzen and Stoermer located another epochal break, the Holocene/Anthropocene boundary.

Some of the symbolic predicaments that come to appear insuperable for the midcentury poet are intensifications of long-standing tensions in Augustan descriptive poetry, such as the competition between pastoral retreat and public duty or concerns about the influence of commercial luxury on the nation's morals. The georgic, from the start, confronts a gap between subject and style, between, in Addison's words, the "low Phrases and Terms of Art that are adapted to Husbandry" and the poem's "Pomp of Numbers and Dignity of words" ("An Essay on the Georgics," 149). This gap grew as poets turned from traditional agriculture to the new infrastructures, technologies, and labor regimes of industrial production. The choice to adopt the georgic is an assertion of historical continuity, a belief that progress can be reconciled with the familiar rhythms of seasonal time and the received wisdom of the past. As David Alff notes, however, georgic poetry in industrializing Britain internalized the future-oriented "world-making pretension" of project ideology, along with its intimations of possible "failure" (intimations, it is worth noting, already harbored in Virgil's attention to accident and entropy).[6] In her account of the "crisis in georgic of the mid-century," Claire Bucknell describes how poems that offered a "macro-economic vision of interconnected industry" sought, not always with success, to synthesize an inherited "moral economy of self-sufficiency" with profit-oriented discourses of improvement and investment.[7] In line with Barrell's analysis, Rudolf Beck sees the "comprehensive" vision of the georgic disintegrate in attempts to overcome "the division between the traditional ethics of the georgic and the economic and political reason governing the 'new' commercial and industrial society."[8]

The representational pressures I identify in this chapter emerge as these poems grapple not only with the rapidity of historical change and new social fault lines, related to dispossession and the violence of the factory system and the slave plantation, but also with socioecological contradiction as well. Classical political economy, according to Wrigley, saw economic growth as "severely and inescapably limited by the fact that one of the triad of factors—land, labour, and capital—upon whose combination all production depended, was in fixed supply" (*Continuity, Chance and Change*, 17). In Thomson's *Summer*, we saw a prophecy of unceasing growth that contravened this sense of intrinsic limit. The "unbounded commerce" of mercantile empire served as a spatial fix, allowing the British economy to grow by appropriating the wealth of other nations. In the poems treated in this chapter, visions of production decoupled from land, climate, and other environmental constraints—and thus of the possibility of unfettered growth—come into sharper focus. Descriptive poetry, I have argued, accords causal significance to the variability of concrete time and space. It is this concrete spatiotemporal diversity that justifies the formal expansiveness of the descriptive poem. Industrial georgics, however, confront the challenge of integrating what Jason Moore, extending Marx's concept of human labor in the abstract, calls "abstract social nature," the representational strategies and modes of exchange that make the natural world recognizable not only as resource and property but also as an essentially interchangeable set of inputs to production (*Capitalism in the Web of Life*, 200).[9] Moore conceptualizes the contributions of nature to value creation in terms of "work/energy," equivalent to waged labor except in that it can be appropriated without compensation. Since capital expands only by increasing labor productivity, and since doing so requires an ever-greater appropriation of that "ecological surplus" that nature gives freely, capitalism tends inevitably toward crisis: a pattern of exhaustion and expansion. "Commodity frontiers"—"bundles of uncapitalized work/energy" accessed through colonial expansion, intensified management, and new technologies of capture and conversion (144)—offer temporary means of increasing productivity, solutions that amplify the scale of capitalization. As Moore notes, abstract social nature includes those racialized and gendered humans excluded from wage labor, property ownership, and territorial possession, offering a way of understanding the strong imperative to naturalize certain types of labor in the industrial georgics.

The crisis in descriptive poetry reflects its attempt to represent an increasingly delocalized economy organized around substitutable resources and energy inputs, accelerating growth, and a fantasy of infinite accumulation decoupled from the constraints of an organic energy economy. Only one of the three poems I discuss, *Edge Hill*, focuses extensively on mineral energy. For Wrigley and other historians, the coal takeoff is the crucial turning point whereby Britain exceeded constraints set by the "annual cycle of insolation": accessing "stores of energy . . . accumulated in past geological ages," it broke through the "energy bottleneck which set limits to growth" (*Energy and the English Industrial Revolution*, 21, 191). In the course of the eighteenth century, annual British coal consumption grew fivefold, from three thousand to fifteen thousand tons, and a large proportion of this increase was due to new uses of coal in manufacturing industries in the Midlands. But the rise of coal—so often the decisive turning point in accounts of modernity and, more recently, the Anthropocene—is part of a bigger story of energy transition. My readings in this chapter lend support to Moore's argument that the mineral energy takeoff is best understood in relation to the broad dynamics of capitalism as a "world ecology." The changeover to fossil fuels was continuous with early capitalism's other "technics" of appropriation. In other words, this early phase of the Industrial

Revolution involves not only the accelerating economic growth made pos-
sible by fossil capitalism but also what Raymond Williams calls the "es-
sential connections between town and country," the infrastructures—of
transport, of investment, and even of symbolic representations—that link
mineral and solar energy sources, the mechanized workhouse, the planta-
tion, and enclosed fields and pastures (Williams, *The Country and the City*,
98). Recognizing coal as a prominent but not definitive feature of industrial
capitalism is important because it reminds us of the role that solar energy
and biological energy converters (including human bodies) continue to play
in industrial society, in the way metabolic and biogeochemical processes are
incorporated into industrial infrastructure, supplemented and intensified
rather than supplanted by fossil fuels.[10]

WOOLEN GEORGIC: DYER'S *THE FLEECE*

Robert Allen contends that Britain's unique path of accelerating economic
growth began not with its colonial projects, its entrepreneurial culture, or
its access to mineral coal but with sheep husbandry. Population decline in
England after the Black Death led to the conversion of arable land to pas-
ture, which allowed England to raise sheep with the longer wool suited for
worsted cloth. Newly competitive with Italian manufactures, English drap-
eries became a major source of export income and urban commercial ac-
tivity, which in turn funded agricultural improvement in the countryside,
manufacturing ventures, and global expansion. "The success of the British
economy was," in Allen's words, "due to long-haired sheep, cheap coal and
the imperial foreign policy that secured the rising volume of trade."[11]

In 1700, wool goods constituted more than two-thirds of British exports.
Though by midcentury this ratio had fallen to half, for John Dyer the cen-
trality of sheep to the national interest was self-evident: "What bales, what
wealth, what industry, what fleets! / Lo, from the simple fleece, how much
proceeds."[12] Dyer approaches sheep husbandry and the trade in wool with
Miltonic aspiration. In the opening lines of *The Fleece*—which Barrell calls
"the most comprehensive and well-informed Georgic in English" (*English
Literature in History*, 107)—Dyer lays out his agenda: "The care of sheep,
the labours of the loom, and the arts of trade" (1.1–2). More than any poem
of the period, *The Fleece* proceeds with the idea that description is the
proper mode for representing an economic system encompassing the Earth,
as totalizing as the ocean and the atmosphere. "Britain's happy trade," as he
writes in the poem's concluding lines, "now spreading wide, / Wide as th'
Atlantic and Pacific seas, / Or as air's vital fluid o'er the globe" (4.694–96).

He attempts what earlier descriptive poets had avoided: to link extensive description of Britain's rural pastures, fields, and villages with its manufacturing towns and ports and the trade networks that extend through what he calls "the whole globe" (4.167).

In book 1, Dyer follows Virgil in directing the agriculturalist first to consider the conditions of terrain and weather. The poem begins by enumerating Britain's "regions on regions" (1.58): the dry pastures of Banstead Downs, Dorchester, and Salisbury Plain; the watery meadows of Ross-on-Wye and Leominster in Herefordshire (famous for its "Lemster ore," a high-grade wool); the peaty soil of Leicester, known for its combing wools. From soil, Dyer turns to climate and inclination, the slope of pasture and its direction with respect to the Sun: "there also must be found / Felicity of clime, and aspect bland, / Where gentle sheep may nourish locks of price" (125–27). The guiding principle here is continuous with the *Georgics* and *The Seasons*. The cultivator's "skillful care" requires him to know "nature; who, in ev'ry change, / In each variety, with wisdom works, / And pow'rs diversif'd of air and soil / Her rich material" (227–30). There is perhaps no better statement than this passage of the georgic principle linking (a personified) nature's productive capacity—its works, its powers—with its variation, the regional diversity of climates and soils. This is the organic energy economy in which sunlight and rain showers, soil and fodder nourish the growth of sheep—"Flocks . . . / Like flakes of gold illumining the green" (168–69)—whose wool is the source of the nation's wealth. To accomplish this transmutation the shepherd must accommodate his practice to his place, by, for instance, choosing the appropriate breed: "Ye shepherds . . . / Be first your purpose to procure a breed, / To soil and clime adapted. Ev'ry soil / And clime, ev'n ev'ry tree and herb, receives / Its habitant peculiar" (185–89). The topographical survey continues, covering the "tempestuous" mountains of Derbyshire and Wales, the downs of the Cotswolds, the mild climate of Herefordshire. In Dyer's hands, georgic bioregionalism transmutes into the encompassing movement of locodescription.[13]

There is, in book 1, already a recognition that place is not entirely fixed. Dyer's injunction to "inclose, inclose" appears in line 109 of book 2, but the first book offers a detailed program of improvement: sinking trenches to reroute rills, amending soil, opening pasture by cutting trees and clearing brambles and pest animals. The emphasis in book 1, however, is the shaping environment, both the distinct regions within Britain and temperate Britain compared with other nations. Dyer presents a familiar portrait of Britain's climate, modeled on Virgil's praise of "the glories of Italy" (*Georgics*, 147). What appears to be a deficit, the absence of tropical warmth and

the prevalence of rain, proves a boon: "Hail noble Albion! Where no golden
mines, / No soft perfumes, nor oils, nor myrtle bow'rs, / The vigorous frame
and lofty heart of man / Enervate: . . . / White-winged snow, and cloud,
and pearly rain, / Frequent attend . . . Rich queen of mists and vapours"
(*The Fleece*, 1.152–58). Lacking the exotic and feminizing luxury goods of
the tropics, Britain's wet climate and "temp'rate air" (249) are conducive
to the growth of wool as well as a hardiness of character. Dyer lists En-
gland's illustrious "sons," for whom the harsh climate served to "twist
their nerves / For deeds of excellence and high renown" (158, 161–62), a list
that culminates with Milton. What Milton called the "cold /Climate," far
from enervating the poet, in Dyer's revisionary geohumoralism, inspired his
epic triumph.

Dyer negotiates dual imperatives in his representation of Britain, ide-
alizing an island nation favored by providence for wool production with
a *pastoral* climate, yet also justifying the labor and improvement neces-
sary to tame a recalcitrant nature as well as the need to establish global
trade networks owing to the *georgic* climate. Not long after his rhapsody on
Britain's "mists and vapours," Dyer warns of the dangers of overprecipita-
tion: "Long rains in miry winter cause the halt; / Rainy luxuriant summers
rot your flock" (1.456–57). Indeed, the decade of the 1750s was the wettest
since 1697, when records were first kept, with summers "averaging 127 per
cent of the modern mean" (Lamb, *Climate, History and the Modern World*,
235). Dyer warns that "sheep no extremes can bear" but then reminds "ye
British swains" to "enjoy / Your gentle seasons and indulgent clime" (1.451,
462–63). He contrasts the rhythmic temporality of agrarian life in Britain,
the "rose-diffusing hours / That dance before the wheels of radiant day"
(470–71), with the six "slow gloomy months" of the Laplander, forced to
retreat indoors where he labors by the "squalid light" supplied by whale
oil (468–75), and with the fate of those who inhabit "warmer zones," sub-
ject to sudden volcanic eruptions (498–505). In ten lines near the end of
book 1, Dyer follows Virgil and Thomson in depicting a destructive flood,
a swollen Cambrian river bearing away the newly shorn sheep "Bleating
in vain" (598) along with huts, trees, and rocks (see generally 590–600). He
then abruptly turns from the distressing reality of natural hazards to an
idealizing description of a harvest festival, which leads to a stylized pastoral
sequence in which two shepherds contrast their rural "prospects" with the
"gardens black with smoke in dusty town, / Where stenchy vapours often
blot the sun" (659–61).

Climate is the representational crux of the first two books of *The Fleece*,
the source of its structuring ambivalence, an uncertainty that produces rhe-

torical excess and self-consciousness. The poem's ideological work involves managing social relations by stabilizing their underlying context, climate, as a source of identity, a condition of production, and a justification for schemes of improvement and investment. In book 2, Dyer seeks to compensate for his earlier idealization of Britain's climate: "There are [those] who over-rate our spungy stores, / Who deem that nature grants no clime, but ours, / To spread upon its fields the dews of heav'n, / And feed the silky fleece" (2.134–37). Piercing such "Illusion" (141)—here awareness of ideological mystification develops precisely with respect to the representation of climate, a self-reflexivity I have traced back to Virgil—Dyer reemphasizes "nature's rigor" (160), an entropic principle, in "the rage of storms" (161) and "chaos drear" (175), that necessitates human labor. How one conceives of natural exigency, Dyer recognizes, plays a role in how one conceives of human identity and the "goal of work" (Frye, *Anatomy of Criticism*, 106). Reference to innate conditions is ideological not because it mystifies social determination but because it posits one particular relation out of many possible relations between natural forces and human world making.

A further explanation for the irresolution in Dyer's representation of the British climate is related to the mercantilist model of value discussed in the previous chapter, in which wealth derives from the movement of commodities from one "clime" to another such that surplus is generated by the free kinetic energy circulating through the Earth. "Each clime," Dyer promises near the end of book 3, "Shall join their various stores, and amply feed / The mighty brotherhood" (3.539–41). For this conception of value to make sense, Britain's climate must be meaningfully distinguished from the harsher "extremes" of the "Hyperborean tracts" and the luxurious airs of the "warmer zones" (1.461, 467, 498). It is only by securing a portrait of what makes Britain or a region within Britain climatically distinct that its potential to contribute to the world market—"trade through various climes" (2.631)—can be identified. Yet the diction of climatic distinction—"torrid climes," "fervid climates," "Luxuriant climes," "hyperborean," "gloomy," "temperate," "airy"—has become vague in its overuse and conventionality, inadequate for accomplishing the work of modeling the political economy of global trade.

In the one sequence in *The Fleece* in which Dyer directly refers to his own labor as a poet and his vision of the role of poetry in society, he concisely identifies the interrelation between three models of value: physiocratic, mercantilist, labor. "'Tis mine," he writes, "to teach th' inactive hand to reap / Kind nature's bounties, o'er the globe diffused." "For this," he adds, "I wake the weary hours of rest" (2.501–3). The depiction of the poet's nighttime labor resonates less with Milton's nightly visits from the muse (*Paradise Lost*, 7.28–29) than with Lucretius's address to Memmius in *De rerum natura*: "urge me to any toil / And lead me on to watch through nights serene / In my long quest for words, for poetry, / . . . / To let you see into the heart of hidden things" (*On the Nature*, 1.141–45). Unlike Lucretius, however, Dyer's concern is not with the hidden forces of nature so much as the hidden sources of social surplus: in human labor power, in nature's uncompensated bounty, and in the global circulation of goods. In the poem's second and third books, a theory of value as constituted by labor begins to dominate, the form of value Dyer associates with his own industriousness and the imperative to wake and work rather than sleep (in contrast with Thomson, whose muse is closely coordinated with diurnal and seasonal cycles of work and rest). The nation's wealth derives not only from the works of nature, its "bounties," and from the transport of commodities, "o'er the globe diffused," but from the value added by human labor: "'Tis art and toil, / Gives nature value, multiplies her stores, / Varies, improves, creates" (2.183–85). Dyer echoes the model of value famously articulated by John Locke in the *Second Treatise of Government* (1689), in which he asserts: "'Tis *Labour* indeed that *puts the difference of value* on every thing." The "effects of labor," he adds, supply nine-tenths of what can be extracted from nature, before revising (in an early anticipation of the self-expanding logic of capital) upward to 99 percent.[14] "What simple nature yields," Dyer writes, "are only rude / Materials, cumbers on the thorny ground; / 'Tis toil that makes them wealth" (3.35–38).

How shall we understand Dyer's growing commitment to an understanding of value that emphasizes human labor over the contribution of nature, especially after the emphasis, in the opening book, on Britain's distinct climate and the local variables that shape agricultural production? Dyer acknowledges in book 2 what he had mystified in book 1: sheep can be—and are—raised in almost any climate. This fact emerges in his deep history of sheep husbandry, from its mythic origins in "Phoenicia's hilly tracts" (2.206) up to the present, when wool is grown in Kashmir, Libya, Spain, France, and even the "new Columbian world" (421). Britain had in the eighteenth century begun to import raw wool, a process that accelerated rapidly with the mechanization of wool manufacturing. Even its unique sheep breeds could be pilfered by other European powers, France in particular, which explains the resonance for Dyer of the story of Jason and the golden fleece. So, if wool is an interchangeable commodity that can be produced anywhere, a new and more complicated set of economic variables must be considered: the relative costs of land, labor, and transport as well as the potential value added in manufacturing.

One solution to the problem of the global wool trade is hinted at in the poem. John Goodridge claims that Dyer's description of the Leicestershire sheep—of a "larger sort," with a "form compact" and "spacious haunches" (1.218–24)—offers one of the earliest references to the new breed being developed through methodical selection by Robert Bakewell (*Rural Life in Eighteenth-Century English Poetry*, 135–36). The "new Leicester" offered a sheep breed optimized for mutton production rather than fine-quality wool, something Dyer suggests when he describes how "fatt'ning flocks" bring "double wealth" (3.367–68). In the course of the eighteenth century, the average weight of sheep sold at London's Smithfield market more than doubled. While wool is a commodity easily transportable, meat markets are much harder to internationalize without fossil-powered transport and refrigeration. The mass production of meat, in turn, plays an important role in Dyer's second solution to the problem of the global wool trade: the growth of urban manufacturing centers, the central topic of book 3. Phyllis Deane estimates that in the very decades that Dyer was laboring over his poem there was a "sharp increase" in the "value added by manufacture" of woolen goods, something the poet recognizes in his detailed accounts of the industrial workhouse, the new water-powered spinning and weaving machines, and the labor unrest caused by their introduction.[15] "But chief by numbers of industrious hands / A nation's wealth is counted," Dyer observes, recanting his earlier emphasis on Britain's environmental assets (3.530–31).

As his repeated references to disembodied hands suggest—the "inactive hand" (2.501), the lock that "from hand to hand / Renews its circling course" (558–59), "unwilling hands" (3.99), a "busy hand" (266), "younger hands" (281), "needless hands" (294)—Dyer works hardest to abstract "grateful toil" (22) precisely in those instances in which he depicts new regimes of industrialized wage labor, "social labor in the abstract." As Wordsworth later noted, the poem's infelicity results not, as Johnson claimed, in its marriage of low subject matter with high diction but in its idealization of factory labor and in Dyer's optimism concerning the effects of mechanization. Mechanized manufacturing adds a new source of input and energy conversion and, accordingly, a new temporality to economic production. The prime mover of the mechanized workhouse was not coal but water, the same hydrologic kinesis a ship captures as it moves down a river, just here captured by a machine. Dyer implies that the system of scaled-up water-powered production is continuous with traditional labor practices in his description of the fulling mill, where the wool is cleaned and prepared for spinning: "tumbling waters turn enormous wheels, / And hammers, rising and descending, learn / to imitate the industry of man" (3.164–66). In fact, mechanization clearly threatened to replace human labor. Dyer describes the supplanting of traditional methods of hand spinning by the "spiral engine"—Lewis Paul's roller spinning machine, patented in 1738—"which, on an hundred spoles, an hundred threads, / with one huge wheel, by lapse of water twines, / Few hands requiring" (81–84). He directly addresses weavers (who had rioted in 1719 and 1739), anxious that their labor was being displaced and devalued by mechanization: "your hands will ever find / Ample employment" (89–90).

Dyer appeals most insistently to generic convention—at times to the point of absurdity—when he wants to assert that the new modes of production are continuous with the old. Book 3 begins with an invocation to the "Arcadian muse" (3.1), implying that mechanized indoor labor befits not only the Virgilian georgic but the pastoral as well: "Let now the fleecy looms / Direct our rural numbers, as of old, / when plains and sheepfolds were the muses' haunts" (11–13). He compares the accelerating "speed" of the hydropowered mechanized workhouse with "fountains sure, / Which, ever-gliding, feed the flow'ry lawn" (91, 93–94). He promises that the "good" of laborers "shall ever rise, / Ever, while o'er the lawns, and airy downs, / The bleating sheep and shepherd's pipe are heard" (100–102). The precise technical language with which he treated sheep husbandry is in these passages replaced with the artificiality of pastoral mystification. The "village nymphs" (43) are called to "begin [their] toils" (47). This rhetorical excess achieves its absurd low point in Dyer's notorious depiction of child labor: "The younger hands / Ply at the easy work of winding yarn / On swiftly-circling engines, and their notes / Warble together, as a choir of larks" (281–84).

What is at stake, rhetorically, in books 2 and 3 is not only historical continuity in an age of new technologies and labor relations but also the problem of connecting the accelerative temporality of mechanized labor in a global market—"Quicken your labours, brace your slackening nerves / Ye Britons; nor sleep careless on the lap / Of bounteous Nature; she is elsewhere kind" (2.426–28)—with regular diurnal and annual patterns "to endow industrial process with a seasonal rhythm," as Barrell writes (*English Literature in History*, 100). Dyer repeatedly acknowledges the imperative to "speed . . . labor" (3.65), to increase the rate of production and profit, but he also asserts that "the round of work goes on, from day to day, / Season to season" (177–78). Already in book 2, Dyer had described how energy-dense fodder crops such as turnips allow the overwintering of the sheep,

who can continue to "swell their fleeces" in "warm cribs" (2.100–101), an
example of production being moved indoors and so removed from seasonal
exigency. His reference to the unfortunate Laplanders seemingly forgotten,
he observes that British weavers are cheered by "sparkling fires," fed with
"stores bituminous," as they work during the long winter months (3.611).
Here it is coal that enables accelerated production.

An understanding of value, as accrued in ever-intensifying labor produc-
tivity, comes to be linked in the poem to abstract social nature, a represen-
tation of nature as a malleable source of essentially interchangeable inputs.
Improvement allows the cultivator to transcend the shaping conditions
of the local environment. In the same passage in which Dyer equates the
"nation's wealth" with the "numbers of industrious hands," he calls for
projects of improvement to be scaled up from the individual estate to the
nation: "teach / The stream a naval course, or till the wild, / Or drain the
fen, or stretch the long canal" (3.542–44). Improvement, mechanization,
and commerce together facilitate a transcendence of the condition physio-
cratic political economy had considered an inexorable check on growth:
the finite stock of land. Indeed, Dyer anticipates David Harvey's spatial fix,
the way environmental constraints and diminishing returns can be over-
come through spatial reorganization and market expansion: "Thus our
isle, / Thus only may Britannia be enlarg'd" (552–53). This prophetic vi-
sion of limits transcended produces a moment of reflexive retrenchment—
"whither strays / the raptur'd muse, forgetful of her task?" (555–56)—an
acknowledgment of the role the poet plays in producing idealizing images
of what David Alff calls a "pliant future" and of the tension between such
"world-making pretension" and the didactic imperative to depict the world
as it is (*The Wreckage of Intentions*, 117, 115).

In the previous chapter, I identified several passages in *The Seasons*
in which the narrator calls attention to his embodied perception and
specifically to the effects of an adverse climate on poetic labor. Such self-
reflexivity takes a different form in *The Fleece*, where the labor of knowing
the world is related not to intense heat or cold but rather to the novelty
and complexity of the historical situation the poem seeks to represent. In
book 1, after the encomium on Albion's "mists and vapours," the narrator
describes London's port, the crux of the networks linking rainy Britain with
the sunny tropics:

> whither strays my muse?
> Pleas'd, like a traveller upon the strand
> Arriv'd of bright Augusta: wild he roves,

From deck to deck, thro' groves immense of masts;
'Mong crouds, bales, cars, the wealth of either Ind;
                    . . . unable yet to fix
His raptur'd mind, or scan in order'd course
Each object singly; with discov'ries new
His native country studious to enrich. (1.175–84)

Barrell notes that, whereas Thomson positions towns in "the penultimate
distance," Dyer brings the city "right before us," in a manner that poten-
tially upsets the "harmony of the landscape" (*English Literature in His-
tory*, 100). Here, the variety of Britain's imported commodities produces
an inability to sustain focus and "scan in order'd course," a condition of
perceptual overload that Dyer explicitly compares with his own difficulty
in organizing his poem's transitions, aligning its diverse scales, topics, and
locales. This scene—which features Dyer's first invocation of the muse,
an intermediary between the poet and the audience he has heretofore ad-
dressed directly—offers an example of the "cognitive dissonance" Good-
man associates with the georgic's medial self-reflexivity, in which an "un-
settling experience of the present" produces "a disturbance in mediation"
(*Georgic Modernity*, 8, 64).

Another instance of such reflexivity occurs later in book 1. The poem has
insisted that, in a world market, British husbandry and the British climate
must be compared with other regions. Dyer details the "perils" and "toils of
life, / In foreign climes." Here again, the muse is called on, redirected, and
made to accelerate: "But speed thy flight, my muse; / Swift turns the year;
and our unnumbered flocks / On fleeces overgrown uneasy lie" (1.551–54).
Too much attention is being dedicated to contrasting Britain with other na-
tions, descriptive expansion interfering with the need to recount the annual
cycle of labor. The two orders of climate that *The Seasons* so masterfully
reconciles—geography and seasonality, space and time—are in active ten-
sion, as if the pressure of foreign markets and mechanized labor is changing
the temporality of animal husbandry in Britain. Dyer's muse is not always
entirely obedient—Goldstein notices that sometimes the poet is subject to
"the mockery of his own muse" (*Ruins and Empire*, 58)—and here the poem
turns not to shearing but to the production of tools, the metal manufac-
turing of Sheffield, a promised pastoral scene interrupted by an image of
"ruddy flames" and clattering hammers (1.557), another site of production
that must be integrated into the system. Where (like Milton and Virgil be-
fore him) Thomson identifies the potential limits of poetic knowledge with
the poet's own geohumoral embodiment, for Dyer such limits emerge as he

attempts to bring into the positive space of representation "the wheels of nature's vast machine" (1.320), the new machinery of mechanized production, and the global "machine of trade," a system to which participants of all sorts contribute even when "unconscious of the union" (4.303–6).

The final book of *The Fleece* surveys the entire globe, naming more than a hundred regions, identified as sources of wool and potential markets for finished woolen goods. Dyer recognizes that the two crucial variables determining the future of wool manufacturing are access to raw wool and the need to expand international markets for the export of finished goods. We see an attenuation of the physiocratic and mercantilist models of value identified earlier, an abstraction of global geography literalized in the final passages of the poem as the poet turns to the "new world," imagining North America remade through the "spread [of] Brittania's flocks o'er every dale" (4.494, 524). Moving northward, the poet wonders why Newfoundland is so frigid while European nations at the same latitude grows grapes. "Must it ever thus? Or may the hand / Of mighty labor drain their gusty lakes, / Enlarge their brightening sky, and, peopling, warm / The opening valleys, and the yellowing plains?" (573–76). The warming of the Arctic clime will be matched by the building of a canal through Panama: "we burst strong Darien's chain" (577). In the poem's final stanza, Dyer's prophetic vision extends further: "That portion too of land, a tract immense, / Beneath the Antarctic spread, shall then be known, / And new plantations on its coast arise" (683–85). Writing more than a decade before the first Cook expedition, Dyer refers to Terra Australis Incognita, the belief going back to Aristotle that a great southern landmass must balance the northern continents. As it happens, it would be the establishment of the Australian wool industry, inaugurated with the arrival of Merino sheep in 1797, that facilitated the continued growth of British wool manufacturing through the nineteenth century.

Unlike so many later romantic-era prophecies, Dyer's premonitions of a warmed Arctic, a canal linking the Atlantic and the Pacific, and sheep plantations on the great southern continent have been largely realized, albeit with certain unintended and catastrophic side effects. Despite these accurate prognostications, *The Fleece*, as Samuel Johnson observed in 1781, "never became popular, and is now universally neglected" (*Lives*, 2:405). Dustin Griffin suggests its optimistic vision of peaceful commerce was ill-timed given the outbreak of the Seven Years' War (*Patriotism and Poetry*, 198). Johnson damned not only the poem but the georgic enterprise itself, asserting that "the woolcomber and the poet" are of "discordant natures": "When Dyer, whose mind was not unpoetical, has done his utmost, by interesting his reader in our native commodity, by interspersing rural imagery, and incidental digressions, by cloathing small images in great words, and by all the writer's arts of delusion, the meanness naturally adhering, and the irreverence habitually annexed to trade and manufacture, sink him under insuperable oppression; and the disgust which blank verse, encumbering and encumbered, superadds to an unpleasing subject, soon repels the reader, however willing to be pleased" (*Lives*, 2:405). Though Wordsworth wrote a sonnet commending the "Bard of the Fleece" and even compared Dyer to Milton, Johnson's opinion largely prevailed, as is evident in a nineteenth-century review in the *Red Dragon*: "It does not require very great critical acumen to perceive that a didactic poem on sheep . . . must in the nature of things end in dullness, and dreariness, and despair; possibly, if one tried to master all four books at once, in suicide."[16] In the mid-twentieth century, Cecil Moore could confidently demean *The Fleece* as a "verse pamphlet on the various departments of the woolen industry"—"there is not a detail of the whole subject too petty or prosaic for the poet's attention"—which makes it "*fortunately* the most elaborate industrial poem, not only of the eighteenth century, but of all English literature."[17]

A more intriguing account of the poem can be found in an 1878 address by John Hays, the secretary of the National Association of Wool Manufacturers, delivered to the US National Agricultural Congress in New Haven. Hays offers an extended reading of *The Fleece*, culminating in a call to extend Dyer's prophetic vision of globalized sheep husbandry to the American West. "There is an area of country," he observes, "between the Missouri River and the Pacific coast containing 1,650,000 square miles, or more than a billion acres, which is one immense pasture ground,—boundless, endless, gateless."[18] Of course, the United States did not become a wool-producing country, in part because of violent opposition from cattle ranchers, in part because the global wool industry was already saturated. Hays explicitly rejects Johnson's criticism of the poem: "Do not believe, with that great moralist, that the poet and the wool-grower or wool-worker are of 'discordant natures.' No grower ever bred a flock of perfect fibre and form, no workman ever designed and executed an artistic fabric, who was not impelled by that enthusiasm, that passion for the ideal, which is the soul of poetry" (7). Such an understanding of poetry and industrial labor as similar world-creating activities, as acts of *poiesis*, quite closely echoes Dyer's comparison of his poetic labor, of collecting and disseminating useful knowledge, with that of the inventor who supplied new techniques for combing wool (2.515–38). Such an understanding of poetry, as an act of labor that can contribute to an ever-more differentiated economy, had, however, grown increasingly untenable.

PLANTATION GEORGIC: GRAINGER'S *THE SUGAR-CANE*

In 1757, a long review of *The Fleece* written by James Grainger, a young phy-
sician with literary pretensions, appeared in the *Monthly Review*. The re-
view begins by acknowledging the marginal status of didactic poetry, which
seeks to "ornament" practical "precepts": "For the lower, or more familiar
the object described, the greater must be the power of language to preserve
it from debasement."[19] To find an audience, Grainger observes, such poems
must address subject matter of a "universal, and especially of a national,
nature" (329). What, he asks, could be a topic of broader interest than that
treated in *The Fleece*: the "Arts of Trade"? He commends Dyer's depictions
of Britain's climate, "the Changes of the Weather"—"the murky cloud, /
Hail, rain, or radiance"—that challenge the shepherd (330). He compares
Dyer's precepts with Virgil's, noting that, whereas the English poet advises
the shepherd to wait on a "balmy morn" for the pasture to dry, Virgil recom-
mends that the sheep be led early to the lawns, "while hoar with virgin-dew
the grass appears." He notes further Dyer's attempts to "rival" Virgil, his
depiction of the global climes compared with Virgil's "description of the
African Shepherd, and the Scythian Winter" ("among the capital paintings
of the Roman Master"), his autumn storm a rewriting of the harvest storm
in the *Georgics* (335). Among the digressive passages expressing the poem's
"benevolent strains," Grainger highlights Dyer's "reflections on the slave
trade" (337). In book 4, Dyer had described—what "in telling, wounds / The
gen'rous heart" (4.193)—the "sale of wretched slaves," who "till our fertile
colonies, which yield / The sugar-cane, and the Tobago-leaf, / And various
new productions, that invite / Increasing navies to their crouded wharfs"
(196–200).

Grainger, it so happens, would soon find himself attempting to tell of
this difficult topic, basing his account on firsthand experience. Two years
after he reviewed *The Fleece*, he agreed to serve as a traveling companion
for his wealthy acquaintance John Bourryau. They first visited the island
of Saint Kitts—or Saint Christopher, as it was then known—to check on
Bourryau's recently inherited properties. After a shipboard romance, how-
ever, Grainger married a local heiress with connections to a number of the
dynastic planter families on the island. He took up work as a physician and
purchased several enslaved Africans. In 1760, he wrote to his friend Thomas
Percy announcing his poetic aspirations: "This Island affords a great fund
of new poetical Images, which I am storing up in my mind to produce on
a proper Occasion."[20] Here is the animating logic of descriptive poetics,
its overlap with an expansionist economic model in which "new poetical

Images"—descriptions of geographic variation—provide a stock that can be exploited. In the preface to his completed four-book "West-India georgic," *The Sugar-Cane*, published in London in 1764, Grainger justifies the poem with similar economic language linking descriptive poetry with accumulation: "The face of the country was wholly different from that of Europe, so whatever hand copied its appearances, however rude, could not fail to enrich poetry with many new and picturesque images."[21]

Part of the Leeward Islands, of which Thomson had been named the surveyor general, Saint Kitts was the first permanent English settlement in the Caribbean. Britain achieved complete control over the small island in 1713 as part of the Treaty of Utrecht. Saint Kitts was one of the earliest islands to see the development of monocultural sugar production, beginning in the mid-seventeenth century. The georgic practices of agricultural improvement occurring in Britain in the seventeenth and eighteenth centuries were being imported to the sugar-producing Caribbean colonies, where they were coordinated with the intensive labor discipline and coercive violence of plantation slavery.[22] Anna Tsing, Jason Moore, and others have highlighted the socioecological novelty of the sugar plantation, with its dependence on speculative investment, global supply chains, the supplanting of native ecosystems by monocultures, and new regimes of labor exploitation.[23] What made the sugar plantation an unusual—if also exemplary—site of production was the need to synchronize field agriculture with industrial processing.[24] A long phase of growth, subject to environmental and climatic vicissitude, is followed by a rapid process of rendering, first through a heavy machine press and then in a boiling vat. Field labor and factory labor combine with a mechanical process (powered by animal, water, or wind) and a heating process (fueled by timber, coal, or, increasingly, dried cane). The human labor directing these varied processes was supplied largely by enslaved Africans, whose health had to be managed and whose varied forms of outdoor and indoor labor coerced and organized to maximize productivity.

In his preface, Grainger points out that only one notable work on plantation agriculture had been written—Samuel Martin's *Essay on Plantership* (1750)—which he terms "an excellent performance."[25] Martin compares the successful plantation to a "well-constructed machine, compounded of various wheels, turning different ways, and yet all contributing to the great end proposed." Yet he also allows that, "if any one part runs too fast or too slow, in proportion to the rest, the main purpose is defeated." As we have seen with Thomson's treatment of the Newtonian clockwork universe, the comparison of the world to a machine was less a way of asserting the perfect regularity of its movement than of defining the relation of order to what

Martin himself calls "disorder." Sounding like Virgil describing agriculture in the Iron Age, Martin continues: "When severe droughts or unseasonable rains happen, contrary to the general course of nature, the wise planter must do the best he can."[26]

Grainger's identification of his poem as a "West-India georgic" is an assertion of historical continuity, the applicability of a classical genre to a new scene of production. The novelty of the sugar plantation includes not only its distinct socioecological machinery but also its tropical locale. Because access to year-round water flows is limited and the growth of the sugar cane depends on regular periods of precipitation, Grainger, invoking the precedent of the "Mantuan Bard," turns in book 1 to the "various signs of future rain."[27] The meteorologic signs that served "once fertile Italy" do not apply. "Other marks," such as the retreat of the speckled lizard and the appearance of black crabs, "portend the approaching shower, in these hot climes" (1.315–16). Yet Grainger's insistence on climatic difference leads to a veritable storm of classical references. An acquaintance killed by a squall is compared with a minor character in the *Iliad*. Cockroaches are likened to harpies. The newly filled streams are enlivened by Naiads, "watery spirits" that dally amorously with the "wood-nymphs" (384–87), an allusion suggesting that Grainger recognized the role forests play in sustaining precipitation. The division of field labor during the rainy season is compared with Homer's account of the industrial smelting and shaping of metal for Achilles's shield in a "vast furnace" (411). This analogy anticipates the extended description of the mills where cane is transformed into sugar, iron furnaces heating the boilers, but it also echoes the depiction of ruinous heat waves, the atmosphere itself a "burning furnace" (2.366). (We have already encountered this evocative analogy, comparing the atmosphere and the furnace as energy converters, in *Paradise Lost* and *The Seasons*.) It was especially important to determine which months "from rain are free" (1.443) since the cane can be harvested only during the dry season. Grainger acknowledges, however, that the "seasons vary" not just on different Caribbean islands but "even in the different parts of the same isle" (445–46). Minute variations of climate and soil that far exceed the enumerating powers of the descriptive poet turn out to be the difference between profit and loss. As Britt Rusert observes, *The Sugar-Cane* is as likely to advocate "experimental practice" as to offer generalizable precepts.[28] "Learn / Of ancient modes to doubt," the poet enjoins, "and new to try" (1.282–83).

Eighteenth-century descriptive poets drew on a stock repertoire of images for representing tropical climes: of luxurious abundance, oppressive heat, and tyrannical governments. As Grainger implies in the preface, *The*

Sugar-Cane was an opportunity to bring a new verisimilitude to descriptions of the tropics as a site of georgic production rather than pastoral fantasy or jingoist projection. Grainger reverts, at times, to a language of idealization, particularly with respect to Saint Kitts, which he apostrophizes in book 1: "a fertility, unknown of old, / To other climes denied, adorns thy hills; / Thy vales, thy dells adorns" (1.75–77). As Gilmore notes (*The Poetics of Empire*, 221), in the longer passage from which these lines are taken Grainger alludes not only to Virgil's *laudes Italiae* but also to Milton's depiction of Eden. He echoes this passage in book 3 when he wistfully invites his London literati friends to join him in this "delicious clime" (3.620) to enjoy fine prospects of a "fair landscape; where in loveliest forms, / Green cultivation hath array'd the land" (524–25). Yet his "strain" in *The Sugar-Cane* is, by and large, far from that of "Arcadian Pan" (1.77, 61). Every idealized image of natural plenty is counterbalanced by a detailed depiction of the hazards faced by the Caribbean planter. Much of the scholarly criticism on *The Sugar-Cane* has focused on Grainger's rhetorical assertion of mastery and legitimacy, a "phantasmagoria of prosperity and plenty" interrupted only, as Shaun Irlam writes, by the "ugly and disagreeable fact of slavery."[29] Yet, following the example of Virgil's *Georgics* as well as Martin's *Essay*, Grainger's poem does not obfuscate the real ecological challenges of plantation agriculture. Sugar cane requires eighteen months to mature, "coction long demands" (1.178), during which time the cane is subject to many threats: "thy plants burnt by the torch of day" (162), "ravening rats destroy / Or troops of monkeys thy rich harvest steal" (172–73), the "Goats baneful tooth; the churning boar" (493), "fire . . . casual or design'd" (494). Even the soil is unstable: "Thy land itself is insecure" (186); the "mining rain" causes landslips (190).

Even more "woes unknown to Britain's Isle" (2.24) confront the planter in book 2, which Grainger considered the high point of the poem. These woes include weeds, infections, and insect invasions, but above all they are climatic. Grainger held off on publishing the poem with the expectation that he would directly experience a tropical hurricane and could draw on that to produce fresh images. He wrote to Percy in 1762, reporting that he had completed the poem, "only as I have seen no hurricane, and have not yet had time to arrange my remarks on a fire by night in a cane field, those parts in the second book are incomplete" (Gilmore, *The Poetics of Empire*, 16). He may have been inspired by the popularity of William Falconer's *The Shipwreck* (1762), a georgic treatment of life on the merchant ship *Britannia* that culminates with a calamitous storm in the Mediterranean. As any reader of Defoe's *Robinson Crusoe* (1719) is aware, hurricanes were recog-

nized as a major threat to life and commerce in the Caribbean. It is esti-
mated that one in twenty ships in the West Indies sunk during storms. In
1757, two years before Grainger's arrival, Saint Kitts had been struck by a
hurricane causing around two hundred deaths. Sixteen years after the publi-
cation of *The Sugar-Cane*, the Caribbean was hit by one of the most power-
ful storms in history, the San Calixto Hurricane of 1780, which caused an
estimated twenty-two thousand deaths (making it the deadliest Atlantic
hurricane on record) and severely damaged the British fleet. According to
one estimate, more British soldiers were killed by San Calixto than died in
action in the American Revolution.

In the end, Grainger's account of the "all-wasting hurricane" (2.71) is sec-
ondhand, much of its diction and imagery unapologetically borrowed from
Paradise Lost, with echoes of Virgil's destructive storm in the first book of
the *Georgics*. The hurricane is preceded by a calm: "the dæmon Heat / High
hurls his flaming brand" (295–96), recalling the "flaming brand" that guards
the gates of Eden (*Paradise Lost*, 12.643). Morning mists dissolve, "the
midday-sun looks red," as the vapors return and darken the sky (*The Sugar-
Cane*, 2.314). The storm begins, its "wild burst" exceeding "all the brazen
engineries of man, / At once exploded," raising an "infernal din" (322, 324–
25). After the hurricane's eye passes, "the aerial war" resumes (344). "A
river foams, which sweeps, with untam'd might, / Men, oxen, Cane-lands
to the billowy main" (352–53). The hurricane is directly followed by a heat
wave, in the description of which Grainger echoes Thomson, personifying
the Sun as a tyrannical sovereign, as well as Milton's culminating image of
postlapsarian climate change: "Even calms are dreadful, and the fiery South /
Oft reigns a tyrant in these fervid isles" (364–65); "Tropic plants hang down /
Their dropping heads; shew arid, coil'd, adust" (370–71). *Adust*, meaning
"desiccated," is a rare word but one that appears in the final lines of *Para-
dise Lost*, when Adam and Eve are expelled from Eden "as the Libyan air
adust / Began to parch that temperate clime" (12.634–35). Though firmly
rooted in literary precedent, Grainger's depiction of the dangerous weather
of the West Indies certainly belies a promise of confident authority and easy
bounty. As in Virgil's relation to Lucretius, here allusion conveys not the
authority of culture but a dangerous necessity in nature. Like earlier poets,
Grainger represents a disordered world that "brings ruins" to human proj-
ects (3.363). During the hurricane, "Earth trembles" (358), just as it did after
Adam ate the fruit (9.1000).

Prior to anthropogenic climate change, hurricanes were, of course, re-
garded as natural disasters, evidence of nature's meteoric unpredictability,
if not of divine judgment. In *The Sugar-Cane*, Grainger also recognizes the

hazardous environmental changes brought about by European colonization. "In the plantation zones," as Tsing pithily writes, "things could easily go awry" ("Unruly Edges," 149). As Richard Grove has shown, in the seventeenth and eighteenth centuries "awareness" of the human capacity for destructive "ecological impact" first began to develop on tropical islands, owing to their bounded geography, ecological fragility, and the intensive interventions brought about by European exploitation.[30] Grainger further recognizes the specific connection between unsustainable agricultural practices and what he calls "avarice" (1.613), the tendency of planters to seek short-term profit, pushing the plantation machinery to its limit, leading, in Moore's words, "to declining productivity, which drove the sugar frontier ever onwards to virgin soil, which in turn required fresh supplies of capital and labor" ("Sugar," 419).

I have already mentioned that among the "ills" that "await the ripening Cane" (2.2) were two invasive species introduced by Europeans: "the monkey-nation" (35), "brought thither by the French" (note attached to line 46), and rats, which, according to Grainger, "came by shipping from Europe" (note attached to line 64). Solutions to one anthropogenic problem, however, introduce new hazards. Grainger includes directions for poisoning rats with arsenic pellets but warns of potential unintended consequences: "Dare not thou, if life deserve thy care / The infected rivulet taste; nor let thy herds / Graze its polluted brinks" (91–93). Early in book 1, Grainger directs the planter to raze the forests "with ceaseless stroke" (1.33), instructing him only to "spare the guava" (37) and other useful trees such as oranges and avocados. He adds that the volcanic hills of Saint Kitts were "formerly covered with wood": "But now the Cane plantations reach almost to their summits, and extend all the way [down]" (note attached to line 60). Grainger, however, worries about the climatic effects of deforestation. He regards with skepticism the local belief that forests harbor tropical disease, which had led the inhabitants to "remorseless fell / Each shrub of shade, each tree of spreading root" (559–60). The "muse," by contrast, values "the woodland tribes, / Earth's eldest birth, and earth's best ornament" (562–65). Grainger recommends that planters maintain trees for shade from "solstitial beams" (570): "in this clime, / Ah, most intensely hot; how he longs / For cooling vast impenetrable shade" (566–68). It is only "ill-judg'd avarice" (572) that leads planters to cut forests that might supply "breezy shade" (574).

Grainger suggests that "lust of gain, unconscious of its end" (1.203), causes planters to pursue quick profits, razing forests, and failing to replenish the soil: "the richest lands grow poor; / And Liamuiga [Saint Kitts] may, in future times, / If too much urg'd, her barrenness bewail" (205–7). He invokes the idea that soil fertility and the growth of plants depend on vital elements that are finite and subject to depletion. Paul Warde notes that the issue of soil fertility was central to the eighteenth-century "invention" of a discourse of sustainability. "Among those seeking to establish ways to raise the productivity of the land," he writes, "the fear emerged that there might also be a systemic logic of *decline*."[31] For Grainger, the solution is compost, as he writes in lines that strain the georgic balance between lowly subject matter and high diction: "Of composts shall the Muse descend to sing, / Nor soil her heavenly plumes? The sacred Muse / Nought sordid deems, but what is base" (218–20). Addressing the planter, Grainger writes: "wouldst thou double thine estate[?]"; to do so, he must "tread" the "dung-heaps" and reclaim the ashes and refuse from the mills in order to produce a compost "of force to fertilize the poorest soil" (222, 223–24, 227). The successful planter must reproduce the natural cycles that circulate the sustenance necessary for growth. Grainger recommends fencing the fields and allowing livestock to refertilize the soil: "There well thy stock with provender supply; / The well-fed stock will soon that food repay" (234–35).

Other challenges involving the management of the forces necessary to drive the machinery of the plantation relate to the mills used to render the cane. Grainger initially depicts the use of windmills to drive the cylinders but then acknowledges that "the faint breeze oft flags on listless wings," stalling production, "and soon (if on the gale thy crop depend,) / Will all thy hopes of opulence defeat" (3.204, 207–8). He advocates instead an animal-powered mill: "two seasoned mules / They pacing round, give motion to the whole" (247–48). Yet animals are subject to debilitating tropical diseases, so he looks to another prime mover, waterpower. The first water-powered mill had been established on the Wingfield estate in the 1680s. As Grainger acknowledges, this energy source is available only to those fortunate planters whose estates enjoy access to a "never-ceasing stream" (280).

Unsurprisingly, much of the criticism on *The Sugar-Cane* has focused on the strains and contradictions that appear in Grainger's fraught adaptation of the Virgilian georgic, with its depiction of virtuous rustic labor, to the regimented and coerced labor of enslaved Africans.[32] This criticism is sophisticated and convincing, but I do want to contribute several points about the climatic dimensions of the poem's depiction of plantation slavery. Grainger recommends that the planter purchase field slaves brought "from barren climes; where want alone, / Offspring of rude necessity, compels / The sturdy native" (4.58–60). Prior experience of environmental dearth and difficulty, he suggests, hardens people for the unrelenting labor of the cane fields.[33] Moreover, the "fervours of the clime" (78) demand that the planter

attend vigilantly to the health of the enslaved and allow for a process of
seasoning to acclimate their bodies to the unfamiliar climate (see generally
103–24). Grainger's muse recognizes that slavery is morally indefensible—
"Did the tender muse possess the power, / Which monarchs have . . . /
'Twould be the fond ambition of her soul, / To . . . knock off the chains / Of
heart-debasing slavery" (232–36)—yet also sees it as an inescapable feature
of the profitable plantation. Grainger's most notorious attempt to justify
plantation slavery occurs when he contrasts the lot of enslaved Africans
working the cane fields, "doom'd to toil from dawn to setting sun" (166),
with that of Scottish coal miners, who

> sweat, sequester'd from the day,
> In dark tartarean caves, sunk far beneath
> The earth's dark surface; where sulphureous flames,
> Oft from their vapoury prisons bursting wild,
> To dire explosion give the cavern'd deep,
> And in dread ruin all its inmates whelm. (168–73)

Though their labor was waged, the Scottish miners were, as Ellis explains,
"bonded," subject to a "contract of service for life."[34] The comparison of
the condition of European miners and Caribbean slaves was quite common.
For Grainger, the difference is environmental: the subterranean mines are
reminiscent of Milton's Hell, and the cane fields, while not edenic, at least
follow the natural rhythms of the Sun. How the dangerous and unceasing la-
bor of the "crackling mills"—where "flames / Bursting thro' many a chim-
ney, bright emblaze / The Æthiop-brow of night" (3.104–7)—fits into this
contrast is left unexplained.

A volatile climate, a finicky tropical island teeming with nonnative
flora and fauna, a novel set of energy converters and industrial technolo-
gies, and a labor regime sustained through extreme violence: together these
conditions account for Grainger's anxious awareness that any system of
production is, at best, imperfect and, at worst, unsustainable and indefen-
sible. Following Dyer, Grainger invokes the muse to lend aid precisely in in-
stances in which he pushes the descriptive mode and georgic convention to
their limits in representing the socioecological challenges of the plantation
economy. Even the poem's opening lines, in which the poet identifies his
topics, including "Afric's sable progeny" (1.4), signal the challenges ahead:
"A Muse, that long hath wander'd in the groves / Of myrtle-indolence,
attempts to sing" (4–5). The more infelicitous the topic—"the dark deep

mould" (127); "Composts" (218); "Joint-racking spasms, and cholic's pungent pang" (3.274); the "horrid whip" (142)—the stronger the imperative to call on the muse explicitly, to define a novel mode of production as essentially continuous with what came before. Yet Grainger calls on the muse and then questions or dismisses her: "other soils abound, / which art may tutor to obtain its smile. / Say, shall the experienc'd Muse that art recite?" (1.139–41). This question is followed by seven further questions about the direction the poem should take. Here, Grainger signals the difficulty of shifting from idealizing panegyrics on the natural fertility of Saint Christopher to the georgic's didactic specificity and recognition of natural limits. Similarly, in book 3, the "heavenly Muse" emerges "joyous" (3.1–2) after representing the tropical hurricane and the heat wave in book 2 (closely echoing Milton's prologue expressing relief after Satan's ascent from Hell in bk. 3). The poem is finally able to expound on the planter's "round" (3.46), the reassuring predictability of cyclic time, only to be confronted yet again with sudden disaster: a fire in the cane fields, the fruits of labor through the "seasons" suddenly made to "perish" (88–89). Milton's invocations of the muse constitute an assertive petitioning for a place in the poetic pantheon. Grainger invokes the muse to register uncertainty about the appropriateness of his subject matter and, more surprisingly, to register the challenge of justifying an enterprise so fraught with danger and injustice, of idealizing an unfamiliar ecosystem that promises "calamity" at every turn (258).

In book 3, Grainger calls on Britons to settle in the West Indies, appropriating and refiguring the rhetoric of climatic plentitude in earlier descriptive poems: "the Cane / Wafted to every quarter of the globe, / Makes the vast produce of the world your own" (3.620–22). Book 4 includes an apostrophe to "mighty commerce" (4.322). The circulatory models of an organic economy of ever-renewed flows of energy that suffuse the poem are supplanted by an extractive language of exhaustible reserve that can be claimed once and for all:

> Parent of wealth! In vain coy nature hoards
> Her gold and diamonds; toil, thy firm compeer,
> And industry of unremitting nerve,
> Scale the cleft mountain, the loud torrent brave,
> Plunge to the center, and thro' Nature's wiles,
> (Led on by skill of penetrative soul)
> Her following close, her secret treasures find,
> To pour them plenteous on the laughing world. (337–44)

Here, we discern a more honest acknowledgment of Grainger's understanding of the plantation economy as a site where a quick fortune can be made. With their dependence on the labor of enslaved humans forcibly imported from Africa and metal tools imported from Britain, with the complexity and contingency of their socioecological machinery, with the strong imperative to maximize short-term gain in a manner that decreases sustainability, sugar plantations were speculative and risky ventures. As Grainger observes, a "sugar-works" requires a "greater fund" to establish and maintain than did plantations dedicated to other commodities (note attached to line 1.60). For Grainger, any moral justification for the Caribbean economy depends on a distinction between "hell-born Avarice" and "winged commerce" (1.116, 124), accumulative extraction and self-sustaining circulation, but the apostrophe to commerce shows that this distinction is unsupportable. Grainger's awareness of the tendency of plantation agriculture toward the maximization of profit and its reliance on the morally indefensible enslavement of human beings (who will, themselves, resist that enslavement) generated at least an intimation of the crisis-prone nature of the plantation economy. This intimation receives its fullest and most surprising articulation in the prophetic vision in the poem's concluding stanza of "wild scenes" (4.656)—"what thunders roll! The sky's on fire!" (654)—of Britain's colonies claiming independence.

In book 1, Grainger had referred somewhat plaintively to his own situation as a recent arrival on a small island the land of which had already been heavily parceled: "when will fate / That long had scowl'd relentless on the bard / Give him some small plantation to inclose, / Which he may call his own? Not wealth he craves, / But independence" (1.544–48). After the conclusion of the Seven Years' War in 1763, new islands were opened to British colonization, and there was a rush to purchase land from the government on Granada, Saint Vincent, Dominica, Saint Lucia, and Tobago. Grainger considered joining the land rush, but his only capital was tied up in slaves, whom he probably rented out as day laborers, a particularly harsh fate. "I have a good number of fine young negroes," he wrote to Percy, "and, as I am well acquainted with West India agriculture, I cannot help think it will be worth my while to sacrifice a few more years in this climate, to the leaving behind me of a little fortune of four or five hundred a-year to my family." Here, climate is a hardship, and the aim of enduring it is the quick accumulation of capital. His work as a physician—"all my Sweat"—would not suffice for Grainger to accrue "an independent fortune." He died of a fever, quite possibly malarial, shortly after writing again to Percy: "I mean to remain some years longer in the torrid zone" (Gilmore, *The Poetics of Empire*, 20).

Early reviewers treated *The Sugar-Cane* much as they had *The Fleece*. Allowing that "Poetry" has long "courted the . . . concurrence of Utility," the *Monthly Review* maintained that the very justification Grainger had cited for his descriptive poem—"novelty of his subject, a manufacture unknown in the European world"—in fact "loaded" it with "many difficulties," including the unfortunate fact that "terms of art to which the ear has never been accustomed have a peculiar uncouthness in poetry."[35] Grainger achieved sufficient repute to have his slight oeuvre included in the hundred-volume *British Poets* series, published in 1822. In a prefatory "Life of James Grainger," the editor, Richard Davenport, identified little to recommend the poet's most ambitious poem: "In selecting as his theme the cultivation of the sugarcane, Grainger was neither fortunate in his choice of a subject, nor of a species of poetry."[36] Davenport sees verse as an inappropriate medium for representing the new forces and relations of production. He notes Grainger's incessant invocations of the muse, whom the poet treats as a "mere servant of all work": "Whether he wishes to describe dark brick mould, or the destroying of weeds and insects . . . or the foddering . . . of mules, she is unceremoniously summoned to his assistance" (15). Yet Davenport avers: "The muses are fastidious, and cannot easily be induced to be teacher of manual processes" (13). While rural labor may once have been amenable to pastoral idealization, Davenport asks: "[By] what art is it possible to make dignified . . . the description of a merely mechanical toil, where, amidst squalor, and privation, and a mournful monotony of existence, man is degraded into something scarcely superior to the machine which is the companion and rival of his efforts[?]" (14). In 1839, another reviewer complained of the poem's "dullness and prosaicalness."[37] Four decades later, *The Sugar-Cane* was called a "curious monument of the misplaced ingenuity of the eighteenth century."[38] More recently, the passage in which the muse is made to sing of "fattening compost" (1.244)—a serious subject for Grainger, as it ensured the continued health of the soil—was included in an edition of *Very Bad Poetry*.[39]

MINERAL GEORGIC: JAGO'S *EDGE HILL*

Richard Jago, a village clergyman in Warwickshire, published *Edge Hill; or, The Rural Prospect Delineated and Moralized* in 1767. He continued to revisit the poem until his death in 1781, and in 1784 a significantly revised version was included in a collection of his complete poems. *Edge Hill* is largely a survey of Warwickshire estates, a four-book locodescriptive tour of the prosperous agrarian Midlands that begins and ends at the eponymous escarpment known not only for its sweeping prospect view but also as the site of the opening battle of the Civil War in 1642. What makes the poem extraordinary is Jago's ambition to narrate, utilizing a set of georgic and locodescriptive conventions concerned with agrarian production, the rising mineral energy economy, from its prehistory in the formation of the Earth's geologic strata, to the economic and technological conditions that shape its growth, to the future geopolitical implications of Britain's mastery of coal and iron. Book 1 includes more than 150 lines of geologic speculation, entering the debate on geogony that followed the publication of Burnet's *Sacred Theory of the Earth*. Book 3 concludes with an extended description linking the Black Country coal mines and iron foundries with the metal workshops of rapidly industrializing Birmingham.

In a preface to *Edge Hill*, Richard Jago identifies his "*Subject*": a specific "*Locality*" known for its pleasing "*Prospect*" and historical significance as the site of the first battle between Charles's forces and the Parliamentarians.[40] As it happens, Samuel Johnson traced the development of a "new scheme of poetry," the locodescriptive—concerned with "some particular landscape, to be poetically described, with the addition of such embellishments as may be supplied by historical retrospection, or incidental meditation"—to a poem published in the immediate aftermath of that battle, John Denham's *Cooper's Hill* (*Lives*, 1:59). Locodescriptive verse had grown immensely popular in the eighteenth century, offering readers a portrait of Britain's geographic variation, a national market contrasted, if also integrated, with the transoceanic trade routes of a developing global economy. Such verse, Johnson noted, was so pervasive that poets "have left scarce a corner of the island not dignified either by rhyme, or blank verse" (60). In *Edge Hill*, the circulatory logic of locodescription, an encompassing movement that follows the pathways of trade, is instantiated formally in the poem's principles of transition and association. Jago's itinerary follows, like trade itself, the course of rivers, "where Avon shapes / His winding way, enlarging as it flows / Nor hastes to join Sabrina's [the Severn's] prouder wave" (1.11–13). Such flow supplies the natural kinetic energy that mobilizes commerce, linking rural England with the "circling ocean" (2). Jago identifies his other generic inheritance with an epigraph from Virgil's *Georgics*, an apostrophe to the fertile earth of Italy highlighting his ambition to connect the present with the past, to "attempt a theme that claimed praise and skill in days of old." Cultivated land, he writes, is the "best source of wealth" (2.40): "the tillag'd plain, / Wide-waving to the sun" (38–39), the "radiant orb" (4). Both these rural descriptive genres, locodescriptive and georgic, emphasize cycles: the periodicity of seasonal patterns, the regular motion of planetary forces. Historical change is understood to be gradual, constrained by the fixed productivity of land, the expense of transport, the climatic distribution of raw materials. Because of this, there is a sense that historical conditions are legible, inscribed in the landscapes the poet surveys. As Jago writes, "from the rural landscape, [we can] learn to know / The various characters of time and place," reading in Britain's productive estates, for example, evidence of a lawful and liberal political order (1.394–95).

There is, however, a tension in each of these genres, an intuition of the volatile history that seethes below or beyond the visual surface of a carefully composed rural prospect. To till the soil is to turn up what is hidden beneath. Even if "sight is the most perfect . . . of all our senses"—as Jago's second epigraph, from Addison's *Spectator*, maintains—the perception of empirical immediacy provided by extended visual description is illusory. *Edge Hill* commences with a prospect view from Edge Hill that destabilizes the epistemological authority of sight. What the narrator gains from the "airy height" (1.37) of the escarpment's summit is not a comprehensive view of nature and human labor harmoniously intermixed but a vision of elemental confusion: "The late-trod plain looks like an inland sea, / View'd from some promontory's hoary head" (38–39). Fields appear like waves "ruffled by the southern gale" (42); trees look like ships' masts; the rural locale promised in the preface and the opening lines seems instead to be a bay harboring imperial fleets. Description is supplanted by uncanny figures that measure a haunted awareness, in a poem written in the aftermath of the Seven Years' War, that the "circling ocean" is always near. "The lab'ring sight" is already "Lost in the bright confusion" (49–50).

Thus Jago, adopting a Lucretian mandate, decides that the muse's "piercing eye" (1.475) must supplement this knowledge, revealing what "mortal ken" (484) cannot see: "earth's profoundest caverns she . . . / . . . makes visible" (481–82). As he stands atop the eponymous escarpment preparing to commence his tour, Jago speculates on the formation of the Earth's uneven topography: "ere the sweet excursion she begins, / O! listen, while, from sacred records drawn, / My daring song unfolds the cause, whence rose / This various face of things—of high, and low" (62–65). I know of no better example than Jago's geologic speculations of what Alan Liu calls the "locodescriptive moment": a sudden introduction of diachronic awareness, the "story of how things fell out in the beginning," a sense of the "metamorphic ground," an apprehension that "the earth could still move."[41] "Sacred records" refers to the mode of scripturally inspired world making popularized by Burnet. In the 1784 edition of *Edge Hill*, Jago not only thoroughly revised these passages but also included extensive notes referring to "Dr. Burnet" and his interlocutors. He takes his own system from Erasmus Warren's 1690 *Geologia*. For Warren, mountains containing cavernous reservoirs preexisted the Deluge, so that, as Jago writes, when man "with horrid crimes / Polluting earth's fair seat" is to be punished, God "loos'd the fountains of the great abyss" (1.120–21, 124). Only "one family" survived as "all the works / Of Art were swept into th' oblivious pool" (129–30). In the image of human artifacts disappearing into the dark abyss of time, their absence itself a measure of geophysical vicissitude, we see the "reciprocal engagement between antiquarianism and natural history" that Noah Heringman has identified as a condition of historicist thinking in the early Anthropocene.[42] In Jago's example, the loss of human "works" reveals the planet's cataclysmic volatility, an extension of Burnet's method of reading the Earth's history from what is displaced or broken. Jago refers to those inexplicable natural "antiquities" that materialize the forces of planetary convulsion—"Stranger-Fossils, in their inmost Bed / of . . . min'ral Strata, found" (144–45 [1767 ed.])—and identifies a problem that had come into sharp relief in an age of intensifying resource extraction: the distribution and layering of "stratum of rock, or ore, / . . . / Orb within orb, earth's secret depths contains" (107–10).[43]

The geologic observations in *Edge Hill* sketch a prehistory of planetary cataclysm that not only explains the present variations in the Earth's surface and mineral depths but also substantiates scripture's account of the conflagration to come: "Such is the structure, such the wave-worn face / Of Earth's huge fabric! . . . / . . . stor'd with wonders, to th' attentive mind / Confirming . . . / . . . / Those sacred pages, which record the past, / And awfully predict its future doom" (1.173–79). It is this rectilinear temporality, this allegory of a conclusive ending, that distinguishes sacred geology from the secular science developed in the later eighteenth century by Buffon and Hutton, which defines planetary time in terms of cyclic processes—uplift, erosion, sedimentation—of which there is, as Hutton put it, "no vestige of a beginning—no prospect of an end."[44] Yet the model of history Jago derives from his geologic conjectures as he returns to rural locodescription is closer to Hutton's desacralized cycles than to the catastrophist geoteleology explored in book 3 of Burnet's *Sacred Theory*. Jago's speculations conclude with a description of the postdiluvian hydrologic cycle, the "never-ceasing round" (1.168). As Thomson did in the final edition of *The Seasons*, Jago in his revisions replaced the waters "ascend[ing] / In secret Tubes" (165–66 [1767 ed.]) with waters "ris[ing] in vapours warm" (164), suggesting a more thorough understanding of the role evaporation plays in the hydrologic cycle.

It is in this context—that of "Nature's . . . flow" (1.439)—that we should read the first explicit reference to coal in *Edge Hill*. A system of sluices and locks had been built on the Warwickshire Avon in the mid-seventeenth century, enabling barge transport to Stratford. Jago describes the import of coal for household use: "STRATFORD her spacious magazines unfolds, / And hails th' unwieldly barge from western shores, / With . . . native ore / Of pitchy hue, to pile the fewell'd grate / In woolly stores, or husky grain repay'd" (247–51). He refers to the robust trade that had formed on the Severn and its tributaries in coal mined from the rich collieries at Coalbrookdale on the Severn Gorge, further from Stratford but more easily transported than that mined from the Black Country coalfields described in book 3.[45] Far from a subterranean wonder predicting "future doom," the "native ore," used for heating and cooking, is here contained in the "never-ceasing round," a stable historical order incorporated into a stable planetary order.

Books 1 and 2 and the first half of book 3 survey the rich estates and bustling agricultural towns of the Midlands, with occasional attention to antiquities, the "spoils of time" (2.336) that prompt meditation on what Jago calls the "fleeting forms" of historical being (333). Jago often acknowledges his preference for rural description, his reticence to tell of the "smoaky arts, taught in the dusky schools / Of Tubal's sons" (2.78–79), Tubal-Cain being the mythic founder of metalwork (as recounted in *Paradise Lost*, 11.564–74). The poet tarries long in the country before finally turning, in book 3, to scenes of "active Industry" (3.350 [1767 ed.]). Readers are led to a "dusky heath": "What? Tho' no grain, / Or herbage sweet, or waving woods adorn / Its dreary surface, yet it bears, within, / A richer treasury" (403, 405–8).[46] The interjection ("What?") signals the oddity of this transition from conventional descriptive topoi (fields, pastures, and forests)—a turn, in Wrigley's terms, from "fungible" solar flows to "consumptible" subterranean stocks. Like precious metals, Jago suggests, coal is a repository of concentrated, unrealized wealth. Indeed, his description of colliery development— "Here many a merchant turns adventurer" (413)—offers the poem's single reference to speculative investment, the nascent model of futurity, of risk and return, that underwrites capital ventures like sugar plantations and coal mines, at least for those speculators able to recognize the latent wealth hidden "beneath a rude, unsightly form," "here useless, like the miser's brighter hoard" (409, 432).[47]

There is a similar apprehension of a law of value and hidden surplus abstracted from sun and soil in Jago's lack of specificity about the location of the coalfields, a notable oversight in a locodescriptive poem otherwise always precise about named locales. The description of mining comes between the remembrance of Solihull, several miles to the southeast of Birmingham, and the discussion of Birmingham itself. Though there were active collieries in the east of Warwickshire around Coventry, Jago implies a direct geographic connection between coal mining, iron mining and smelting, and Birmingham metal manufacturing, which was largely fueled by the South Staffordshire coalfields. That Jago describes the coal as destined for both household and manufacturing use—"Thus the grim ore, / Here useless, like the miser's brighter hoard, / Is from its prison brought, and sent abroad, / The frozen hours to cheer, to minister / To needful sustenance, and polish'd arts" (3.431–35)—does little to clarify the issue. This absence of geographic reference may reflect the logic of spatial abstraction instantiated by the mineral energy regime. As Andreas Malm explains, fossil capitalism facilitated the production of "abstract space": "By virtue of being concentrated in subterranean sites of no other use or meaning, coal could be brought into the world of earthlings as loose fragments . . . circulating freely inside the commodity circuits and releasing the forces of accumulation."[48] When Jago's narrator travels underground—charting the process whereby the "sable rock inflammable" is raised to the surface, "from its prison brought, and sent abroad" (496, 433)—he shifts attention from the absolute space of agricultural production and mercantile commerce to the abstract space of fossil capitalism.

What Jago's account of the mines lacks in terms of geographic specificity it makes up for in technical depictions of test boring, mine construction, the division and culture of labor, and the technologies that were transforming British coal mining.[49] "A cunning artist tries the latent soil" (3.422) is how Jago represents speculative test boring, "a highly skilled craft . . . undertaken by specialized teams," the techniques for which had been developed in the early eighteenth century (see Flinn, *History of the British Coal Industry*, 70–72). Jago details the process of building a mine (426–29) and the division of labor between the hewers who cut the coal loose and the putters who bring it the surface (429–31). He identifies the horrific conditions of mine labor, attributing the imperative to work underground not to economic necessity but to "the force of Custom's pow'rful laws!" (439). He also describes two novel technologies, each of which found a practical application for Boyle's recognition of atmospheric weight: "Philosophy two curious arts supplies, / To drain th' imprison'd air, and, in its place, / More pure convey, or, with impetuous force, / To raise the gath'ring torrents from the deep (447–50). The first invention is the ventilation bellows designed by Stephen Hales. The second is the atmospheric engine developed by the ironmonger Thomas Newcomen and first employed at the Coneygree Coal

Works near Dudley Castle in South Staffordshire. A machine less iconic but no less significant than Watt's double-acting engine, the Newcomen directly exhibits energy conversion: the fact that, channeled through the engine, coal can drive a piston and produce what was an unprecedented amount of sustained mechanical power. While it is not the first technology to convert combustion into pressure into kinesis—that would be the musket or the cannon—the Newcomen can be regarded as the inceptive Anthropocene technology because of the way it generates an energy surplus, a condition of autocatalytic systemic amplification.[50] By pumping water from mines and so opening deeper shafts, the Newcomen combusts coal to enable the extraction of more coal. In his description of the engine's workings—"its influence owes to air / By cold, and heat alternate now condens'd, / Now rarefied" (455–57)—however, Jago stresses its familiarity. He includes the first of five notes in Latin, recalling relevant passages in the *Georgics*, in this case Virgil's description, in the famed storm sequence, of modulations in atmospheric pressure: Jove "thickens what just now was rare, and makes rare what now was thick" (*Georgics*, 129). The reference is not entirely infelicitous. The Newcomen drew on the counterintuitive discovery that atmosphere has weight and so could perform the physical work of pushing a piston to the bottom of a vacated cylinder. A coal-fired boiler produces steam, which fills a cylinder; the steam is cooled by water, producing a vacuum, which allows the piston to return to the bottom of the cylinder by the force of atmospheric pressure. As Jago writes: "how seeming weak, in act how powerful" (458).

What is notable about this representation is not only that Jago overlooks the actual prime mover of the Newcomen, coal combustion, but also that for the first time since the epigraph he directly invokes the *Georgics*, calling on the literary past as a precedent for the present.[51] He does this four more times in book 3, in the descriptions of iron smelting and manufacturing. Like Dyer and Grainger, he appeals most actively to generic continuity precisely when he attempts to represent novel conditions of production, which may express an intuition that, like the industrializing city, the mines—fed by speculative investment, made efficient by new technology—constitute a disconcerting new energy regime not easily integrated into the fixed horizons of eighteenth-century political economy or millennia-old genres of agrarian labor.

That something like an "energy unconscious"—an anxious awareness of a novel energy economy that cannot be fully integrated into inherited frames of reference—is active here becomes evident in the next sequence, the culminating description of the coal mines.[52] Jago depicts firedamp—the explosive mixture of coal dust and methane—as an accelerating, self-amplifying conflagration:

> But who that fiercer element can rule?
> When, in the nitrous cave, the kindling flame,
> By pitchy vapours fed, from cell to cell,
> With fury spreads, and *the wide fewell'd earth*,
> Around, with greedy joy, receives the blaze
> By its own entrails nourish'd, like those mounts
> Vesuvian, or Ætnean, still it wastes,
> And still new fewel for its rapine finds
> *Exhaustless.* (461–69; my emphasis)

His language of combustive intensification, of a planet primed to burn, echoes not only Milton's depiction of Hell—for example, "thundering Etna, whose combustible / And fueled entrails thence conceiving fire, / Sublimed with mineral fury, aid the winds" (*Paradise Lost*, 1.233–35)—but also Burnet's startling prophecy in *The Sacred Theory of the Earth*, a touchstone for Jago. In the third book, Burnet had speculated about the material causes of the final conflagration, asking: "Where are the Seeds of this universal Fire, or fewel sufficient for the nourishing of it?" (240).[53] He solved the problem of the Earth's "dissolution" in a manner analogous to his solution to the problem of the Deluge. What corresponds to "the fountains of the great deep," hidden beneath the Earth's crust, is the mineral reserve, "subterraneous store-houses of Fire": "hidden invisible Materials within the Veins of the Earth; Such are all Minerals . . . that are igniferous" (277). In Jago's language of intensifying flame and exhaustless fuel we catch a glimpse of cataclysmic latency, a demonic principle of change harbored in the Earth's mineral reserve. Yet, as in the prophecy of "future doom" in book 1, the vision of catastrophic potential in "the wide fewell'd earth" is quickly sidestepped as the poet's gaze shifts to another scene of production, the Black Country iron smelters.

In his depiction of iron smelting, Jago is vague about the fuel that fires "the furnace's impetuous rage" (3.500). In the 1750s and 1760s, forge masters had begun developing new methods for replacing charcoal with coal in smelting and refining iron. A "sharp upturn" in the domestic production of pig iron—so-called because its "mazy moulds" were thought to resemble nursing piglets—and the development of a workable iron bar contributed significantly to the rapid midcentury growth of Birmingham manufacturing.[54] In linking the coal and iron mines of the Black Country with the smelters and smithies of the industrial city—"Soon o'er thy furrowed pavement, Bremicham! / Ride the loose bars" (512–13)—Jago characterizes an emerging network, a loop between capital expenditure, fossil-resource extraction, industrial processing, and manufacturing. In the very year that Jago first published *Edge Hill*, Parliament passed the Birmingham Canal Act, authorizing construction of a canal linking Birmingham with the Black Country, the completion of which significantly reduced transportation costs, almost halving the price of coal.

Jago identifies the specific technical challenge of refining iron with coal, producing "malleable ore" (3.517), "ductile Ore . . . ready to obey / The Workman's Will, and take its destined Form" (516–18 [1767 ed.]). And he is explicit about coal's place in the workshops where knives and scissors, buttons and buckles, rings and "letter'd type" ("the poet's pride") were being manufactured (567–68). Enumerating the variety of metalwork produced in Birmingham, he comes up against a representational limit, a definitive phenomenon of industrial modernity, the ever-expanding multitude of commodities, familiarized with another Virgilian reference. He asks "who can count the forms / That hourly from the glowing embers rise[?]" (551–52): "what art / Can, in the scanty bounds of measur'd verse, / Display the treasure of a thousand mines / To wond'rous shapes by stubborn labour wrought?" (554–57). Virgil had found himself unable to catalog all the vines of Italy: "there is no numbering—nor, indeed, is the numbering worth the pains" (*Georgics*, 143). Jago's reference to Virgil masks a significant contrast, however. The passage in the *Georgics* leads to an assertion of natural limits: "Nor yet can all soils bear all fruits"; "trees have their allotted climes" (145). What produces the sublime variety of metal commodities is, by contrast, the ductility of the ore subject to human refashioning. For Virgil, representation is inadequate to natural variation; for Jago, it is the human capacity to remake nature, in producing what in *Capital* Marx called an "immense collection of commodities," that strains poetic representation.

Though sublimely unrepresentable in their variety, these finished forms of iron animate Jago's culminating apostrophe: "Hail, native British Ore! / For thine is trade, that with its various stores, / Sails round the world, and visits ev'ry clime, / And makes the treasures of each clime her own" (3.626–29). In addressing iron, not the "parent fires" (554) and the labor that enable iron's metamorphoses, Jago overlooks the fuel, the role of Britain's other "native ore." In fact, Britain's growing global "manufacturing and commercial supremacy" was premised on a particular form of unequal exchange, in which, as Debeir, Deleage, and Hemery put it, "industrial goods produced with increasing flows of fossil energy were traded for imported agricultural goods" (*In the Servitude of Power*, 96). Britain, in essence, exchanged its underground energy "stocks" for the labor and produce of other countries. Jago misses this condition of unequal exchange, but he does notice something significant. Contrasting British iron, "real wealth" (3.603), with the precious metals of the New World mines, he foresees the possibility of unending accumulation, the transcendence of fixed limits to growth. Silver and gold are valued according to their "outward form," their "sparkling" surfaces (576–78). In the Birmingham workshops, by contrast, the "malleable ore" is given shape, transformed, producing plows and horseshoes, planes and chisels, spades and combs. Iron is not only a raw material that can, within a given mode of production, be transformed into various commodities. Iron tools and weapons themselves alter the conditions of production and circulation. "The sounding axe," for instance, turns "gloomy forests" into cultivated fields (617). There were emerging markets for Britain's ironwork—the early historian of Birmingham, William Hutton, ascribed its "rapid increase" to its cultivation of "the foreign market"—but, in Jago's formulation, it is iron that secures those markets.[55] It is here that Jago offers his most vivid prophecy, a prospect of the future—imperial and secular rather than eschatological—as the addressee shifts from native iron to the Britain nation itself: "ply / Your Iron arts, and rule the vanquish'd world" (605–6).[56] Birmingham was well-known for its weaponry: "The glitt'ring faulchion, and the thund'ring tube! /At whose tremendous gleam, and volley'd fire, / Barbarian kings fly from their useless hoards, / And yield them all to thy superior pow'r" (635–38). Notably, Jago had earlier compared subterranean coal with "the miser's brighter hoard" (432). The "useless hoards" of foreign nations, not yet circulating on the global market, are, like subterranean minerals, a manifestation of unexploited reserve. In this prophecy of unbounded expansion, Jago reconceptualizes political economy. As Britain gains access to coal and colonies, accumulation is no longer constrained by the fixed supply of land and the variable flow of solar rays.

In the poem's final book, Jago returns to the more familiar ground of the solar energy economy. The four books of *Edge Hill* are structured around the Earth's internal rotation, the diurnal rhythm. At the beginning of the final book, Jago acknowledges that what "the morning-sun, or noon-tide ray," had, in the first two books, "distinctly mark'd," the "meridian blaze" of book 3 illumined "more confus'dly" (4.18–20). Book 4, set at dusk, returns to the legible domain of the Earth's surface, the country estate "whose champaigns wide / With plenteous harvests wave" (193–94) Yet "descriptive song" once again finds an insufficiency in "the surfaces of things" (221, 231). A plowman turns up artifacts buried in the soil, remnants from the

Battle of Edge Hill. With the hope of ensuring "future peace" (399), Jago of-
fers a nonpartisan recounting of this inconclusive battle. The crescendo is
a scene of abstracted violence orchestrated by a personified "Death": "on
the cannon's brazen orb / He . . . with fatal aim, / Involves whole squad-
rons in the sulph'rous storm" (489–91). A century later, all that remains in
the "monumental mould" are weapons and bones (511): "as the plowman
breaks the clotted glebe, / He . . . some trophy finds / . . . rusty spear, / Or
canker'd ball" (513–16). No reader would have missed this Virgilian allu-
sion, which has to do less with exhuming or burying "history in nature,"
as Alan Liu reads the georgic motif (Wordsworth, 19–20), than with a meta-
bolic inseparability between history and nature. To till the soil is to channel
planetary forces in the service of civilizational ends. It is also to turn up
what is hidden beneath. The work of the plow, of the driver and his draft
animals, furrowing the soil, like the work of the foundries and smithies
that once produced the cannon and the ball, continues even as it redirects
a process of planetary work. Perhaps a literary artifact like Edge Hill is not
unlike the weapons turned up in the "monumental mould," all instances
of time's "fleeting forms" that, in what remains of a shape through which
energy once coursed, hint at the broader forces of history, the channeling
and the conversion of energy, whether in a field or a factory, an engine or a
musket, the oceans or the planetary atmosphere.

Despite the novelty of its subject, as the first poem and one of few poems
to offer a sustained description of the new mode of production associated
with the Industrial Revolution, Edge Hill has received little critical atten-
tion. The first reviewers treated it as yet another rural topographical poem,
barely commenting on book 3. An unsympathetic review in the Monthly
Review began: "That poetry which is employed in rural description lies
under many disadvantages. Though there is a variety, there is, likewise, an
uniformity in the works of nature, which renders it difficult to embellish
such subjects with images that have not been exhibited by former writ-
ers."[57] The Critical Review was no more enthusiastic. While noting echoes
of Thomson and Milton, the reader reported that the very "locality of the
subject" lacked the necessary "warmth and animated colouring" to engage
the imagination. Descriptive poetry, in its very commitment to the par-
ticular, had lost any claim to speak of the general, as the reviewer noticed
in identifying a contradiction between the "abstracted nature" of "moral
truths" and the attempt to illustrate them "by objects of the senses."[58] The
Annual Register of 1767 saw fit to quote the four pages from Edge Hill
in which Jago represents coal mining and metal manufacturing, and the

entry for "Birmingham," "the greatest manufacturing town in England," in the 1819 *Cyclopaedia* cites a twelve-line passage from *Edge Hill*, beginning "The noise, and hurry all," in order to acquaint the "stranger and foreigner" with "the general character of this place."[59] The most notable characteristic of *Edge Hill*'s reception is the sheer absence of notice, popular or critical. The poem has a strong claim to offer the first extended poetic description of the definitive energy transition of modernity, and it links that description with unusually precise and extended geologic speculations. That it has hardly been read tells us more about what we expect of poetry than about its quality or noteworthiness. Indeed, while *The Fleece* and *The Sugar-Cane* have each in recent years been republished in well-annotated editions and have received significant scholarly notice, *Edge Hill* has never been reprinted and has received minimal attention from literary historians.

CHAPTER FOUR

Uncertain Atmospheres: Romantic Lyricism in the Time of the Anthropocene

LYRICIZING GEOHISTORY

Writing in 1836, Robert Southey deemed *The Task* (1785) "more popular than any other poem of equal length in the English language." Cowper's recasting of georgic as the poet's search for a meaningful vocation found such a receptive audience because, according to Southey, Cowper enlivens natural description with subjective presence, foregrounding the thinking, feeling self that counterintuitively brings the poem closer to wild nature. The "descriptive parts," Southey observes, "bore evidence of a thoughtful mind . . . ; and the moral sentiment which pervaded them, gave a charm in which descriptive poetry is often wanting. The best didactic poems, when compared with the Task, are like formal gardens in comparison with woodland scenery." Southey's analogy echoes Cowper's own account of the poem's unifying theme, which Southey quotes: "If the work cannot boast a regular plan . . . it may yet boast that the reflections are naturally suggested always by the preceding passage; and that . . . the whole had one tendency,—to discountenance the modern enthusiasm after a London life, and to recommend rural ease and leisure as friendly to the cause of piety and virtue." Southey, however, does not entirely accept the poet's claim about lessons in rural virtue, proposing a different interpretation of the poem's unifying principle and resonance with readers: "Cowper himself, perhaps, was not aware of what it was that supplied the place of plan, and with happier effect that the most skillful plan could have produced. . . . In the Task . . . the reader feels that the poet is continually present; he becomes intimately acquainted with him, and this it is which gives to this delightful poem its unity and its peculiar charm."[1]

This final chapter offers a geohistorical perspective on a problem that has been central to the formation of historical poetics, the field of romanticism, and literary studies itself: lyricization and, specifically, what Clifford Siskin calls the shift from the "georgic-descriptive hierarchy of forms" to a "lyricized hierarchy."[2] Of the three blank-verse descriptive poems I discuss— Cowper's *The Task* (1785), Wordsworth's "Tintern Abbey" (1798), and Charlotte Smith's "Beachy Head" (1807)—only "Tintern Abbey" makes a claim to be "lyrical," being the concluding poem in *Lyrical Ballads*. All three, however, have been read lyrically in the manner Southey reads *The Task*, the heightened presence of an autobiographical narratorial persona providing the measure of their historical novelty, importance, and popular resonance. In this chapter, I argue that, as a modal pressure that remakes inherited genres, romantic lyricization provides a solution to the crisis in description discussed in chapter 3, much as descriptive naturalism emerged as a counterpressure to the symbolic temporality of sacred history in Miltonic allegory.

Like the novel, and unlike other verse modes, lyric invites a theory because its development, or at least its claim to literary preeminence, is coextensive with modernization. In his lectures on aesthetics (1818–29, published 1835), Hegel contrasted the lyric, as a distinctly "modern form," with the ancient epic. While epic poetry, the "oldest" of the genres, derives from the "need to listen to something which is unfolded as an independent and self-complete totality, objective over against the subject," the lyric expresses an imperative to apprehend the "mind in its own self-expression," the "inwardness of mood or reflection."[3] Epic expands, while lyric concentrates. Though the lyric poet may "incorporate the natural environment [or] locality," Hegel observes, such external conditions—the exigencies of time and place—are regarded as secondary: "The proper *unity* of the lyric is not provided by the occasion and its objective reality but by the poet's inner movement of soul and his way of treating his subject" (1119). A poetry organized around "the inwardness of mood or reflection," Hegel maintains, will flourish only in societies that "have achieved a more or less complete organization of human relationships" (1123).

The Frankfurt school critics, in turn, read lyricization as an expression not of the maturation of the nation-state but of the accelerated temporality and reifying grasp of industrial capitalism. For Benjamin, as I discussed in the introduction, the lyric evocation of ritual time, however retrospective and nostalgic, serves as a counterweight to the "alienating, blinding experience of the age of large-scale industrialism," allowing the poem to register in the stimuli and speed of modern life the "disintegration of the aura" ("Motifs in Baudelaire," 314, 343). Adorno reads the lyric's retreat into interiority as a protest against generalized commodification. "The lyric spirit's idiosyncratic opposition to the superior power of material things," he writes, "is a form of reaction to the reification of the world, to the domination of human beings by commodities that had developed since the beginning of the modern era, since the industrial revolution became the dominant force in life."[4] In *Aesthetic Theory*, Adorno attributed the modern love of natural beauty, which is so often the subject of the lyric, to similar conditions. It is our experience of a fully "objectified world"—in which the mark of the human is pervasive—that underlies the modern preoccupation with natural beauty, the imperative to seek "consolation in first nature," to step "out into the open," to take "a breath of fresh air."[5]

Even for critics whom we might call *lyric readers*, the lyric, however triumphant its appearance, is approached as a historical problem, a modal transition. For M. H. Abrams, "the Greater Romantic lyric"—defined by the "free flow of consciousness, the interweaving of thought, feeling, and perceptual detail, and the easy naturalness of the speaking voice"—is "the earliest Romantic formal invention."[6] What Abrams's account shares with Southey's reading of *The Task* is a narrative of literary history in which the "local poem," or "descriptive" poetry, is lyricized. Subjective response replaces the "landscape as the center of poetic interest" (90). The lyricization of topographical and georgic verse is a solution to the problem of description's "want of method," the absence of a principle that would coordinate its varied "images," its tendency, as Donald Wesling puts it, toward "sheer aggregation."[7] Descriptive poetry discovers justification for transition and resolution in the external world, an infinitely various planetary economy connecting the works of nature with human labor. Lyricization, by contrast, allows the poet's own consciousness, however divided or diffuse, to organize the poem's expansion and contraction.

Lyric criticism, in and beyond romanticism, has developed as a particularly reflexive avenue of metacommentary, interrogating the modern reading and teaching practices organized around an understanding of lyric as the paradigm of poetry.[8] Decades before the appearance of a school of "historical poetics" organized, in part around a critique of "lyric reading," historicist-minded romanticists began questioning triumphalist accounts of the lyric, even if, as Siskin observes, no amount of historicization can counter the "hegemonic" association of lyric with romantic aesthetics because this association is constitutive of romanticism. Recent scholarship has significantly deepened our understanding of the range, context, and social work of romantic-era lyric. Rachel Crawford, for example, characterizes the lyric tendency toward compression and containment as a preexisting "bedrock that was jolted to the surface by a seismic shift in public perception that took place during the final quarter of the century," after Britain's defeat in the American War of Independence.[9] Other scholars, expanding on the Frankfurt school's dialectical approach, identify lyricization with the assertion of a particularized subjectivity, haunted by an awareness of economic exchangeability and performing a redemptive self-making that can be contrasted with the alienation of industrial labor or even staging a communitarian commitment through the very conventionality of subjective expression.[10]

To read lyricization as responding to a geohistorical pressure registered in descriptive poetry, as I do here, is to suggest a genealogy of lyric that begins not with Sappho's fragments, or with the formal compression and subjective orientation of the ode or the sonnet, but with Virgil's *Georgics*, in which, in book 2, having addressed his nominal audience ("O farmers"), the poet for the first time offers himself as a subject of attention: "But as for me" (171). Virgil calls on the muse to support his Lucretian ambition to discern nature's hidden forces before accepting a less expansive mandate: "But if the chill blood about my heart bar me from reaching those realms of nature, let my delight be the country, and the running streams amid the dells—may I love the waters and the woods, though I be unknown to fame" (171). This is a difficult and perhaps disingenuous passage since Virgil's practical-minded georgic didacticism splits the difference between cosmologic speculation and pastoral love of the countryside. I have already shown how Addison and Thomson invoke this passage. With these examples in mind, we might identify the lyric not as a realized genre but as a modal strategy within description, one in which a predicament is acknowledged, an interruption of the poet's claim to narrate or describe, the solution of which is to foreground the poet's own situation as a condition of poetic labor, knowledge, or desire.

In the *Georgics*, it is not the corruption and violence of the human-made world—the court, the city, or the empire—that engenders the fantasy of pastoral escape, as it often is in the *Eclogues*. Nature, the inexorable forces described by atomic philosophy as well as the oppressive climate that is the most immediate instance of our embodied susceptibility to those forces, is the real against which poetry produces its compensatory ideals. Similar pressures shape romantic-era poems, the existence of a difficult reality located not in society, however naturalized, but in nature itself. Yet, more often in the poems I discuss in this chapter, the impasse that suspends description, stalling the return from inwardness to worldly knowing, is an experience of temporal division and epistemological uncertainty related to modernization and the disconcerting indistinguishability of natural givens and the human-made. In chapter 2, I explored how Thomson aligns planetary and human history within a descriptive poetics concerned with the flows of solar energy, a synthesis that required him to exclude the productive forces embodied in coal-polluted London. The industrial georgic poets, discussed in chapter 3, invoke the muse and literary antecedents when confronted with socioecological contradictions no longer safely contained in the metropole. For the three poets treated in this chapter, the contrast between the country and the city was growing even more difficult to sustain as evidence of a new and disconcerting energy regime became omnipresent, even in the air itself. Rather than calling on the muse, the romantic poet draws attention to his or her own constrained positionality and incertitude.

The final decades of the eighteenth century were a period of unprecedented economic expansion, associated especially, as Dyer had predicted, with the growth of manufacturing exports. Total industrial production doubled in the final two decades of the eighteenth century, and foreign trade tripled. As Harold Perkins writes of the period between 1783 and 1802: "These years spanned the central phase of a transition which was to carry the British economy from a lower to a higher plane of productiveness, and create the framework for a modern industrial system."[11] Whether or not this period can be retrospectively identified in terms of the beginning of self-sustaining growth and a decoupling of economic cycles from planetary vicissitudes, for observers on the ground it was marked by a return of climatic disorder. The very decade, the 1780s, that has been identified with the first boom/bust cycle of the industrial stage of capitalist development was also the first decade since the 1740s and 1690s when sustained climatic disruptions caused significant social upheaval and dearth in Britain and Europe.[12] The years 1781 and 1782 saw a return of the wet summers and frigid winters that had caused such turmoil in those earlier decades. Then in 1783, with the eruption of the Icelandic volcano Laki, a sulfurous fog descended on Europe, bringing a scorching summer—in central England, July was the warmest month in the 320-year temperature record—followed by a glacial winter. The year 1785 recorded the coldest March ever, and 1788 was one of the driest years in the 250 years for which there are precipitation records (Lamb, *Climate, History and the Modern World*, 237–38). In France, drought and another atypically cold winter in 1788–89 caused escalating food costs, contributing to political instability and, finally, revolution.[13] The eruptions of Laki and then of Tambora in 1815, John Brooke observes, temporarily recreated "the harsher world of the Little Ice Age" (*Climate Change*, 470).

It is now a commonplace that this age of revolutions brought about a heightened sense of historicity, a new experience of living in historical times or modern times, an awareness of what Wordsworth called "a multitude of causes unknown to former times."[14] However, any such sense of history in process, of a present defined by its break with the past or its uncertain relation to the future, whether attributed to industrialization and accelerating economic growth, an unprecedented expansion of media, the ferment of political revolution, or secularization, would have existed in unreconciled tension with an experience of the stochastic temporality of planetary disorder. Emily Rohrbach proposes that "mist" offered romantic-era writers a particularly resonant figure for the experience of being unable to "fully know the historical dimensions of the age in which they were living," particularly in its relation to "an unknown and unpredictable time, yet to come."[15] Tom Ford also identifies this "period's emergent sense of historical specificity" with its increasingly sophisticated language of atmosphere, given specificity by the new sciences of weather, atmospheric chemistry, and respiratory physiology.[16] I have, in this book, tracked a longer history of air as an auratic medium of poetic inspiration and imaginative flight. I agree with Ford's point that, at the end of the eighteenth century, in this period of accelerating industrialization, air comes to bear the elusive impress of "modernity's own constitutive vagueness and urgency, its paradoxical blend of categorical imperatives and affective and cognitive disorientations" (13–14). I want to suggest, however, that this atmospheric reflexivity reflects not only literature's dialogue with science but also an experience of the air itself. What gave the present its atmosphere of uncertainty was not mist so much as smog.

To interpret the misty, mystifying, mystified romantic atmospheres and the displaced geohistoricity of the romantic lyric as examples of the climatological unconscious, as I do in this chapter, is to return to the sort of Althusserian reading against which Jonathan Bate and Karl Kroeber reacted. If these early ecocritics seemed, in turn, to recapitulate certain forms of the romantic ideology, ecocriticism has in recent decades revitalized our sense of romanticism's unrealized possibilities and untimely afterlives, including forms of planetary awareness—and unawareness—valuable because they are less familiar than a Wordsworthian love of nature. In *Natures in Translation*, Alan Bewell shows that "natures" in the romantic period were less local than cosmopolitan, less a site of retreat than a means of following the global lineaments of empire: of exchange and circulation, translation and comparison. From Noah Heringman's study of romantic rocks to Amanda Jo Goldstein's recovery of a Lucretian "poetic materialism," scholars have shown how romantic writers engaged science in ways that showcased the affordances of literary form and figure to mediate the deep time and emergent properties of planetary history.[17] David Higgins, Gillen D'Arcy Wood, and others have focused on the extraordinary cultural response to the global climate change and social disruption brought about by the massive Tambora eruption.[18] Other scholars have identified detranscendentalized, if not always secularized, intimations of disastrous possibility, precarity, and extinction in this period as an outgrowth of geologic catastrophism and early industrialization.[19] Indeed, the central socioecological paradox of this period is the appearance of a new historical pessimism, a sense of depletion or immanent crisis coincident with the radical expansion of productive power enabled by empire and industry. Malthus's *Essay on the Principle of Population* (1798) is the most acute manifestation of this paradox, a theory of inescapable environmental limit written just as Britain appeared to have escaped long-standing energy constraints. Malthusian demography, in turn, justified a biopolitical sovereignty organized around the management of a growing but precarious human population.[20] Anne-Lise François sees a new apprehension of risk in this period, such that even avoidance or repair can produce an unintended "response or counterpunch that, far from averting the disaster, disseminates and distributes it."[21] François and Anahid Nersessian have each articulated immensely compelling challenges to maximalist romanticism, discovering an ecological aesthetics and politics based on acknowledgment of finitude and precarity, a staging of recessive action or curtailment, what Nersessian calls a "utopian doing-with-less."[22]

François asks whether lyric might itself offer a distinctly versatile representational medium for assembling the diverse temporalities of an anthropogenic epoch: "To what extent does the formalization of scale variance and of the play of different techniques for condensing and extending, slowing and accelerating time, which goes by the name of 'lyric,' anticipate and even neutralize the shock of the Anthropocene?"[23] She invokes the principle of lyric time first articulated by Sharon Cameron, who in her reading of Emily Dickinson showcased the lyric's power to suspend, multiply, dilate, and transcend time.[24] Rachel Crawford offers a prehistory of such lyric time in the very poetic archive this book has examined, identifying "lyric moments"— defined by their "extracability" from "context"—in eighteenth-century descriptive long poems (*Poetry, Enclosure, and the Vernacular Landscape*, 177). That she refers to these as "embowered episodes," however, returns us to the alternative genealogy of lyricism I have already identified. For poets from Virgil to Thomson, the retreat offered by the forest bower, as lyric recess, was an escape not from history but from summer heat.[25]

As a way of understanding the cultural resonance of lyric time we might recall Andreas Malm's argument that societies organized around "the flow of energy" are distinctly bound to "absolute" time and space. The transition to fossil fuels facilitates spatiotemporal "abstraction"; mineral energy stands "outside of time," "cut off from diurnal, seasonal, historical, and even civilizational time" (*Fossil Capital*, 42). The subjective correlative of the abstract space-time of carbon modernity, generated in the "closed system" of the "steel-enclosed heat engine," is, as Nigel Clark and Bronislaw Szerszynski explain, an understanding of the individual as enclosed and self-moving, defined by "psychic closure from wider energetic flows."[26] In other words, a material analogue of the romantic lyric self is the steam engine, an energy converter independent of the ambient energy circulating in the environment, a technology that fully encloses the process of conversion within a secret interior that cannot operate and be visible at the same time. The abstraction of time and space under fossil capitalism intensifies, to the point of qualitative difference, a way of thinking about nature's plasticity as energy input because fossil-powered energy conversion is separate from the climatic energy in the environment, the flow of light, water, and wind. It is no wonder then that Milton's Satan has often been identified as a precursor to the egotistical sublime of the romantic lyric self.

Romantic lyricization expresses an emergent experience of the self as internal and insulated, defined by energetic closure. Yet, when this self turns to the world, she or he finds no satisfying objective correlative, no knowable history written in the landscape, no inspiring air. I would like to propose, then, that the lyric turn, including what Ford calls "Romantic lyric poetry's distinctive claims to transhistorical agency" (*Wordsworth and the Poetics of Air*, 3), can be understood as evidence of growing access at the end of the eighteenth century to fossil energy and the abstraction from concrete space-time it enables. This would offer us a different take on Siskin's account of the alignment of critical and poetic interest in the rise of lyric as the mode with which "man reconstituted himself as the modern psychologized subject: a mind, capable of limitless growth" (*Historicity*, 11). I would not hang my entire argument on such a hypothesis, but I do wonder whether we might see this "limitless growth" as the psychological correlate of the economic expansion unleashed by capitalism as a world ecology, including fossil capitalism, just as we might see the decontextualized temporalities of the lyric as expressions of industrial modernity's (apparent) transcendence of concrete time. In turn, as the dominant productive forces in society migrate from the field and the forests to the factories and the furnaces, it becomes possible to see nature as dematerialized, a source of spiritual succor that can compensate for the alienation of the commodified world. "Tintern Abbey" provides my surest evidence for this argument. The poem crystallizes and its reception consolidates a broader cultural transformation (including the invention of the romantic lyric) that is less complete in the two other poems I discuss. *The Task* and "Beachy Head" are more divided, modally, than "Tintern Abbey" and ultimately less confident in their allegorization of the landscape and in the psychological compensations the love of nature might offer. In these poems, the lyricization of description expresses the uncertainty of a world out of joint.

THE "PRESENT OBFUSCATION": CLIMATE AND THE POET'S CALLING IN COWPER'S *TASK*

In a June 13, 1783, letter to John Newton, his close friend and fellow Evangelical, William Cowper reflects on whether one can recognize the onset of the end times. He alludes to Isaiah's prophecies concerning the events that precede the last day, which begin: "Beware, the Lord is about to strip the earth, split it and turn it upside down, and scatter its inhabitants" (Isa. 24:1). Remarking on the "singularity of the present season," he wonders how one can distinguish millennial presages from meteorologic extremes within regular seasonal cycles.[27] Earthquakes had devastated southern Italy in the spring, and in Cowper's Buckinghamshire village of Olney the June weather had taken a turn eerily reminiscent of Isaiah's apocalyptic prophecies: "The earth dries up and withers" (Isa. 24:4). "The fogs," Cowper writes, "continue, though 'till yesterday the Earth was as dry as intense Heat could make it" (2.143). "The moon will grow pale and the sun hide its face in shame" (Isa. 24:23), according to the prophet. In Olney, the sun rises and sets "without his rays, and hardly shines at noon even in a cloudless sky," and the moon is "the colour of heated brick," an effect of a "misty atmosphere" unlike any in "remembrance." Calling his perspective "perfectly Scriptural," Cowper decides that, while "some will look for" Judgment Day "at one period and some at another," there is no point in seeking signs of its imminence. There will be no meteorologic premonitions because the Last Judgment constitutes a total interruption of nature's spatiotemporal continuity, an apocalyptic unveiling recognizable only on "the day itself." (*Letters*, 2:143).

Over the next year, as he composed the six-book georgic *The Task* (1785), Cowper continued to ask what the weather—a summer of scorching heat and noxious haze followed by the coldest winter in memory—might reveal about an uncertain present. As he wrote his poem of "modern times," what troubled him was not the inevitable approach of the End, which he expected any day, but the possibility that the very means of keeping time, of recognizing what endures and what gives way, were being lost.[28] *The Task* is marked by the uncertainties and anxieties of a modern climate, a sky that has lost its capacity to signify. In his 1967 study of eschatology as narrative form, Frank Kermode observes that the Greeks distinguished between *chronos*, time's steady succession, and *kairos*, "the season, a point in time filled with significance, charged with a meaning derived from its relation to the end."[29] Like the French *temps*, *kairos* refers to time and weather, indexing an etymological connection between temporal perception and meteorologic periodicity. In modernity, according to Kermode, "perpetual crisis," reckoned in chronological time, supplants both the punctuations of *kairos* and an "apocalypticism" that anticipates the End as an "imminent historical event" (27–28). In a year of atmospheric disturbance, in an age of temporal acceleration, Cowper, I argue, grappled with the insufficiency of *chronos* as a measure of crisis, as a means of apprehending the unique conditions of the present.

Jameson identifies temporal self-reflexivity, the hallmark of modernist aesthetics he calls "sensitivity to deep time," as reflecting a "comparativist perception" of contrasting rural and urban "socioeconomic temporalities."[30] Unlike the modernist writers who lived in London but retained experience of seasonal rhythms and dilatory rural time, Cowper, writing in the 1780s, witnessed the incipient stages of modernization—mercantile imperialism, urbanization, enclosure, and industrialization—from a rural village. Like the modernists, he was profoundly alert to variable speeds, durations, and time scales as well as what Mary Favret calls "time's utterance," the perceptual and representational measures that make time articulate.[31] Indeed, in a letter to Newton he deemed himself an "Œconomist of time" (*Letters*, 2:186). As Favret and Kevis Goodman have shown, *The Task* is a poem preoccupied with temporal forms and figures, particularly with the challenge of representing historical eventfulness.[32] Building on their insights, I suggest that Cowper understood "modern times" as a structure of temporal consciousness characterized by the intensification of present awareness and short-term expectation. In *The Task*, he contrasts the disordered temporality of the modern metropole with several modes of climatic time: cumulative experience within a stable, if not always pleasant, English climate; the georgic synchronization of human cultivation with recurrent seasonal cycles; and a providential or prophetic hermeneutics that looks to the atmosphere for signs of divine judgment. Yet he is, I argue, unable to escape modernity's temporal disorientation. The heat and sulfuric haze he describes in his June 1783 reflections on eschatology had, we now know, a natural cause, the massive eruption of the Icelandic volcano Laki. As he composed

The Task, however, Cowper came to regard the atmospheric turmoil as a symptom of modern times. The climatic measures with which he sought to record the passing historical moment themselves seemed occluded, as if the calendar was changing according to a hidden logic. "The weather is an exact emblem of my mind in its present state," he wrote to Newton in January 1784. "A thick fog envelops every thing" (*Letters*, 2:200).

Much is revealed about the ascendance of empirical meteorology when a poet as saturnine as Cowper, writing to his most devout friend, reacted to the biblical weather of June 1783 by designating himself "a great Observer of natural appearances, but . . . not a superstitious one" (*Letters*, 2:143). Reporting on the toxic haze, violent storms, and deafening fireballs, Cowper distinguishes between natural time and messianic time, the book of nature and the fate of man; he does not read "Scripture by the contingencies of the day." He defends his weather reportage in Enlightenment terms: "Misty however as I am, I do not mean to be *Mystical*, but to be understood like an Almanac maker" (144). The almanac, as Jan Golinski explains, had undergone a significant redefinition in the eighteenth century as astrological prediction gave way to daily record keeping. The new almanacs bound the contingency of unpredictable atmospheric events within the sequential forward movement of the "civic calendar."[33] Weather became a "quotidian occurrence" rather than a singular event (a "meteor") when inscribed within the chronological time of the almanac, the newspaper, the calendar, the clock. The analogical worldview gave way, the sky was emptied of portent, and the weather, silenced and secularized, came to mark time's movement in its most prosaic register. Rejecting an anthropomorphic meteorology that would see in strange weather a presage of historical eventfulness, Cowper claims to understand even the most unusual atmospheric phenomena within the uniformity of nature. Yet, having adopted an Enlightenment understanding of climatic time, he does not altogether eschew the possibility that the singular weather tells a different story: "As a poet nevertheless I claim, if any wonderfull event should follow, a right to apply [it] . . . to the purposes of the tragic Muse" (*Letters*, 2:144).

Unbeknownst to Cowper, on June 8, a sixteen-mile volcanic fissure in southern Iceland opened. Laki was the most powerful and devastating volcanic eruption between Huaynaputina in 1600 and Tambora in 1815. During its early eruptions, it produced as much sulfur dioxide in two days as European industry does today in one year. Observers reported the progress of the toxic cloud as it drifted over Scandinavia, France, and Britain, triggering a "range of extreme atmospheric, meteorological, and environmental phenomena."[34] The accumulation of sulfur dioxide in the lower atmosphere

amplified the natural greenhouse effect, leading to the hottest summer re-
corded in England until 1995.[35] Extreme summer heat, along with the mi-
asma of poisonous gas, aerosol, and ash, amplified the typical mortality rate
by 40 percent.[36] Laborers died during the harvest, as Cowper noted in a Sep-
tember 7 letter to William Unwin (*Letters*, 2:157). As the volcanic gases
accumulated in the upper atmosphere, they deflected solar energy back into
space (much like the global cooling that followed Mount Pinatubo's erup-
tion in 1991), leading to a severe winter and another mortality peak. The
average temperature in 1784 in Europe was 2°C below the norm, and global
weather patterns remained abnormal for years, causing famines in France,
Egypt, Japan, and Alaska.

Over the following decade, naturalists correctly correlated the meteo-
rologic disturbance with Laki's eruption. In 1784, Benjamin Franklin, the
American ambassador to France, linked the "universal fog" of 1783 with
"the vast quantity of smoke, long continuing to issue during the summer
from Hecla," a volcano near Laki, "which might be spread by various winds,
over the northern part of the world."[37] Immersed in the thick haze, how-
ever, even as empirical an observer as the Selborne naturalist Gilbert White
found himself wondering what the remarkable atmospheric phenomena
might portend. "The country people began to look with a superstitious awe
at the red, louring aspect of the sun," he wrote to Daines Barrington, "and
indeed there was reason for the most enlightened person to be apprehen-
sive."[38] Though 1783 was an eventful year—Britain recognized American
independence; the first hot-air balloon rose over France—it was not an
obvious candidate for the Apocalypse. Observers did not look to the skies
expecting portent; rather, the ominous weather made them reconsider the
present. As Cowper explained to Newton on June 29, the weather—the sun
rising and setting with "the face of a red hot salamander"—had precipitated
anxious "speculation among the *connoscenti*." Some wondered whether the
earth's orbit had tilted, a sure sign of "the last times" (*Letters*, 2:148–49).

Although no miraculous event occurred, Cowper's tragic muse was
awakened. In the June 29 letter to Newton, he associates his own surprising
"Sally of Genius," a witty rhyme at the start of the letter, with the "Boeo-
tian atmosphere"—Boeotia being a region in central Greece known for its
fogs (*Letters*, 2:148). He also recalls *Paradise Lost*, the simile describing
Satan's sublime obscurity that echoed in the minds of many of his contem-
poraries that June: "We never see the sun but shorn of his beams."[39] In this
inspired, agitated state, Cowper began writing *The Task*. He first discusses
the poem in his correspondence as it neared completion during the freezing
winter of 1783–84, one of the coldest winters in the eighteenth century.[40]

Writing to William Bull on February 22, he reports the end of a long frost: "The Ice in my Ink however is not yet dissolved. It was long before the frost seized it but at last it prevailed. The Sofa [the original title of the poem] has consequently received little or no addition since" (*Letters*, 2:217).

As had Milton in the previous century, Cowper often reflected on the quality of his nation's climate and its implications for politics and poetry. He considered himself uniquely sensitive to seasonal extremes. In book 5, he addresses England: "My native nook of Earth! Thy clime is rude, / Replete with vapours, and disposes much / All hearts to sadness, and none more than mine" (5.462–64).[41] For him, the composition of poetry offered a way of managing climatic affliction. As he wrote to John Newton in December 1780: "At this season of the year, and in this gloomy uncomfortable climate, it is no easy matter for the owner of a mind like mine to divert it from sad subjects, and fix it upon such as may administer its amusement. Poetry, above all things, is useful to me in this respect. While I have held in pursuit of pretty images, or a pretty way of expressing them, I forget every thing that is irksome."[42] In another instance, however, the climate—in this case, the extreme heat of summer—interrupts the sensitive poet's work, providing him with a new perspective on Virgil's *Georgics*. In July 1779, Cowper wrote to William Unwin, who was enjoying a holiday on the coast:

> We envy you your sea-breezes. In the garden we feel nothing but the reflection of the heat from the walls; and in the parlour, from the opposite houses. I fancy Virgil was so situated when he wrote those two beautiful lines,—
>
> —*Oh quis me gelidis in vallibus Hæmi*
> *Sistat, et ingenti ramorum protegat umbra!*
>
> [O for one to see me in the cool glens of Haemus and shield me under the branches' mighty shade.]
>
> The worst of it is, that though the sunbeams strike as forcibly upon my harp-strings as they did upon his, they elicit no such sounds. (*Letters*, 1:297)

Perhaps concerned about her friend's susceptibility to climatic influence, early in the awful summer of 1783 Lady Austen suggested to Cowper, who had seen his first public success with his 1782 volume of moral satires, that he divert himself by writing a poem on an indoor theme, the sofa. Cowper acknowledged the arbitrariness of his choice to "sing the Sofa," but what is clear from *The Task*'s opening is that the theme of the domestic interior initially served his intention to reflect critically on the state of English society without the sententiousness of his previous volume (1.1). It is in the sitting room, after all, that he read both "the historian's page" (4.158) and the newspaper, which, by bringing "intelligence [from] ev'ry clime," provided "a map of busy life / Its fluctuations, and its vast concerns" (111, 55–56). The furniture that is the setting of historical inquiry, Cowper decides, can also be its object. *The Task* commences with a historical account in which trade and labor contribute to the invention of the sofa. The bathos of the sofa as a synecdoche for "the manners and the arts of civil life," however, suggests that history's tendency is not unequivocally progressive (1.596). Advancement and decline are inseparable, for what Cowper uncovers in domestic furniture are not only the comforts of home but also the ills of the present: imperial war, fashionable consumption, even deforestation.

Genteel repose offers an unsatisfactory posture for a poet who aspires to rouse his urbane readers by "speak[ing] to purpose" (3.25). To judge the present requires an untimely voice, an alternative vantage. Seeking an understanding of the present beyond that available in the nightly reading of the newspaper, the poet heads outdoors. "For I have lov'd the rural walk" (1.109), he explains, and here the eddying temporality of the continuous present perfect, the tense in which the past cumulates in the present, establishes the poem's crucial spatiotemporal distinction between the accretion of experience within natural cycles and the dizzying motion of historical succession.[43] The *once again* of a return that measures change, which Wordsworth learned from Cowper, reflects the periodic temporality of a stable climate: a region and its prevailing weather. Rural scenes and cycling seasons sustain a continuous cadence in a world of accelerating change. Recurrence—paths and prospects revisited, the daily and seasonal round—is perceived as renewal because experience accumulates unconsciously: "we have borne / The ruffling wind scarce conscious that it blew" (155–56).

A careful "observer of natural appearances" who flirts with natural theology and amateur natural history, Cowper describes a dynamic system he calls an "economy" (6.579), adopting the term popularized by Linnaeus. His conception of nature's economy is essentially climatic, stressing not stasis but a stability that prevails within fluctuation, cycles that recur amid variation, global systems with local permutations. This economy is defined by the periodic motion of the earth's rotation and its orbit around the sun, by the hydrologic cycle, and by the passage of winds and vapors: "By ceaseless action all that is subsists. / Constant rotation of th' unwearied wheel /

That nature rides upon maintains her health, / Her beauty, her fertility"
(1.367–70). Cowper is describing a global circuit—"Winds from all quarters
agitate the air" (373)—but its perceptible manifestation is decidedly local.
The locodescriptive account of Olney, its natural cycles generating a tempo
of recollection and return, is followed, in book 1, by scenes of displacement
across an "earth . . . so various" (506): the mariner longing for home, the
widow whose fancy follows her lost sailor "to distant shores" (540), the dis-
placed Tahitian Omai. In contrast with these dislocated imperial subjects,
only one who remains "still" in place—in his "native nook"—recognizes the
"revolency" that "upholds the world" (143, 372). As Favret notes, stillness
has a "peculiar charge" in *The Task*, as a state of "hesitation" encompassing
"ongoing-ness" and completion (*War at a Distance*, 106). Cowper understands
the cumulative, what is *still*, as the condition for registering change, what is
new. It is neither his knowledge of historical events nor an all-encompassing
prospect view that offers a critical vantage on modern times but rather settled
experience of a familiar—if at times oppressive—English clime.

   Though its title, "The Time-Piece," suggests the regularized measure
of time passing, book 2 opens with the poet seeking to elude the demands
historical awareness places on his moral sensibility by retiring to a "lodge
in some vast wilderness / Some boundless contiguity of shade" (2.1–2). The
fantasy of a "boundless contiguity of shade" expresses, in this instance,
a need to escape not from history into nature but from the climate itself.
What interrupts the rhythm of rural time is not the news from the "noisy
world" of London (4.5) but rather bad weather: "Fires from beneath, and
meteors from above, / Portentous, unexampled, unexplain'd, / Have kindled
beacons in the skies" (2.57–59). The time of weather has become *meteoric*,
in the sense of the "unstable, unpredictable, aleatory, turbulent, disruptive,
and chaotic" atmospheric event.[44] Cowper recounts the awful harbingers
and natural calamities of recent years, beginning with the massive October
1780 hurricane in the Caribbean: "When were the winds / Let slip with such
a warrant to destroy, / When did the waves so haughtily o'erleap / Their
ancient barrier, deluging the dry?" (53–56). He includes a note clarifying
that he is referring to the "late calamities at Jamaica," the hurricane and the
tidal wave that destroyed the town of Savannah-la-Mar. In a letter to Joseph
Hill, he had considered the geohistorical and eschatological implications of
this event:

   Since the first Tour that Columbus made into the Western World it
   never before experienced such a convulsion, perhaps never since the
   foundation of the globe. You say the state grows old, and discovers many

symptoms of decline. A writer possessed of a genius for hypothesis, like that of Burnet, might construct a plausible argument to prove that the world itself is in a state of superannuation. . . . When that just equilibrium that has hitherto supported all things seems to fail, when the elements burst the chain that had bound them, the wind sweeping away the worlds of man, and man himself together with his works, and the ocean seeming to overlook the command, "Hitherto shalt thou come, and no further, and here shall thy proud waves by stayed," these irregular and prodigious vagaries seemed to bespeak a decay, and forebode, perhaps, not a very distant dissolution. (*Letters*, 1:443)

The hurricane was followed by earthquakes in Calabria, violent thunderstorms, and the inexplicable, interminable toxic fog. "The Time-Piece," Cowper later explained to Newton, "is intended to strike the hour that gives notice of approaching judgment, . . . dealing pretty largely with the *signs* of the *times*" (*Letters*, 2:309). The natural-historical scrutiny of his initial reports on the Laki haze has been supplanted by a "mystical" meteorology. Although "prophecy" (2.66) may require a "longer respite" (67), deferring the "end" (65) augured by these "frowning signals" (68), here it is not climatic regularity but its rupture that sustains moral-social critique. The poet gains his authority to judge modern times not as one who has experienced the comprehensive workings of general providence but as one who recognizes special providence, interpreting the "voice" that speaks in atmospheric violence (52). Correlating the apocalyptic weather with urbanization, the slave trade, and imperial warfare, Cowper contends that a wrathful God "involves the heav'n / In tempests, quits his grasp upon the winds / And gives them all their fury" (180–82). In "The Time-Piece," Enlightenment natural philosophy gives way to the doctrine Vladimir Janković refers to as "Divine steering," according to which God acts as a "moral coordinator," maintaining a *"causal* link between nature and human affairs."[45]

Cowper initially interpreted the Laki haze as a contingent meteorologic event within the uniform flow of seasonal time, and then, in "The Time-Piece," he identifies it as a portent of Judgment Day, when God arrests nature's recurrent temporality. Within these two interpretive modes, which would seem to distinguish religious from scientific knowledge, allegory from description, the weather is understood as constituting a time and measuring an agency distinct from human action. But what is truly disconcerting to Cowper is the possibility that the haze may be related to the modernizing processes that are obscuring meteorologic signs and times. This concern is anticipated in the June 29 letter to Newton. In rejecting a millennial understanding of the sulfuric fog—"the present obfuscation"—he asks how "signs in the heavens" could allow Londoners to predict the end times when, enveloped as they were in a "dingy atmosphere" from burning coal, they would be unlikely to notice the sky (*Letters*, 2:149). The city, he observes, generates its own smoggy weather, a secularized atmosphere devoid of divine signatures. London keeps its own time.

The two-line description of the Laki haze in "The Time-Piece"—"Nature with a dim and sickly eye / [seems] to wait the close of all" (2.64–65)—is so peculiar that Cowper added a note (attached to line 64) clarifying that it refers "to the fog that covered both Europe and Asia during the summer of 1783." The personification is confusing because it designates not the occluding agent but what has been occluded, the Sun, which is represented, paradoxically, as both an instrument of vision and a source of illumination. The Sun is imbued with what Benjamin calls "aura": "To perceive the aura of an object we look at means to invest it with the ability to look back at us. This experience corresponds to the data of the *mémoire involontaire*" ("Motifs in Baudelaire," 338).[46] If long experience reflects the role of a given climate's diurnal and seasonal cycles as a subconscious calendar, the haze interposes between self and sky, which no longer serves as a container for memory. This waning of atmospheric aura, a sky that has lost its periodicity, will be linked to the crisis in perception that comes to shape the poet's own experience of modern times. The status of the haze is indeterminate: as sign or context, natural, divine, or human artifact, physical or perceptual condition. It is a visible manifestation of obscuration, what Goodman calls a figure of "expressive inarticulateness" (*Georgic Modernity*, 97), and, while it interrupts the rhythm of time, it also alerts the poet to the problem of the present, which is why he clarifies its standing as a historic event.

What must have been most distressing about the Laki haze was how physically reminiscent it was of the everyday atmosphere of London: a noxious mix of ash, sulfur dioxide, and other gases. In the opening book of *The Task*, Cowper refers repeatedly to the revitalizing purity of Buckinghamshire's "fresh air" (1.138) and "wholesome air" (589). This enlivening atmosphere is replaced with "smoke . . . the eclipse / That Metropolitan volcanos make, / Whose Stygian throats breathe darkness all day long" (3.736–38). Serendipitously figuring smokestacks as volcanoes, Cowper aligns the infernal Laki haze with London's perpetual smog. In *The Botanic Garden* (1790), Erasmus Darwin made the same connection: "The dry mist of summer 1783, was probably occasioned by volcanic eruption . . . and therefore more like the atmosphere of smoke which hangs on still days over great cities."[47] Cowper draws attention to London's noisome atmosphere, its worsening industrial pollution, the "smoke of lamps," and "the pent-up breath of an unsav'ry throng" (4.195–96). "All for smoke," he writes, dismissing modern industriousness and ingenuity (3.174). The city is plagued by haze and miasma but also by an artificially bright ambience, lighting that upsets circadian rhythms and obscures the sky. In the famous Brown Study scene that influenced Coleridge, the refulgent urban atmosphere is contrasted with "slow-moving" (4.246) natural twilight and diurnal repetition, the gentle approach of evening that encourages untimely ruminations (see generally 243–66).

London's obscuring smog and bright lights intensify awareness of a fleeting present, which becomes more consuming as it becomes less knowable. Unhitched from the Earth's steady "revolency," modern time moves so quickly and is perceived so acutely that those who live in the city "know no pause" (4.283). Time passes without accumulating in memory. Cowper worries that the time of the *beau monde*—the annual migration to London, "time in masquerade" he calls it (213)—has displaced seasonal time. Fashions, which "change with ev'ry moon," provide an example of time unnaturally quickened and so incapable of ripening in experience (2.599). For the shopper who lives *à la mode*, "constant revolution" fails to bring satisfaction because the spell of "fancy" remains tilted toward the immediate future (1.462). Newness is experienced as enervating repetition. The gambler exemplifies this mode of life lived in a present so demanding that all times beyond the coming instant disappear.[48] The "hour-glass" is transformed into "a dice-box," a speculative temporality defined by unceasing anticipation of what is just about to occur (4.220–21).

As readers have long noticed, *The Task* is unable to sustain its symbolic moral topography—"God made the country, and man made the town" (1.749)—because the climatic temporalities (languid, periodic, cumulative) of rural life are being subsumed by modern time. "The town has ting'd the country" as "fashion runs / Down into scenes still rural" (4.553, 555–56). Viewed according to picturesque principles, estates become "landscapes," subject to altering acts of "Improvement" (3.755, 764). Without considering seasonal patterns, the landscape architect Lancelot "Capability" Brown refashioned the English countryside as swiftly as the earthquakes upended Calabria: "The lake in front becomes a lawn, / Woods vanish, hills subside, and vallies rise" (774–75). The loss of forest shade is, for Cowper, the starkest example of this remaking of rural time and clime. In his initial account of country rambles, in lines composed during the severest summer in memory—indeed, what turned out to be the hottest July recorded in England between 1659 and 1983—he describes the relief of entering the "cooler clime" of a leafy forest, like the dusk-lit parlor, a recess in which time eddies, duration expands, and consciousness is emancipated from the demanding present (1.335–37). In *The Task*, Cowper complains that shade had grown "obsolete" (265). While previous generations "knew the value of a screen / From sultry suns" (255–56), changing fashions and the short-term calculations of absentee landowners, who sell timber to pay gambling debts (3.752–63), have contributed to England's deforestation. Cowper celebrates the decision of the local squire, John Throckmorton, to leave uncut a chestnut grove on his estate at Weston Underwood, yet it is the poet's elegy for lost shade and lost time—"Ye fallen avenues! Once more I mourn / Your fate unmerited" (1.338–39)—that registered so acutely with nostalgic nineteenth-century readers (such as Austen's Fanny Price, who responds to Mr. Rushworth's plan to raze an avenue of trees by quoting these lines from *The Task*). As he was completing *The Task*, Cowper published one of his most popular short poems, "The Poplar Field," in the *Gentleman's Magazine* (January 1785). It laments the local climate change caused by deforestation.

When, acknowledging his debt to the "Mantuan bard" (3.453), Cowper turns to the art of cultivating cucumbers in book 3, "The Garden," it is with the aim of regaining a rhythm of human action harmonized with natural cycles, the "employs of rural life, / Reiterated as the wheel of time / Runs round" (625–27). As Thomson had demonstrated in *The Seasons*, the georgic is the proper genre in which to treat the cultivation of temporal synchronization. As in Virgil's *Georgics*, which offers a key to those atmospheric "signs" that predict "the heat, and the rain, and the cold-bringing winds" (123), in "The Garden" Cowper teaches his readers to slow down and attend to meteorologic and horticultural signs. Time slackens as Cowper narrates the process of cultivating cucumbers, an art acquired through "Experience, slow preceptress" (3.505). The gardener must yield to the tempo of the garden, patiently accepting a "discreet delay" in order to catch "Th' auspicious moment" when "time subdues / The rage of fermentation" (504, 518–19). Here, Cowper's narration becomes self-reflexive.[49] Even so prolix a genre as the blank-verse georgic, he worries, is inadequate for narrating the pace of gardening, especially given the impatience of modern readers. If his account of cultivating cucumbers fails to accord with the time and temperature of his readers, they will "judge the song / Cold as its theme" (563–64). Yet, if Cowper's contemporaries inhabit the accelerated temporality of an overheated atmosphere, so does the hothouse gardener. He builds a cold frame, "overlaid with clear translucent glass," which keeps the rain out and the warmth in, allowing a pile of manure to ferment (485). Here, in this greenhouse atmosphere, a surprising vapor and a familiar simile enter the poem: "behold! / A pestilent and most corrosive steam, / Like a gross fog Boeotian, rising fast, / . . . / Asks egress" (493–97). The only other use of this stock figure recorded in Cowper's correspondence or verse is his description of the toxic Laki haze—which, like a cold frame, intensified heat and, like the fermenting compost, was noxious to plants. Although "fog Boeotian" refers to "smoking manure" (517), the figurative migration is revealing, for, throughout the poem, haze appears at moments of temporal opacity. The influx of a "vapour dank" (499), figured in the very terms as the portentous summer haze, indexes the disordered time of the greenhouse.

Although Cowper associates horticulture with the perceptual slow time of seasonal periodicity, the reappearance of the haze suggests that there is a point at which cultivation—the "Assistant art" to "nature's office" (3.541–42)—becomes history and the timeless becomes irrevocably new. Cucumber gardening is, after all, a recent innovation, "an art / That toiling ages have but just matur'd" (449–50). The hothouse enables the gardener to escape the capriciousness of spring in a "clime so rude" as England's (431), producing artificial and perhaps ill-begotten blooms: "hence ev'n winter fills his wither'd hand / With blushing fruits, and plenty, not his own" (428–29). The dream image of the greenhouse, which collects the world's floral plenitude within its imperial grasp, is of a cornucopia unhitched from seasonal cycles and climatic variability. The greenhouse offers an ultimately unsatisfactory site for the georgic task of harmonizing human acts with seasonal recurrence, for its climate is exotic, inundated by the fog of history.[50]

The final three of *The Task*'s six books—largely composed between December and March of the frigid Laki winter, which, Cowper reported to Newton, saw "a frost of nine weeks' continuance" (*Letters*, 2:214 [February 22, 1784])—narrate the condensed span of a single evening and morning. Time pools up as the poet seeks the still clarity of an ending. The moment is given palpable duration by a winter storm, first recognized in book 4 with the closing of the shutters that precedes the reading of the news. The scene that follows perfectly stages Cowper's experience, both bewildering and illuminating, of inhabiting a present riven among contending temporalities. The newspaper promises "intelligence [from] ev'ry clime" (4.111), access to the synchronic social simultaneity of a present projected onto global space. Its temporality is one of anticipation (for "who can say / What are its tidings?" [24–25]) and addiction, modernity's obsession with its present ("I long to know them all" [33]). "'Tis pleasant through the loop-holes of retreat / To peep at such a world" (88–89), Cowper writes, identifying the newspaper as a medium that connects the poet with the world even as it allows him to remain at a safe remove.

Writing to Thomas Park, Anna Seward suggested that Cowper borrowed the "loophole" from Thomson's description in *Autumn* of the man who hears, "at distance safe, the human tempest roar" (*Au*, 1301).[51] We can detect, however, an instance of a displaced climatic referent in another possible source, Milton's description of the Indian shepherd who retreats to the cool shade of the giant banyan trees: "There oft the Indian herdsman, shunning heat, / Shelters in cool and tends his pasturing herds / At loopholes cut through the thickest shade" (*Paradise Lost*, 9.1108–10). Of course, for Cowper what is held at a remove is not the heat of summer but "the globe and its concerns" (4.95). Indeed, what keeps him in place, "still at home," is the regularity (if unusual frigidity) of "Winter" (119–20), a perception of the stable climate that underlies the vicissitudes of a season. As he scans the catastrophic news—falling stocks, battles lost, the exploits of empire (16–30)—he also tracks the blizzard, its "sleet like ashes" (121). In this fluctuating temporal weave, he remembers his own intention not only to record the digressions of a "wand'ring muse" (3.692) but also to narrativize and thus make knowable the present: "Roving as I rove, / Where shall I find an end?" (4.232–33). He hesitates, safely ensconced beside the fire, his fancy freed in the "slow moving" twilight, before being revived, his question apparently answered, by the storm's "freezing blast" rattling the shutters (303).[52] The events of distant climes dissipate as the snow accumulates, for it is in the weather of a recognizable season that tomorrow (and thus today) can be known:

> To-morrow brings a change, a total change!
> Which even now, though silently perform'd
> And slowly, and by most unfelt, the face
> Of universal nature undergoes.
> Fast falls a fleecy show'r. (322–26)

The snowstorm measures time silently but surely, its incessant drift clarifying by obscuring—"Assimilat[ing] all objects" (329)—a world of human acts and artifacts.

The promise of clarity is short-lived. Tomorrow does arrive, and the present remains hazy. The reassurance of climatic periodicity as countermeasure gives way to unsettling modern weather. In book 5, "The Winter Morning Walk," the poet wakes to the sun rising on the wintry scene: "the clouds / That crowd away before the driving wind, / More ardent as the disk emerges more, / Resemble most some city in a blaze" (5.2–5). The clouds are like an urban crowd and the sky a burning city. Obscuring resemblance supplants the clarity of juxtaposition. As the poet walks through the snow-covered landscape, a frozen waterfall reminds him of the notorious ice palace built in Saint Petersburg for the empress Anna Ivanovna. While the palace exemplifies the correlation between climatic and political extremism explored by Montesquieu, Cowper emphasizes not environmental determinism but the artificial time of tyrannical rule: "'Twas transient in its nature, as in show / 'Twas durable" (173–74). More unsettlingly, the absolutism of "barb'rous climes" is, like the blossoms of equatorial flora, coming to England (1.604). In these Whiggish ruminations on sovereignty, climate change indexes the anxieties of imperial expansion.[53] Cowper sees the development of English liberty as recompense for an intemperate climate, preferring freedom in a "fickle clime" to arbitrary governance in a temperate one (5.484). Yet, as he reflects on increasing faction, corruption, and absolutism, he admits that under a tyrannous English crown he would prefer to live "under skies / Milder" (487–88). As his jeremiad heats up, the meteorologic tropology of the Laki summer is applied to a nation in decline. The haze reappears as a figure for kingcraft: "They semi-deify and fume him so / That in due season he forgets" he is a man (266–67). Partisanship produces "factious fumes," and irreligion is the "eclipse that intercepts truth's heavenly beam" (513, 683). The storm of history causes the "tempest-beaten turrets [to] shake" on the "old castle of the state" (525, 527). The English climate is infused by history.

The snowstorm and the "morning sharp and clear" (6.58) are followed by May-like warmth at noon, a return to time's reassuring periodicity after the unprecedented Laki winter. Book 6 begins with Cowper observing signs of seasonal change—bleating lambs and budding primroses—that "Deceive no student" (114). These auguries of spring reveal the "pow'r divine" (118) evident in the "constancy of nature's course" (122), the providential consistency of the English climate. Yet the restoration of spring, "the renovation of a faded world" (124), also anticipates the Resurrection: "from death to life, / Is Nature's progress when she lectures man / In heav'nly truth" (181–83). This narrative contradiction—spring's return affirms both a cyclic and an eschatological conception of time—encapsulates the hermeneutical problem that haunts Cowper's weather reports. If every atmospheric occurrence is a miracle, the "regular return of genial months" (123) no less than the "punctual sun" frozen at Gibeon (127), then there is no way of interpreting the specific implications of the Laki haze. Everywhere Cowper looks—the English state, its capital, London, its growing empire, his own garden and native countryside—he discovers a smoggy intermingling of human affairs and atmospheric phenomena. Ascribing this murky atmosphere to "a present God" (252) does nothing to dispel it, for what is illuminated by providential meteorology is the opacity of natural signs, the "veil [that] / Hangs over mortal eyes" (3.233–34). Turning from almanac maker to mystic, from natural history to the designs of an inscrutable God, Cowper finds himself no closer to understanding the sky's "frowning signals." In a world in which human acts and meteorologic facts are indistinguishable, in which an urban haze obscures divine portent, providential explanations fail to clear the opacity of the present.

If rural time and modern time, the garden and the empire, the skies and the state are inseparably mixed, the poet must reclaim a more absolute temporal measure, the clarity of the End. Rather than prognosticating the future by casting his gaze on the present, the prophet identifies himself as the medium by which the illumination of futurity, "a flash from heav'n," casts its backward glow (5.884). Invoking the apocalyptic tradition, he speaks of the promise of time's legibility, "that blest moment [when] Nature throwing wide / Her veil opaque, discloses with a smile / The author of her beauties" (891–93). As do Milton and Thomson, when Cowper accepts the burden of prophecy, the allegorical imperative to transmute the concrete facts of history into a total story, what he envisages is not the cataclysmic transition described by Isaiah or John but a timeless world to come where people "from ev'ry clime" congregate in a sacred city under cloudless skies (6.814). But for the absence of smog, however, this reparative end of time is indistinguishable from Cowper's own time. As in the greenhouse, climatic variation disappears, "Rivers of gladness water all the earth, / And clothe all climes with beauty" (763–64), and the yearly cycle is suspended, "The various seasons woven into one, / And that one season an eternal spring" (769–70). Of course, this ancient fantasy of a renovated world, the eschatological vision that promises release from the vicissitudes of nature, is precisely what empire offers as its utopian end of history: weather managed, climate overcome, natural limits transcended.

In the final stanzas of *The Task*, Cowper turns from his readers to address God directly. Plaintive apostrophe replaces prophetic meteorology, as if the poet's own power to speak is all that remains secure in a foggy world. He calls on the seasons to accelerate—"Haste, then, and wheel away a shatter'd world, / Ye slow-revolving seasons!" (6.823–24)—and then speaks to God: "The very spirit of the world is tir'd / Of its own taunting question, ask'd so long, / 'Where is the promise of your Lord's approach?'" (869–71). He is left waiting, wondering about the weather, and hearing only his own voice. In the final stanza, he reflects on his distance from "the haughty world": "Perhaps she owes / her sunshine and her rain, her blooming spring / and plenteous harvest, to the pray'r [the poet] makes" (945–47). As the poem ends, he is more confident about his capacity to influence the seasons, entreating for a final revolution even as he prays for steady revolvency, than he is about his capacity to recognize the prevailing weather. The weatherman has become a weather maker. Cowper continues to wander, he assures us near the end: "Neither mist, / Nor freezing sky, nor sultry, checking me" (296–97).

LYRICIZING LOCODESCRIPTION AND
LOVING NATURE IN "TINTERN ABBEY"

"Lines Written a Few Miles above Tintern Abbey, on Revisiting the Banks of the Wye during a Tour. July 13 1798" is the culminating poem—added, in fact, while the volume was in press—in the first edition of *Lyrical Ballads* (1798). In his snarky ("the 'experiment,' we think, has failed") anonymous review of the collection in the *Critical Review*, Southey singled out "Tintern Abbey" for praise, writing of the rhapsodic fourth verse paragraph: "In the whole range of English poetry, we scarcely recollect any thing superior."[54] In a note to the second edition, Wordsworth remarked on the poem's uncertain generic status: "I have not ventured to call this Poem an Ode; but it was written with a hope that in the transitions, and the impassioned music of the versification, would be found the principal requisites of that species of composition."[55] Much critical attention has been dedicated to unpacking this short comment.[56] Some readers see in "Tintern Abbey" the formal structure and precise dialectical turns of the Pindaric ode, while others, sensitive to Wordsworth's own taxonomic hesitation, detect the emergence of an innovative and thus not yet fully nameable lyric mode less formally structured than the ode, organized around subtle shifts of consciousness rather than sharp inversions and reconciliations.[57]

"Tintern Abbey" is a poem that asks what is learned in a return, what can be gained in repetition, and readers continue to return to the poem, to read it again and again, in order to consider the legacies of the lyric and the romantic "love of nature."[58] The fact that critics still cannot agree on how to title the poem attests to the rich and contentious discussion it has inspired. As I did, many readers first come to romanticism through "Tintern Abbey," drawn as much by a referentiality apparently unburdened by history as by the poem's intimate first-person voice. Here, I ask why, specifically, a poem that may be "Wordsworth's greatest poem on love of nature," as Seth Reno writes, should also be, as Paul Frye claims, Wordsworth's "greatest lyric," which in turn makes it, in Harold Bloom's words, "*the* modern poem proper . . . [which] most good poems written in English since . . . inescapably repeat, rewrite, or revise."[59] Why should a poem often identified as the exemplary romantic lyric also be read as a poem that models a new salutary mode of ecological consciousness, offering a new way "to look at and dwell in the natural world," as Jonathan Bate writes (*Romantic Ecology*, 7)?[60]

I map the poem's "insights and oversights" not by reconstructing its historical scene, as did Marjorie Levinson in her bravura reading in *Wordsworth's Great Period Poems*, but by highlighting its departure from descriptive convention. If Wordsworth considered "Tintern Abbey" a not quite ode and so a poem lacking an identifiable genre, in its title he pointed to another precursor: locodescriptive poetry.[61] Wordsworth's first two published poems, brought out as separate volumes by Joseph Johnson in 1793, were each intended and received as locodescriptive: *Descriptive Sketches Taken during a Pedestrian Tour among the Alps* and *An Evening Walk*. In a conversation with Isabella Fenwick, Wordsworth characterized the aim of his early topographical efforts in descriptive terms: to catalog "the infinite variety of natural appearances."[62] Yet such infinitude had come to seem a burden. Of "descriptive poetry," the *Monthly Review*, reviewing *An Evening Walk*, asked: "Have we not yet had enough?"[63] Thomsonian description had run its course.

"Tintern Abbey" announces its lyric itinerary in its opening lines: "Five years have passed; five summers, with the length / Of five long winters! and again I hear / These waters, rolling from their mountain-springs / With a sweet inland murmur" (1–4). Disturbed seasonal time is being made to stand for psychological experience, the elongation of time under conditions of distress. We may detect a hint of the *Georgics* here since one of the enigmas to be examined under the Lucretian mandate was the length of winter nights and the shortness of winter days. We may also sense the impress of geohistory itself, the insistent remainder of a geophysical referent not fully subsumed by the metaphoric tenor, in this case psychologized time. The winter of 1794–95 was severe and extended, unusually cold from November until the end of March, with the coldest January—indeed, the coldest month ever—recorded in the Central England Temperature Index. The Severn and the Thames both froze. The Thames froze again in December 1796, although the cold spell was briefer. Whether the disturbance of time is psychological or climatic, in the mind or in the world, for Wordsworth the return to the Wye valley promises to set time aright. Revisiting a

familiar place, itself unchanged, offers the narrator an opportunity to reflect
back and project forward, measuring loss and gain. Because the landscape
remains as it was, the self can identify its alteration. It is a landscape condu-
cive to self-reflection, what Hegel calls the "apprehension of the mind in its
own self-expression" (*Aesthetics*, 1113), because it is knowable, its deictic
availability—"These waters," "these steep and lofty cliffs" (5), "this dark
sycamore" (10), and perhaps, above all, "this season" (12)—the enabling
condition of the poet's "Thoughts" (7).

As an object of perception and memory, the River Wye supports the con-
trast the poem develops between the unreflective pleasure of the younger
self and the wiser, if more chastened, man who seeks intellectual consola-
tion in the natural scene. The younger Wordsworth was the sort of poet
who would compose topographical poems, satisfied by what he saw and
perceived in the external world: "the tall rock, / the mountain, and the deep
and gloomy wood, / Their colours and their forms" (78–80). Personal matu-
ration recapitulates the history of English poetry in which "Tintern Abbey"
intervenes, the development from a descriptive poetics concerned with the
world in its geophysical variation to a lyricized poetics in which the natural
scene is refracted through contemplative self-examination.

The long-standing analogy between the flow of water through the Earth
and the flow of blood through the body organizes the sequence that begins in
the second stanza. "[M]id the din / Of towns and cities" (26–27), the "forms"
of remembered natural "beauty" (24), the poet asserts, lent him, "In hours
of weariness, sensations sweet, / Felt in the blood" (28–29), sensations sup-
porting his capacity for kindness and love in the alienating city. This con-
ceit is then repeated a second time as the basis for a more expansive claim,
one that recalls as it revises the Lucretian mandate for poetry concerned
with the causes of things. The same remembered images of natural beauty
produce a mood of "lighten'd" (42) consciousness "until, the breath of this
corporeal frame, / And even the motion of our human blood / Almost sus-
pended, / We are laid asleep / In body, and become a living soul": "We see
into the life of things" (44–50). The short third stanza begins with equivo-
cation, an example of the semantic slippage and controlled vagueness that
make the poem so enduringly fascinating: "If this / Be but a vain belief"
(50–51). The translation of seeing beyond surfaces ("into the life of things")
into believing (that things have life?) may, the poet hints, be psychologi-
cally motivated. The idea of the previous stanza is then repeated in a way
that inverts its physiology. Lost in the obscurity of urban life, now figured
in atmospheric terms, "In darkness, and amid the many shapes / Of joyless
day-light," the narrator says, "the fretful stir / Unprofitable, and the fever of

the world, / Have hung upon the beatings of my heart" (52–55). A number of readers have sought to elucidate this enigmatic sequence with reference to late eighteenth-century medical discourse and aesthetic theory.[64] Ford offers a particularly ingenious reading, according to which Wordsworth's long, enjambed blank-verse stanzas exhaust the breath, slowing the blood and so replicating the aesthetic experience described, offering "poetic mechanisms for suspending modernity's dissolution of the old and ceaseless outpouring of the new" (*Poetics of Air*, 164). Ford has little to say, however, about this third stanza, where the conceit is repeated but with the implication that slowed circulation ("the fever of the world / . . . hung upon the beatings of my heart") is a consequence of modern life rather than remembered scenic beauty.

Here, especially, Wordsworth is revisiting the key passage in book 2 of the *Georgics*: "But if the chill blood about my heart bar me from reaching those realms of nature, let my delight be the country, and the running streams amid the dells—may I love the waters and the woods, though I be unknown to fame." Wordsworth resists the geohumoralism taken up by Milton, Thomson, and Cowper. Slowed circulation is an effect not of the climate but of the experiential *contrast* between life in "towns and cities" and the beauty of the natural scene conjured in memory. The slowing of the blood promises to resolve this disjunctive experience, to *still* the displaced self sufficiently so that he can once again discover animacy in things. Like Virgil, Wordsworth stages a lyric turn that acknowledges the imperative—in his case psychological rather than geohumoral—motivating the retreat from a difficult reality. Once again, the transformation of didactic poetry, as a medium of knowledge and an act of labor, into pastoral retreat and wish fulfillment produces lyricization.

The poet has not simply remembered but has turned to the Wye: "How oft, in spirit, have I turned to thee / O sylvan Wye! Thou wanderer through the woods" (56–57). While the 1798 *Lyrical Ballads* explores a number of complex rhetorical situations, there is only one other instance of apostrophe directed to a nonhuman (indeed nonliving) addressee, also a river, in "Lines Written Near Richmond, upon the Thames, at Evening." In these poems, Wordsworth is following a convention, what David Fairer terms the "riverbank revisited" poem, the most famous instance of which, Thomas Warton's sonnet "To the River Lodon," also contains a restrained address to the "Sweet native stream."[65] The personification of rivers was a commonplace of descriptive poetry, as in Pope's personification of the Thames, prophesizing the growth of Britain's mercantile empire, in *Windsor-Forest*. Given Wordsworth's stated allergy to Augustan poetic diction and personification, however, we still require an explanation for this apostrophic turn to a personified Wye—yet another residual personification and an embellished figurative language so unlike the diction of everyday language. What is clear is that Wordsworth's apostrophe differs from Pope's in the absence of a public context. An insistently private self enters into an I/thou relation with the river, which embodies the most minimal kind of external auditor, an audience that will ask or expect nothing. Indeed, the effect of the personification may be to deanimate the river, to isolate it as an object of personal perception. There is, as Levinson notes, a degree of empirical obfuscation in the descriptions of the river (*Wordsworth's Great Period Poems*, chap. 1). Wordsworth's "sylvan Wye" was, in fact, busy with traffic. In his *Observations on the River Wye* (1782), a guide Wordsworth may have carried on his 1798 tour, William Gilpin, like many tourists, traveled the river by boat. Approaching Tintern, he describes numerous small harbors "where little barks lay moored, taking in ore and other commodities from the mountains": "These vessels, designed plainly for rougher water than they at present encountered, shewed us . . . that we approached the sea."[66] Wordsworth's failure to describe this commercial traffic requires a significant revision of descriptive convention. For poets like Thomson and Jago, rivers are transport networks, sources of kinetic flow linking places and facilitating commerce. It is this locodescriptive understanding of rivers as phases in the hydrologic cycle and nodes in an energy infrastructure that Wordsworth rejects, characterizing the Wye in terms of retreat rather than connection, its "inland" source rather than its global course. The absence of boats on the river is as notable as the absence of laborers in the landscape.

A similar overturning of descriptive convention can be seen in the representation of the atmosphere. On a summer afternoon the poet stands beside the river and beholds a scene that has long dwelled in his memory: of lofty cliffs, orchards, hedgerows, and

> wreaths of smoke
> Sent up, in silence, from among the trees,
> With some uncertain notice, as might seem,
> Of vagrant dwellers in the houseless woods,
> Or of some hermit's cave, where by his fire
> The hermit sits alone. (18–23)

When Wordsworth visited—first in 1793 and then in 1798—the Wye Valley was home to a major ironworks. The region played a major role in early industrialization, being the site of the first coal-fire smelting of copper, the

first water-powered wire works, and some of the earliest brass and tin pro-
duction in Britain. The Forest of Dean had been decimated, and the local
forests were managed for charcoal production. Any "vagrant dwellers" may
have been charcoal burners, producing fuel for Tintern's furnaces. I read
the syntactic contortion in Wordsworth's description of the rising smoke
as a symptom of the strenuous compositional labor—of displacement, of
not seeing in order to see—that enables the poet to view an industrial land-
scape as a "wild secluded scene" (6). The first two lines *describe* the visible
object world, but somewhere in the third line a *lyric* subject is introduced
whose limited point of view is supplemented by the conjectures recorded
in the fourth, fifth, and sixth lines. The poet's gaze momentarily extends
"up" with the smoke as it clears the trees, but then, as he stops describing
and begins imagining, his mind returns to the terrestrial world of vagrants,
woods, and caves. "Some uncertain notice" initially appears to describe a
property of the smoke. *Uncertain* may mean indefinite, without clear out-
line, and *notice*, a word appearing nowhere else in *Lyrical Ballads*, can be
used as a noun meaning "information." There is, however, an inescapable
suggestion of a perceiving subject, of someone in doubt or misinformed.
The identity of this someone is itself uncertain, however, for the uncer-
tainty that the poet claims, with the conjectures introduced by the oddly
tentative "as might seem," has to do specifically with the provenance of the
smoke, a not irrelevant issue given the proximity of the blast furnaces and
charcoal burners. Two material conditions are lost to consciousness in the
transition from object perception to imagination, description to "uncertain
notice." First is the source of the rising smoke. Second is its destination:
the atmosphere. The difficult third line of the passage seems to enact this
double obfuscation, the condition, attributable to neither subject nor object,
of "some uncertain notice."[67]

For Levinson, the poem's ideological displacement is evident in the
"gratuitous allusion to the vagrants. The strictly notional being of these
figures ("as might seem . . .") marks an attempt to elide the confessed fac-
tual intelligence" (*Wordsworth's Great Period Poems*, 43). Wordsworth,
however, does recognize a sociohistorical condition, rural destitution. What
is elided is the relation of the vagrants to energy production, their marginal
status (as charcoal burners) in an increasingly industrialized economy. That
industry, not poverty, is at the root of Wordsworth's dissociative logic is
further implied by the description of the smoke as "sent up, in silence,"
given that Gilpin had noted the "noise and bustle" of the scene around Tin-
tern (*Observations on the River Wye*, 54). Challenging Levinson's reading,
Charles Rzepka observes that during Wordsworth's 1798 visit the Tintern

furnaces were temporarily shuttered; moreover, he reminds us, the poet explicitly set his meditations "a few miles" upriver from both the abbey and the ironworks. The bellows, forge hammers, and wire-drawing machinery were situated not on the Wye but up the Angidy valley—and, in all probability, would not have been seen by William and Dorothy. "I hope to allay suspicions still entertained by many," Rzepka writes, "that Wordsworth deliberately excluded from his poem unmistakable signs of environmental and social degradation caused by the iron industry at Tintern in 1798."[68] Yet simply to localize the poem, to say that in some positive sense it represents a scene several miles above Tintern Abbey on July 13, 1798, is perverse, given that what Wordsworth so explicitly seeks to represent is a fraught *experience* of spatial and temporal interpenetration, knowledge and non-knowledge, reality and desire.

Like the depiction of the river, Wordsworth's dematerialization of the air—the transformation of atmosphere into something subjective, an indistinct space between the mind and the world's surfaces—revises descriptive convention. As I argued in earlier chapters, eighteenth-century poets, drawing on Boyle's pneumatic chemistry and the detailed atmospheric lexicon of *Paradise Lost*, were highly attuned to air's matter and motion, air as medium and aggregate. Descriptive poets were particularly attuned to the flow of air, which, like the flow of water, energized transport, as in Grainger's "prosperous breezes," which "wafted" the sugar cane "to every quarter of the globe" (2.497, 3.621). By contrast, for Wordsworth, the wind is something felt on the skin, as he asserts in the culminating address to Dorothy: "let the misty mountain winds be free / To blow against thee" (137–38).[69] Here, too, we can hear an echo of Virgil's resolution: "let my delight be the country, and the running streams amid the dells." Virgil, however, immediately recasts his wish as a desire to inhabit the distant glens of Haemus, highlighting its fantastic impossibility.

Descriptive poetry, this book has argued, gives expression to the advanced organic energy economy defined by an expansionist tendency but limited by the finite and fluctuating flows of energy through the Earth system, the solar radiance that enables plants to grow, rivers to flow to the sea, ocean currents and trade winds to connect the Earth's diverse climes. Beauty, for the descriptive poet, is found in the harmony between human and planetary work, in images, for instance, of sunlight falling on fertile fields. For Wordsworth, by contrast, natural beauty appears in nature's nonproductivity, the separation rather than the synthesis of the human-made and the naturally given. As Adorno writes of the invention of "natural beauty," which he sees as coextensive with industrialization: "Nature is exclusively appearance, never the stuff of labor and the reproduction of life" (*Aesthetic Theory*, 65). According to the prevailing reading, "Tintern Abbey" narrates the process whereby "forms of beauty" (24)—the picturesque geometries described in the opening stanza, nature's "colours and . . . forms" (80)—resolve, for a poet who has learned to hear "the still, sad music of humanity" (92), into

> Something far more deeply interfused,
> Whose dwelling is the light of setting suns,
> And the round ocean, and the living air,
> And the blue sky, and in the mind of man,
> A motion and a spirit, that impels
> All thinking things, all objects of all thought,
> And rolls through all things. (97–103)

We hear an echo of the "rolling" (3) waters of the opening lines, the hydrologic cycle transmuted, in the course of the poet's meditation, into a deified nature. In these rhapsodic lines, we see a further example of the dematerialization of energy I have been tracking. Consider the contrast between Wordsworth's "motion and a spirit" and Thomson's apostrophe to the sun in *Summer*: "O Sun!" "Prime cheerer, Light! / Of all material beings first and best! / Efflux divine!" Thomson is explicit about the source of the energy the flows of which his poem describes. It comes from the Sun, and the intensity and variable availability of this solar energy is the condition of all human world making. By contrast, Wordsworth's "setting sun," the only direct reference to the Sun in the poem, is a beautiful sunset, with no relation to production. Writing a half century after Thomson and a decade before Thomas Young articulated the first properly thermodynamic definition of energy, Wordsworth abstracts planetary energy flux into a "motion and a spirit," a dematerialized natural supernaturalism. Yet we do not term this transfiguration of the concrete details of a particular time and place into "a motion and a spirit" *allegory*. We call it *lyric* because the poem supplies the key that mediates its levels: the psychic imperatives that necessitate the consolation of the transcendent.

"Tintern Abbey" is not a representative poem in Wordsworth's oeuvre, which is replete with images of hardship and human precarity in inclement weather as well as sustained philosophical engagement with the sciences of Earth history.[70] Compare the mountain winds that Wordsworth encourages to blow freely with the "storm and rain" and "wind full ten times over" that confront the narrator in "The Thorn."[71] Indeed, *Lyrical Ballads* presents us with a number of unhoused characters exposed to the dangerous elements. Or consider the way the "Two blighting seasons when the fields were left / With half a harvest," described in *The Ruined Cottage*, combine with the war in North America and unemployment to produce socioecological disaster.[72] Levinson characterizes Wordsworth's transmutation in "Tintern Abbey" of an industrial landscape into a "pastoral" prospect as an exemplary instance of the romantic mystification of social determination, its presentation of "culture as Nature" (*Wordsworth's Great Period Poems*, 39). Yet what is more surprising is the way "Tintern Abbey" mystifies not social but climatic exigencies: the role played by water and wind in energizing production as well as the hazards of unpredictable and extreme weather. That in doing so it gives birth to the modern lyric and the romantic love of nature tells us something about the energy imaginary that underlies both.

SOLAR POETICS AND THE LYRIC IMPULSE IN SMITH'S "BEACHY HEAD"

The use of *energy* to describe a unified physical phenomenon that can be reduced to specific units is often traced to Thomas Young's *Course of Lectures in Natural Philosophy and the Mechanical Arts*, published in 1807. "The term energy," he writes, "may be applied, with great propriety to the product of the mass or weight of the body, into the square of the number expressing its velocity."[73] The force of an object moving through space in time, kinetic energy, can be understood in terms of a quantifiable unit. Over the next decade, Humphry Davy and others extended this to "chemical energy" and "electrical energy." Young himself had proposed that light and heat were manifestations of the same underlying phenomenon.[74] As Young was preparing his *Lectures*, Charlotte Smith was writing a poem that expresses, in form and theme, a prethermodynamic conception of energy: of energy equivalence and feedback across systems, of energy flux as a measure of time. Smith's "Beachy Head," the major poem in a posthumously published collection of the same title, is, as Smith described it, a "local poem" that "embraces a variety of subjects,"[75] moving vertiginously across geographic and temporal scales, from sublime scenes of history to "objects more minute" (372). If allegory projects the possibility of aesthetic unification into anagogic expectation, and if lyric discovers the analogue of the poem's formal coherence in biographical continuity, the referential horizon and formal correlative of descriptive poetry is, as I have been arguing, the variable Earth itself. What underlies the shifts of scale and subject in "Beachy Head"— from geohistorical world making and the climatic exigencies of conquest and commerce to the daily toil of the agriculturalist and the descriptions of flora and weather—is the prethermodynamic advanced organic energy imaginary I have been exploring in this book. To read "Beachy Head," as John Anderson does, as a cacophonous "mosaic" lacking "system" may, as we have seen with *The Seasons*, reveal more about our principles of formal coherence than those that structure the poem.[76]

Readers have in recent years often compared "Beachy Head" to "Tintern Abbey" as part of a larger case for the introduction of Smith into the romantic canon.[77] Yet Smith's trajectory as a poet can be seen to invert the first stage of Wordsworth's career. She established her reputation publishing autobiographical lyrics in her popular *Elegiac Sonnets* (1784–97), which influenced both Cowper and Wordsworth, before turning to more didactic and descriptive projects with *The Emigrants* (1793) and especially the poems included in *Beachy Head, Fables, and Other Poems* (1807).[78] This turn was an outgrowth of Smith's progressive political commitments but also of her work composing educational texts on natural history addressed to children, such as *Rural Walks* (1795) and *Conversations Introducing Poetry; Chiefly on Subjects of Natural History* (1804).[79] Unlike a lyric poem, a didactic tract cannot even pretend to turn its back on its readers. Generically, "Beachy Head" is, like *Edge Hill*, locodescriptive, organized through its sustained attention to a place, the eponymous chalk headland and its South Downs environs. As she was writing "Beachy Head," in the final years of her life, Smith reread Michael Drayton's *Poly-Olbion* (1612–22), often identified as the first topographical poem in English. However, as Theresa Kelley notes, critics have tended to read Smith's descriptive poetry through the lens of the sonnets, as defined by "self-inscription" and the staging of a "Romantic poetic persona," a mode of gendered lyric reading that begins in the earliest reviews of *The Emigrants* and remains a significant critical approach to Smith's later poetry.[80] In my reading of "Beachy Head," I show how Smith develops a distinctly sophisticated and reflexive treatment of the forms of poetic idealization and lyric desire I have been discussing. Indeed, if Wordsworth's project in "Tintern Abbey" is to find "recompense" (89) in a spiritualized "motion" that "rolls through all things," Smith in "Beachy Head" is investigating, with Lucretian rigor, the psychological motives that compel such consolatory fantasies.

Like *Edge Hill*, "Beachy Head" commences with a "locodescriptive moment": the introduction into the temporal immediacy of spatial perception of geohistorical awareness, "a sudden recitation of narrative catastrophe," attention to "metamorphic ground" (Liu, *Wordsworth*, 119–20). Smith's initial apostrophe to the "stupendous summit, rock sublime" (1), names a

geohistorical puzzle widely discussed in the eighteenth century: the plan-
etary past that would explain the asymmetrical distribution of matter, in
this case the unconformity of the English Channel. Indeed, in fancying an
"impetuous . . . flood" rushing "between / The rifted shores" (8–9)—"some
convulsion of Nature," as she adds in the second of the poem's sixty-two
scientific and historiographic notes (attached to line 6)—Smith was not far
from the truth: the Channel was carved 400,000 years ago by an immense
glacial lake outburst flood. Smith returns to such world-making "Fancy"
in the passage later in the poem where the narrator suspends her motion,
holding "still" and looking down to examine "objects more minute, / . . .
the strange and foreign forms / Of sea-shells" (372–74). Assuming that the
apparent fossils were once organic, their presence in the upland soil means
either that the ocean was once higher or that underwater sediment has been
raised:

> What time these fossil shells,
> Buoy'd on their native element, were thrown
> Among the imbedding calx: when the huge hill
> Its giant bulk heaved, and in strange ferment
> Grew up a guardian barrier, 'twixt the sea
> And the green level of the sylvan weald. (384–89)

No lines in the poem have garnered as much critical scrutiny as these and
the passage that follows, in which, adopting the view of the "peasant" who
labors on the land, Smith questions "Science" as mere "conjecture" (390–
93). In a note attached to line 375, she claims never to have "read any of the
late theories of the Earth," or, as she clarifies, never to have been "satisfied"
with the explanations offered in what books she has read. Noah Hering-
man reads her as critiquing the "emergence of scientific specialization,"
aligning her geologic interests with an amateur natural history of obser-
vation, defined in opposition to (French) theory.[81] As Kevis Goodman ob-
serves, Smith may momentarily disavow "conjecture," but the whole of
"Beachy Head" practices it, insofar as *conjecture* (from the Latin *conjectus*,
"thrown together") refers to assemblage, the "composite quality" that the
Earth shares with the poem, "an unabashedly heterogenous assembly, mix-
ing lyric song and narrative verse, myths and histories of Britain with de-
tails of botany and other sciences."[82]

Following Goodman, I read "Beachy Head" as a stratigraphic poem and
not only because of its sustained thematic interest in planetary history: in
climate, in erosion, in ruins and fossils. It is the culminating poem in this

study because of the richness with which it revisits and reworks the modes
and themes I have been reading as expressions of geohistorical transition.
Goodman highlights the way in which Smith integrates phrasing from ear-
lier poets, wording that "pervades *Beachy Head* as fossil forms" ("Conjec-
tures on *Beachy Head*," 997), offering as an example the echo in the lines
on marine fossils of Raphael's account of cosmogenesis in *Paradise Lost*:
"the mountains huge appear / Emergent, and their broad backs upheave"
(7.285–86). The allusion goes deeper, returning us to the language of Earth-
system complexity I associated with the persistence of personification in
chapter 1. Raphael characterizes life as beginning in the ocean: "over all the
face of earth / Main ocean flowed, not idle, but with warm / Prolific humor
softening all her globe, / Fermented the great mother to conceive, / Satiate
with genial moisture" (278–83). Like Milton and the other poets treated in
this study, Smith is, despite the momentary claim of empirical modesty, a
world maker who sees in the Earth's forms a history of intersecting forces.

In the opening passage of the poem, Smith shifts from conjectural geo-
history to the immediacy of the present, from catastrophism to uniformi-
tarianism, from the enigmatic forces registered in the Earth's asymmetrical
forms to the daily operation of planetary systems driven by the Sun's "radi-
ance" (96): "Emerging, brilliant rays of arrowy light / Dart from the horizon;
when the glorious sun / Just lifts above it his resplendent orb" (15–17). *Ra-
diance* had first been employed in a technical sense seven years before the
publication of "Beachy Head" by William Herschel, who used it to describe
the common medium of solar heat and light. The language of force used
to describe sunlight in the opening stanzas hints at the conversion of the
radiant energy of the Sun into the kinetic energy of the hydrologic cycle,
an equivalence between the activity of water (rippling, rushing, rifting) and
light (darting, touching, shooting, firing). "Beachy Head" opens by linking
the Earth-shaping flow of water and the stream of radiant solar energy. The
next description, in the poem, is of metabolic flows within the living world:
"The terns, and gulls, and tarrocks, seek their food" (23). And then we have
another site of energy conversion, in the first representation of a human
artifact, a sailing ship, a definitive preindustrial technology for capturing
planetary flow: "The sloop, her angular canvas shifting still, / Catches the
light and variable airs" (33–34). This is the first of numerous references to
the flow of wind, whether at large—"conflicting winds" (186), "wintry tem-
pests blow" (199)—or channeled to human ends: "Where the knoll / More
elevated takes the changeful winds, / The windmill rears its vanes" (470–
72). Locodescription formalizes, I have claimed, the mercantilist principle
that, in a world of climatic variation, value is created in the transport of

commodities. And what the narrator notices as she gazes out is "the ship of commerce richly freighted, . . . / Bound to orient climates, where the sun / Matures the spice within its odorous shell, / And, rivaling the gray worm's filmy toil, / Bursts from its pod the vegetable down" (42–47). Here, Smith's comparison of the "toil" of the silkworm with the radiance energizing the growth of spice and cotton expresses the georgic principle that surplus derives from the uncompensated labor of nature.

The third stanza ends with an extended description of a sunset, "the sun . . . verging to the sea," "Till the last ray shot upward, fires the clouds" (75, 94). The opening ninety-nine lines of "Beachy Head," in other words, depict a single day, from the "Emerging, brilliant rays of arrowy light" to the "last ray." Daytime, the phase during which sunlight reaches a portion of the Earth, is the poem's operative unit of power. After all, it is the phase during which plants photosynthesize, the primary biospheric energy conversion whereby solar output is transformed into planetary surplus. This process is evoked strikingly in another poem in the *Beachy Head* collection, "The Horologe of the Fields," where Smith describes the diurnal cycles according to which flower species "open, expand, and shut": "the course of Time their blooms describe," "faithful monitors, who tell / How pass the hours and seasons by."[83] In "Beachy Head," there is a pervasive attunement to patterns of available sunlight, such as the way "a richer tract of cultur'd land / Slopes to the south; and burnished by the sun / Bend in the gale of August, floods of corn" (456–58), or the manner in which a ridgeline catches "the last rays of the evening sun" (493), or the way a fallen elm creates an opening in the canopy and "lighter grows the forest scene" (586), or the way "with Spring's return the green blades rise" (200), or the way a lamb seeks "shelter from the noon-day sun" (303).

This variable flux of solar energy, of shortage and excess, shapes life at every scale, from the local to the planetary. Like Milton's and Thomson's, Smith's broad view of history emphasizes the shaping role of climate. Not long after describing ships of commerce bound for "orient climes," the narrator recounts the prehistory of the Norman Conquest. A long note explains: "The Scandinavians . . . began, towards the end of the 8th century, to leave their inhospitable climate in search of the produce of more fortunate countries" (attached to line 126). In "Studies by the Sea," also included in the *Beachy Head* collection, Smith describes the "Sons of the North"—echoing Milton's "multitude" from "the populous North"—whose "venturous toils" are "Urged by imperious want."[84] Climatic conditions compel hard labor and migration. As I have noted, Smith decries the injustices of imperial trade, including the forced "toil" of the slave ("Beachy Head," 54).

Like many of her contemporaries, she personally experienced the profit and pain of British empire. Her father-in-law—who died in 1776, leaving a will the contestation of which was the defining issue of Smith's life—built his fortune from sugar plantations in the West Indies, and her son Charles died of yellow fever in Barbados in 1801.

The organizing movement of "Beachy Head" is an oscillation between expanded and contracted vision, attention to large-scale systems and minute particulars. Kelley sees this scale shifting as staging "an impasse in romantic historiography created by the presence of two historiographical models," the first of which proposes grand narratives, the second of which focuses on a "single place or group over a few years" ("Romantic Histories," 287). The poem, however, defines the pull of the particular as psychological rather than epistemological: "From even the proudest role by glory fill'd, / How *gladly the reflecting mind* returns / To simple scenes of peace and industry, / Where, bosom'd in some valley of the hills / Stands the lone farm (167–71; my emphasis). The sheltered farm, "partially shaded" (174) by elm and ash, and the "hind" (193) with his "independent hut / . . . whence the slow white smoke / Of smouldering peat arises" (195–97) fit within an enclosed, stable system. "Simple scenes of peace and industry" (169) are repeatedly contrasted with the violence, danger, and the illicit profit of smuggling, trade, and conquest. Yet what the reflecting mind discovers is that the planetary conditions that shape empire and global commerce no less shape the labor of the locals who eke out a marginal living from the "hostile" soil of the South Downs (231): the "daily task" (395) of the rural peasant who works "with no care / But that the kindly change of sun and shower / Fit for his toil the earth he cultivates" (396–98). What exposes the fantasy of autonomous locality as a "poet's fabling dreams / Describing Arcady" (209–10) are the exigencies of scarcity and surplus within the advanced organic energy economy: variable access to the Sun's energy among the Earth's climates and across its seasons. The disequilibrium that drives history precedes and informs social relations, which is why I do not entirely agree with Heringman's suggestion that the root of Smith's skepticism about theories of the Earth is the concern that geologic speculation "runs the risk of naturalizing the social history of that landscape": "*Beachy Head*'s insistent antipastoral attention to social inequality and war struggles against such a naturalization of social conditions" ("'Very vain . . . ,'" 255). Without in any way diminishing her attention to "human crimes" (690), Smith recognizes that distributive asymmetries within society are inseparable from the uneven or oscillating allotment of dearth and superfluity in nature. The day laborer who watches a fancy carriage pass by, for instance, "thinks how one day's expenditure, like this, / Would cheer him for long months, when to his toil / The frozen earth closes her marble breast" (252–54). It should be no surprise that the laborer, who sells his work for a wage, so fluently commensurates economic and energy outlays, comparing the cost of the horse-drawn carriage to the cost of the coal that would "cheer" his winter home. The peat fires and rushlight Smith earlier idealized—as when the peasant gathers "the long green rush / That well prepar'd hereafter lends it light / To her poor cottage, dark and cheerless else / Thro' the drear hours of Winter" (216–19)—are insufficient. Smith herself complained, in her destitute final years, about being unable to afford to heat her home: "I am without coals & have only been able to obtain some logs of green wood which will not burn, & my sufferings from cold are dreadful in this cold house" (*Letters*, 535).

In her interpretation of "Beachy Head," Goodman emphasizes Smith's attunement to imperceptibly interlinked scales, the connection between local phenomena and the "global system—a system in which ecological, economic, and political elements intertwine" ("Conjectures on *Beachy Head*," 994). What I would add to this reading of "Beachy Head" as a poem that uses geology to figure absent causality is a recognition that the macro scale of this economy is not planetary but solar. Our models of ecology and economy generally take the planet as the scope of systemic totality. The *Beachy Head* collection returns us to an era in which any conception of the local, any account of surplus and scarcity, would have been organized in relation to what Smith calls, in "Studies by the Sea," the "Day's bright star" (31), not as a historical constant but as an originary surplus the "fluctuating" (18) organization of which constitutes the climate of history.

This solar energy economy of stochastic flux and spatiotemporal variation also generates the lyric impulse. "Beachy Head" is a descriptive poem that integrates several discrete lyric moments. The narrator, whose "Fancy" (4), "Contemplation" (117), and "reflecting mind" (167) organize its dilations and expansions is not explicitly an autobiographical self until line 282: "*I* once was happy." The conventional personifications of mental activity as well as the didactic first-person plural, as in "let us turn" (440), are reminders that this is an insistently public poem rather than a soliloquy overheard. There are, in "Beachy Head," two lyric poets: one male, one female. There is the lovelorn "stranger" (507) who lives "among the ruins" (510) of an old fortress, having suffered from "cold neglect" (527). For this "lonely man" (518), the "flattering pencil" (557) of poetry offers its consolations: "rear'd to sooth his soul / Ideal bowers of pleasure" (558–59). While rural laborers work the land, the poet leaves his "scatter'd rhymes" (574) and "Unfinishe'd sentences" (575) strewn about, nearly a hundred lines of

which are interpolated in "Beachy Head." These lyrics are precisely of the
sort that one imagines Virgil composing as he longs for the cool glens of
Haemus. A harsh climate is the real against which dreamy visions of mild
labor and reciprocal love play out: "I'll contrive a sylvan room / Against
the time of summer heat" (613–14); "I'll dress the sand rock cave for
you, / . . . That you, against the autumnal air / May find securer shelter
there" (621–24). Smith's narrator comments on these poetic consolations,
interpreting the stranger's lyrics (and developing her own version of a *geo-
historical poetics*):

> The visionary, nursing dreams like these,
> Is not indeed unhappy . . .
> And as above him sail the silver clouds,
> He follows them in thought to distant climes,
> Where . . .
> He, in some island of the southern sea,
> May happy build his cane-constructed bower. (655–64)

A countervailing reality principle is, however, asserted in a note (attached to
line 663) that characterizes the idealization of Polynesia as pure projection.
    Smith's own appearance as a lyric presence in "Beachy Head" also in-
volves the staging of certain wish-fulfilling compensations for an experi-
ence of personal loss. In the poem's most autobiographical sequence, Smith
describes her early "exile" (288) from the South Downs and the stark "con-
trast" (290) between London's "polluted smoky atmosphere" (291) and

> the southern hills
> That to the setting Sun, their graceful heads
> Rearing, o'erlook the frith, where Vecta [the Isle of Wight] breaks
> With her white rocks, the strong impetuous tide,
> When western winds the vast Atlantic urge
> To thunder on the coast. (292–97)

Smith moved from Sussex to London at age eight to attend a school in Ken-
sington, although the nostalgia and sense of exile in her poetry is surely more
closely related to her marriage in 1765 to Benjamin Smith and the tumult
that followed. Lyricism emerges, as it does for Cowper and Wordsworth, in
the narrator's experience of a rupture between past and present registered in
atmospheric change. The introduction of the poet's situatedness as a mea-
sure of history and a condition of poetic labor is a response to the same loss

of "pure air" (60) that Eve experienced after the Fall. What embodies the difficult reality that induces the turn to fantasy or nostalgic reminiscence is not heat or cold, as it is for Virgil and for Smith's stranger, but London's "polluted smoky atmosphere." Smith had staged a similar scene in *The Old Manor House* (1793), a historical novel in which the hero, Orlando, recalls his first visit to London at the age of sixteen: "He remembered that he never was so happy as when they left it, and, on a fine evening of May, returned from the smoke of the Strand . . . to his dear native county, where only there seemed to be any happiness for him. Since that time he had never felt a wish to revisit London." Returning to London as an adult on a "dreary, foggy evening in December," he is jostled by crowds, "deafened" by noise, and disgusted by the "thickness of the air."[85] I cite this passage to emphasize how acutely Smith seems to have experienced this contrast, how much biography is, in this poem, filtered through the stark contrast between London's polluted atmosphere and the pure air of the Sussex Downs.

When Smith turns from the Channel—and the war with France and the imperial commerce it brings to mind—to the north, this is what she sees, or sees herself not seeing:

> How wide the view!
> Till in the distant north it melts away,
> And mingles indiscriminate with clouds:
> But if the eye could reach so far, the mart
> Of England's capital, its domes and spires
> Might be perceived—Yet hence the distant range
> Of Kentish hills, appear in purple haze. (481–87)

She echoes the prospect sequence in *The Seasons*, in which Thomson looks out on the capital from Richmond Hill: "what a goodly prospect spreads around, / Of hills, and dales, and woods, and lawns, and spires, / And glittering towns, and gilded streams, till all / The stretching landscape into smoke decays!" (*Su*, 1438–41). London is sixty miles to the north of Beachy Head, so it is a stretch to imagine that the capital would be visible from the low escarpments of the South Downs. What the speaker does see between her position and London, just visible beyond the High Weald, is a chalk hill in the North Downs of Kent, perhaps Saltbox Hill. The "purple haze," in other words, may well be the air pollution of London as it settles on the North Downs. Indeed, the passage resonates with Wordsworth's "some uncertain notice" in the "Might" and the "hence" and the confusion of subjective perception with physical conditions, the way it is impossible to know whether the limit of vision is in the "eye" or in the opacity of the "purple haze." This perceptual confusion is matched by a temporal ambiguity when the narrator exclaims: "Ah! Hills so early loved! In fancy still / I breathe your pure keen air" (368–69). These are difficult lines in that they suggest that an insistently deictic and descriptive poem can, in some way, also be the retrospective projection of "fancy." Fancy is, throughout the poem, the medium of reminiscence and (geo)historical conjecture (e.g., 4, 409).

The "pattern of geological skepticism" Heringman identifies in "Beachy Head" is equaled by a skepticism about lyric poetry's idealizations and consolations ("'Very vain . . . ,'" 250). "Happiness!" exclaims the narrator, "a word / That like false fire, from marsh effluvia born, / Misleads the wanderer, destin'd to contend / In the world's wilderness, with want or woe— / Yet *they* are happy, who have never ask'd / what good or evil means" (255–60). Given that Satan tempting Eve is compared to the *ignis fatuus*, "a wandering fire," these lines can be read as a miniaturized retelling of Milton's epic. Yet, unlike Milton and the other British poets treated in this study, Smith offers no compensatory vision of the future. She insists on what Lucretius calls "the strong force of time" (*On the Nature*, 5.314).[86] She compares the finitude to which all living beings are subject with the "transient" (438) clouds, windblown, casting shifting shadows on the landscape: "All, with the lapse of Time, have passed away" (434). Fading flowers and changing skies tell the same story, of a human condition that cannot be separated from planetary vicissitude, as do the artifacts discovered "beneath the green sward" (429), marine fossils in the high chalk cliffs, the bones of Roman elephants and the "remains of men" in "half obliterated mounds" (402). For Thomson, it is the "bold ambition" of the European explorers that led to the "rising world of trade" (*Su*, 1004–7). To this, Smith replies: "Hither, Ambition, come! / Come and behold the nothingness of all / For which you carry thro' the oppressed Earth, / War, and its train of horrors" (419–22).

If lyricization registers a psychological imperative, the drive to discover a refuge or enclosure, Virgil in the *Georgics* is quick to return from the pastoral dream of "cool glens" to the task of conveying in verse "the laws of nature's working." Smith too, in the final passages of "Beachy Head," returns from fantasies of an exotic clime or an untouched atmosphere to Lucretian hard truths and the practical question of how to live with others in a tempestuous world. In doing so, she revises a key passage in *De rerum natura*, the opening lines of book 2: "A joy it is, when the strong winds of storm / Stir up the waters of a mighty sea, / To watch from shore the troubles of another" (*On the Nature*, 1–3). In the final three stanzas of "Beachy Head," she celebrates the life of an actual historical personage, Parson Darby, who in the early eighteenth century inhabited a cavern in the limestone cliffs. "Outraged / . . . By human crimes" (689–90), Darby retreated to this "flint-surrounded home" (686), yet remained "feelingly alive to all that breath'd" (688). Like the Virgilian husbandman, he learned to read the skies, "to augur from the clouds of heaven / And from the changing colours of the sea / . . . / When tempests were approaching" (692–97). When storms are predicted, he watches for foundering ships. When he is able, he rescues the sailors from the "wild billows" (708), and, when he fails to save them, he buries their bodies, offering his prayers to some "helpless stranger" (716) on a beach where the sea meets the land. Darby practices a form of care that transcends the nation, attending to those made precarious in the networks of global capitalism. Responsibility for others extends beyond borders; as Goodman and Gurton-Wachter have shown, Smith works incessantly to denaturalize the jingoism and enmity the predominated during the Napoleonic Wars.[87] The relation between Darby and the sailors is, as Nigel Clark describes an ethics of planetary life, "forged in response to the incitements of an out-side": "For it is the raw and the processed physicality of the earth—howling wind, surging waters, failing levees—that unravels pre-existing bonds and propels exposed beings into each other's paths—and in this way re-enacts an originary imperative to being-in-common" (*Inhuman Nature*, 156, 159).

The concluding stanza of "Beachy Head" recounts Darby's death, when "One dark night / The equinoctial wind blew south by west, / Fierce on the shore" (716–18). The wind is so strong that fragments of stone are blown from the cliff. The following morning, local shepherds recover Darby's corpse from the waves and bury him. A poem that begins atop Beachy Head concludes in a recess within it:

> Those who read
> Chisel'd within the rock, these mournful lines,
> Memorials of his sufferings, did not grieve,
> That dying in the cause of charity
> His spirit, from its earthly bondage freed,
> Had to some better region fled for ever. (726–31)

"Beachy Head," like *De rerum natura*, is a poem that discovers no solace in the workings of providence or anagogic anticipation. The expectation of a "better region," as a reward for good works and compensation for the suffer-ing of "earthly bondage," is ascribed to the shepherds, those who read the "mournful lines." Beyond the reference to the cosmogenic "Omnipotent" in the opening stanza (naturalized as a "convulsion" in the corresponding note [attached to line 6]), nowhere does the narrator invoke the salvific solar deity of Milton, Thomson, and Cowper. Also like *De rerum natura*, "Beachy Head" is unfinished; according to the advertisement, it was "not completed according to the original design."[88] Smith has left unwritten the parson's epitaph, unless, as some readers have suggested, we take the poem itself to provide the "mournful lines," Smith's own self-memorializing epitaph. The missing epitaph, words written on stone but not reproduced on the page, is a textual unconformity. It thus stages the dilemmas of interpretation this study has examined, asking us, as readers, to read what earlier readers read yet is not present to us. It posits an inscription in the Earth that is also an absence, and it does so in a poem in which, I have been suggesting, one governing absence is, as in so much of the solar energy poetry I have discussed, the emergent fossil-fuel energy regime embodied in London's "polluted smoky atmosphere."

The Literary Past and the Planetary Future

As a work of metacommentary, this study has foregrounded the persistent failure of historical criticism to recognize the Earth's climate as a referent. This critical failure is evidence of what, following Jameson, I call the *climatological unconscious*. The first condition of the climatological unconscious is not historical, an expression of the accelerative growth of industrial modernity, but simply phenomenal: the unavailability of the Earth, as a spherical totality, and the absent causality of energy itself.[1] Lucretius draws on the affordances of verse to figure forth the hidden causes of things, to narrate the natural history of the Earth as an assemblage—"earth and sea and sky / . . . Three forms so unalike, so interwoven" (*On the Nature*, 5.92–94)—and to teach his readers to face up to this hazardous world, "burnt / By constant sun" (231–32). Even as subsequent poets are drawn to his audacity and rigor, they never entirely accept this mandate. Virgil already softens the hard medicine, in the injunction to worship the rural gods, in the panegyrics to Italy's climate and sovereign, and in the fantasy of pastoral retreat. In Virgil, then, we see a second version of the climatological unconscious, psychological rather than phenomenal: "the conflict of desire and reality," as Frye writes, "which has for its basis the work of the dream" first theorized by Freud (*Anatomy of Criticism*, 105).[2] The British poets I have discussed returned to each of these Virgilian strategies for wishing away planetary necessity in the very modes I have been distinguishing: in the allegorical sublimation of natural-historical time in anagogic expectation, in the descriptive investment in projects of nation building and imperial expansion, and in the lyric staging of individual desire.

The climatological unconscious as a critical blind spot is, in other words, not merely a projection of modern criticism. It is, rather, a selective and insufficiently dialectical way of reading since it misses the planetary real that precedes and provokes these compensatory wishes. This third sense of the climatological unconscious—a habit of thinking shared with culture broadly—is, I have been arguing, a specific symptom of an industrial economy that gives temporary (and, finally, illusory) material form to the idea that, by channeling the forces of nature, humans can free themselves from planetary constraints.

This project has been inspired at every turn by Jameson's reading of the oversights in Frye's capacious "poetics" (*Anatomy of Criticism*, 14), including Jameson's insistence that the mode of production, not nature, is the alienating reality against which literature imagines its worlds, which are to be understood as both compensatory and critical, ideological and utopian in their recasting of the real. In "Marxism and Historicism," Jameson observes that the concept of the mode of production may solve the problem of the "logic of the historical object" while leaving unanswered the question of the "place of the historian-subject, or of the present" (59, 69). To interpret the cultural past, he observes, is to establish an untimely vantage on our own historical situation, on the modes of production that are the condition of possibility for our interpretive agendas, the ways we read and think now. Frye had identified in "the culture of the past . . . not only the memory of mankind, but our own *buried life*," such that the study of literary history "leads to a recognition scene, a discovery in which we see, not our past lives, but the total cultural form of our present life" (*Anatomy of Criticism*, 346). For Jameson, what we recognize in the history of literature is not ourselves but "a radically different life form which rises up to call our own form of life into question and to pass judgment on us, and through us, on the social formation in which we exist": "[It] judges us, imposing the painful knowledge of what we are not, what we are no longer, what we are not yet" ("Marxism and Historicism," 70). In this "not yet," the unfulfilled futures of the literary past, Jameson discovers a "Utopian impulse" (71).

Jameson's own persistent misreading of modern history in terms of an "imminent abolition of nature"—and no less his utopian vision of the "collective struggle to wrest a realm of Freedom from a realm of Necessity" (*The Political Unconscious*, 19)—itself reflects the productivist fantasy of an Earth system that can be reshaped to human ends, which many strands of Marxism share with capitalist ideologies of growth. "History," Jameson writes, "is a product of human labor just like the work of art itself, and obeys analogous dynamics" (*Marxism and Form*, 328). In Jameson's thought, then, we see again this climatological unconscious, this failure to recognize the Earth as the untranscendable condition of production. His hermeneutic can be read as itself one of those "specialized interpretive codes whose insights are strategically limited" by their "situational origin" (*The Political Unconscious*, 21) in a brief phase of industrial modernity defined by an "unprecedented upsurge in energy mobilization" (*Shock of the Anthropocene*, 9). The limit I am identifying is evident in the second epigraph to *The Political Unconscious*, from Émile Durkheim's *The Elementary Forms of Religious Life*, part of which I quote here: "The very concept of totality is but the abstract form of the concept of society: that whole which includes all things." It is the principle of the "unity of the social"—an idea Jameson associates with the romantic period, as an expression of the first stage of the Industrial Revolution—that supports a theory of mediation linking culture with society, the work of art with the mode of production. The principle of a unified social field sustains the interpretive work, figured as a "sudden exchange of energy," that "involves the jumping of a spark between two poles, the coming into contact of two unequal terms, of two apparently unrelated modes of being," such as aesthetics and economics (*Marxism and Form*, 4). The idea of the social as the horizon of totality, the unity in which the "semi-autonomy" of the levels is subsumed, underlies Althusser's structuralist account of the mode of production as "the synchronic system of social relations as a whole" (*The Political Unconscious*, 36–37). Like the labor theory of value, the concept of the mode of production as the total form of society draws on a nineteenth-century conception of energy that decouples work from the planetary forces that enable and exceed social reproduction.

Here we see the presupposition that Jameson's strong theory shares with liberal and positivist forms of criticism, including a vast swathe of weakly theoretical historical-contextualist projects: the identification of society or the social relation as the privileged explanatory principle, the condition of historicity that literary texts represent or repress, resolve or resist. The belief that there exists a social world analytically separable from the Earth and its dynamic agencies underwrites the humanistic disciplines, which study those phenomena—identities and institutions, texts and technologies—that humans have made. There are perfectly valid reasons for this emphasis on social production. Ideology, it is assumed, works through naturalization, where nature stands for the inevitable, the necessary, the inescapable. To constitute a horizon of political possibility—to imagine the world being made otherwise, which is one task criticism shares with literature—seems to require that we emphasize, in Nigel Clark's words, "the various achievements and potentialities of human agency" (*Inhuman Nature*, 13).

One might wonder whether the concept of the Anthropocene is not the very fulfillment of such a mode of thought, in that the Earth system itself has come to be a human artifact. Is not nature now a social construct in a material as well as an ideological sense? It turns out that this is not the case at all. The semantic inadequacy of the term *Anthropocene* has less to do with the attribution of a unified species identity to the human, given that nothing precludes us from recognizing conflict and variation within the Anthropos, than with its failure to recognize planetary forces, including the unpredictability of tipping points related to internal feedback mechanisms in the Earth system, such as Arctic methane release. The Anthropocene is so difficult to conceptualize and periodize because it names a twofold energy transition, a change in the social organization of energy production that introduces, as an unintended consequence, a wholesale alteration of the planetary energy system—the climate. What appeared to be a vast increase in human productive power turned out to be a disruption of Earth system processes that catastrophically rebounds on human world making, exposing the limits of our agency, the vulnerability of our infrastructure, and the inadequacy of our political institutions. The shock of the Anthropocene is not the geologic scaling up of the human—which is, after all, a story we have been telling for two centuries—but the fact that human societies have succeeded in intensifying planetary processes in ways that reveal our inability fully to control, contain, and capture the Earth's energies. The Anthropocene is not, as it is been characterized, a terminal crisis: the end of the human, the end of time, or the exhaustion of planetary resources. As Fredrik Albritton Jonsson observes, such entropic anxieties are themselves a by-product of the fossil age, as the unprecedented amplification of productive power was shadowed by fears of resource exhaustion.[3] Apprehensions of entropic finitude turn out to be no more appropriate than ecomodernist fantasies of geoengineered sustainability in orienting us toward the definitive condition of this new epoch we are entering: increased absorption of solar radiation in the atmosphere and of heat in the ocean, a catastrophic upsurge in the flow of energy through the Earth system.

"A genealogy of energy," Cara New Daggett writes, "helps [us] in understanding why it is so difficult to imagine energy otherwise" (*The Birth of Energy*, 3). The aim of this book has been to recover a prethermodynamic solar energy imaginary, the otherwise of which—the possible future toward which I read the literary past—is not the utopian otherwise of human emancipation but the otherwise of Lucretian necessity, the "danger and disaster" that exist in "sky and sun and earth and sea's deep waters" (*On the Nature*, 5.369, 374). We are, in these early days of the Anthropocene, once again confronting the sort of planetary limits and hazards that preindustrial societies recognized as inescapable. "Climate," as Jesse Oak Taylor writes, "is a discourse of limits" (*The Sky of Our Manufacture*, 13). Climate determines human project not as an all-controlling law but in the sense Raymond Williams recovers in the root meaning of *determine* as "setting bounds," a "complex and interrelated process of limits and pressures."[4] Williams's language of determination parallels that of climate historians, who have sought to nuance climatic determinism by describing climate change as a catalyst, trigger, or intensifier in social life.

The claim that I have developed in this book is that there is no social totality because the social—the symbolic categories we draw on to know ourselves, our labor, and our world, as well as the institutions and infrastructures that organize the reproduction of human life—is constitutively open to the planetary. Whatever surfaces and depths, crises or cruxes of meaning operate within a text give expression to historical conjunctures that are necessarily socioecological. The climate crisis, then, requires us to develop a new critical theory of society in which we account for the way in which a turbulent and self-differing Earth intensifies, mediates, triggers, and asymmetrically distributes in ways that exceed sociological explanation. Ideology is not only the mystificatory naturalization of the social but also the mystificatory socialization of the natural. Any vision of a more just collective life, including one retrieved from the unrealized futures of the literary past, must integrate an appreciation of a necessity that exists in the Earth itself. In the past decade, scholars across the humanities have begun developing such a critical social theory of the Earth in a multidisciplinary conversation this study has drawn on and to which it seeks to contribute. I am thinking, in particular, of the work Jason Moore and Andreas Malm have done to rethink value form theory, offering a new history of extraction and accumulation as "world ecology" or "fossil capital"; of the challenge to the historian's code in the work of Julia Adeney Thomas and Dipesh Chakrabarty; of the incitement to "think social life through the Earth" in the work of British sociologists such as Nigel Clark, Kathryn Yusoff, and Bronislaw Szerszynski; of Joel Wainwright's and Geoff Mann's rethinking of sovereignty for the Anthropocene; and of the work of Michel Serres, Bruno Latour, Donna Haraway, and others who recognized the need for such a reformulation of critical social theory long before the shock of the Anthropocene.

In this study, I have identified poetry, in its stratigraphic density and shifting modes, as a unique archive of geohistory, tracking a literary genealogy of revision and repression that runs from the world making of Lucretius to romantic lyricization. If romanticism expresses an initial industrial stage of the Anthropocene, in the post-1945 Great Acceleration, poetry, as Margaret Ronda recounts, came to associate itself with other remaindered forms, "with what lives on and what is beyond repair," including nature itself in its fragility and transience.[5] Even earlier, the novel, in its pretensions as modern epic, claims from poetry the ambition to represent the system entire. As Jesse Oak Taylor argues, Victorian realism does not just oversee the work of mediating rifts between the subject and the social totality. Drawing on similar narrative resources, novels such as *Bleak House* can represent climate by integrating "discrete atmospheric events into a broader totality of long-term global patterns," attesting "to the presence of climate as such, and recast[ing] human agency (and accountability) within it" (*The Sky of Our Manufacture*, 10–11). For an even longer history of climate fiction, we can revisit *Frankenstein*, Mary Shelley's secular retelling of *Paradise Lost*, a novel that, as David Higgins and Gillen D'Arcy Wood have each shown, was birthed in the disorienting aftermath of Tambora.[6] We can look back further still, as Annette Hulbert explains, to the way in which the Great Storm of 1703, and the risk to life and capital it represents, haunts Defoe's realist novels.[7]

Despite these examples, as it supplants poetry as the dominant literary mode the modern novel can also be seen to forget about the Earth and its climate, as recurrent rhythm and stochastic unpredictability.[8] The novel, in fact, may be inherently anthropocentric, owing to basic formal features or its development in industrial modernity.[9] Because of its rhythmicity, its figurativeness, its materialization of the signifier, and its flexible modes of address, poetry may be intrinsically closer to an Earth that is itself animate. It may preserve an earlier language, like Adam's first speech, in which the auditor is not always already human.

With alacrity and inventiveness, contemporary novelists have been testing such a claim, experimenting with generic patterns of expectation to imagine a present and future in which climate is once again a condition of human world making. The burgeoning of climate change fiction over the past two decades has, in turn, inspired (and been inspired by) a new critical conversation about the adequacy and affordances of realism for what Jennifer Wenzel calls "world-imagining," bringing into the space of fictive representation the diverse scales, times, and actors involved in planetary crisis.[10] Yet, if fiction today seeks to make itself anew under the pressure of geohistory, a recurrent feature of the new climate change novels is the reappearance of older literary modes. Consider Lauren's Earthseed verse in Octavia Butler's *Parable of the Sower*, the Khembalung myth in Kim Stanley Robinson's *Green Earth*, the "stone lore" in N. K. Jemisin's *Broken Earth* trilogy, the swan poems of Blake and Baudelaire entering Aboriginal dream time in Alexis Wright's *The Swan Book*, and the retelling of the Manasa Devi legend in Amitav Ghosh's *Gun Island*. New novels, searching for imaginative resources with which to take the measure of accelerating geohistorical change, return to the cultural past because humans have been trying to find the modes with which to know a precarious and changeable Earth for as long as they have been imagining worlds.

ACKNOWLEDGMENTS

A properly "historicist perspective," Jameson observes in *The Political Unconscious*, is one in which "our readings of the past are vitally dependent on our experience of the present." I wrote this book about climate as something difficult to apprehend and know over the course of a decade in which nothing has seemed more ineluctably real than the planetary climate crisis. I began working on this project in the fall of 2009, when I was teaching a first-year interdisciplinary seminar at Willamette University on climate change and the human imagination. The seminar coincided with the Copenhagen Summit, President Obama's first opportunity to contribute to the negotiation of a global climate accord. COP 15 was an abysmal failure, concluding with a nonbinding and unratified "accord" that contained no legal commitments for the reduction of carbon emissions. This project began with an experience, which is ongoing, of real historical pessimism. As I completed an initial draft of the first chapter, writing about Milton's depiction of the expulsion of Adam and Eve and the fiery loss of Eden, the deadliest wildfire in California history incinerated the town of Paradise.

In these dark and difficult times, I am very grateful for the support of the serious-minded and generous people and the institutions that have nourished this project.

It is in the classroom, especially, that old books find new life. I thank the undergraduates and the graduate students at Willamette University, Miami University, and the University of California, Davis, who have, over the past decade, taken classes or worked on projects with me in which we look squarely at planetary crisis. In particular, thanks to Chris Washington, Caroline Heller, Annette Hulbert, Elizabeth Giardina, Kristin Hogue, Jumana Esau, and Isabel Realyvasquez.

Over the past decade, many colleagues and friends have inspired me, challenged me, read drafts, invited me to present work, and shared their ideas with me. In particular, I would like to thank Derek Woods, Julian Yates, Jeffrey Jerome Cohen, John Havard, Alysia Garrison, Jason Moore, Julia Adeney Thomas, Fredrik Albritton Jonsson, Tim Campbell, Hannes Bergthaller, Bryan Rasmussen, Benjamin Morgan, Devin Griffiths, Scott Hess, Lynn Voskuil, Anne-Lise François, Antoine Traisnel, Joe Albernaz, Jeremy Davies, Lynn Badia, Tom Ford, David Craig, Erin Drew, Robert Markley, Rajani Sudan, David Collings, Jesse Molesworth, Rebecca Spang, Mary Favret, Noah Heringman, Tommy Davis, Chuck Rzepka, Jennifer Wenzel, and Deidre Lynch.

I owe a particular debt to those intellectual comrades who have stuck with me for so many years and who sustain the most serious interlocution on matters scholarly and existential without always insisting on the decorum and indoor settings of academic exchange: Jesse Oak Taylor, Kevis Goodman, Eric Gidal, Stan Robinson, David Moser, Yutan Getzler, Annie McClanahan, and Theodore Martin.

The University of California, Davis, is an extraordinary place to teach and study the environmental humanities. I thank, in particular, my Davis colleagues and friends who have supported this project: Alessa Johns, David Simpson, Margie Ferguson, Fran Dolan, Matthew Stratton, Kathleen Frederickson, Louis Warren, Gina Bloom, Flagg Miller, Tiffany Werth, and Sudipta Sen. Special thanks to my fellow energy critics Mike Ziser and Liz Miller, who have been close ecocritical collaborators since I arrived at Davis.

An earlier version of the reading of Cowper's *Task* in chapter 4 was published as an article, "'The Present Obfuscation': Cowper's *Task* and the Time of Climate Change," *PMLA* 127.3 (May 2012): 477–92 (reprinted by permission of the copyright owner, The Modern Language Association of America). The reading of Smith's "Beachy Head" in chapter 4 is derived in part from my "Late Holocene Poetics: Genre and Geohistory in *Beachy Head*," *European Romantic Review* 28.3 (2017): 307–14, copyright Taylor and Francis, https://www.tandfonline.com/doi/full/10.1080/10509585.2017.1314669. Several sentences in the introduction and chapter 4 on the figuration of atmosphere in the work of Benjamin and Adorno are taken from "Anthropocene Air," *Minnesota Review* 83 (2014): 93–101 (reprinted by permission of Duke University Press).

Making a book is a lot of work (and not only for its author). Alan Thomas has guided this project from a germ of an idea to a book in a hand for almost a decade. Randy Petilos and the staff at the University of Chicago Press provided timely and professional support. Thank you to the anonymous readers whose incisive feedback spurred significant revisions.

My son, Rowan, was born in 2010, the year I began working on this project. It is with his future in mind that I have written this book. I am fortunate to share my household with a companionate thinker, Margaret Ronda; our daily conversations and shared world making have, in so many ways, shaped this book and its author.

NOTES

INTRODUCTION

1. See Jeremy Davies, *The Birth of the Anthropocene* (Oakland: University of California Press, 2016).

2. See Andreas Malm: "Climate change does not produce natural disasters of the garden variety present since time immemorial, but a very peculiar form of the phenomenon: namely, extreme weather caused by the large-scale combustion of fossil fuels. The same distance separates our present and future from Prospero's storm, Dante's wastelands or the jeremiads of the Hebrew prophets, which have nothing to do with the source of the problem." "'This is the hell that I have heard': Some Dialectical Images in Fossil Fuel Fiction," *Forum for Modern Language Studies* 53.2 (April 2017): 121–41, 126.

3. Jennifer Wenzel, "Stratigraphy and Empire: *Waiting for the Barbarians*, Reading under Duress," in *Anthropocene Reading: Literary History in Geologic Times*, ed. Tobias Menely and Jesse Oak Taylor (University Park: Pennsylvania State University Press, 2017), 167–83, 170.

4. Walter Benjamin, "Commentary on Poems by Brecht," in *Selected Writings* (Cambridge, MA: Harvard University Press, 2003), 4:215–50, 215–16.

5. See, e.g., Barbara Leckie, "Sequence and Fragment, History and Thesis: Samuel Smiles's Self-Help, Social Change, and Climate Change," *Nineteenth-Century Contexts* 38.5 (2016): 305–17; and Adeline Johns-Putra, "Climate and History in the Anthropocene: Realist Narrative and the Framing of Time," in *Climate and Literature*, ed. Adeline Johns-Putra (Cambridge: Cambridge University Press, 2019), 246–62.

6. Walter Benjamin, "On the Concept of History," in *Selected Writings*, 4:389–400, 395 (hereafter cited in text).

7. Walter Benjamin, "On Some Motifs in Baudelaire," in *Selected Writings*, 4:313–55, 314 (hereafter cited in text).

8. Walter Benjamin, "The Storyteller: Observations on the Works of Nikolai Leskov," in *Selected Writings* (Cambridge, MA: Belknap Press of Harvard University Press, 2006), 3:143–66, 144.

9. Walter Benjamin, *The Arcades Project* (Cambridge, MA: Belknap Press of Harvard University Press, 2002), 474.

10. Jonathan Culler, "Apostrophe," in *The Pursuit of Signs: Semiotics, Literature, Deconstruction* (Ithaca, NY: Cornell University Press, 1981), 135–54, 142.

11. Marjorie Levinson, *Wordsworth's Great Period Poems: Four Essays* (Cambridge: Cambridge University Press, 1986), 37–39 (hereafter cited in text).

12. See Mark Canuel, "Historicism, Formalism, and 'Tintern Abbey,'" *European Romantic Review* 23.3 (June 2012): 363–71.

13. Northrop Frye, *Anatomy of Criticism: Four Essays* (Princeton, NJ: Princeton University Press, 1957), 160 (hereafter cited in text).

14. Amanda Jo Goldstein, *Sweet Science: Romantic Materialism and the New Logics of Life* (Chicago: University of Chicago Press, 2017), 7, 20 (hereafter cited in text).

15. Michel Serres proposes that Lucretius initiated a physics of fluid dynamics and temperature differentials, with the "clinamen" standing for "the minimal angle of deviation from a laminar flow required to create turbulence, which is the condition for atoms to meet and combine and thereby also for the emergence of order." *The Birth of Physics*, trans. Jack Hawkes (Manchester: Clinamen, 2000), 5.

16. John L. Brooke, *Climate Change and the Course of Global History: A Rough Journey* (Cambridge: Cambridge University Press, 2014), 1 (hereafter cited in text). For insightful overviews of the field, see Franz Mauelshagen, "Redefining Historical Climatology in the Anthropocene," *Anthropocene Review* 1.2 (2014): 171–204; and Benjamin Lieberman and Elizabeth Gordon, *Climate Change in Human History: Prehistory to the Present* (London: Bloomsbury, 2018).

17. Hubert Lamb, *Climate, History and the Modern World* (London: Methuen, 1982), xviii, 3 (hereafter cited in text).

18. See, e.g., Anthony McMichael, *Climate Change and the Health of Nations: Famines, Fevers, and the Fate of Populations* (Oxford: Oxford University Press, 2017); Kyle Harper, *The Fate of Rome: Climate, Disease, and the End of an Empire* (Princeton, NJ: Princeton University Press, 2017); William J. Burroughs, *Climate Change in Prehistory: The End of the Reign of Chaos* (Cambridge: Cambridge University Press, 2005).

19. See Thomas B. van Hoof et al., "Forest Re-Growth on Medieval Farmland After the Black Death Pandemic: Implications for Atmospheric CO_2 Levels," *Palaeogeography, Palaeoclimatology, Palaeoecology* 237, nos. 2–4 (August 2006): 396–409; and Alexander Koch et al., "Earth System Impacts of the European Arrival and Great Dying in the Americas After 1492," *Quaternary Science Reviews* 207 (2019): 13–36.

20. Sam White, "The Real Little Ice Age," *Journal of Interdisciplinary History* 44.3 (Winter 2014): 327–52, 328.

21. See Dagomar Degroot, *The Frigid Golden Age: Climate Change, the Little Ice Age, and the Dutch Republic, 1560–1720* (Cambridge: Cambridge University Press, 2018) (hereafter cited in text); Sam White, *The Climate of Rebellion in the Early Modern Ottoman Empire* (Cambridge: Cambridge University Press, 2011), and *A Cold Welcome: The Little Ice Age and Europe's Encounter with North America* (Cambridge, MA: Harvard University Press, 2017); Brian Fagan, *The Little Ice Age: How Climate Made History, 1300–1850* (New York: Basic, 2000); Philipp Blom, *Nature's Mutiny: How the Little Ice Age of the Long Seventeenth Century Transformed the West and Shaped the Present* (New York: Norton, 2019); and Sugata Ray, *Climate Change and the Art of Devotion: Geoaesthetics in the Land of Krishna, 1550–1850* (Seattle: University of Washington Press, 2019).

22. Geoffrey Parker, *Global Crisis: War, Climate Change and Catastrophe in the Seventeenth Century* (New Haven, CT: Yale University Press, 2013) (hereafter cited in text).

23. See also John Richards, *The Unending Frontier: An Environmental History of the Early Modern World* (Berkeley and Los Angeles: University of California Press, 2005), chap. 6. On the first-wave "organic Anthropocene," see John L. Brooke and Christopher Otter, "Concluding Remarks: The Organic Anthropocene," *Eighteenth-Century Studies* 49.2 (Winter 2016): 281–302.

24. Kenneth Pomeranz, *The Great Divergence: China, Europe, and the Making of the Modern World Economy* (Princeton, NJ: Princeton University Press, 2000).

25. Jason Moore, "Climates of Crisis, 376–2019" (lecture presented at the Fifth Annual Conference of the World-Ecology Research Network, San Francisco, May 30, 2019). David Harvey defines the *spatial fix* in terms of "capitalism's insatiable drive to resolve its inner crisis tendencies by geographical expansion and geographical restructuring." See "Globalization and the 'Spatial Fix,'" *Geographische Revue* 3 (2001): 23–30.

26. Ji-Hyung Cho, "The Little Ice Age and the Coming of the Anthropocene," *Asian Review of World Histories* 2.1 (January 2014): 1–16, 16 (my emphasis).

27. Jason Moore, *Capitalism in the Web of Life: Ecology and the Accumulation of Capital* (London: Verso, 2015), 196 (hereafter cited in text). Elsewhere, Moore writes that "*geohistory* . . . includes biogeological changes as fundamental to human histories of power and production": "Early capitalism's most serious political crises—until the mid-twentieth century—coincided with the most severe decades of the Little Ice Age in the seventeenth century. Climate determines nothing, but climate changes are woven into the fabric of production, reproduction, governance, culture . . . in short, everything!" Jason Moore, "Capitalocene and Planetary Justice," *Maize* 6 (2019): 49–54.

28. Bruno Latour, "Agency at the Time of the Anthropocene," *New Literary History* 45.1 (2014): 1–18.

29. Andrew Ford, *The Origins of Criticism: Literary Culture and Poetic Theory in Classical Greece* (Princeton, NJ: Princeton University Press, 2002), 130, 139, 146, 169–70, 168–69 (hereafter cited in text). See also Jesper Svenbro, *La parole et le marbre: Aux origins de la poétique grecque* (Lund: Klassika Institutionen, 1976), which connects early Greek poetics specifically to the introduction of waged labor.

30. Jesse Oak Taylor thus advocates for a practice of "atmospheric reading": "Rather than lying either on the surface or concealed in the depths, atmosphere extends outward to envelop the interpenetrating contexts of composition, production, and reception." *The Sky of Our Manufacture: The London Fog in British Fiction from Dickens to Woolf* (Charlottesville: University of Virginia Press, 2016), 8 (hereafter cited in text).

31. Sir Philip Sidney, *The Defense of Poesy*, ed. Albert Cook (Boston: Athenaeum, 1890), 6, 7, 7–8, 58 (hereafter cited in text).

32. Catherine Bates reads Sidney's "layered" conception of poetics as including an "unofficial" voice opposed to an "idealist" bourgeois conception of poetry as productive and profitable. She notes: "The Golden Age can only be named as such recursively, from the perspective of a later, fallen Age, by which time gold had become the signifier of value." *On Not Defending Poetry: Defence and Indefensibility in Sidney's "Defence of Poesy"* (Oxford: Oxford University Press, 2017), 34. Todd Borlik emphasizes the metaphor of cultivation in his discussion of the *Defense*, poetry being like gardening a practice "of

mutual construction that celebrates nature's agency within human art." *Ecocriticism and Early Modern English Literature* (New York: Routledge, 2011), 16.

33. Percy Bysshe Shelley, "A Defense of Poetry," in *Shelley's Prose*, ed. David Lee Clark (New York: New Amsterdam, 1988), 275–97, 277, 294, 291, 293, 294 (hereafter cited in text).

34. Martin Heidegger, "Poetically Man Dwells," in *Poetry, Language, Thought*, trans. Albert Hofstadter (New York: Harper Perennial), 209–27, 215, 216.

35. Fredric Jameson, "Metacommentary," *PMLA* 86.1 (January 1971): 9–18, 17 (hereafter cited in text).

36. Fredric Jameson, *Allegory and Ideology* (London: Verso, 2019), 35–36 (hereafter cited in text).

37. Fredric Jameson, *The Political Unconscious: Narrative as a Socially Symbolic Act* (Ithaca, NY: Cornell University Press, 1981), 110 (hereafter cited in text).

38. Fredric Jameson, *Marxism and Form: Twentieth-Century Dialectical Theories of Literature* (Princeton, NJ: Princeton University Press, 1971), 342 (hereafter cited in text).

39. Fredric Jameson, "Marxism and Historicism," *New Literary History* 11.1 (Autumn 1979): 41–73, 56 (hereafter cited in text).

40. Joseph Addison, "An Essay on the Georgics," in John Dryden, *Poems: The Works of Virgil in English, 1697*, ed. William Frost, vol. 5 of *The Works of John Dryden* (Berkeley and Los Angeles: University of California Press, 1987), 145–53, 51 (hereafter cited in text). In his translation of the *Georgics*, Joseph Warton contextualizes Virgil's reference: "Thrace was full north of Greece, and some of the Greeks therefore might talk of the coldness of that country as strongly, perhaps, as some among us talk of the coldness of Scotland. The Roman writers speak just in the same stile of the coldness of Thrace, tho' a considerable part of Italy lay in as northern a latitude, and some of it even farther north than Thrace." *The Works of Virgil in English Verse* (London, 1753), 1:199 n. 592.

41. On Virgil's dialogue with Lucretius, particularly the shared concern with natural laws and limits, see Monica Gale, *Virgil on the Nature of Things: The Georgics, Lucretius and the Didactic Tradition* (Cambridge: Cambridge University Press, 2004).

42. I have in mind Michel Foucault's reading of Nietzschean genealogy, as concerned with "an unstable assemblage of faults, fissures, and heterogeneous layers that threaten the fragile inheritor from within or from underneath." "Nietzsche, Genealogy, History," in *Essential Works* (New York: New Press, 1998), 2:369–91, 375.

43. Reinhard Koselleck, *Sediments of Time: On Possible Histories* (Stanford, CA: Stanford University Press, 2018).

44. Virginia Jackson, *Dickinson's Misery: A Theory of Lyric Reading* (Princeton, NJ: Princeton University Press, 2005), 7.

45. Wai Chee Dimock, "Introduction: Genres as Fields of Knowledge," *PMLA* 122.5 (October 2007): 1377–88, 1380.

46. Kevis Goodman, *Georgic Modernity and British Romanticism: Poetry and the Mediation of History* (Cambridge: Cambridge University Press, 2004), 28 (my emphasis; hereafter cited in text). As Goodman writes: "The glorious labouriousness of reading the *Georgics* results from a complex, non-mimetic practice of reference; *verba* in the poem point in two directions at once—ostensibly, but not transparently, toward the details and cycles of agricultural work, and diachronically toward layers of previous poetic works" (ibid.).

47. John Leonard, *Faithful Labourers: A Reception History of Paradise Lost, 1667–1970*, 2 vols. (Oxford: Oxford University Press, 2017), 1:vii–viii. See also Ralph Cohen, *The Art of Discrimination: Thomson's "The Seasons" and the Language of Criticism* (London: Routledge & Kegan Paul, 1964).

48. Jonathan Bate, *Romantic Ecology: Wordsworth and the Environmental Tradition* (New York: Routledge, 1991), 11.

49. Karl Kroeber, *Ecological Literary Criticism: Romantic Imagining and the Biology of Mind* (New York: Columbia University Press, 1994), 14. Ursula Heise notes that early ecocriticism defined its own critical practice through "allegiance to the scientific study of nature," particularly ecology, which was seen to validate the normative values of balance and interrelation. In her account, ecocriticism emerges as a response not to Marxist criticism but to similar hermeneutical impulses in French poststructuralist theory, with its emphasis on the "disjunctures between forms of representation and the realities they purported to refer to." "The Hitchhiker's Guide to Ecocriticism," *PMLA* 121.2 (2006): 503–16, 505.

50. On description, see Cannon Schmitt, "Interpret or Describe?" *Representations* 135 (Summer 2016): 102–18, and "Tidal Conrad (Literally)," *Victorian Studies* 55.1 (Autumn 2012): 8–29. On paraphrase, see Andrew Piper, "Paraphrasis: Goethe, the Novella, and Forms of Translational Knowledge," *Goethe Yearbook* 17 (2010): 179–201. For a bracing critique of descriptive reading, see Ellen Rooney, "Live Free or Describe: The Reading Effect and the Persistence of Form," *Differences* 21.3 (2010): 112–39. "Symptomatic reading," Rooney argues, "implies a kind of unfreedom, an imposition, the *trace of a force* never entirely in the control of either reader or writer" (116; my emphasis).

51. Bruno Latour, "Why Has Critique Run Out of Steam? From Matters of Fact to Matters of Concern," *Critical Inquiry* 30 (Winter 2004): 225–48, 227.

52. Sharon Marcus and Stephen Best, "Surface Reading: An Introduction," *Representations* 108.1 (Fall 2009): 1–21, 15 (hereafter cited in text).

53. Rita Felski, *The Limits of Critique* (Chicago: University of Chicago Press, 2015), 5 (my emphasis; hereafter cited in text).

54. Marjorie Levinson, *Thinking through Poetry: Field Reports on Romantic Lyric* (Oxford: Oxford University Press, 2018), 9 (hereafter cited in text). Jameson writes: "Dialectical thinking can be characterized as historical reflexivity, that is, as the study of an object which also involves the study of the concepts and categories that we necessarily bring to the object." *The Political Unconscious*, 109.

55. Levinson echoes not only Jameson but also Latour, who defines the "mediation, translation, and networks" that connect "social needs and natural reality, meanings and mechanisms" as the "unconscious of the moderns." Bruno Latour, *We Have Never Been Modern* (Cambridge, MA: Harvard University Press, 1991), 37. Mediation is a "trajectory," within a given mode of knowledge production, "characterized . . . by a particular hiatus between elements so dissimilar that, without this trajectory, they would never have lined up in any order." Bruno Latour, *An Inquiry into Modes of Existence* (Cambridge, MA: Harvard University Press, 2013), 39. Jameson writes: "One cannot enumerate the differences between things except against the background of some more general identity. Mediation undertakes to establish this initial identity, against which . . . local identification can be registered." *The Political Unconscious*, 42.

56. Dipesh Chakrabarty, "The Climate of History: Four Theses," *Critical Inquiry* 35.2 (Winter 2009): 197–222, 218, 220, 198 (hereafter cited in text).

57. See Patricia Yaeger, "Editor's Column: Sea Trash, Dark Pools, and the Tragedy of the Commons," *PMLA* 125.3 (2010): 523–45; Leerom Medovoi, "The Biopolitical Unconscious: Toward an Eco-Marxist Literary Theory," in *Literary Materialisms*, ed. Mathias Nilges and Emilio Sauri (New York: Palgrave Macmillan, 2013), 79–92; Nathan Hensley and Philip Steer, introduction to *Ecological Form: System and Aesthetics in the Age of Empire*, ed. Nathan Hensley and Philip Steer (New York: Fordham University Press, 2019), 1–17.

58. On the figure of "the great stone book of nature," see Bronislaw Szerszynski, "The End of the End of Nature: The Anthropocene and the Fate of the Human," *Oxford Literary Review* 34.2 (2012): 165–84.

59. See Noah Heringman, "The Anthropocene Reads Buffon; or, Reading Like Geology," in Menely and Taylor, eds., *Anthropocene Reading*, 59–77.

60. Nigel Clark, *Inhuman Nature: Sociable Life on a Dynamic Planet* (London: Sage, 2011), 82 (hereafter cited in text).

61. Eric Gidal, *Ossianic Unconformities: Bardic Poetry in the Industrial Age* (Charlottesville: University of Virginia Press, 2015), 5 (hereafter cited in text).

62. Michel Foucault, *The Order of Things: An Archaeology of the Human Sciences* (New York: Vintage, 1994). Only in the nineteenth century, claims Foucault, is "history restored to the irruptive violence of time" (132). For a critique of Foucault, see Noah Heringman, *Sciences of Antiquity: Romantic Antiquarianism, Natural History, and Knowledge Work* (Oxford: Oxford University Press, 2013).

63. Devin Griffiths, *The Age of Analogy: Science and Literature between the Darwins* (Baltimore: Johns Hopkins University Press, 2016), 2–4.

64. Martin Rudwick, *Bursting the Limits of Time: The Reconstruction of Geohistory in the Age of Revolution* (Chicago: University of Chicago Press, 2005), 6.

65. Thomas Ford, "The Romanthropocene," *Literature Compass* 15.5 (May 2018): 4.

66. John Keill, *An Examination of Dr. Burnet's Theory of the Earth together with Some Remarks on Mr. Whiston's New Theory of the Earth* (Oxford, 1698). Keill identifies Epicurus as the first world maker: "But who without indignation can hear . . . Epicurus the World-maker assert, that the Earth was in the shape of a Drum, and that we dwell upon the plain surface of it. . . . With an unpardonable boldness he pretended to tell us, how the World was made" (4–5). Burnet acknowledged that Epicurean atomism was an important precursor to his own attempt to reconstruct the Earth's history on the basis of "no causes . . . but Matter and Motion" (*Sacred Theory*, 121).

67. Later readers saw Milton's world making as an influence on Burnet. Edward Gibbon praised "the third part of Burnet's *Sacred Theory* [where] he blends philosophy, Scripture, and tradition, into one magnificent system; in the description of which he displays a strength of fancy not inferior to that of *Milton* himself." *The History of the Decline and Fall of the Roman Empire* (London, 1825), 2:141. Charles Lyell also drew a connection between Milton and Burnet: "Even Milton had scarcely ventured in his poem to indulge his imagination so freely in painting scenes of the Creation and Deluge, Paradise and Chaos, as this writer, who set forth pretensions to profound philosophy." *Principles of Geology* (1830; London: Penguin, 1997), 37–38 (hereafter cited in text).

68. See Paolo Rossi, *The Dark Abyss of Time: The History of the Earth and the History of Nations from Hooke to Vico*, trans. Lydia Cochrane (Chicago: University of Chicago Press, 1984) (hereafter cited in text). The historicism of the early world makers has been overshadowed in histories of science that regard Newton's confirmation of a harmonious cosmos as this period's decisive contribution to scientific knowledge. See also William Poole, *The World Makers: Scientists of the Restoration and the Search for the Origins of the Earth* (Peter Lang: Oxford, 2010).

69. Stephen Jay Gould credits Burnet with first treating planetary history as a "sequential narrative," "a story line of pasts that determine presents and presents that constrain futures." *Time's Arrow, Time's Cycle: Myth and Metaphor in the Discovery of Geological Deep Time* (Cambridge, MA: Harvard University Press, 1987), 44.

70. Simon Lewis and Mark Maslin, "Defining the Anthropocene," *Nature* 519 (March 12, 2015): 171–80.

71. Karl Marx, *Capital* (1867; London: Penguin, 1990), 1:492 (hereafter cited in text).

72. In Lyell's *Principles of Geology*, we find language resonant with Marx's: "The line of demarcation between the actual [current] period and that immediately antecedent, is quite evanescent, and the newest members [fossils] of the tertiary series will be often found to blend with the formations of the historical era" (368).

73. Fredric Jameson, "'End of Art' or 'End of History'?" in *The Cultural Turn: Selected Writings on the Postmodern, 1983–1998* (London: Verso, 1998), 73.

74. Will Steffen et al., "Stratigraphic and Earth System Approaches to Defining the Anthropocene," *Earth's Future* 4.8 (August 2016): 324–45, 29 (hereafter cited in text).

75. Consider Joseph North's *Literary Criticism: A Concise Political History* (Cambridge, MA: Harvard University Press, 2017), which reads "Always historicize!" as the mantra of the "historical-contextualist" paradigm within literary studies when it is, in fact, a critique of an untheoretical historicism.

76. Patricia Yaeger, "Editor's Column: Literature in the Ages of Wood, Tallow, Coal, Whale-Oil, Gasoline, Atomic Power and Other Energy Sources," *PMLA* 126:2 (2011): 305–10, 309.

77. Jean-Claude Debeir, Jean-Paul Deleage, and Daniel Hemery, *In the Servitude of Power: Energy and Civilization through the Ages*, trans. John Barzman (London: Zed, 1991), 7 (hereafter cited in text).

78. Heidi Scott, *Fuel: An Ecocritical History* (London: Bloomsbury, 2018), 12.

79. See Frederick Buell, "A Short History of Oil Cultures; or, The Marriage of Catastrophe and Exuberance," *Journal of American Studies* 46.2 (May 2012): 273–93; and Stephanie LeMenager, *Living Oil: Petroleum Culture in the American Century* (Oxford: Oxford University Press, 2015).

80. Paul Crutzen and Eugene Stoermer, "The 'Anthropocene,'" *International Geosphere-Biosphere Programme (IGBP) Global Change Newsletter* 41 (May 2000): 17–18.

81. Andreas Malm, *Fossil Capital: The Rise of Steam Power and the Roots of Global Warming* (London: Verso, 2016) (hereafter cited in text). "Fossil capital," as Malm succinctly defines it, "is self-expanding value passing through the metamorphosis of fossil fuels into CO_2" (290).

82. Cara New Daggett, *The Birth of Energy, Thermodynamics, and the Politics of Work* (Durham, NC: Duke University Press, 2019) (hereafter cited in text). Clark and

Yusoff describe a "contraction in thinking about what energy 'does'" in the modern age, "a diminution from its role in a generalized metamorphosing of matter toward more calculable and controllable mechanical or kinetic functions." Nigel Clark and Kathryn Yusoff, "Combustion and Society: A Fire-Centered History of Energy Use," *Theory, Culture, and Society* 31.5 (2014): 203–26, 222. Allen MacDuffie identifies "a particular tension . . . between energy defined as a usable resource, and energy defined as ambient agency circulating endlessly through the world." *Victorian Literature, Energy, and the Ecological Imagination* (Cambridge: Cambridge University Press, 2014), 2.

83. E. A. Wrigley, *Energy and the English Industrial Revolution* (Cambridge: Cambridge University Press, 2010), 42 (hereafter cited in text). Anson Rabinbach similarly maintains that until the middle of the nineteenth century "the equivalence of labor and natural power was not a generally accepted concept in the vocabulary of political economy." *The Human Motor: Energy, Fatigue, and the Origins of Modernity* (Berkeley and Los Angeles: University of California Press, 1992), 70.

84. Guy Lemarchand, Emmanuel Le Roy Ladurie, and Karine Rance, "Regards croisés," *Annales historiques de la Révolution française* 351 (2008): 177–95.

85. Georges Bataille, *The Accursed Share: An Essay on General Economy*, vol. 1, *Consumption*, trans. Robert Hurley (New York: Zone, 1991), 20. Bataille discovered the planetary solar energy economy by reading Vladimir Vernadsky's *The Biosphere* (1926; New York: Copernicus, 1997), a foundational work of Earth-system science that compares the living Earth to a "thermodynamic engine" powered by the Sun (26). "Activated by radiation," Vernadsky writes, "the matter of the biosphere collects and redistributes solar energy, and converts it ultimately into free energy capable of doing work on Earth" (44). On the implications of Bataille's project, Antti Salminen and Tere Vadén write: "In Bataille's view, homogenic economy—say, fossil capitalism in its liberalist form—has been separated out of a general economy, also called the solar economy. . . . The general economy is heterogeneous since its energies have not been objectified according to a measure or goal." *Energy and Experience: An Essay in Nafthology* (Chicago: MCM, 2015), 31–32 (hereafter cited in text).

86. Christophe Bonneuil and Jean-Baptiste Fressoz, *The Shock of the Anthropocene: The Earth, History and Us*, trans. David Fernbach (London: Verso, 2015), 101 (hereafter cited in text).

87. See E. A. Wrigley, *Continuity, Chance and Change: The Character of the Industrial Revolution in England* (Cambridge: Cambridge University Press, 1988) (hereafter cited in text).

88. Frye's "epochs of Western literature" (*Anatomy of Criticism*, 35) define a trajectory from the aggrandized agency of myth to the minimal agency of naturalism. As Angus Fletcher reminds us, such usage is appropriate "because in each of the five [modes] the hero is a protagonist with a given strength relative to his world, and as such each hero— whether mythic, romantic, high mimetic, low mimetic, or ironic—is a *modular* for verbal architectonics; man is the measure, the *modus* of myth." "Utopian History and the Anatomy," in *Northrop Frye in Modern Criticism*, ed. Murray Krieger (New York: Columbia University Press, 1966), 31–73, 34–35. Shaobo Xie observes that "the five epochs of Western literature designated in the *Anatomy of Criticism* can be interpreted, from a Marxist perspective, as indicative of five phases of the mode of production, which partly

determines and subsumes the literary mode of production." "History and Utopian Desire: Fredric Jameson's Dialectical Tribute to Northrop Frye," *Cultural Critique* 34 (Autumn 1996): 115–42, 121.

89. See Burroughs, *Climate Change in Prehistory*, 217–23.

90. Walter Benjamin, *The Origin of German Tragic Drama*, trans. John Osborne (London: Verso, 1998), 165 (hereafter cited in text).

91. William Cowper, *The Task*, in *The Task and Selected Other Poems*, ed. James Sambrook (London: Longman, 1994), 1.372, 462 (verse from *The Task* hereafter cited in text by book and line numbers).

92. Charlotte Smith, "Beachy Head," in *The Poems of Charlotte Smith*, ed. Stuart Curran (New York: Oxford University Press, 1993), line 690 (hereafter cited in text by line number).

93. See Ted Underwood, *Why Literary Periods Mattered: Historical Contrast and the Prestige of English Studies* (Stanford, CA: Stanford University Press, 2013).

94. On the Miltonic tradition, see Raymond Dexter Havens, *The Influence of Milton on English Poetry* (Cambridge, MA: Harvard University Press, 1922); and Dustin Griffin, *Regaining Paradise: Milton and the Eighteenth Century* (Cambridge: Cambridge University Press, 1986).

95. Hugh Blair, *Lectures on Rhetoric and Belles Lettres* (1783; Carbondale: Southern Illinois University Press, 2005), 177–80 (hereafter cited in text).

96. Angus Fletcher, *A New Theory for American Poetry: Democracy, the Environment, and the Future of Imagination* (Cambridge, MA: Harvard University Press, 2004), 39 (hereafter cited in text).

CHAPTER ONE

1. Hiltner identifies the association of Hell with sulfurous smoke and "brimstone" as distinctly English. See Ken Hiltner, *What Else Is Pastoral? Renaissance Literature and the Environment* (Ithaca, NY: Cornell University Press, 2011), chap. 5.

2. John Hatcher, *The History of the British Coal Industry* (Oxford: Clarendon, 1993), 1:40.

3. J. U. Nef, *The Rise of the British Coal Industry* (Chicago: University of Chicago Press, 1932), 1:256. See also William Cavert, *The Smoke of London: Energy and Environment in the Early Modern City* (Cambridge: Cambridge University Press, 2016).

4. John Evelyn, *Fumifugium; or, The Inconveniencie of the Aer and Smoak of London Dissipated* (London, 1661), 5–6.

5. Patrick Hume, *Annotations on Milton's Paradise Lost wherein the Texts of Sacred Writ, Relating to the Poem, Are Quoted, the Parallel Places and Imitations of the Most Excellent Homer and Virgil Cited* (London, 1695), 15 (hereafter cited in text).

6. See Franz Mauelshagen, "Climate as a Scientific Paradigm—Early History of Climatology to 1800," in *The Palgrave Handbook of Climate History*, ed. Sam White, Christian Pfister, and Franz Mauelshagen (London: Palgrave, 2018), 565–99. While Mauelshagen claims that any synthesis of cartographic, meteorologic, and Hippocratic ideas of climate did not occur until the eighteenth century, Sara Miglietti identifies instances, speculative if not systematic, of such synthesis among classical and early modern

thinkers. See "Mastering the Climate: Theories of Environmental Influence in the Long Seventeenth Century" (PhD diss., University of Warwick, 2016).

7. William Cowper, "The Fragment of an Intended Commentary on Paradise Lost," in *Cowper's Milton* (London, 1810), 2:434.

8. In an ingenious reading of this scene, J. P. Conlan observes that Satan's shield—"Hung on his shoulders like the moon" (1.287), emblematizing his ongoing defiance of God—works to concentrate the heat of Hell, suggesting that his torment and his ongoing exercise of free will remain inseparable. " 'Vaulted with fire': The Thermodynamics of Infernal Justice in Book 1 of *Paradise Lost*," *Explorations in Renaissance Culture* 43 (2017): 232–47.

9. Two short articles were published in the mid-twentieth century on the topic of Milton and climate. Z. S. Fink argues that "the notion of climatic influence . . . had some partial hold upon [Milton], but that he was in active rebellion against it." "Milton and the Theory of Climatic Influence," *Modern Language Quarterly* 2.1 (March 1941): 67–80, 73 (hereafter cited in text). Thomas Stroup notes the persistent association of Satan with the north. See "Implication of the Theory of Climatic Influence in Milton," *Modern Language Quarterly* 4.2 (June 1942): 185–89. On the long history of ideas about climatic influence, see Clarence Glacken, *Traces on the Rhodian Shore: Nature and Culture in Western Thought from Ancient Times to the End of the Eighteenth Century* (Berkeley and Los Angeles: University of California Press, 1967). Hard climate determinism is more common in late nineteenth- and early twentieth-century imperial discourse, frequently linked with notions of race. See Mike Hulme, "Reducing the Future to Climate: A Story of Climate Determinism and Reductionism," *Osiris* 26 (2011): 245–66; and David Livingstone, "Race, Space and Moral Climatology: Notes toward a Genealogy," *Journal of the History of Geography* 28 (2002): 159–80.

10. Edward Philips, "The Life of Mr. John Milton," in *The Early Lives of Milton*, ed. Helen Darbishire (New York: Barnes & Noble, 1965), 49–82, 73.

11. John Toland, "The Life of John Milton," in Darbishire, ed., *The Early Lives of Milton*, 83–198, 178. For "In adventum veris" (*Poems* [1645]), see *The Riverside Milton*, ed. Roy Flannagan (Boston: Houghton Mifflin, 1998), 191.

12. John Milton, *The History of Britain*, in *Complete Prose Works* (New Haven, CT: Yale University Press, 1971), 5:450.

13. John Milton, "Ad Salsillum" (*Poems* [1645]), in Flannagan, ed., *Riverside Milton*, 229.

14. John Milton, *Reason of Church-Government*, in *Complete Prose Works* (New Haven, CT: Yale University Press, 1953), 1:813–14.

15. John Evelyn, *The Diary of John Evelyn: 1647–1676* (New York: Macmillan, 1906), 181.

16. On the historiographic controversy, see "The Little Ice Age: Climate and History Reconsidered," special issue, *Journal of Interdisciplinary History*, vol. 44 (Winter 2014).

17. Gustav Utterström, "Climatic Fluctuations and Population Problems in Early Modern History," *Scandinavian Economic History Review* 3.1 (1955): 3–47, 38. Utterström notes that Scandinavian historians have been atypically attentive to the role of climate given the marginal agricultural conditions of far northern Europe.

18. Wolfgang Behringer, *A Cultural History of Climate* (Cambridge: Polity, 2010), 86.

19. Emmanuel Le Roy Ladurie, *Times of Feast, Times of Famine: A History of Climate since the Year 1000*, trans. Barbara Bray (Garden City, NY: Doubleday, 1971), 7, 11 (hereafter cited in text).

20. Emmanuel Le Roy Ladurie, *Histoire humaine et comparée du climat*, 3 vols. (Paris: Librairie Arthème Fayard, 2004–9).

21. "Histoire et climat" (debate between Emmanuel Le Roy Ladurie and Geoffrey Parker, German Historical Institute, Paris, January 26, 2012), quoted in Geoffrey Parker, "From the General Crisis to the Global Crisis" (lecture delivered at the conference "History After Hobsbawm," London, April 30, 2014). See also Mike Davis, "Taking the Temperature of History: Le Roy Ladurie's Adventures in the Little Ice Age," *New Left Review* 110 (March–April 2018): 85–129.

22. Paul Warde, "Global Crisis or Global Coincidence?" *Past and Present* 228.1 (August 2015): 287–301, 293, 287 (my emphasis).

23. Michael Murrin notes that Spenserian personification functions "in a manner opposite to that of allegory" since personification works to limit the range of interpretation; a personified "figure like Excess . . . requires no interpretation." "Renaissance Allegory from Petrarch to Spenser." *The Cambridge Companion to Allegory*, ed. Rita Copeland and Peter Struck (Cambridge: Cambridge University Press, 2010), 162–76, 175. On neoclassical theories of allegory, see Angus Fletcher, *Allegory: The Theory of a Symbolic Mode* (Ithaca, NY: Cornell University Press, 1964), chap. 4 (hereafter cited in text); and Gordon Teskey, *Allegory and Violence* (Ithaca, NY: Cornell University Press, 1996), chap. 5 (hereafter cited in text).

24. Unpublished "poetic notebook" quoted in William Poole, *Milton and the Making of "Paradise Lost"* (Cambridge, MA: Harvard University Press, 2017), 112 (hereafter cited in text).

25. Anne Ferry, *Milton's Epic Voice: The Narrator in Paradise Lost* (Chicago: University of Chicago Press, 1983), 108 (hereafter cited in text). For Ferry, personification allegory is replaced with a form of "sacred metaphor" that ritualistically unites specific and abstract meaning, anticipating the Coleridgean distinction between allegory and symbol. Other readers see Milton rejecting allegory for a more realist representational mode in line with his monism and the wider currents of nominalism and empiricism emerging in the late seventeenth century. While allegory depends on an apprehension of the "layering of reality," Stephen Fallon claims, Milton, rejecting Platonic universals, develops a leveling mimetic practice continuous with his "animist materialism." The two residual personified abstractions are presented ironically, Fallon maintains, since allegory still offered "an ideal vehicle for presenting deficient ontology." *Milton among the Philosophers: Poetry and Materialism in Seventeenth-Century England* (Ithaca, NY: Cornell University Press, 1991), 177, 1, 183 (hereafter cited in text).

26. Scholars have, in recent decades, developed a refined account of Milton's Protestant monism, working to square poetry with doctrine, Raphael's claim that there is "one first matter all" (5.473) with Milton's heterodox ruminations in *Christian Doctrine*, where he observes that in Hebrew the word *to create*, the second word in Genesis, means to "make something out of matter"—to give it form and boundary—and that, since matter did not preexist God, God must be at once spirit and substance, meaning that "God did not produce all things out of nothing but out of himself." John Milton, *Christian*

Doctrine, in *Complete Prose Works* (New Haven, CT: Yale University Press, 1973), 6:305–10 (hereafter cited in text).

27. Mindele Anne Treip, *Allegorical Poetics and the Epic: The Renaissance Tradition to Paradise Lost* (Lexington: University Press of Kentucky, 1994), 229 (my emphasis), 188 (hereafter cited in text).

28. See Christopher Kendrick, *Milton: A Study in Ideology and Form* (New York: Methuen, 1986); and Carrol B. Cox, "Citizen Angels: Civil Society and the Abstract Individual in *Paradise Lost,*" *Milton Studies* 23 (1987): 165–96. On a broad scale, Immanuel Wallerstein defines *liberalism* as "a geoculture for the modern world-system." *The Modern World-System IV: Centrist Liberalism Triumphant, 1789–1914* (Berkeley and Los Angeles: University of California Press, 2011), xiii.

29. Catherine Gimelli Martin, *The Ruins of Allegory: "Paradise Lost" and the Metamorphosis of Epic Convention* (Durham, NC: Duke University Press, 1998), 323 (hereafter cited in text).

30. John Milton, "Of Education" (1644), in Flannagan, ed., *Riverside Milton,* 980–86, 980.

31. On Benjamin's "vindication of allegory," see Hans-Georg Gadamer, *Truth and Method,* trans. Joel Weinsheimer and Donald G. Marshall (New York: Crossroad, 1989), xxxi; and Paul de Man, "The Rhetoric of Temporality," in *Blindness and Insight* (Minneapolis: University of Minnesota Press, 1983), 187–228. The nineteenth century's "asserted superiority of the symbol over allegory" turns out to be simply a rhetorical form of "tenacious self-mystification" (de Man, "The Rhetoric of Temporality," 208), related to the collapse of the distinction between description and experience, something I explore in chapter 4.

32. Teskey sees Benjamin as inverting the traditional meaning of allegory as "a discourse that acknowledges incommensurable registers in itself." This inversion occurs in a historical moment in which "the hierarchical transcendentalism of the Renaissance gave way to what Benjamin regarded as the dialectical transcendentalism of the baroque." *Allegory and Violence,* 4.

33. Bruce Clarke, *Energy Forms: Allegory and Science in the Era of Classical Thermodynamics* (Ann Arbor: University of Michigan Press, 2001), 6. Clarke follows Benjamin and Jameson in seeing allegory as the mode that internalizes diachronicity: "Allegorical forms are intrinsically anachronistic structures that interfold the historical past, the perceived present, and the imagined future" (ibid.).

34. Simon Lewis and Mark Maslin, *The Human Planet: How We Created the Anthropocene* (London: Pelican, 2018), 167–68.

35. See Brooke, *Climate Change and the Course of Global History,* 438–42.

36. If Milton saw the Americas as a territory rife with the anxieties of colonization, he shared with contemporaries a mercantilist vision of the East as a source of spices and other luxury commodities. David Quint has drawn attention to this other imperial subtext in the poem, one oriented toward the Indian Ocean rather than the Atlantic. See *Epic and Empire: Politics and Generic Form from Virgil to Milton* (Princeton, NJ: Princeton University Press, 1993), chaps. 6–7. Robert Markley suggests that the simile comparing Satan in Chaos to the fleet of ships carrying "spicy drugs" from the East (2.636–43) clearly associates Satan with the Dutch, who retained a "near monopoly" on the East Indies spice trade. "'The destin'd Walls / Of Cambalu': Milton, China, and the Ambiguities of

the East," in *Milton and the Imperial Vision*, ed. Balachandra Rajan and Elizabeth Sauer (Pittsburgh, PA: Duquesne University Press, 1999), 191–213.

37. J. Martin Evans, *Milton's Imperial Epic: "Paradise Lost" and the Discourse of Colonialism* (Ithaca, NY: Cornell University Press, 1996), 5 (hereafter cited in text). Evans suggests that Milton's own views on the "colonization of the New World" and colonialism more generally were "deeply divided" (146), on the basis of a distinction between Virginia, affiliated with Charles I, and New England, a refuge for Puritans (147).

38. See Suman Seth, *Difference and Disease: Medicine, Race, and the Eighteenth-Century British Empire* (Cambridge: Cambridge University Press, 2018), chap. 3. Seth cites the demographer John Graunt, who applied the principle of seasoning to London's coal-fouled air: "As for unhealthiness, it may well be supposed, that although seasoned Bodies may, and do live near as long in *London*, as elsewhere, yet new-comers and Children do not: for the *Smoaks, stinks,* and close *Air,* are less healthful than that of the Country." *Natural and Political Observations . . . upon the Bills of Mortality* (London, 1676), 100.

39. See Warren Tormey, "Milton's Satan and Early Industry and Commerce: The Rhetoric of Self-Justification," *Interdisciplinary Literary Studies* 13.1–2 (Fall 2011): 127–59; and Diane McColley, *Poetry and Ecology in the Age of Milton and Marvell* (London: Routledge, 2016), chap. 2.

40. See Anya Zilberstein, *A Temperate Empire: Making Climate Change in Early America* (Oxford: Oxford University Press, 2016).

41. Thomas Hariot, *Briefe and True Report of the New Found Land of Virginia* (London, 1588), 45.

42. Richard Hakluyt, *Principal Navigations, Voyages, Traffiques, and Discoveries of the English Nation* (Edinburgh, 1889), 13:311.

43. Robert Crosman, *Reading "Paradise Lost"* (Bloomington: Indiana University Press, 1980), 32.

44. See Andrew Mattison, *Milton's Uncertain Eden: Understanding Place in "Paradise Lost"* (New York: Routledge, 2007); and Ken Hiltner, *Milton and Ecology* (Cambridge: Cambridge University Press, 2003) (hereafter cited in text).

45. Dennis Danielson, *Paradise Lost and the Cosmological Revolution* (Cambridge: Cambridge University Press, 2014), xvi (hereafter cited in text).

46. On this simile and its allusions, see esp. John R. Mulder, "Shades and Substance," in *Milton in Italy: Contexts, Images, Contradictions*, ed. Mario A. Di Cesare (Binghamton, NY: Center for Medieval and Early Renaissance Studies, 1991), 61–70; Neil Harris, "The Vallombrosa Simile and the Image of the Poet in *Paradise Lost*," in ibid., 71–95; and Charles A. Huttar, "Vallombrosa Revisited," in ibid., 95–112. See also John Evans, "The Leaves of Vallombrosa: Milton's Great-Rooted Simile," *English Studies* 71.5 (1990): 395–409.

47. It is not clear whether Milton would have known that the reference in Hebrew is not to the Red Sea but to the Yam Soof, a "reed sea," the marshes to the east of the Nile delta. See Daniel Hillel, *The Natural History of the Bible: An Environmental Exploration of the Hebrew Scriptures* (New York: Columbia University Press, 2006), 114–15.

48. See Behringer, *A Cultural History of Climate,* 56–57.

49. L. D. Lerner, "The Miltonic Simile," *Essays in Criticism* 4.3 (July 1954): 297–308.

50. Geoffrey Hartman, "Milton's Counterplot," *ELH* 25.1 (March 1958): 4.

51. *The Iliad*, trans. A. T. Murray (New York: G. P. Putnam's Sons, 1925), 565. See C. A. Martindale, "Milton and the Homeric Simile," *Comparative Literature* 33.3 (Summer 1981): 224–38.

52. J. A. [John Aikin], "The Similes of Homer, Virgil, and Milton, Examined and Compared" (1796–98), in *Milton, 1732–1801: The Critical Heritage*, ed. John Shawcross (London: Routledge & Kegan Paul, 1972), 387.

53. Abbé Le Blanc, *Letters on the English and French Nations* (Dublin, 1747), reprinted in Shawcross, ed., *Milton, 1732–1801: The Critical Heritage*, 133.

54. Paul the Deacon, *History of the Langobards* (ca. 720), trans. W. D. Foulke (New York, 1907), 1. See also Samuel Kliger, *The Goths in England: A Study in Seventeenth and Eighteenth Century Thought* (Cambridge, MA: Harvard University Press, 1952), 10–15, 241–52.

55. Giovanni Botero, *Relations of the Most Famous Kingdoms and Common-Weales* (London, 1611), 6.

56. On the discourse of population in *Paradise Lost*, see David Glimp, *Increase and Multiply: Governing Cultural Reproduction in Early Modern England* (Minneapolis: University of Minnesota Press, 2003), chap. 5; and Charlotte Sussman, *Peopling the World: Representing Human Mobility from Milton to Malthus* (Philadelphia: University of Pennsylvania Press, 2020), chap. 1.

57. On Milton's rejection of Aristotle's "two-storey universe" and the poem's (ambivalent) integration of Copernican heliocentrism, see Danielson, *"Paradise Lost" and the Cosmological Revolution*; and Harinder Singh Marjara, *Contemplation of Created Things: Science in "Paradise Lost"* (Toronto: University of Toronto Press, 1992) (hereafter cited in text). Both scholars definitively overturn the view—presented in Kester Svendsen, *Milton and Science* (Cambridge, MA: Harvard University Press, 1956)—that Milton's science is completely premodern.

58. Milton, "Prolusion III," in Flannagan, ed., *Riverside Milton*, 854.

59. Ayesha Ramachandran, *The Worldmakers: Global Imagining in Early Modern Europe* (Chicago: University of Chicago Press, 2015) (hereafter cited in text).

60. See also Elizabeth Sauer, *Barbarous Dissonance and Images of Voice in Milton's Epics* (Montreal: McGill-Queens University Press, 1996).

61. Theodore Hiebert, *The Yahwist's Landscape: Nature and Religion in Early Israel* (Oxford: Oxford University Press, 1996) (hereafter cited in text).

62. For an argument that primordial chaos is evil, see Regina Schwartz, *Remembering and Repeating: Biblical Creation in "Paradise Lost"* (Cambridge: Cambridge University Press, 1988).

63. John Rumrich associates chaos with a generative "indeterminacy." See "Milton's God and the Matter of Chaos," *PMLA* 110.5 (October 1995): 1035–46. So does Catherine Gimelli Martin. See *The Ruins of Allegory*.

64. In his work as a private teacher in the 1640s, Milton always included *De rerum natura* on his syllabi. See Poole, *Milton and the Making of "Paradise Lost,"* chap. 5. On Lucretius and Milton, see Philip Hardie, "The Presence of Lucretius in *Paradise Lost*," *Milton Quarterly* 29.1 (March 1995): 13–24.

65. For an argument linking the prospect view with colonial vision, see Bruce Macleod, "The Lordly Eye: Milton and the Strategic Geography of Empire," in Balachandra

and Sauer, eds., *Milton and the Imperial Vision*, 48–66. On the long history of representing the Earth as a unitary form, see Dennis Cosgrove, *Apollo's Eye: A Cartographic Genealogy of the Earth in the Western Imagination* (Baltimore: Johns Hopkins University Press, 2001).

66. Barbara Kiefer Lewalski, *"Paradise Lost" and the Rhetoric of Literary Forms* (Princeton, NJ: Princeton University Press, 1985), 132–35.

67. Richard DeRocher finds a precedent for such personifications of an animate Earth in Roman stoicism. See "The Wounded Earth in *Paradise Lost*," *Studies in Philology* 93.1 (Winter 1996): 93–115. Leah Marcus links Milton's personified Earth with seventeenth-century *vitalism*, according to which "all natural things, not only the earth itself, are infused with sentience and purpose." "Ecocriticism and Vitalism in *Paradise Lost*," *Milton Quarterly* 49.2 (2015): 96–111. Hiltner links the Earth's "wound" with the "uprooting" of Adam and Eve. See *Milton and Ecology*, 54. All three critics suggest that the personified Earth can be assimilated into Milton's monist Christianity. More adventurously, Steven Swarbrick reads the figure as a "queer personification in which the figure of the 'face' (Greek *prosopon*) derives from inhuman forces." "Milton's Queer Earth: A Geology of Exhausted Life," in *Queer Milton*, ed. David Orvis (Cham: Palgrave Macmillan, 2018), 255–91, 274 (hereafter cited in text).

68. Bruno Latour, *Facing Gaia: Eight Lectures on the New Climate Regime* (Cambridge: Polity, 2017), 75 (hereafter cited in text). See also James Lovelock, *Gaia: A New Look at Life on Earth*, 1979 (Oxford: Oxford University Press, 2000) (hereafter cited in text).

69. David Quint, *Inside "Paradise Lost": Reading the Designs of Milton's Epic* (Princeton, NJ: Princeton University Press, 2014), 99–100 (hereafter cited in text).

70. John Milton, "On the Morning of CHRISTS Nativity" (*Poems* [1645]), in Flannagan, ed., *Riverside Milton*, 38–47 (lines 79–83). See also Mother M. Christopher Pecheux, "The Image of the Sun in Milton's Nativity Ode," *Huntington Library Quarterly* 38 (1973–74): 315–33.

71. On the links between Jewish and Christian monotheism and older forms of solar veneration, see J. Glen Taylor, *Yahweh and the Sun: Biblical and Archeological Evidence for Sun Worship in Ancient Israel* (Sheffield: Sheffield Academic, 1993).

72. See Quint, *Inside "Paradise Lost*,*"* chap. 4; Raymond Waddington, "Here Comes the Sun: Providential Theme and Symbolic Pattern in *Paradise Lost*, Book 3," *Modern Philology* 79.3 (February 1982): 256–66; and Albert Cirillo, "'Hail holy light' and Divine Time in *Paradise Lost*," *Journal of English and Germanic Philology* 68.1 (January 1969): 45–56.

73. Dimitri Levitin, *Ancient Wisdom in the Age of New Science: Histories of Philosophy in England, c. 1640–1700* (Cambridge: Cambridge University Press, 2015), 415–16.

74. Edward Herbert, *Pagan Religion*, ed. John Anthony Butler (Ottawa: Dovehouse, 1996), 82.

75. Richard Serjeantson writes: "We might even go so far as to suggest that the orthodox tradition of investigation into the origins of pagan idolatry contained within itself the seeds of its own destruction. The answers it offered, after all, quickly became double-edged. If the origin of false religion could be explained in terms of tendencies in human nature, might not ultimately even true religion—Christianity—itself succumb to such a critique?" "David Hume's *Natural History of Religion* (1757) and the End of Modern Eusebianism," in *The Intellectual Consequences of Religious Heterodoxy, 1600–1750*, ed. Sarah Mortimer and John Robertson (Leiden: Brill, 2012), 267–95, 271.

76. Max Müller, *Physical Religion* (London: Longmans, Green, 1891), 11 (hereafter cited in text).

77. Max Müller, *Natural Religion* (London: Longmans, Green, 1889), 393–94 (hereafter cited in text).

78. Along these lines, Vladimir Vernadsky observes that "ancient religious institutions that considered terrestrial creatures, especially man, to be children of the sun were far nearer to the truth than is generally thought." *The Biosphere*, 44.

79. Geoffrey Hartman, "Adam on the Grass with Balsamum," in *Beyond Formalism: Literary Essays, 1958–1970* (New Haven, CT: Yale University Press, 1970), 124–50. Hartman links the interpretive problem of defining the "decorum" of this exorbitant image to the inescapable dilemma of any hermeneutical situation: "The theory of criticism does not seem sufficiently advanced to solve problems even of this elementary kind, since two quite opposite types of justification could be entertained: one demonstrating that the image is in its place, and a link contributing to the poem's unity; the other that it is displaced, yet expressive of some extraordinary feature of Milton's poetry or mind" (125).

80. On Adam's names, see Harold Toliver, "Symbol-Making and the Labors of Milton's Eden," *Texas Studies in Literature and Language* 18 (1976): 433–50; Lee Jacobus, *Sudden Apprehension: Aspects of Knowledge in "Paradise Lost"* (The Hague: Mouton, 1976); and John Leonard, *Naming in Paradise: Milton and the Language of Adam and Eve* (Oxford: Clarendon, 1990).

81. On these parallel scenes, see Stephen Wigler, "The Poet and Satan Before the Light: A Suggestion about Book III and the Opening of Book IV of 'Paradise Lost,'" *Milton Quarterly* 12.2 (May 1978): 59–64; and Louis Martz, "Paradise Lost: *The Realms of Light*," *English Literary Renaissance* 1.1 (December 1971): 71–88.

82. *Lucy Hutchinson's Translation of Lucretius: "De rerum natura,"* ed. Hugh de Quehen (Ann Arbor: University of Michigan Press, 1997), 2.210–17.

83. See Marjara, *Contemplation of Created Things*, chap. 6.

84. See Henry Guerlac, "The Poets' Nitre," *Isis* 45.3 (September 1954): 243–55.

85. Neil Forsyth, *The Satanic Epic* (Princeton, NJ: Princeton University Press, 2003), 57–58.

86. Jonathan Sawday, *Engines of the Imagination: Renaissance Culture and the Rise of Machines* (London: Routledge, 2007), 266.

87. In *Energy and Experience*, Salminen and Vadén link "the death of God" with "the birth of the age of oil" (2). They observe: "Like the notions of force, will, work, and the sacred, energy seems to name at the same time something internal, immaterial, and spiritual and something material, concrete, and physical" (7). See also Hannes Bergthaller, "Insidious Alchemy: God and Oil in the Petrofiction of John Updike," *Green Letters* 23.2 (2019): 130–40.

88. George Coffin Taylor, *Milton's Use of Du Bartas* (Cambridge, MA: Harvard University Press, 1934), 106–70.

89. Robert Burton, *The Anatomy of Melancholy*, ed. Holbrook Jackson (New York: New York Review Books, 2001), 133–34.

90. Amitav Ghosh suggests that catastrophism may be the default mode of human storytelling until the "instinctive awareness of the earth's unpredictability was gradually supplanted by a belief in uniformitarianism." *The Great Derangement: Climate Change and the Unthinkable* (Chicago: University of Chicago Press, 2016), 25.

91. Arthur Golding, trans., Ovid's "Metamorphoses," ed. Peter Scupham (Manchester: Carcanet, 2005), 1.122 (hereafter cited in text).

92. See Richard Grove, Green Imperialism: Colonial Expansion, Tropical Island Edens and the Origins of Environmentalism, 1600–1860 (Cambridge: Cambridge University Press, 1995), and Ecology, Climate and Empire: Colonialism and Global Environmental History, 1400–1940 (Cambridge: White House, 1997). See also Brant Vogel, "The Letter from Dublin: Climate Change, Colonialism, and the Royal Society in the Seventeenth Century," Osiris 26.1 (2011): 111–28.

93. Although the cause is still debated, climate historians today regard the prolonged sunspot minimum as having contributed to the Maunder Minimum. See J. A. Eddy, "The Maunder Minimum," Science 192 (June 1976): 1189–1202; and M. Lockwood et al., "Are Cold Winters in Europe Associated with Low Solar Activity?," Environmental Research Letters 5.2 (April 2010): n.p.

94. See Quint, Inside Paradise Lost, chap. 4.

95. John Rogers identifies God's retributive justice and naturalistic causality as providing two incompatible philosophies of history. See The Matter of Revolution: Science, Poetry, and Politics in the Age of Milton (Ithaca, NY: Cornell University Press, 1996), chap. 5.

96. For readings linking the postlapsarian labor of poetic representation with scientific inquiry, see Karen Edwards, Milton and the Natural World: Science and Poetry in Paradise Lost (Cambridge: Cambridge University Press, 1999); and Denys Van Renen, Nature and the New Science in England, 1665–1726 (Oxford: Oxford University Press, 2018), 25–43.

97. Srinivas Aravamudan, "The Catachronism of Climate Change," Diacritics 41.3 (2013): 6–30, 8.

98. Flannagan, ed., Riverside Milton, 354 n. 14. On the idea of a "paradise within," see Philip Almond, Adam and Eve in Seventeenth-Century Thought (Cambridge: Cambridge University Press, 1999); N. H. Keeble, The Literary Culture of Nonconformity in Later Seventeenth-Century England (Leicester: Leicester University Press, 1987); Thomas Blackburn, "Paradises Lost and Found: The Meaning and Function of the 'Paradise Within' in Paradise Lost," in Milton Studies 5, ed. James D Simmonds (Pittsburgh: University of Pittsburgh Press, 1973), 191–211; and Beverley Sherry, "A 'Paradise Within' Can Never Be 'Happier Farr': Reconsidering the Archangel Michael's Consolation in Paradise Lost," Milton Quarterly 37.2 (May 2003): 77–91.

99. Joanna Picciotto, "Reforming the Garden: The Experimentalist Eden and Paradise Lost," ELH 72.1 (Spring 2005): 23–78, 51.

CHAPTER TWO

1. William Wordsworth, "Essay, Supplementary to the Preface," in The Prose Works of William Wordsworth, ed. W. J. B. Owen and Jane Worthington Smyser (Oxford: Clarendon, 1974), 3:72–75.

2. William Hazlitt, Lectures on the English Poets (London, 1818), 173.

3. John Aikin, "An Essay on the Plan and Character of the Poem," in The Seasons, by James Thomson (London, 1779) (hereafter cited in text).

4. I have drawn on the extensive notes in James Sambrook, ed., *The Seasons and The Castle of Indolence* (Oxford: Clarendon, 1972).

5. "Arthur's Seat," in *Poems . . . by the Author of The Sentimental Sailor* (London, 1774), 34.

6. Sarah Dimick, "Disordered Environmental Time: Phenology, Climate Change, and Seasonal Form in the Work of Henry David Thoreau and Aldo Leopold," *ISLE* 25.4 (Autumn 2018): 700–721.

7. See Karen J. Cullen, *Famine in Scotland: The "Ill Years" of the 1690s* (Edinburgh: Edinburgh University Press, 2010).

8. M. L. Parry, "Secular Climate Change and Marginal Land," *Transactions of the Institute of British Geographers* 64 (1975): 1–13.

9. James Thomson to William Cranstoun, ca. October 1, 1725, in *James Thomson (1700–1748): Letters and Documents*, ed. Alan Dugald McKillop (Lawrence: University of Kansas Press, 1958), 15–18 (letters hereafter cited in text by page).

10. Thomas Van der Goten, "Eschatology and the Pindaric Ode in James Thomson's *Winter* (1726)," in *The Genres of Thomson's "The Seasons,"* ed. Sandro Jung and Kwinten Van De Walle (Bethlehem, PA: Lehigh University Press, 2018), 83–98, 84.

11. See Michael Ketcham, "Scientific and Poetic Imagination in Thomson's Poem to Newton," *Philological Quarterly* 61 (Winter 1982): 33–50; Carson Bergstrom, "James Thomson's *A Poem Sacred to the Memory of Sir Isaac Newton* and the Revisions to *The Seasons*: New Science and Poetics in the Eighteenth Century," in *Experiments in Genre in Eighteenth-Century Literature*, ed. Sandro Jung (Gent: Academia, 2011), 33–59; and Stefanie Lethbridge, *James Thomson's Defence of Poetry: Intertextual Allusion in "The Seasons"* (Tübingen: Niemeyer, 2003).

12. James Thomson, *Liberty* (1735–36), in *Poetical Works*, ed. J. Logie Robertson (London: Oxford University Press, 1971), 309–421 (book 4, line 260) (hereafter cited in text by book and line numbers).

13. Blanford Parker, *The Triumph of Augustan Poetics: English Literary Culture from Butler to Johnson* (Cambridge: Cambridge University Press, 1998), 148 (hereafter cited in text).

14. In *Liberty*, Thomson describes Pythagoras as anticipating Newton in scanning the heavens and discovering the basis for a solar physicotheology: "There [he] first discerned the secret band of love, / The kind attraction that to central suns / Binds circling earths, and world with world unites. / Instructed thence, he great ideas formed / Of the whole-moving, all-informing God, / The Sun of beings! Beaming unconfined / Light, life, and love, and ever-active power" (3.45–51).

15. Edmund Halley had drawn the same comparison in an ode attached to the 1687 *Principia*. Thomson's epigraph was removed when the poem was included in an edition with the complete *Seasons* in 1730, effacing the Lucretian precedent.

16. James Thomson, *To the Memory of Sir Isaac Newton* (1727), in Robertson, ed., *Poetical Works*, 436–42, lines 69–72 (hereafter cited in text by line numbers). On Thomson's Newtonian education in Edinburgh, see Herbert Drennon, "James Thomson's Contact with Newtonianism and His Interest in Natural Philosophy," *PMLA* 49.1 (March 1934): 71–80.

17. Bentley quoted in Alan Dugald McKillop, *The Background of Thomson's "Seasons"* (Hamden, CT: Archon, 1961), 32 (hereafter cited in text). See Courtney Weiss Smith,

Empiricist Devotions: Science, Religion, and Poetry in Early Eighteenth-Century England (Charlottesville: University of Virginia Press, 2016), chap. 1. In his unpublished writing, David Kubrin explains, Newton wondered whether providence could be identified in a principle of energetic renewal, a divinely supplied "fuel" or "food" that would explain all forms of activity: "gravity, fermentation, light, heat, cohesion, and life." David Kubrin, "Newton and the Cyclical Cosmos: Providence and the Mechanical Philosophy," *Journal of the History of Ideas* 28.3 (July–September 1967): 325–46, 331–32.

18. Joseph Addison in *Spectator* no. 120, in *The Spectator* (London, 1753), 2:149–53.

19. Anne Janowitz, "The Sublime Plurality of Worlds: Lucretius in the Eighteenth Century," *Tate Papers*, no. 13 (April 2010), https://www.tate.org.uk/research/publications/tate-papers/13/the-sublime-plurality-of-worlds-lucretius-in-the-eighteenth-century.

20. Henry More, *Philosophical Poems* (1647), quoted in Gerard Passannante, *The Lucretian Renaissance: Philology and the Afterlife of a Tradition* (Chicago: University of Chicago Press, 2011), 195.

21. Catherine Wilson notes that Descartes describes God as having made corpuscular matter before he "agitated it" and withdrew. See *Epicureanism at the Origins of Modernity* (Oxford: Oxford University Press, 2008), 98.

22. Robert Markley, "Literature, Climate, and Time: Between History and Story," in Adeline Johns-Putra, ed., *Climate and Literature*, 15–30, 18.

23. Burnet had suggested that there may be germs of geohistorical truth in the "fictions" of the Ancients (*Sacred Theory*, 190–91), a theme explored in his dangerously heterodox *Archaeologiae philosophicae* (1692), which treats the Mosaic cosmogony as myth.

24. In the last query appended to the second edition of the *Optics* (London, 1718), Newton articulates an essentially atomistic understanding of matter as being composed of "primitive Particles" that "never . . . break to pieces" (376).

25. See Sean Silver, "Making Weather: Communication Networks and the Great Storm of 1703," *Eighteenth-Century Fiction* 30.4 (Summer 2018): 495–518.

26. Fagan, *The Little Ice Age*, 138.

27. See José L. Martínes-González, "Did Climate Change Influence English Agricultural Development? (1645–1740)," Working Paper no. 75 (Vienna: European Historical Economics Society, April 2015); and Axel Michaelowa, "The Impact of Short-Term Climate Change on British and French Agriculture and Population in the First Half of the 18th Century," in *History and Climate: Memories of the Future?*, ed. P. D. Jones et al. (New York: Springer, 2001), 201–17.

28. Frans De Bruyn discusses connections between the georgic revival and agrarian science. See "Eighteenth-Century Editions of Virgil's *Georgics*: From Classical Poem to Agricultural Treatise," *Lumen* 24 (2005): 149–63; and "Reading Virgil's *Georgics* as a Scientific Text: The Eighteenth-Century Debate between Jethro Tull and Stephen Switzer," *ELH* 71.3 (January 2004): 661–89.

29. See M. Owen Lee, *Virgil as Orpheus: A Study of the "Georgics"* (Albany: State University of New York Press, 1996), chap. 5.

30. Kurt Heinzelman, "Roman Georgic in the Georgian Age: A Theory of Romantic Genre," *Texas Studies in Literature and Language* 33.2 (Summer 1991): 182–213, 188 (hereafter cited in text).

31. John Chalker, *The English Georgic: A Study in the Development of a Form* (London: Routledge & Kegan Paul, 1969), 92.

32. James Thomson, "Notes to Winter," in Robertson, ed., *Poetical Works*, 239–44, 239 (hereafter cited in text).

33. Robertson, ed., *Poetical Works*, 241–42. In his translation Thomson repeats a mistake made by Dryden ("what cause delays / The summer nights, and shortens winter days"), rendering "vel quae tardis mora noctibus obstet" as referring to "lazy summer-night." Joseph Warton corrects the error: "Why wintry suns roll down with rapid flight, / And whence delay retards the lingering night." *Works of Virgil in English Verse*, 1.198.

34. See Cutler J. Cleveland, "Biophysical Economics: Historical Perspectives and Current Research Trends," *Ecological Modelling* 38 (September 1987): 47–73.

35. Stephen Hales, *Vegetable Staticks* (London, 1727), 324 (my emphasis; hereafter cited in text).

36. Hales cites Newton: "Are not gross bodies and light convertible into one another, and may not bodies receive much of their activity from the particles of light, which enter their Composition? The changing of bodies into light, and of light into bodies, is very conformable to the course of nature, which seems delighted with Transmutations." *Vegetable Staticks*, 327. Lucretius describes "the sun's light and its heat" as "particles," "made of minute elements." *On the Nature*, 4.184–85.

37. Paul Warde, *The Invention of Sustainability: Nature and Destiny, c. 1500–1870* (Cambridge: Cambridge University Press, 2018), 249.

38. A. H. John, "Aspects of English Economic Growth in the First Half of the Eighteenth Century," *Economica* 29.110 (May 1961): 176–90.

39. Edmund Gosse, "Descriptive Poetry," *Encyclopedia Britannica* (1911), 8:91–92. In the 1815 preface to *Lyrical Ballads*, Wordsworth distinguished five "moulds" or "forms" of poetry, including narrative, dramatic, lyric, didactic, and idyllium, which is "descriptive chiefly either of the processes and appearances of external nature, as the *Seasons* of Thomson; or of characters, manners, and sentiments." Owen and Smyser, eds., *Prose Works*, 3:28. Blanford Parker observes that "the whole notion of descriptive poetry is the invention of that period": "The natural world and the world of incidental appearances, stripped for the first time of their iconic burden, burst forth and flooded the scene of eighteenth-century descriptive writing." *The Triumph of Augustan Poetics*, 18.

40. Warton, *Works of Virgil in English Verse*, 1:ii.

41. Joseph Warton, *An Essay on the Genius and Writings of Pope* (London, 1772), 41.

42. James Sambrook, *James Thomson, 1700–1748* (Oxford: Clarendon, 1991), 101 (hereafter cited in text).

43. Heather Keenleyside, "Personification for the People: On James Thomson's *The Seasons*," *ELH* 76 (2009): 447–72, 449. Keenleyside notes: "Thomson suggests that personification and natural description are not clear and distinct modes. Every action is an animation: something that is described by means of personification" (457).

44. John More, *Strictures, Critical and Sentimental, on Thomson's "Seasons"* (London, 1777), 108–10 (hereafter cited in text).

45. Robert Story, *Love and Literature* (London, 1842), 154.

46. John Barrell, *The Idea of Landscape and the Sense of Place, 1730–1840* (Cambridge: Cambridge University Press, 2011), 21, 24.

47. John Barrell, *English Literature in History: An Equal, Wide Survey* (London: Hutchinson, 1983). Recent criticism has challenged Barrell's reading. Kevis Goodman examines the poem's techniques for managing overwhelming sensory stimulation, an "inchoate, amorphous, and incompletely realized awareness of history," by reflexively foregrounding its status as a representational medium. *Georgic Modernity and British Romanticism*, 41. Adam Potkay attends to the poem's sonic concerns, the way its own music joins with birdsong and the wind "attach[ing] us to a world that exceeds linguistic or scientific comprehension and control." "Ear and Eye: Counteracting Senses in Loco-Descriptive Poetry," in *A Companion to Romantic Poetry*, ed. Charles Mahoney (Malden, MA: Blackwell, 2011), 176–94. Elizabeth Oldfather examines Thomson's staging of embodied perception, especially the manner in which, rather than exerting control, the narrator's gaze is often (pleasingly) captured and compelled by what he perceives. See "'Snatched' into 'The Seasons': The Cognitive Roots of Loco-Descriptive Form," *The Eighteenth Century* 56.4 (Winter 2015): 445–65.

48. W. B. Hutchings, "'Can pure description hold the place of sense?': Thomson's Landscape Poetry," in *James Thomson: Essays for the Tercentenary*, ed. Richard Terry (Liverpool: Liverpool University Press, 2000), 35–65, 55.

49. The exceptions are several figures of human petrification, what Katarina Stenke calls Thomson's "still lives." "'The well-dissembled Mourner': Lightning's (Dis)course in the Still Lives of Thomson's 'Celadon and Amelia,'" *Studies in the Literary Imagination* 46.1 (Spring 2013): 19–46.

50. As Jayne Lewis observes in her study of atmosphere and the rise of the novel, the "ludic and elusive qualities" of air invited (in fact, required) "linguistic experiment" and literary self-reflexivity. *Air's Appearance: Literary Atmosphere in British Fiction, 1660–1794* (Chicago: University of Chicago Press, 2012), 23. To write about air, which is discernible primarily as a medium (of heat, of moisture, of sound), was often to write about the mediation of language itself.

51. Robert Boyle, *Suspicions about Some Hidden Realities of the Air* (London, 1674), 2. Boyle was responsible for importing the word *atmosphere* into English, showing that the atmosphere has weight and varies with altitude and weather conditions. See Craig Martin, "The Invention of Atmosphere," *Studies in History and Philosophy of Science* 52 (August 2015): 44–54. As Martin notes, the early modern science of atmosphere was inspired by Lucretius. Pierre Gassendi had challenged Aristotle's meteorology, drawing on Lucretian atomism to suggest that atmospheric pressure and variability result from a "weaving [*textura*] of exhalations or corpuscles emanating from earth and water" (48–49 [quoting Gassendi]).

52. Edmund Halley, "An Account of the Circulation of the Watry Vapours," *Philosophical Transactions of the Royal Society* 17 (1686): 468–73. See Yi-Fu Tuan, *The Hydrologic Cycle and the Wisdom of God: A Theme in Geoteleology* (Toronto: University of Toronto Press, 1968); and Dilip Da Cunha, *The Invention of Rivers: Alexander's Eye and Ganga's Descent* (Philadelphia: University of Pennsylvania Press, 2019).

53. Gertrude Greene Cronk, "Lucretius and Thomson's Autumnal Fogs," *American Journal of Philology* 51.3 (1930): 233–42.

54. Thomas Reisner, "The Vast Eternal Springs: Ancient and Modern Hydrodynamics in Thomson's 'Autumn,'" *Mosaic* 10.4 (Summer 1977): 97–110.

55. As Mary Floyd-Wilson explains, most classical thinkers, with the notable exception of Hippocrates, posited "a counteractive relationship between internal and external temperatures, that is, cold air makes for hot blood" (and vice versa). See *English Ethnicity and Race in Early Modern Drama* (Cambridge: Cambridge University Press, 2003), 25. Michael Putnam argues that it is specifically the fear of death that causes the poet's blood to chill. See *"Frigidus sanguis*: Lucretius, Virgil and Death,"* in *Roman Literature, Gender and Reception*, ed. Donald Lateiner, Barbara K. Gold, and Judith Perkins (London: Routledge, 2013), 28–39.

56. Christopher Miller, "The Lyric Self in *The Seasons,"* in Jung and Van De Walle, eds., *The Genres of Thomson's "The Seasons,"* 61–81, 64–65.

57. John Wilson Foster notes that in topographical poetry the river "represents both the local and the broadly geographic in its flowing from the mountains to the far-flung oceans": "The river is a genuine conjunction of time and space." "A Redefinition of Topographical Poetry," *Journal of English and Germanic Philology* 69.3 (July 1970): 394–406, 402.

58. Cavert, *The Smoke of London*, 23.

59. Daniel Defoe, *A Tour through the Whole Island of Great Britain* (London: Dent, 1928), 1:167–68.

60. *Georgics*, in Dryden, *The Works of Virgil in English*, 5.320–27.

61. Warton, *The Works of Virgil in English Verse*, 1:237 n. 432.

62. Fredrik Albritton Jonsson, *Enlightenment's Frontier: The Scottish Highlands and the Origins of Environmentalism* (New Haven, CT: Yale University Press, 2013), 44–45, 124.

63. Beth Fowkes Tobin asserts that "some of the most powerful and influential" representations of tropical bounty "can be found in English georgic poetry," including *The Seasons. Colonizing Nature: The Tropics in British Arts and Letters, 1760–1820* (Philadelphia: University of Pennsylvania Press, 2004), 35.

64. Leo Spitzer, "Milieu and Ambiance: An Essay in Historical Semantics," *Philosophy and Phenomenological Research* 3.1 (September 1942): 1–42, 22. The ancients, Spitzer claims, were "embraced" by their atmosphere; in the Newtonian world, the "aetherial medium" becomes the abstract intermediary for the play of forces.

65. In chap. 34 of *Leviathan* (Cambridge: Cambridge University Press, 1996), Thomas Hobbes observes that our perception of air's fluid motion—a cloud moving through the sky or wind roiling the water—provides us with the metaphoric resources by which we characterize other forms of apparent immateriality, such as "inspiration," "Imagination," and the "Spirit of God."

66. George Hadley had in 1735 published an explanation of the trade winds correctly incorporating both "the action of the sun" in "the rarefaction of the air" and the "Motion of the Earth." "Concerning the Cause of the General Trade-Winds," *Philosophical Transactions of the Royal Society* 39 (1735–36): 58–62. But Thomson's account of the "general breeze" in the final edition remained imprecise, despite the inclusion of an authorial note describing how the "trade winds" are "caused by the pressure of the rarefied air on that before it, according to the diurnal motion of the sun."

67. Wolfram Schmidgen, *Eighteenth-Century Fiction and the Law of Property* (Cambridge: Cambridge University Press, 2002), 107.

68. Laura Brown, *Fables of Modernity: Literature and Culture in the English Eighteenth Century* (Ithaca, NY: Cornell University Press, 2001), 63, 71.

69. Fredrik Albritton Jonsson offers a genealogy of cornucopianism that begins with natural theology and alchemy, is sharply inflected by colonial expansion, but takes its modern form in the early nineteenth century in Ricardo's concept of rent, according to which endless growth is supported by the substitutability of natural resources, most crucially the substitutability of fuels. See "The Origins of Cornucopianism: A Preliminary Genealogy," *Critical Historical Studies* 1.1 (Spring 2014): 151–68, 153–54.

70. Robert Markley, "Nation and Environment in Britain, 1660–1705," in *Emergent Nation: Early Modern British Literature in Transition, 1660–1714,* ed. Elizabeth Sauer (Cambridge: Cambridge University Press, 2019), 295–312, 297, 301. See also Robert Markley, " 'Land enough in the world': Locke's Golden Age and the Infinite Extension of 'Use,' " *South Atlantic Quarterly* 98.4 (1999): 817–37. Steve Pincus argues that, after the Revolution of 1688, a Whig political economy based on the idea that "wealth was potentially infinite and created by human labor" took hold. *1688: The First Modern Revolution* (New Haven, CT: Yale University Press, 2009), 383.

71. See William Levine, "Collins, Thomson, and the Whig Progress of Liberty," *Studies in English Literature* 34.3 (Summer 1994): 553–77; and Alan Dugald McKillop, "The Background of Thomson's *Liberty*," Pamphlet 38.2 (Houston: Rice Institute, July 1951).

72. In 1734, the clergyman Dr. Alured Clarke wrote to Charlotte Clayton about Thomson's *Liberty*: "And as Italy, with all its fruitfulness, its warm clime, and every other natural advantage, is yet become a barren and desolate, miserable country, merely by losing its liberty, he draws from thence a very useful lesson to Britons to take care to preserve that blessing which enabled us to make ourselves more than amends for every disadvantage of our soil and climate." *Letters and Documents*, 88–89.

73. Alan Bewell, *Natures in Translation: Romanticism and Colonial Natural History* (Baltimore: Johns Hopkins University Press, 2017) (cited hereafter in text). See also Jonsson, *Enlightenment's Frontier*, 60–61.

74. Raymond Williams, *The Country and the City* (New York: Oxford University Press, 1982), 69 (cited hereafter in text). Tim Fulford similarly notes: "At his best he makes landscape speak of British liberty retreating to rural margins, the wildness of which left them uncultivated." *Landscape, Liberty and Authority: Poetry, Criticism and Politics from Thomson to Wordsworth* (Cambridge: Cambridge University Press, 1996), 35 (hereafter cited in text).

75. On shifting eighteenth-century representations of common lands, wastes, and wilderness, see Vittoria Di Palma, *Wasteland: A History* (New Haven, CT: Yale University Press, 2014).

76. Anthony Ashley Cooper, Third Earl of Shaftesbury, *Characteristics of Men, Manners, Opinions, Times* (1711), ed. Lawrence Klein (Cambridge: Cambridge University Press, 1999), 315.

77. Michael Marder, "Cornucopia," *The Turnip Truck(s)* 3.1 (Spring/Summer 2017): 24–27.

78. John Veitch, *The Feeling for Nature in Scottish Poetry* (Edinburgh, 1887), 2:69 (hereafter cited in text).

79. Ralph Cohen, *The Unfolding of "The Seasons"* (London: Routledge, 1970), 75.

80. See Utterström, "Climatic Fluctuations and Population Problems," 5.

81. Lucretius, *His Six Books of Epicurean Philosophy, Done into English Verse*, trans. Thomas Creech (London, 1699), 146.

82. Richard Mead, *Short Discourse concerning Pestilential Contagion* (London, 1722), 29–31, quoted in McKillop, *The Background of Thomson's "Seasons,"* 167–68.

83. Glynnis Ridley, "The Seasons and the Politics of Opposition," in *James Thomson: Essays for the Tercentenary*, ed. Richard Terry (Liverpool: Liverpool University Press, 2000), 93–116, 97.

84. Denys Van Renen, "'Sick Nature blasting': The Ecological Limits of British Imperialism in Thomson's *The Seasons*," *Journal of Scottish Historical Studies* 38.1 (2018): 121–42, 134.

85. In a letter to Cranstoun after the death of his brother—who, suffering from consumption, had returned home with the hope that his "native Air" would support his "Recovery" (*Letters and Documents*, 94 [August 7, 1735])—Thomson echoes Lucretius on "the Death of Relations and Friends": "They then are past our Regret: the Living are to be lamented, and not the Dead" (ibid., 99 [October 20, 1735]).

86. Fulford notes that the peasant poet Stephen Duck showed how "the farmworker's need to labour in all weather was determined by a social and economic order in which farmers and landowners demanded it of him" (*Landscape, Liberty and Authority*, 26). On depictions of extreme weather in laboring-class poetry, see Bridget Keegan, "Snowstorms, Shipwrecks, and Scorching Heat: The Climates of Eighteenth-Century Laboring Class Poetry," *ISLE* 10.1 (Winter 2003): 75–96.

87. Patrick Murdoch, "A Life of the Author," in *The Poetical Works of James Thomson* (London, 1849), xv–xxxiv, xxix.

88. See Paul Reiter, "From Shakespeare to Defoe: Malaria in England in the Little Ice Age," *Emerging Infectious Diseases* 6.1 (February 2000): 1–11.

89. Jonathan Swift, *Correspondence*, ed. Harold Williams (Oxford: Clarendon, 1965), 4:53.

90. Robert Shiels, "The Life of Mr. James Thomson," in *Lives of the Poets of Great Britain and Ireland* (London, 1753), 5:190–218.

91. Thomas B. Gilmore tracks Johnson's appreciation of Thomson's scientific diction in his *Dictionary of the English Language* (1755), which uses 614 quotations from the poet's verse. See "Implicit Criticism of Thomson's 'Seasons' in Johnson's 'Dictionary,'" *Modern Philology* 86.3 (February 1989): 265–73.

92. Samuel Johnson, *Dr. Johnson's Table Talk* (London, 1807), 2:189.

93. Samuel Johnson, *Idler*, no. 11 (June 24, 1758), in *The Idler* (London, 1767), 1.59–64, 62 (hereafter cited in text). Johnson does acknowledges that "it is the present state of the skies, and of the earth, on which plenty and famine are suspended, on which millions depend for the necessaries of life" (61).

94. John Wilson, "An Hour's Talk about Poetry," in *Recreations of Christopher North* (Edinburgh, 1868), 1:220–21.

95. Gerrit de Maar, *A History of Modern English Romanticism: Elizabethan and Modern Romanticism in the Eighteenth Century* (New York: Haskell, 1970), 176. On critical debates regarding the Scottishness of *The Seasons*, see Mary Jane W. Scott, *James Thomson, Anglo-Scot* (Athens: University of Georgia Press, 1988).

96. The debate between Johnson, on one side, and More and Aikin, on the other, on the coherence of *The Seasons* plays out in recent criticism. James Sambrook—who was, along with Ralph Cohen, Thomson's most committed and careful reader in the twentieth century—argues that seasonal change is sufficient to encompass the poem's many topics:

"For all the digressions, the varied material of the poem is contained within a natural framework, so that all the minutely-observed weather signs and other natural features of the seasons, together with the seasonal activities of insects, birds, animals, and men, are described in due order" (*Life*, 100). Yet a number of other critics have read the poem in terms of what Sandro Jung calls its "digressive and fragmentary form." See *The Fragmentary Poetic: Eighteenth-Century Uses of an Experimental Mode* (Bethlehem, PA: Lehigh University Press, 2009), 73. My argument is that the critical debate on the poem's formal and thematic unity hinges on whether a given critic regards seasonal change and the effects of climate as meaningful sources of coherence.

97. Robert Heron is an exception in insisting that the poem's organizing principle is the "relation" of man and nature: "From the change which Spring happily produces on the temperature of the atmosphere, on the face of the sky, and by the influence of the kindlier air, on the soil and on the labours of man;—the transition is natural, to the renewed energy of Vegetation." *A Critical Essay on The Seasons* (Perth, 1793), 9. See also Cohen, *The Art of Discrimination*, 93–94.

98. Anna Seward to Thomas Park, May 10, 19, 1798, in Seward, *Letters of Anna Seward*, 5:84–96.

99. James Russell Lowell, *My Garden Acquaintance and A Good Word for Winter* (Boston, 1877), 55. Of Thomson, Lowell observes: "The poet of Winter himself is said to have written in bed, with his hand through a hole in the blanket" (56), which explains why his "view of winter is a hostile one" (61). "In truth, it is no wonder that the short days of that cloudy northern climate should have added to winter a gloom borrowed of the mind" (62).

100. Hugh Miller, *First Impressions of England and Its People* (Edinburgh, 1847), 559–60.

101. See Cohen, *The Art of Discrimination*, 382.

102. Review of *The Poetical Works of James Thomson*, *The Academy*, April 17, 1897, 417.

CHAPTER THREE

1. Paul Hohenberg and Lynn Hollen Lees, *The Making of Urban Europe, 1000–1994* (Cambridge, MA: Harvard University Press, 1995), 184. "The best examples of the transforming power of rapid industrial growth are to be found in the coal-mining regions," Hohenberg and Lees write. "Since coal was needed to run the engines and smelt the ores, factories and furnaces tended to locate very near coal supplies or in places where they had good access to transportation. . . . These coal basins grew by a kind of regional implosion, whereby a rural milieu crystallized into a densely urban one" (184–85).

2. Sidney Mintz, *Sweetness and Power: The Place of Sugar in Modern History* (New York: Penguin, 1986), 47–51.

3. Barrell, *English Literature in History*, 29, 14.

4. James Boswell, *The Life of Samuel Johnson* (London: J. M. Dent, 1973), 1:621–22 (hereafter cited in text).

5. Markman Ellis, "'The Cane-Land Isles': Commerce and Empire in Late Eighteenth-Century Georgic and Pastoral Poetry," in *Islands in History and Representation*, ed. Rod

Edmond and Vanessa Smith (New York: Routledge, 2003), 42–63, 60 (hereafter cited in text).

6. David Alff, *The Wreckage of Intentions: Projects in British Culture, 1660–1730* (Philadelphia: University of Pennsylvania Press, 2017), 115 (hereafter cited in text).

7. Claire Bucknell, "The Mid-Eighteenth-Century Georgic and Agricultural Improvement," *Journal for Eighteenth-Century Studies* 36.3 (2013): 335–52, 338.

8. Rudolf Beck, "From Industrial Georgic to Industrial Sublime: English Poetry and the Early Stages of the Industrial Revolution," *Journal for Eighteenth-Century Studies* 27.1 (March 2004): 17–36, 27.

9. On the rendering of global nature as material that can be combined, exchanged, and transported, see also Bruno Latour, *Science in Action: How to Follow Scientists and Engineers through Society* (Cambridge, MA: Harvard University Press, 1987); and Noel Castree, "Commodifying What Nature?," *Progress in Human Geography* 27.3 (2003): 273–97.

10. William Boyd, W. Scott Prudham, and Rachel Schurman see a shift from extractive industries that treat nature as an "exogenous" stock of resources to what they call the "real subsumption of nature," whereby "biophysical systems are industrialized"—augmented or rerouted—to serve as "productive forces." "Industrial Dynamics and the Problem of Nature," *Society and Natural Resources* 14.7 (2001): 555–70, 557.

11. Robert Allen, *The British Industrial Revolution in Global Perspective* (Cambridge: Cambridge University Press, 2009), 130.

12. John Dyer, *The Fleece: A Poem in Four Books* (1757), ed. John Goodridge and Juan Christian Pellicer (Cheltenham: Cyder, 2007), 3.630–31 (hereafter cited in text by book and line numbers). The definitive question in modern criticism on *The Fleece* is Dyer's degree of awareness regarding the contradictions his poem stages. Laurence Goldstein sees a degree of self-consciousness in the poem but claims that Dyer is "evasive of *bedrock realities.*" See *Ruins and Empire: The Evolution of a Theme in Augustan and Romantic Literature* (Pittsburgh: University of Pittsburgh Press, 1977), 57. Richard Feingold argues that Dyer shows "no clear sense" of the novel historical energies his poem features. See *Nature and Society: Later Eighteenth-Century Uses of the Pastoral and the Georgic* (New Brunswick, NJ: Rutgers University Press, 1978), chap. 3. John Barrell offers a Jamesonian reading in which Dyer foregrounds certain contradictions so as to sublimate the reality of class conflict. See *English Literature in History*, chap. 1. Dustin Griffin links Dyer's explicit "doubts and misgivings" to new forms of luxury consumerism. See *Patriotism and Poetry in Eighteenth-Century Britain* (Cambridge: Cambridge University Press 2002), 181 (and chap. 7 generally) (hereafter cited in text). John Goodridge's immensely detailed study of the poem shows how Dyer's optimistic vision is grounded in a technical knowledge of sheep husbandry. See *Rural Life in Eighteenth-Century English Poetry* (Cambridge: Cambridge University Press, 1995), pt. 2 (hereafter cited in text).

13. Dustin Griffin notes that Dyer's reference to Drayton's *Poly-Olbion* places the poem in a "chorographical" tradition that also includes Camden's *Britannia* (1586), a major source for Defoe's *Tour*. See *Patriotism and Poetry*, 187.

14. John Locke, *Two Treatises of Government*, ed. Peter Laslett (Cambridge: Cambridge University Press, 1988), 296.

15. Phyllis Deane, "The Output of the British Woolen Industry in the Eighteenth Century," *Journal of Economic History* 17.2 (June 1957): 207–23. On the manner in which mechanization decouples value from "the limitations of seasonal rhythms, climatic uncertainties and soil variations," see Debeir, Deleage, and Hemery, *In the Servitude of Power*, 91.

16. W. Arthur, "John Dyer," *The Red Dragon: The National Magazine of Wales* 10, no. 3 (1886): 208–28, 223–24.

17. Cecil Moore, *Backgrounds of English Literature, 1700–1760* (Minneapolis: University of Minnesota Press, 1953), 127–28.

18. John Hays, *The Resources of the United States for Sheep Husbandry and the Wool Manufacture: An Address Delivered Before the National Agricultural Congress, in New Haven* (Boston, 1878), 27 (hereafter cited in text).

19. James Grainger, review of *The Fleece, Monthly Review* 16 (1757): 328–40, 329 (hereafter cited in text).

20. James Grainger to Thomas Percy, June 1, 1760, cited in John Gilmore, *The Poetics of Empire: A Study of James Grainger's "The Sugar Cane" (1764)* (London: Athlone, 2000), 15.

21. James Grainger, preface to *The Sugar-Cane*, reprinted in Gilmore, *The Poetics of Empire*, 89–90, 89.

22. See Richard Drayton, *Nature's Government: Science, Imperial Britain and the "Improvement" of the World* (New Haven, CT: Yale University Press, 2000).

23. Anna Tsing, "Unruly Edges: Mushrooms as Companion Species," *Environmental Humanities* 1 (2012): 141–54 (hereafter cited in text); Jason Moore, "Sugar and the Expansion of the Early Modern World-Economy: Commodity Frontiers, Ecological Transformation, and Industrialization," *Review (Fernand Braudel Center)* 23.3 (2000): 409–33 (hereafter cited in text).

24. See Justin Roberts, *Slavery and the Enlightenment in the British Atlantic, 1750–1807* (Cambridge: Cambridge University Press, 2013).

25. Grainger, preface to *The Sugar-Cane*, 89.

26. Samuel Martin, *An Essay upon Plantership* (Antigua, 1750), 37.

27. James Grainger, *The Sugar-Cane*, reprinted in Gilmore, *The Poetics of Empire*, 1.312–13 (hereafter cited in text by book and line numbers).

28. Britt Rusert, "Plantation Ecologies: The Experimental Plantation in and against James Grainger's 'The Sugar-Cane,'" *Early American Studies* 13.2 (Spring 2015): 341–73. Rusert sees the poem's extensive notes as harboring an ecological disorder, a kind of "wild overgrowth" that exists in tension with the authority claimed in the verse, an interesting but not entirely convincing interpretation given how much danger and disorder is acknowledged in the verse.

29. Shaun Irlam, "'Wish you were here': Exporting England in James Grainger's *The Sugar-Cane*," *ELH* 68.2 (Summer 2001): 377–96, 384. For a reading that shows how Grainger's personifications strain and transform under the pressure of a challenging colonial environment, see Monique Alewaert, "Insect Poetics: James Grainger, Personification, and Enlightenments Not Taken," *Early American Literature* 52. 2 (2017): 299–332.

30. Grove, *Green Imperialism*, 6.

31. Warde, *The Invention of Sustainability*, 228–29.

32. See Ellis, " 'The Cane-Land Isles' "; Stephen Thomas, "Doctoring Ideology: James Grainger's *The Sugar-Cane* and the Bodies of Empire," *Early American Studies: An Interdisciplinary Journal* 4 (2006): 78–111; and Tobin, *Colonizing Nature*, chap. 1.

33. James Fenske and Namrata Kala identify a correlation between warmer temperatures, which lowered agricultural production, and a decrease in slave trading, suggesting that the African slave trade was rooted in economic surplus rather than scarcity. See "Climate and the Slave Trade," *Journal of Development Economics* 112 (2015): 19–32.

34. Markman Ellis, " 'Incessant labour': Georgic Poetry and the Problem of Slavery," in *Discourses of Slavery and Abolition*, ed. Brycchan Carey et al. (Basingstoke: Palgrave Macmillan, 2004), 45–62, 55. See also Michael Morris, *Scotland and the Caribbean, c. 1740–1833: Atlantic Archipelagos* (New York: Routledge, 2015), chap. 2.

35. *Monthly Review* 31 (1764): 105–18.

36. Richard Davenport, "The Life of Grainger," in *The Poems of Grainger, and Boyse* (Chiswick, 1822), 7–16, 13 (hereafter cited in text).

37. Review of F. W. P. Greenwood, *A Description of the Principal Fruits of Cuba*, *Christian Examiner and General Review*, May 1839, 259–62.

38. "Literature and Medicine," reprinted in *Eclectic Magazine of Foreign Literature, Science, and Art* 30.93 (July 1879): 110.

39. *Very Bad Poetry*, ed. Kathryn Petras and Ross Petras (New York: Vintage, 1997), 43–44.

40. Richard Jago, *Edge-Hill; or, The Rural Prospect Delineated and Moralized* (London, 1767), v–vi. Unless otherwise noted, subsequent references are to book and line numbers in the posthumous edition, *Poems, Moral and Descriptive* (London, 1784).

41. Alan Liu, *Wordsworth: The Sense of History* (Stanford, CA: Stanford University Press, 1989), 120.

42. Noah Heringman, "Deep Time at the Dawn of the Anthropocene," *Representations* 129.1 (Winter 2015): 56–85, 60.

43. On the relation between the professionalization of geology and coal-mine surveying, see Roy Porter, *The Making of Geology: Earth Science in Britain, 1660–1815* (Cambridge: Cambridge University Press, 1977).

44. James Hutton, "Theory of the Earth," *Transactions of the Royal Society of Edinburgh* 3.2 (1788): 209–304.

45. See Hatcher, *The History of the British Coal Industry*, 1:142–44.

46. Jago's "grain, / Or herbage sweet, or waving woods" perfectly coincide with what Rolf Peter Sieferle identifies as the "three different types of land" that "can be attributed to metabolic, mechanical and thermal energy in agricultural space: arable, pasture, and woods," in Rolf Peter Sieferle, *The Subterranean Forest: Energy Systems and the Industrial Revolution* (Cambridge: White Horse, 1982), 25.

47. See Michael Walter Flinn, *The History of the British Coal Industry* (Oxford: Clarendon, 1984), 2:73–74 (hereafter cited in text).

48. Malm, *Fossil Capital*, 302.

49. As Rachel Crawford notes in the one extended critical reading of *Edge Hill*, the poem "ignores the agricultural arts for which Warwickshire was famous," drawing on georgic conventions—the depiction of active labor, the concern with practical technique

and instruction—to describe the world of mining, metallurgy, and manufacturing. *Poetry, Enclosure, and the Vernacular Landscape, 1700–1830* (Cambridge: Cambridge University Press, 2002), 153 (hereafter cited in text).

50. James Lovelock identifies the Newcomen as an important precipitant of the Anthropocene, as "the first occasion in the Earth's history that a sustained continuous source of energy above a critical threshold flux of approximately 1 kW per square meter was used purposefully, successfully and economically for periods as long as days." *A Rough Ride to the Future* (London: Penguin, 2014), 7. E. A. Wrigley identifies the "fundamental change" instantiated by the Newcomen engine in terms of positive feedback: "a device dependent upon a mineral power source to solve the problems of an industry devoted to the production of a mineral raw material" (*Continuity, Chance and Change*, 79).

51. By contrast, in a poem published in 1755, John Dalton describes how the engine operates in such a way that "Discordant elements agree, / Fire, water, air, heat, cold unite." *A Descriptive Poem, Addressed to Two Ladies, at Their Return from Viewing the Mines Near Whitehaven* (London, 1755), 136–37. On eighteenth-century poetic representations of the Newcomen engine and other new technologies, see Ivanka Kovacevich, "The Mechanical Muse: The Impact of Technical Inventions on Eighteenth-Century Neoclassical Poetry," *Huntington Library Quarterly* 28.4 (May 1965): 263–81.

52. Yaeger, "Literature in the Ages of Wood, Tallow, Coal . . . ," 309.

53. Burnet cites Pliny the Elder's extraordinary inquiry into the inexplicable ontology of fire in *Historia naturalis*. Given the pervasiveness of fuel and fire's tendency toward intensification, Pliny remarks: "It really exceeds all other wonders, that one single day should pass in which everything is not consumed." *The Natural History* (London, 1893), 3:142. Identifying the volcanoes Aetna and Vesuvius as two examples of the inexhaustible, though mysterious, element that "supplies this most greedy voracity without destroying itself," Pliny sees in fire's capacity to assimilate other forms into its own an implied directionality in time; in fire, "nature rages, threatening to consume the earth" (141). As Gaston Bachelard observes, there is a persistent association between combustion—as a symptom of the tendency within matter to burn, as a force of irreversible metamorphosis—and the expectation of Earth's end: an imperative to accelerate time and "bring all of life to its conclusion, to its hereafter." "In order to obtain the essence of fire," he writes, "one must go to its source, to its reserve, where it husbands its strength and concentrates itself, that is to say, to the mineral" (73). *Psychoanalysis of Fire*, trans. Alan Ross (London: Routledge & Kegan Paul, 1964), 16, 73.

54. Eric Hopkins, *Birmingham: The First Manufacturing Town in the World, 1760–1840* (London: Weidenfeld & Nicolson, 1989), 31–33. Abraham Darby's revolutionary technique for smelting iron with coke (coal with its sulfur content reduced), introduced in 1709 at Coalbrookdale, had been slow to spread because of its high cost and inferior product. The second half of the century saw "much faster growth" in overall domestic iron output than had any time in the previous century and a half, argues P. Riden. See "The Output of the British Iron Industry Before 1870," in *The Steel Industry*, ed. T. Boyns (London: I. B. Tauris, 1997), 1:1–20, 14–15. Rachel Crawford claims that "Jago permits ambiguities concerning the historic role of mineral coal in the iron-founding process." She cites Flinn's *History of the British Coal Industry* to substantiate her claim that "the region around Birmingham produced a form of coal unsuited for coke and thus did not

profit from the coke revolution." See *Poetry, Enclosure, and the Vernacular Landscape,* 155. But Flinn is describing the Cannock Chase field, not the Black Country. C. K. Hyde notes that, like Darby's Coalbrookdale coal, South Staffordshire coal has a relatively low sulfur content, which enabled the production of higher-quality pig iron. See "The Adoption of Coke-Smelting by the British Iron Industry, 1709–1790," in Boyns, ed., *The Steel Industry,* 1:273–91, 274.

55. William Hutton, *An History of Birmingham,* 3rd ed. (London, 1795), 99. We can read Jago's fervent linking of "native British ore" to foreign "trade" with two historical conditions. As Hopkins notes, the years 1760–81 saw significant stagnation in export activity, and, in the same decades, imports of high quality Swedish and Russian iron bar were also accelerating.

56. Hutton writes: "It is easy to see, without the spirit of prophecy, that Birmingham has not yet arrived at her zenith, neither is she likely to reach it for ages to come. Her increase will depend upon her manufactures; her manufactures will depend upon the national commerce; national commerce upon a superiority at sea; and this superiority may be extended to a long futurity." *An History of Birmingham,* 69–70.

57. *Monthly Review* 37 (1767): 16–21, 16.

58. *Critical Review* 24 (1767): 166–72, 172.

59. *The Annual Register; or, A View of the History, Politicks, and Literature, for the Year 1767* (London, 1768), 235–38; "Birmingham," in *The Cyclopaedia; or, Universal Dictionary of Arts, Sciences, and Literature* (London, 1819), vol. 4 (n.p.).

CHAPTER FOUR

1. Robert Southey, "Life of Cowper," in *The Works of Cowper* (London, 1836), 174, 184–85.

2. Clifford Siskin, *The Historicity of Romantic Discourse* (Oxford: Oxford University Press, 1988), 11.

3. G. W. F. Hegel, *Aesthetics: Lectures on Fine Arts,* trans. T. M. Knox (Oxford: Clarendon, 1975), 2:1113 (hereafter cited in text).

4. Theodor Adorno, "On Lyric Poetry and Society," in *Notes to Literature* (New York: Columbia University Press, 1991), 1:50, 40.

5. Theodor Adorno, *Aesthetic Theory* (Minneapolis: University of Minnesota Press, 1997), 62–63 (hereafter cited in text).

6. M. H. Abrams, "Structure and Style in the Greater Romantic Lyric," in *The Correspondent Breeze: Essays on English Romanticism* (New York: Norton, 1984), 76–108, 88, 79. (hereafter cited in text).

7. Donald Wesling, *Wordsworth and the Adequacy of Landscape* (New York: Barnes & Noble, 1970), 13.

8. See Rei Terada, "After the Critique of Lyric," *PMLA* 123.1 (January 2008): 195–200.

9. Crawford, *Poetry, Enclosure, and the Vernacular Landscape,* 4–5.

10. For David Simpson, lyric individuation is inseparable from the capitalist value form, "the rhetoric of self-making . . . shadowed by a paranoia that intuits everything as evanescent, about to slip away into a forgetting that is a psychological reflection of the formation of economic value as relentlessly unstable." *Wordsworth, Commodification,*

and Social Concern: The Poetics of Modernity (Cambridge: Cambridge University Press, 2011), 141. Anne Janowitz asserts that romanticism's "lyric modality" was produced in the "unrelieved tension" between an unrealized communitarian utopianism still available in the "customary language of the past" and "the limits imposed by an ineluctable alienation offered by the individualist language of the future." *Lyric and Labour in the Romantic Tradition* (Cambridge: Cambridge University Press, 1998), 1, 5. Noel Jackson has shown that the new "sciences of sensation" in this period helped lyric poets define a "uniquely social logic of this inward-turning language." *Science and Sensation in Romantic Poetry* (Cambridge: Cambridge University Press, 2008), 1.

11. Harold Perkins, *The Origins of Modern English Society* (London: Routledge, 1972), 1.

12. In *Class Struggle and the Industrial Revolution: Early Industrial Capitalism in Three English Towns* (London: Methuen, 1974), John Foster correlates the Industrial Revolution with the first appearance of the secular "boom-slump cycle": "While economic fluctuations were . . . nothing new . . . they had previously been largely the result of harvest failure and war. The new form of crisis was very different. It marked the arrival of the industrial stage of capitalist development, one demanding an increasing body of fixed investment which would only be sustained by the fundamentally contradictory private profit incentive" (141). That is, social crisis would be defined in terms of not food costs but unemployment and wage cutting. Foster dates this new mode of cyclic crisis to the mid-1780s, with downturns in 1785, 1788, 1793, 1797, and 1800. This entire period is defined by significant climatic instability.

13. See J. Neumann and J. Dettwiller, "Great Historical Events That Were Significantly Affected by the Weather: Pt. 9, The Year Leading to the Revolution of 1789 in France," *Bulletin American Meteorological Society* 71.1 (January 1990): 33–41.

14. William Wordsworth, preface to *Lyrical Ballads* (London, 1800), 1:xviii.

15. Emily Rohrbach, *Modernity's Mist: British Romanticism and the Poetics of Anticipation* (New York: Fordham University Press, 2015), 1.

16. Thomas H. Ford, *Wordsworth and the Poetics of Air* (Cambridge: Cambridge University Press, 2019), 2 (hereafter cited in text).

17. See Noah Heringman, *Romantic Rocks, Aesthetic Geology* (Ithaca, NY: Cornell University Press, 2004); Goldstein, *Sweet Science.*

18. See David Higgins, *Writing Tambora: British Romanticism, Climate Change, and the Anthropocene* (Cham: Palgrave Macmillan, 2017); Gillen D'Arcy Wood, *Tambora: The Eruption That Changed the World* (Princeton, NJ: Princeton University Press, 2014).

19. See Jacques Khalip, *Last Things: Disastrous Form from Kant to Hujar* (New York: Fordham University Press, 2018); Jacques Khalip and David Collings, "Introduction: The Present Time of 'Live Ashes,'" in "Romanticism and Disaster," ed. Jacques Khalip and David Collings, special issue, *Romantic Circles*, January 2012, https://romantic-circles.org/praxis/disaster/HTML/praxis.2012.khalip.html; Chris Washington, *Romantic Revelations: Visions of Post-Apocalyptic Life and Hope in the Anthropocene* (Toronto: University of Toronto Press, 2019); and David Collings, *Disastrous Subjectivities: Romanticism, Modernity, and the Real* (Toronto: University of Toronto Press, 2019).

20. See Sara Guyer, *Reading with John Clare: Biopoetics, Sovereignty, Romanticism* (New York: Fordham University Press, 2015).

21. Anne-Lise François, " 'Shadow boxing': Empty Blows, Practice Steps, and Nature's Hold," *Qui Parle* 25.1–2 (Fall/Winter 2016): 137–77 (hereafter cited in text).

22. Anne-Lise François, *Open Secrets: The Literature of Uncounted Experience* (Stanford, CA: Stanford University Press, 1999); Anahid Nersessian, *Utopia, Limited: Romanticism and Adjustment* (Cambridge, MA: Harvard University Press, 2015), 3.

23. Anne-Lise François, "Ungiving Time: Reading Lyric by the Light of the Anthropocene," in Menely and Taylor, eds., *Anthropocene Reading*, 239–58, 243.

24. Sharon Cameron, *Lyric Time: Dickinson and the Limits of Genre* (Baltimore: Johns Hopkins University Press, 1979). Jonathan Culler extends Cameron's argument, proposing that it is apostrophic address that best exemplifies "the special 'now,' of lyric articulation" as a transcendence of chronological or historical time. *Theory of the Lyric* (Cambridge, MA: Harvard University Press, 2015), 226.

25. In an essay that reminds us that the celestial time—days, lunar months, and years—of everyday experience is also geological time, Jeremy Davies points to the way in which romantic poems register a new unease about the "convergence between lyric and celestial temporality." "Lyric's Diurnal Course: Reading with Geology," *Mosaic* 52.3 (September 2019): 1–17, 5.

26. Nigel Clark and Bronislaw Szerszynski, *Planetary Social Thought: The Anthropocene Challenge to the Social Science* (Cambridge: Polity, 2020), 44.

27. William Cowper to John Newton, June 13, 1783, *The Letters and Prose Writings*, ed. James King and Charles Ryskamp (Oxford: Clarendon, 1981), 2:143 (letters from this volume hereafter cited in text by volume and page numbers).

28. Cowper, *The Task*, ed. Sambrook, 178n.

29. Frank Kermode, *The Sense of an Ending: Studies in the Theory of Fiction* (New York: Oxford University Press, 1967), 47 (hereafter cited in text).

30. Fredric Jameson, "The End of Temporality," *Critical Inquiry* 29.4 (Summer 2003): 695–718, 699.

31. Mary Favret, *War at a Distance: Romanticism and the Making of Modern Wartime* (Princeton, NJ: Princeton University Press, 2010), 53 (hereafter cited in text).

32. Goodman characterizes Cowper's verse as managing the process whereby the cacophonies of information conveyed by the daily newspaper can be registered in silence, stillness, and inarticulate affect. See *Georgic Modernity and British Romanticism*, chap. 3.

33. Jan Golinski, *British Weather and the Climate of Enlightenment* (Chicago: University of Chicago Press, 2007), 101–4.

34. John Grattan and Mark Brayshay, "An Amazing and Portentous Summer: Environmental and Social Responses in Britain to the 1783 Eruption of an Iceland Volcano," *Geographical Journal* 161.2 (July 1995): 125–34, 126.

35. "The Summer of Acid Rain," *Economist*, December 19, 2007, 132–34.

36. C. S. Witham and C. Oppenheimer, "Mortality in England during the 1783–4 Laki Craters Eruption," *Bulletin of Volcanology* 67 (2005): 15–26, 18.

37. Benjamin Franklin, *The Works* (Philadelphia, 1809), 3:287–89.

38. Gilbert White, *The Natural History of Selborne* (1789; Oxford: Oxford University Press, 1993), 247–48 (hereafter cited in text). See also Stuart Peterfreund, " 'Great frost and . . . some very hot summers': Strange Weather, the Last Letters, and the Last Days in Gilbert White's *Natural History of Selborne*," in *Romantic Science: The Literary Forms*

of Natural History, ed. Noah Heringman (Albany: State University of New York Press, 2003), 85–110.

39. White recalled the same simile—"As when the sun, new risen, / Looks through the horizontal, misty air, / Shorn of his beams"—which captured the "superstitious kind of dread, which with the minds of men are apt to be impressed by such strange and unusual phenomena." *Natural History of Selborne*, 248. So did Horace Walpole, writing to the Countess of Upper Ossory on July 15: "A sun shorn of his beams, and a moon that only serves to make darkness visible, are mighty homogeneal to a distracted state." *The Letters of Horace Walpole* (Oxford: Clarendon, 1905), 8:21 (hereafter cited in text).

40. David E. Parker, "Uncertainties in Early Central England Temperatures," *International Journal of Climatology* 30.8 (2010): 110–13.

41. Like Milton, Cowper sees English liberty as a never entirely secure compensation for an unpleasant climate. See *Paradise Lost*, 4.465–90. On this association, see Eric Gidal, "Civic Melancholy: English Gloom and French Enlightenment," *Eighteenth-Century Studies* 37.1 (Fall 2003): 23–45.

42. William Cowper to John Newton, December 21, 1780, *The Letters and Prose Writings*, ed. James King and Charles Ryskamp (Oxford: Clarendon, 1979), 1:425 (letters from this volume hereafter cited in text by volume and page numbers).

43. See Jonathan Sachs, "Eighteenth-Century Slow Time: Seven Propositions," *The Eighteenth Century: Theory and Interpretation* 60.2 (Summer 2019): 185–205, 200.

44. Arden Reed, *Romantic Weather: The Climates of Coleridge and Baudelaire* (Hanover, NH: Brown University Press, 1983), 9.

45. Vladimir Janković, *Reading the Skies: A Cultural History of English Weather, 1660–1820* (Manchester: Manchester University Press, 2001), 56.

46. As Elissa Marder explains: "When one receives the returned gaze of the world, one is 'remembered' by the world through those very parts of the self—the unconscious memory traces—that one has forgotten." *Dead Time: Temporal Disorders in the Wake of Modernity* (Stanford, CA: Stanford University Press, 2002), 27.

47. Erasmus Darwin, *The Botanic Garden* (London, 1790), 116n.

48. Martin Priestman sees Cowper's focus on the ills of gambling as exaggerated: "Gambling was indeed one of the luxuries to which the country's fair dues were being diverted, but to make this specific sin the whole cause of large-scale social change is just wishful thinking." *Cowper's "Task": Structure and Influence* (Cambridge: Cambridge University Press, 1983), 105. But, if one understands gambling, as Benjamin does, as a trope for the temporality of both speculative capitalism and factory labor, in which a subject is "completely liquidated [of his] memories" ("On Some Motifs in Baudelaire," 329–32), Cowper's critique seems prescient.

49. Cowper defines poetic labor as the cognitive act of slowing the mental phantasmagoria: "'I' arrest the fleeting images that fill / The mirror of the mind, and hold them fast" (2.290–91). Here is a surprising echo in Benjamin's "On the Concept of History": "Thinking involves not only the movement of thoughts, but their arrest as well. Where thinking suddenly comes to a stop in a constellation saturated with tensions, it gives the constellation a shock. . . . In this structure [the historical materialist] recognizes the messianic arrest of happening" (396). Cowper worries that, in an accelerated media culture, the authority of literature—and perhaps the claims of a prophetic poet to recognize

"messianic arrest"—will be supplanted: "At a time [like the] present, what Author can stand in competition with a Newspaper" (*Letters*, 2:220).

50. Deidre Lynch has identified alongside "green Romanticism" a parallel tradition she felicitously terms "greenhouse Romanticism," concerned with the global circulation of natural objects and the tropes of rhetorical naturalization within national and domestic spaces, above all the "artificial climates" of the increasingly popular greenhouses. See "'Young ladies are delicate plants': Jane Austen and Greenhouse Romanticism," *ELH* 77.3 (Fall 2010): 689–729, 692.

51. Anna Seward, *Letters of Anna Seward: Written between the Years 1784 and 1807* (Edinburgh, 1811), 5:97 (May 19, 1798).

52. Favret sees this interruption as a turning point in the poem: "With the inrush of noise," from the storm outside, "the poet takes up an alternative mode for telling the time of war, one that turns its untimeliness not to wayward vacancy but to fullness and conviction," the "voice of prophecy." *War at a Distance*, 82.

53. During the awful Laki summer, Walpole expressed a similar concern: "I begin to think that the Rumbolds and Co. have robbed the Indies of their climate as well as of their gold and diamonds." *Letters*, 8:38.

54. Robert Southey, *Critical Review* 24 (October 1798): 197–204, reprinted in *Lyrical Ballads, 1798 and 1800*, ed. Michael Gamer and Dahlia Porter (Peterborough, ON: Broadview, 2008), 148–50, 149.

55. Gamer and Porter, eds., *Lyrical Ballads, 1798 and 1800*, 289.

56. For an overview, see J. Douglas Kneale, "Wordsworth, Milton, and a Question of Genre," *Modern Philology* 109.2 (November 2011): 197–220.

57. See Stuart Curran, *Poetic Form and British Romanticism* (Oxford: Oxford University Press, 1990), 76–77; and Lee Johnson, *Wordsworth's Metaphysical Verse: Geometry, Nature, and Form* (Toronto: University of Toronto Press, 1982). Johnson claims that Abrams misses "the precision and rigour of Wordsworth's geometrical adaption of the Pindaric ode" (60). Douglas Lane Patey notes that the eighteenth century considered itself "*the* lyric age" and considered the ode the most lyric of genres. See "'Aesthetics' and the Rise of Lyric in the Eighteenth Century, *Studies in English Literature, 1500–1900* 33.3 (Summer 1993): 587–608, 588. On Wordsworth and Coleridge's appropriation of the ballad form, see Ian Newman, "Moderation in the *Lyrical Ballads*: Wordsworth and the Ballad Debates of the 1790s," *Studies in Romanticism* 55 (Summer 2016): 185–210.

58. Virginia Jackson and Yopie Prins attribute the creation of the "abstract literary lyric" to Coleridge and Wordsworth's 1798 collection. Virginia Jackson and Yopie Prins, introduction to *The Lyric Theory Reader*, ed. Virginia Jackson and Yopie Prins (Baltimore: Johns Hopkins University Press, 2014), 3.

59. Seth Reno, "Rethinking the Romantics' Love of Nature," in *Wordsworth and the Green Romantics: Affect and Ecology in the Nineteenth Century* (Durham: University of New Hampshire Press, 2016), 28–58, 38. Reno writes: "Wordsworth's love of nature reveals how affective engagement with the natural world can unlock the bodily, material processes of interconnectedness and transcendence" (31). Paul Fry, *The Poet's Calling in the English Ode* (New Haven, CT: Yale University Press, 1980), 179; Harold Bloom, *Poetry and Repression: Revisionism from Blake to Stevens* (New Haven, CT: Yale University Press, 1976), 59.

60. For his detailed engagement with "Tintern Abbey," see Jonathan Bate, *The Song of the Earth* (Cambridge, MA: Harvard University Press, 2000), 139–52.

61. Robert Mayo notes that literary magazines in the 1790s were replete with "moral and philosophic poems inspired by physical nature, and lyrical pieces in a variety of kinds describing rural scenes, the pleasures of the seasons, flora and fauna, and a simple life in the out-of-doors." He claims that the "novelty" of "Tintern Abbey" has to do with its "*air* of spontaneity," which sounds right to me. "The Contemporaneity of the Lyrical Ballads," *PMLA* 69.3 (June 1954): 486–522, 490, 493.

62. William Wordsworth, *An Evening Walk*, ed. James Averill (Ithaca, NY: Cornell University Press, 1984), 319 (app. A). Wordsworth recounts a specific line of the poem describing an oak and the moment where "this first struck me": "The moment was important in my poetical history; for I date from it my consciousness of the infinite variety of natural appearances which had been unnoticed by the poets of any age or country, so far as I was acquainted with them: and I made a resolution to supply in some degree the deficiency" (301).

63. *Early Reviews of English Poets*, ed. John Louis Haney (Philadelphia: Egerton, 1904), 16–18, 16.

64. See Nicholas Roe, "'Atmospheric air itself': Medical Science, Politics and Poetry in Thelwall, Coleridge and Wordsworth," in *1798: The Year of the Lyrical Ballads*, ed. Richard Cronin (Basingstoke: Palgrave Macmillan, 1998), 185–202; and Jackson, *Science and Sensation*, 144.

65. David Fairer, *Organising Poetry: The Coleridge Circle, 1790–1798* (Oxford: Oxford University Press, 2009), chap. 4.

66. William Gilpin, *Observations on the River Wye* (1792; London, 1800), 47 (hereafter cited in text).

67. As François observes, this scene "makes it impossible to mark the moment at which human violence passes into natural phenomena of dissipation and dispersion—the point at which the wind begins to carry the smoke" ("'Shadow boxing,'" 161). See also the reading in Scott, *Fuel*, 101.

68. Charles Rzepka, "Pictures of the Mind: Iron, Charcoal, 'Ouzy' Tides and Vagrant Dwellers, at Tintern, 1798," *Studies in Romanticism* 42.2 (Summer 2003): 155–85, 155.

69. As Abrams observes, for romantic writers "air-in-motion" becomes "a metaphor for change in the poet's mind." *The Correspondent Breeze*, 113.

70. On Wordsworth and bad weather, see Elias Greig, "Wordsworth in the Tropics of Cumbria," *Romantic Climates: Literature and Science in an Age of Catastrophe*, ed. Anne Collett and Olivia Murphey (Cham: Palgrave Macmillan, 2019), 33–58. On Wordsworth and Earth science, see Alan Bewell, *Wordsworth and the Enlightenment: Nature, Man, and Society in the Experimental Poetry* (New Haven, CT: Yale University Press, 1989), chap. 6.

71. William Wordsworth, "The Thorn," in Gamer and Porter, eds., *Lyrical Ballads, 1798 and 1800*, 103–10, lines 190–94.

72. William Wordsworth, *The Ruined Cottage and the Pedlar*, ed. James Butler (Ithaca, NY: Cornell University Press, 1979), 52.

73. Thomas Young, *A Course of Lectures in Natural Philosophy and the Mechanical Arts* (London, 1807), 1:78. In the *Lectures*, Young uses *power* to describe a measure of

energy flux in time, and he compares the rate of work—the change introduced in a physical system across a certain temporal duration—of different energy converters. "Mechanical power," he writes, can be quantified by comparing the "daily labour" of a certain number of men with different "natural and artificial agents," such as gunpowder or the "force of the wind acting on the sails of a windmill" (358–59).

74. See Jennifer Coopersmith, *Energy, the Subtle Concept: The Discovery of Feynman's Blocks, from Leibniz to Einstein* (Oxford: Oxford University Press, 2010), chap. 9.

75. *The Collected Letters of Charlotte Smith*, ed. Judith Phillips Stanton (Bloomington: Indiana University Press, 2003), 705 (hereafter cited in text by page).

76. John Anderson, "*Beachy Head*: The Romantic Fragment Poem as Mosaic," *Huntington Library Quarterly* 63.4 (2000): 547–74.

77. See, e.g., Jacqueline Labbe, "Beachy Head," in *A Companion to Romanticism*, ed. Duncan Wu (Malden, MA: Blackwell, 1999), 221–27. Labbe reads "Beachy Head" as an aggressive rewriting of "Tintern Abbey"—"Wordsworth, too, is buried in *Beachy Head*"— but also as a poem no less concerned with "self-construction, self-placement, and even self-promotion" (221–22).

78. On the relationship of mutual influence between Wordsworth and Smith, see Bishop C. Hunt, "Wordsworth and Charlotte Smith: 1970," *Wordsworth Circle* 35 (2004): 80–91; and Jacqueline Labbe, *Writing Romanticism: Charlotte Smith and William Wordsworth, 1784–1807* (Basingstoke: Palgrave Macmillan, 2011).

79. Melissa Bailes explores how "natural history techniques" allowed Smith to revise and resist "literary concepts of individualism." See *Questioning Nature: British Women's Scientific Writing and Literary Originality, 1750–1830* (Charlottesville: University of Virginia Press, 2017), 97.

80. Theresa Kelley, "Romantic Histories: Charlotte Smith and *Beachy Head*," *Nineteenth-Century Literature* 59.3 (2004): 281–314, 285–26 (hereafter cited in text). For a lyric reading of "Beachy Head," see Donelle Ruwe, "Charlotte Smith's *Beachy Head* and the Lyric Mode," *Pedagogy* 16.2 (April 2016): 300–307. Kari Lokke argues that "Smith creates in *Beachy Head* a complex tribute to herself." "The Figure of the Hermit in Charlotte Smith's *Beachy Head*," in *Charlotte Smith in British Romanticism*, ed. Jacqueline Labbe (London: Pickering & Chatto, 2008), 45–56, 49. Christoph Bode offers a more sophisticated account of the "radicalization of subjectivity" in "Beachy Head"— which, along with "Tintern Abbey" and Shelley's "Mont Blanc," are poems that appear locodescriptive "but are really meditations on the placement of the subject"—but the fluidly shifting narrative perspective he describes would be familiar to any reader of a poem such as *The Seasons*. See "The Subject of *Beachy Head*," in *Charlotte Smith in British Romanticism*, 57–69, 62.

81. Noah Heringman, "'Very vain is Science' proudest boast': The Resistance to Geological Theory in Early Nineteenth-Century England," in *The Revolution in Geology from the Renaissance to the Enlightenment*, ed. Gary D. Rosenberg (Boulder, CO: Geological Society of America, 2009), 247–57, 248 (hereafter cited in text). Heringman importantly draws attention to Smith's "distance from natural theology" (249).

82. Kevis Goodman, "Conjectures on *Beachy Head*: Charlotte Smith's Geological Poetics and the Ground of the Present," *ELH* 81.3 (Fall 2014): 983–1006, 996 (hereafter cited in text).

83. Charlotte Smith, "The Horologe of the Fields," in *The Poems of Charlotte Smith*, lines 35, 15–16.

84. Charlotte Smith, "Studies by the Sea," in *The Poems of Charlotte Smith*, lines 103–5 (hereafter cited in text by line).

85. Charlotte Smith, *The Old Manor House* (London, 1793), 3:106–7.

86. Anne Wallace identifies in "Beachy Head" "conceptions of a deep earth, of deep time, and of continual exchanges of energy and form through these containing spatial-temporal structures." "Interfusing Living and Nonliving in Charlotte Smith's 'Beachy Head,'" *Wordsworth Circle* 50.1 (Winter 2019): 1–18, 9.

87. Goodman, "Conjectures on *Beachy Head*"; Lily Gurton-Wachter, *Watchwords: Romanticism and the Poetics of Attention* (Stanford, CA: Stanford University Press, 2016), chap. 4.

88. For the advertisement, see *The Poems of Charlotte Smith*, ed. Stuart Curran (New York: Oxford University Press, 1993), 215.

AFTERWORD

1. On planetarity "as the species of alterity," see Gayatri Chakravorty Spivak, "Planetarity," in *Dictionary of Untranslatables*, ed. Barbara Cassin (Princeton, NJ: Princeton University Press, 2014), 1223.

2. See also Jameson, *The Political Unconscious*, 66–69.

3. Jonsson, "The Origins of Cornucopianism."

4. Raymond Williams, *Marxism and Literature* (Oxford: Oxford University Press, 1977), 87.

5. Margaret Ronda, *Remainders: American Poetry at Nature's End* (Stanford, CA: Stanford University Press, 2018), 5.

6. See Higgins, *Writing Tambora*, chap. 3; and Wood, *Tambora*, chaps. 3, 7.

7. Annette Hulbert, "Defoe's Storm Forms," *Digital Defoe* 11.1 (Fall 2019): 1–16.

8. See Ghosh, *The Great Derangement*.

9. See Hannes Bergthaller, "Climate Change and Un-Narratability," *Metaphora* 2 (2018): 1–12.

10. Jennifer Wenzel, *The Disposition of Nature: Environmental Crisis and World Literature* (New York: Fordham University Press, 2019), 1. See also Stephanie LeMenager, "Climate Change and the Struggle for Genre," in Menely and Taylor, eds., *Anthropocene Reading*, 220–38; and Adeline Johns-Putra, *Climate Change and the Contemporary Novel* (Cambridge: Cambridge University Press, 2019)

Unless otherwise noted, references to primary texts are citing the following editions:

Burnet, Thomas. *The Sacred Theory of the Earth*. Carbondale: Southern Illinois University Press, 1965. Cited by page number.

Johnson, Samuel. *Lives of the English Poets*. Vols. 1 and 2. Oxford: Oxford University Press, 1929. Cited by volume and page numbers.

Lucretius. *On the Nature of the Universe*. Translated by Ronald Melville. Oxford: Oxford University Press, 1999. Cited by book and line numbers. N.B.: The line numbering in this edition refers to the Latin text.

Milton, John. *Paradise Lost*. Edited by David Scott Kastan. Indianapolis: Hackett, 2005. Cited by book and line numbers.

Thomson, James. *The Seasons*. In *Poetical Works*, ed. J. Logie Robertson, 1–244. London: Oxford University Press, 1971. Cited by season (*Wi* = *Winter*, *Sp* = *Spring*, *Su* = *Summer*, *Au* = *Autumn*) and line number. N.B.: This variorum edition contains the 1726 stand-alone edition of *Winter* and the 1746 (final) edition of *The Seasons* as well as all variations in the 1730 and 1744 editions and the first stand-alone editions of *Spring* (1728), *Summer* (1727), and *Autumn* (1730), which are given in the notes. Unless otherwise indicated, I cite the 1746 edition.

The Oxford Study Bible. New York: Oxford University Press, 1992.

Virgil. *Aeneid*. In *Eclogues, Georgics, Aeneid I–VI*, trans. H. Rushton Fairclough, 261–597. Cambridge, MA: Harvard University Press. Cited by page number.

———. *Georgics*. In *Eclogues, Georgics, Aeneid I–VI*, trans. H. Rushton Fairclough, 97–259. Cambridge, MA: Harvard University Press. Cited by page number.

Wordsworth, William. "Lines Written a Few Miles above Tintern Abbey." In *Lyrical Ballads, 1798 and 1800*, ed. Michael Gamer and Dahlia Porter, 282–86. Peterborough, ON: Broadview, 2008. Cited by line number.

INDEX

Abrams, M. H., 167
abundance, 101, 112, 116
Academy, The, 126
acclimatization, 115, 119. *See also* climate
Act of Union of 1707, 85
Addison, Joseph, 14, 90, 94, 130, 155
Adorno, Theodor, 166–67, 194–95
Aeneid (Virgil), 54, 122
aesthetics, 5, 12–13, 166, 191, 210
Aesthetic Theory (Adorno), 167
Africa, 111, 115–16
Agricultural Revolution, 94
agriculture: after the Fall, 79; and crop failure,
   41, 117; descriptions of, 145; develop-
   ment of, 94–96, 127, 149, 237n28;
   economics of, 26, 152; and nature, 133,
   149; unsustainable practices of, 148.
   See also cultivation
Agriculture (Dodsley), 127
Aikin, John, 57, 84, 98, 124–25
air: dematerialization of, 194; flows of, 194,
   240n65 (*see also* wind); as a medium,
   9, 170; and the planetary system, 112;
   purity of, 81, 181, 204; scientific studies
   of, 101–2; as unchanging, 3. *See also*
   atmosphere
Akkadian Empire, 78
alchemy, 75, 89, 101
Alff, David, 130
allegory: critical reading of, 43; decline of, 64,
   99; description as response to, 166; and
   personification, 64; places as, 54; role of,
   8, 33, 44–46, 187, 196; stability of, 47–48,
   82; and theology, 75; traditional meaning

of, 230n32. *See also* baroque allegory;
   description; lyricism
Allegory and Ideology (Jameson), 12–13,
   47–49
Allen, Robert, 132
allusion, 33, 54, 99, 145, 147, 163, 199
Althusser, Louis, 18, 48, 170, 210
Anatomy of Melancholy (Burton), 77
Anderson, John, 197
animal-powered mills, 149
Annual Register, The, 163
Antarctica, 141
Anthropocene: critical reading in the, 20; lyric
   as the genre of the, 32; and modernity, 1,
   27; and planetary forces, 210–11; recogni-
   tion of the, 7, 13, 22, 24, 27, 49, 129,
   247n50; and sovereignty, 212; technol-
   ogy of the, 159; temporality of the, 171;
   trajectory of the, 24. *See also* geologic
   epochs
Anthropocene Working Group, 24
anthropocentrism, 115, 213
apostrophe, 4, 34, 66, 81–82, 86, 103–6, 151–
   52, 161, 187, 191–92, 195
Aravamudan, Srinivas, 81
Arctic warming, 141
Aristotle, 79, 93, 141, 232n57
Armstrong, John, 121
Art of Discrimination, The (Cohen), 16
assemblages, 18, 32, 198, 208, 222n42
astronomy, 59, 79
atmosphere: economy of, 95, 109–10; etymol-
   ogy of, 38, 239n51; influence of, 121, 123;
   as a medium, 112; as mode of reading,